"Neal Johnson and I have been friends for maenced several generational leaps in the practithis book, Neal has jumped to a new BAM best-practices woru .is a must-read for those already doing BAM as well as for those considering BAM. May this book also catalyze closer working relationships and trust between mission agencies and the business people and especially entrepreneurs of the world."
DWIGHT NORDSTROM, CHAIRMAN, PACIFIC RESOURCES INTERNATIONAL

"Neal Johnson has provided a systematic, strategic and tactical approach in answering the important question on how to conduct business as mission in a God-honoring way."
LUIS BUSH, INTERNATIONAL FACILITATOR, TRANSFORM WORLD CONNECTIONS

"C. Neal Johnson's *Business as Mission* would be my first choice for a single textbook on the subject. It is comprehensive, up-to-date, theoretically lucid and instructive for implementation. Business is a strategic tool for a new breed of cross-cultural workers in the twenty-first-century mission. Not only will it be used for evangelism but also for securing the economic well-being of the people."
TETSUNAO YAMAMORI, LAUSANNE SENIOR ADVISER AND PRESIDENT/CEO OF WORLDSERVE MINISTRIES

"Neal Johnson's *Business as Mission* is the most comprehensive manual in the history of the marketplace movement. For years to come this will be the foundational text used by mission agencies, universities and seminaries, and business leaders interested in BAM. It identifies and simplifies the definitions, strategies, practical steps and key players in the worldwide BAM movement."
KENT HUMPHREYS, AMBASSADOR, FCCI / CHRIST@WORK

"Be prepared to have your view of the marketplace launched into a new orbit! This is easily the most comprehensive and valuable guide to business as mission ever written, perhaps because no one is better qualified to write it than Neal Johnson. This book will serve multitudes who are finding that business may be *the* primary gateway to extending God's kingdom into every corner of the earth in the decades just ahead."
JOHN D. BECKETT, CHAIRMAN, THE BECKETT COMPANIES, AND AUTHOR OF *LOVING MONDAY* AND *MASTERING MONDAY*

"The global business as mission (BAM) movement has for many years been on a journey toward holistic transformation through business and the quadruple bottom lines. Dr. Neal Johnson has developed an important road map for our journey. Fellow BAM travelers everywhere: Use this map!"

Mats Tunehag, Senior Associate for Business as Mission for the Lausanne Movement and the World Evangelical Alliance

"Masterfully combining 'how come' and 'how to,' Neal Johnson has crafted an instant classic on marketplace missiology. His unusually rich experiences in work, ministry and education prepared him to offer in a single volume almost everything we need to know philosophically, theologically, scripturally and practically with the greatest mission opportunity in the twenty-first century—business as mission. While elaborating the complexities and ambiguities of definition and implementation—this is no slick quick-fix book—Johnson leaves us with a heart panting after God's own heart in the words of Jesus: 'As the Father has sent me, I am sending you' (John 20:21), a fully incarnational mission."

R. Paul Stevens, Emeritus Professor, Marketplace Theology, Regent College, Vancouver, B.C.; part-time faculty, Bakke Graduate University, Seattle; and adjunct professor, Biblical Graduate School of Theology, Singapore

"There is a growing awareness throughout the world church that in the twenty-first century business as mission (BAM) may well prove to be one of God's primary, if not the principle, instrument of world evangelization and kingdom transformation. Neal Johnson's presentation of BAM is masterful, comprehensive, clear, wonderfully readable, motivating and challenging—the best in the field. May this work help to motivate and mobilize biblical Christians around the globe to new, creative and committed missionary action to, within and through the marketplace to proclaim in word and deed the coming of the kingdom of God in Jesus Christ, by the power of the Holy Spirit."

Charles Van Engen, Arthur F. Glasser Professor of Biblical Theology of Mission, Fuller Theological Seminary

C. NEAL JOHNSON

FOREWORD BY STEVE RUNDLE

BUSINESS AS MISSION

A COMPREHENSIVE GUIDE TO THEORY AND PRACTICE

IVP Academic

An imprint of InterVarsity Press
Downers Grove, Illinois

InterVarsity Press
P.O. Box 1400, Downers Grove, IL 60515-1426
World Wide Web: www.ivpress.com
E-mail: email@ivpress.com

InterVarsity Press® is the book-publishing division of InterVarsity Christian Fellowship/USA®, a movement of students and faculty active on campus at hundreds of universities, colleges and schools of nursing in the United States of America, and a member movement of the International Fellowship of Evangelical Students. For information about local and regional activities, write Public Relations Dept., InterVarsity Christian Fellowship/USA, 6400 Schroeder Rd., P.O. Box 7895, Madison, WI 53707-7895, or visit the IVCF website at <www.intervarsity.org>.

All Scripture quotations, unless otherwise indicated, are taken from the Holy Bible, New International Version®. NIV®. *Copyright 1973, 1978, 1984 by International Bible Society. Used by permission of Zondervan Publishing House. All rights reserved.*

Appendix 3 on pp. 497-99 is taken from Table 1. "Checklist for Making a Differential Diagnosis," from The End of Poverty *by Jeffrey D. Sachs, copyright ©2005 by Jeffrey D. Sacks. Used by permission of The Penguin Press, a division of Penguin Group (USA) Inc.*

Every effort has been made to trace and contact copyright holders for materials quoted in this book. The authors will be pleased to rectify any omissions in future editions if notified by the copyright holders.

Design: Cindy Kiple
Images: Robert Daly/Getty Images

ISBN 978-0-8308-3865-3

Printed in the United States of America ∞

 InterVarsity Press is committed to protecting the environment and to the responsible use of natural resources. As a member of Green Press Initiative we use recycled paper whenever possible. To learn more about the Green Press Initiative, visit <www.greenpressinitiative.org>.

Library of Congress Cataloging-in-Publication Data

Johnson, C. Neal, 1942-
  Business as mission a comprehensive guide to theory and practice /
  C. Neal Johnson.
      p. cm.
  Includes bibliographical references and index.
  ISBN 978-0-8308-3865-3 (pbk.: alk. paper)
  1. Business enterprises—Religious aspects. 2. Mission statements.
  I. Title.
  HF5388.J64 2009
  658.4'01—dc22

                                                                    2009032078

P 23 22 21 20 19 18 17 16 15 14 13 12 11 10 9 8 7 6 5 4 3 2

Y 29 28 27 26 25 24 23 22 21 20 19 18 17 16 15 14 13 12 11 10

To my mother, Frances Johnson,
who introduced me to Jesus.

To my marketplace colleague, Robert Runyan,
who brought me back home when I strayed.

To my precious wife, Frecia,
who showed me the true meaning
of unconditional love.

Contents

Figures

FOREWORD

IN THE SUMMER OF 1998 I RECEIVED AN E-MAIL from a friend who
was participating in a series of meetings at the Oxford Center for Mission
Studies. He was seeking input on a discussion they were having about the difference between what they were calling "Business as Mission" and "Business
with a Christian Hat." I remember being intrigued by those terms because
they captured something I too had been thinking about, namely, how to explain the difference between Christian-owned businesses that are actively
seeking to advance the cause of Christ in the neediest parts of the world and
those that are "merely" doing business, albeit with integrity and grace. Eventually, Tom Steffen and I adopted the term *Great Commission Companies* to
describe the former. The latter term quietly, and thankfully, disappeared.

Much has changed in the ten years since those meetings. The term *Business as Mission* (BAM) is now almost ubiquitous in mission circles, and it is
hard to find anyone who does not support the idea or claim to be involved in
it in some form or fashion. However, many are feeling ill-equipped or confused. With the passage of time the term is now being applied to a much wider
range of activities than originally envisioned. Some are even starting to push
back, asking, in effect, Where's the beef? Much of the ambivalence or skepticism can be attributed to the fact that theologians and missiologists are still
catching up, trying to understand the many different facets of BAM and how
they fit (or don't) with God's timeless plan for humankind and the purpose of
the church.

One thing is clear: BAM is not the be-all and end-all of missions. Economic
transformation alone does not educate children nor eradicate disease, for example. But there is now abundant and compelling evidence that a properly
motivated and managed business can, in its own unique way, draw attention

to Christ and be a profound blessing to a community. The question of what defines a "properly motivated and managed business" is the subject of this book. Neal Johnson is uniquely qualified to write it. After a distinguished business career in international and domestic law and banking, and years on the mission field as a pastor, tentmaker, educator, marketplace ministry leader, and BAM advocate, he pursued an M.A. in international community development and a Ph.D. in intercultural studies and missiology, both from Fuller Theological Seminary's School of World Mission. His Ph.D. focused on the emerging "marketplace mission" movement and all its many facets and players. This book represents a convergence of those varied experiences.

In this book Dr. Johnson does a masterful job of explaining that movement and its missiological significance. He also moves the conversation forward by providing insights—drawing from his personal experience and his research—into the how-to questions that so many aspiring practitioners are asking. His book will be extremely useful to anyone interested in BAM, students as well as practitioners.

Steve Rundle
Associate Professor of Economics, Biola University
Coauthor of Great Commission Companies:
The Emerging Role of Business in Mission

ACKNOWLEDGMENTS

THIS BOOK IS THE PRODUCT OF OVER thirteen years of engagement in the Marketplace Mission Movement and a lifetime career in business, banking, law, government and education. So many people have helped shape my life, faith and views on what God is doing to, within and through the marketplace that it is impossible to thank each of them (which I do) in this limited space. Accordingly, let me simply mention those who have been more directly related to the final production of this book. First, without a doubt, is my wife, Frecia, who not only put up with countless weeks, weekends, holidays and evenings without her computer-bound husband, but who also has read every manuscript draft thoroughly and, through her insightful editing, has added immeasurably to this book's content and form. Second, my IVP editor, Al Hsu, and the copyeditor, Drew Blankman, who have patiently helped me through each phase of this process with professionalism and sensitivity, and their IVP colleagues who had enough faith in this project to see it through to the end.

I am also indebted to Roger Parrott and Dan Fredericks, president and provost, respectively, of Belhaven College in Jackson, Mississippi, for giving me the freedom to devote months of time to this project as a scholar in residence. Similarly, Brad Smith and Grace Barnes, president and academic dean, respectively, of Bakke Graduate University, who helped me see it through to the finish.

Special thanks also goes to my close friend, colleague and fellow pilgrim-pioneer in today's BAM frontier, Steve Rundle, for the countless hours and penetrating discussions we have had trying to discern what God and his people are doing in today's global marketplace. So, too, to my dear friends Charles Dunn, whose heart for the poor of the world was second to none, and Steve Brown, who provided generous encouragement, stimulating ideas and much-needed humor during the research and drafting phases of this endeavor.

Last, but far from least, my heartfelt gratitude to Debby Thomas and Michael Chapman, missionaries in Rwanda, who field-tested my proposals and provided invaluable comments during the process; to Paul Stevens, Edgar Elliston, Charles Van Engen, Doug Lainson, Bill Wimberley, Tom Sudyk and Colleen Ramos, who served as outside readers and commentators; to my hardworking, ever-cheerful, invaluable assistants Jessica Moore and Ruby Allen; and to my bright, gregarious, insightful intern, Andrew Haas.

Without all of you, and your love, encouragement and critical thinking, this book would not have been possible.

Abbreviations

ACA	Association of Christian Accountants
BAM	Business as Mission (see also GCC, KC)
BAMer	an individual who practices BAM
BBL Forums	Beyond the Bottom Line Forums
BK	BAMer's Kid (see also MK)
BPN	Business Professional Network
CAN	Creative Access Nation (see also RAN)
CCCU	Christian Community Credit Union
CBMC	Christian Businessmen's Committees (also known as Connecting Businessmen in the Marketplace to Christ, Connecting Businessmen to Christ, and Concerned Businessmen for Christ)
CBMC-F	CBMC Forums
CCC	Campus Crusade for Christ
C-CSR	Christian Corporate Social Responsibility (see also CSR)
CD	community development
CEO	chief executive officer (see also, CFO, COO, CMO)
CFO	chief financial officer (see also CEO, CMO, COO)
CiW	*Christen in der Wirtschaft* (Christians in the Workplace)
CMO	chief mission officer (see also CEO, CFO, COO)
COO	chief operating officer (see also CEO, CFO, CMO)
CSR	corporate social responsibility (see also C-CSR)
EC	Evangelistic Commerce
EIS	environmental impact statement
ESL	English as a second language
Ex-pat	expatriate (a person temporarily or permanently residing in a country and culture other than that of the person's upbringing or legal residence)
FCCI	Fellowship of Companies for Christ International (AKA Christ@Work)

FSU	former Soviet Union
GCC	Great Commission Company
GCOWE '95	Global Consultation on World Evangelization in Seoul, Korea, 1995
GO	global opportunities
GOK	government of Kazakhstan
HR	human resources
IHP	inner healing prayer
IVCG	*Internationale Vereinigung Christlicher Geschaftsleute* (International Association of Christian Businessmen)
KBF	Kingdom Business Forum
KC	kingdom company (see also BAM, GCC)
KIO	Kingdom Impact Opportunities
KJV	King James Version of the Holy Bible
K-ROI	kingdom return on investment (see also ROI, $-ROI)
LCWE	Lausanne Committee for World Evangelization
LDC	lesser developed country (see also MDC)
MDC	more developed country (see also LDC)
MK	missionary kid (see also BK)
MM	marketplace ministry
MP	marketplace
NGO	nongovernmental organization (see also NPO)
NPO	nonprofit organization (see also NGO)
OPE	overseas private equity
QC	quality control
RAN	restricted access nation (see also CAN)
Rb	rubles (the currency of Russia)
ROI	return on investment (see also K-ROI, $-ROI)
$-ROI	financial return on investment (see also K-ROI)
SAA	strategic area/country analysis (see also SBP, SMBP, SMA)
SBP	strategic business plan (see also SAA, SMBP, SMA)
SMA	strategic mission analysis (see also SAA, SBP, SMBP)
SMBP	strategic master BAM plan (see also SAA, SBP, SMA)
SME	small and medium enterprise development
WWJD	What Would Jesus Do?

Introduction

"Faith by itself, if it is not accompanied by actions, is dead."
JAMES 2:17

"I am only one,
But still I am one.
I cannot do everything,
But still I can do something.
And because I cannot do everything,
I will not refuse to do the something that I can do."
EDWARD HALL, 1822

Whenever I speak to groups about integrating biblical principles into their businesses, leading their companies for Christ, becoming kingdom companies, practicing Business as Mission (BAM), and engaging others in the God-ordained mission of city and national transformation, I am always asked, How?

Businesspeople everywhere see the concept, become excited about it and want to embrace it. The natural next step is implementation—doing it. And they haven't a clue where to begin. That is the reason for this book. There are a number of truly excellent books on the market now for the chief executive officer (CEO) who wants to be intentional about integrating the Christian faith into the workplace or to use his or her God-given skills and business acumen for mission. But unfortunately, there are virtually no books that address the nagging *how* questions I am continually confronted with.

There are simply no set formulas or models for faith integration, let alone the even greater task of BAM. That is understandable when we think of the myriad facets to our Lord's interactions with humanity. So, too, the ways of doing BAM are as varied and complex as the Christians who practice it.

There is, however, a systematic, strategic and tactical approach to the *how* challenge that can provide a guideline for motivated CEOs, entrepreneurs and business students who are eager to engage in BAM. This book will explore that challenge in depth as well as the reasons for making BAM the book's primary focus.

Of all the mission initiatives being practiced today, BAM has perhaps the highest potential for effecting sustainable, transformational, holistic *kingdom impact* to a hurting world. There is virtually no person on earth who is not directly or indirectly affected by the marketplace. That is true now and has been true in every era and every society throughout history. BAM's capacity to reach the marketplace in every culture and nation in today's world is nothing short of mind-boggling. Unfortunately, BAM is also by far the most complex and challenging mission strategy, especially in the *how* area. It requires a mastery of both the worlds of business and of missions (which includes the complex arena of holistic community development), and it must merge and contextualize into something significantly different than either can be alone. Further, in today's pluralistic society, BAM's outreach is not only international, it can also be domestic, even next door. Further, BAM is not solely oriented toward evangelism or discipleship; it is holistic—reaching the whole needs of the whole of humanity everywhere.

But first, to build sustainability into the BAM movement, we need to educate the next generation of Christian leaders as well as CEOs, owners and entrepreneurs on both *what* BAM is and *how* to do it. My hope and prayer are that

- this book will stimulate broad-ranging discussions and in-depth soul-searching as to how faith and work should and can intersect, and how Christian mission and the marketplace can be brought together in support of God's kingdom

- it will help people develop an intense interest in BAM and an in-depth understanding of how to do BAM in a crosscultural context

- it will contribute to a massive new grassroots, holistic approach to mission through business that will spread globally

- in BAM's wake, people's lives and their communities will be permanently and eternally transformed as they encounter Jesus and his followers in business

- the church will come to see the enormous potential of this movement and wholeheartedly embrace it, and in so doing, will release the army of business men and women in their pews to engage the community for Christ and equip them with new forms of *doing church* to match the new forms of *doing mission*

- this book will also cause each Christian business student, awakening entrepreneur and established businessperson to seriously consider engaging the world of BAM and using their calling to further his kingdom on earth

PART ONE

BUSINESS AS MISSION

An Overview

"[The] idea is . . . simple: It assumes that the main players in overseas kingdom work are not trained cross-cultural missionaries or NGO professionals, but laypeople who take their current expertise (whether it is teaching, plumbing, electronics, or so forth) and use it to serve people in other nations. . . .

"I view the church as an army of missionaries sitting in the pews. My job is to mobilize them. . . .

"Some people talk about 'business as mission,' how we're going to use business to do mission work. That's an insult to the businessman, because to him business is his mission. His mission is the kingdom of God."

BOB ROBERTS JR., INTERVIEWED BY MARK GALLI

1

What Is Business as Mission?

*"The commercial business marketplace may well be the
primary mission field of the twenty-first century."*
CHARLES VAN ENGEN

*For a blessing upon all human labor,
And for the right use of the riches of creation,
That the world may be freed from poverty,
famine, and disaster,
We pray to you, O Lord.
For the poor, the persecuted, the sick, and all who suffer;
For refugees, prisoners, and all who are in danger;
That they may be relieved and protected,
We pray to you, O Lord.*
BOOK OF COMMON PRAYER

TODAY THE TERM *BUSINESS AS MISSION* (BAM) is bandied about as a new church fad or mission buzzword. It has garnered a great deal of attention but not a great deal of action for three reasons: (1) it is difficult to define exactly what BAM means, (2) many people love the concept of BAM, but few really understand how to do it, and (3) those who do understand and undertake a BAM initiative seldom stop to count the true cost of the undertaking. I will attempt to clarify all three of these difficulties with this text.

A Working Definition

BAM is broadly defined as a for-profit commercial business venture that is

Christian led, intentionally devoted to being used as an instrument of God's mission *(missio Dei)* to the world, and is operated in a crosscultural environment, either domestic or international. BAM companies are themselves ministries at two levels. First, they minister to all those who are directly in the business's spheres of influence, such as their workforce and their families, suppliers and vendors, investors and creditors, customers and clients, even competitors. Second, they engage the community they operate in and undertake holistic, people-impacting community-development initiatives. Some might say that BAM is crosscultural business plus community development. BAM is, however, not that easily pigeonholed.

In modern times the idea of business as mission was revived and promoted as a means to gain access to countries that close their borders to traditional missionaries. The reasons that these so-called closed (or creative) access nations (CANs) or restricted access nations (RANs) deny visas to Christian missionaries are varied, but frequently they arise from either the church's association with the nation's colonial past or the church and its missionaries posing a threat to the country's politically dominant religion or other power structures. Not infrequently, the secular or sectarian national government is simply anti-Christian. In practice these nations are frequently in the world's undeveloped (predeveloped) countries that are usually characterized by rampant corruption, a wide gulf between rich and poor, a small or nonexistent middle class, endemic poverty, economic stagnation and hopelessness, limited actual religious and political freedom, and pervasive abuse of human rights.

Having said this, I am compelled to state that any definition of BAM—including my own working definition on the previous page—is by its nature limiting and therefore inadequate. The 2004 Lausanne Working Group 30 on Business as Mission was composed of sixty-eight BAM activists from twenty-eight countries. After a week of meetings, our group concluded that it was virtually impossible to achieve a universally satisfactory definition of BAM. The best that the group could do was to note the almost infinite variety of connections between business and mission, and to discuss some of BAM's key characteristics:

- BAM is based on the principle of holistic mission

- BAM has a kingdom perspective, kingdom business

- BAM is different but related to
  - workplace ministries (marketplace ministries)
  - tentmaking
  - business for mission (donation of business profits for mission)

- BAM does not condone nonbusiness and nonmissions (it must be real business and real missions, simultaneously)

- BAM pursues profit

- BAM comes in all shapes and sizes

- BAM is not about jobs and money—per se

- BAM's ultimate bottom line is *ad majorem Dei gloriam*, "for the greater glory of God"[1]

Nonetheless, one of the participants, Tom Sudyk, the founder and CEO of a BAM enterprise, the EC Group (Evangelistic Commerce) in Grand Rapids, Michigan, proffered a definition: BAM is "the Strategic use of authentic business activities to create cross-cultural opportunities to minister and evangelize within the business's spheres of influence with the aim of holistic transformation."[2] Mats Tunehag, the BAM track facilitator at the 2004 Lausanne Conference in Thailand, takes a more negative line, describing what BAM *is not*:

> BAM is real business, not Christian charity in a business disguise. But it is more than just business. Two approaches to business that do not come within the scope of "business as mission" by any definition are: (1) Fake businesses that are not actually functioning businesses, but exist solely to provide visas for missionaries to enter countries otherwise closed to them. (2) Businesses that purport to have Christian motivations but which operate only for private economic advantage and not for the king-

---

[1]Adapted from "Business as Mission," Lausanne Occasional Paper No. 59, September 29-October 5, 2004, in The Lausanne Movement <www.lausanne.org/documents/2004forum/LOP59_IG30.pdf>. This website contains a wealth of information on BAM and should be actively reviewed by all would-be BAMers.

[2]Evangelistic Commerce Institute, "EC Institute," conference brochure (n.d.), p. 1.

dom of God. Neither do we mean businesses run by Christians with no clear and defined kingdom strategy in place.[3]

Tunehag later gave his own definition of what BAM *is:* "Business as Mission is about real, viable, sustainable and profitable businesses; with a Kingdom of God purpose, perspective and impact; leading to transformation of people and societies spiritually, economically, socially and environmentally—to the great glory of God."[4]

Ken Eldred says, "Kingdom businesses [BAMs] are for-profit commercial enterprises in the mission field of the developing world through which Christian business professionals are seeking to meet spiritual, social and economic needs."[5] Notwithstanding the differences in definition, the essence is the same: crosscultural Christian mission in and through business.

R. Paul Stevens, quoting Sunki Bang of the Business Ministry of Seoul, Korea, offers some additional, useful distinguishing features of BAM:

- business *and* mission—two isolated activities

- business *for* mission—using the proceeds of business as a way of financing mission

- business *as a platform for* mission—work and professional life as means of channeling mission throughout the world (in Korea such people are called *businaries*)

- mission *in* business—hiring nonbelievers and offering chaplaincy services with a view to leading them to Christ

- business *as* mission—business as part of the mission of God in the world[6]

---

[3]Mats Tunehag, "God Means Business! An Introduction to Business as Mission, BAM," unpublished monograph, 2008, p. 9.

[4]Ibid., p. 8.

[5]Ken Eldred, *God Is at Work: Transforming People and Nations through Business* (Ventura, Calif.: Regal, 2005), p. 61.

[6]Sunki Bang, cited in R. Paul Stevens, *Doing God's Business: Meaning and Motivation for the Marketplace* (Grand Rapids: Eerdmans, 2006), p. 80. While I have some difficulty with these definitions—especially the BAM definition, which is too vague to offer much help to those who would grasp the essence of BAM—the basic distinctions are important to grasp. In part, they help define what BAM is by looking at what it is not. It should be noticed, however, that BAM is both mission *in* the business and a *platform for* mission outside the business. We will spend a good deal of time on both the internal and external components of BAM, but hopefully Bang's distinctions are useful fodder for insightful discussions.

A HISTORICAL PERSPECTIVE

BAM arises from a deep, abiding concern for the impoverished people of the world, especially those in the area that has come to be known as the 10/40 Window, which was coined by Luis Bush in 1990 and describes a geographic rectangle from 10 degrees north to 40 degrees south of the Equator and stretches from West Africa to East Asia. This area contains half of the world population (about 3.2 billion people), 95 percent of whom are unevangelized (in fifty-five of the least evangelized nations), and 85 percent of whom are among the world's poorest of the poor. The 10/40 Window's dominant religions are Islam, Hinduism and Buddhism.[7]

Historically, God's people have responded to their concern for these people through traditional church or mission-agency missionaries. Some of these missionaries were supported by their sponsors, but many were not. William Carey, the father of modern missions, was a cobbler who set up a printing business in India to support himself, his family and their ministry. In fact, business has been used for centuries to support missionaries on the field, but it was not until the last two decades that it was approached as a specific mission strategy in and of itself.

BAM'S REBIRTH: FROM THE ASHES OF COLONIALISM

The shift in perception and practice primarily resulted from the collapse of colonialism. During that era the church was often a useful and complicit tool in the colonial powers' foreign policies. In most situations the colonialist state and the church worked hand in glove to subdue, occupy, govern and convert conquered peoples and nations. As such, the church incurred the enmity that was directed at the colonial powers themselves. When independence came, the colonials left almost overnight. Amid the reactionary responses, the newly independent states passed laws and policies that restricted the church's activities and forbade missionaries from entering their countries. That is where the term *restricted access nations* (RANs) originated.

The church noted that these new nations were eager, even desperate, to initiate economic reforms and to grow their business sectors. While they

---

[7]For more on the 10/40 Window, see Howard Culbertson's missions website at <http://home.snu .edu/~HCULBERT/1040.htm>. For other noteworthy examples see William J. Danker, *Profit for the Lord* (Grand Rapids: Eerdmans, 1971).

would not allow Christian church workers or missionaries into their countries, they welcomed Western businessmen, Christian or not, with open arms. The church saw this as an opening and began sending missionaries into these countries under the guise of business. They lied on their visa applications, entered the countries, set up shell businesses and then proceeded to use those businesses as covers to initiate mission activities. That creativity led to the term *creative (or closed) access nations* (CANs).

People of those nations may have been poor and underdeveloped, but they were not stupid. They saw through the ruse and realized that these missionaries had not only lied but were adding nothing of value to the country's economic growth. Accordingly, many missionaries were forced to leave their assignments and return home. This was tragic in several ways, but in particular it shut down the mission outreach within those countries and conveyed the wrong message to their officials and people. It told them in unequivocal terms that Christianity is a foreign, Western religion that uses lies, deception and trickery to get its way. Further, its God, this Jesus and its emissaries are not people of honesty and integrity and are not to be trusted or associated with.

BAM IS REAL BUSINESS

BAM arose from this hotbed of controversy. Christian businessmen and women saw that while missionaries were excluded or even evicted, businesspeople were welcomed into these nations. They witnessed, often with dismay and disdain, the church's counterproductive strategies. Being businesspeople who understood adding value to a society and—being moved by God—they purposed to use their business skills to succeed where the church had failed. That required creating (or purchasing) and operating real, legitimate, profit-oriented businesses in those countries and using them not simply for evangelism but also for holistic ministry to the people they targeted. They realized that *establishing a real, for-profit business in the country was an ideal way to find legitimacy within the society; to add value to that society through the creation of jobs, products and services that benefit the people; and to develop credibility and trust for the gospel.*

This is not to say that BAM businesses were not faced with real, substantial barriers to their entry into the market. On close inspection it became apparent to these Christian businesspeople that the host countries were doing all they could to develop their nations economically, but that their businesses were in a primitive, often embryonic state. This was especially true for businesses producing exportable products; there were few that could compete on the global market. And many of these nations lacked the infrastructure so useful (essential) to rapid business growth and economic progress.

Further, most businesses were being crippled by rampant corruption at every level of government and society. The reasons for the corruption were legion, from simple survival strategies by individuals in minipower positions to well-organized, brutal gangs and mafia, to despotic rulers at the highest levels of government. In each instance, justice, righteousness and fairness were subverted, leaving an unhealthy society in serious need of political reform, economic growth, jobs and Jesus. But such conditions—while imposing for BAM companies—ironically embody the essence of why BAM is needed. These countries are fertile, uncultivated soil that is ripe for the seeds of the gospel—seeds coming not merely from words but from seeing Christ in action through Christian businesspersons and their activities.

BAM IS FOR JOB-MAKERS

In fall 2002, Tetsunao (Ted) Yamamori, who served for seventeen years as president of Food for the Hungry, and businessman Kenneth Eldred, founder of Kingdom Business Forums (KBF), convened a Consultation for Holistic Entrepreneurs. The purpose was to explore the BAM theme. The consultation unequivocally concluded that a BAM business is about job creation, value enhancement, wealth generation and product/service distribution at both the business and spiritual levels. To accomplish this, BAM must be about job making, never about job taking. In that sense BAM distinguishes itself from the classical concept of tentmaking. As Yamamori wrote in the preface to a compilation of the consultation's BAM papers:

> Most tentmakers are "job-takers." . . . In contrast to regular tentmakers, kingdom entrepreneurs [i.e., BAM practitioners] are job *makers*, starting small to large for-profit businesses. These businesses are not fronts to get into closed countries (with the attendant ethical problems), but real enterprises that meet real human needs. . . . Their goal is to share the gospel and make disciples across cultural divides while

starting and maintaining for-profit businesses that produce tangible goods and services. . . .

Kingdom entrepreneurs are business owners, called by God, to do ministry through business. They are business owners rather than business employees. They are entrepreneurs rather than salaried men and women. They are engaged full-time in business. They are more like Aquila and Priscilla than like Paul (Ac. 18:1-5, 24-26).[8]

Tunehag takes the same tack, albeit a bit more caustically. He divides the business-mission world into three categories, "job takers, makers and fakers," respectively: tentmakers, BAMers and missionaries pretending to be businesspersons.[9]

A STRATEGIC ECONOMIC PARADIGM

When approaching mission, the church learned long ago that its colonialist and postcolonialist mission paradigm was broken. Since then it has struggled with how to conduct mission in today's globalized world in a way that is incarnational, holistic *and* strategic. BAM seems well-suited for that role, not as a replacement for traditional mission but as a strategic supplemental approach. Let's examine some ways in which BAM is an ideal strategy to simultaneously provide economic stimulation, to be a key player in community transformation (both within the United States and abroad) and to be a specific mission strategy for evangelizing and discipling the world for Christ.

An economic stimulus strategy. During the past two decades, mission-minded Christian businesspeople have seen that BAM—aside from its evangelistic component—has a formidable holistic, economic development component. Not only do the BAM companies create valuable products and services to meet people's chronic needs, but in so doing, they create jobs. Those jobs in turn create wages, which give people buying power. With their increased purchasing power these new employees are now able to buy goods and services that will improve living standards, health, housing, food, education and opportunities—not only for themselves but for their children and their children's children. Further, this process will allow people to retain the dignity, self-

---

[8]Tetsunao Yamamori and Kenneth Eldred, *On Kingdom Business: Transforming Missions Through Entrepreneurial Strategies* (Wheaton, Ill.: Crossway, 2003), pp. 8-9.
[9]Mats Tunehag, "Business as Mission," unpublished manuscript, 2002, p. 4.

esteem, healthy pride and realistic hope that come from being usefully employed and economically self-sufficient.

Economically, this increased purchasing power ignites the economic multiplier effect and spreads the economic benefit to the entire community. This occurs when the money circulates from the new employee's hands into the hands of other shopkeepers, thereby boosting their businesses, profits and purchasing power as well. The multiplier effect also provides an increased demand for goods and services that motivates others to see a profit-making opportunity, which then creates additional jobs and produces an upward spiral of economic activity.

This cycle is the heart of BAM's business-development component: creating businesses that create jobs that put money in the hands of marginalized people and thereby allows them to climb onto the bottom rung of the economic development ladder. Once on the ladder the free-market economic engine begins to move, allowing them to slowly ascend upward from one rung to the next. With each higher rung the economic engine moves at a faster pace and allows the people and their communities (and nations) to develop the capacity to realize better, fuller, healthier, richer lives. It also gives these people a stake in the stability of the society and, collectively, can begin raising their hopes, aspirations and expectations. While such upward personal mobility can be potentially destabilizing in a traditionally stagnate society, it can also have a healthy political effect. If not thwarted by repressive governmental reaction, war or other catastrophic events, the end result is predictably positive: an increase in the quality of the community's civic life, pressure for greater societal democratization and, hopefully, enhanced official accountability and even reduced corruption.[10]

The potential economic, social, political and cultural implications of a suc-

---

[10]Corruption, wholly corrosive corruption, is rampant throughout the world today, especially in the developing and emerging economies. Not only does it impede (even totally stifle) economic development, but it corrodes the people's respect for authority and government. It also bleeds off capital that could otherwise be used by people to improve their lives, invest in their businesses and purchase goods and services from others. Perhaps most tragically, it thwarts the efforts, morale and motivation of those hard-working, honest people who are the foundation of any society, especially one that is struggling to provide a decent life for its citizens, to grow and to come into the modern world. The result: people stop trying, caring and working—and things get worse rather than better. Corruption can easily prevent a people or nation from actually experiencing economic recovery and development. It can lead to both economic bankruptcy and deep spiritual, moral and ethical bankruptcy as well.

cessful BAM strategy are mind-boggling. This is not to say that the solutions to all urban ghetto problems are economic. Clearly they are not. Economics is, however, a major factor in virtually every such situation. People with productive, dignified, well-paying jobs have a greater capacity for, as the saying goes, being part of the solution rather than part of the problem. Many of the problems facing inner cities globally—drugs, violence, crime, gangs, prostitution, trash, graffiti, safety, sanitation, disease, education, welfare, health services, housing, youth and family displacement—can be positively affected when local people who are unemployed or underemployed have meaningful, society-building jobs.[11]

In its essence BAM could be a major factor in the proverbial tide that raises all boats and all nations. There is the old saying, "Give a man a fish and you feed him for a day, but teach him to fish and you feed him for a lifetime." BAM goes the next step and says, "Teach a man (or a woman) how to start a fishing business that creates jobs and you feed the community for generations."

A community transformation strategy. It has been said that a BAM firm's chief characteristic is to "exhibit fruits, which become evident in the community" and that lead to community transformation: "A business working, creating, producing, and multiplying wealth, causes transformation to take place in the community. What was dead before takes on life. The poor become rich, the weak become strong, cities are rebuilt, houses and dwellings spring up, children are enabled, and the next generation is strengthened."[12]

To these BAM advocates and many others, God-honoring city and national transformation is the end game and the essence of BAM. Here are some of their thoughts:

> Simply stated . . . Kingdom business is for-profit business ventures designed to facilitate God's transformation of people and nations. Business becomes a missions tool for ministering to those with real needs, both economic and spiritual. Addressing both needs is important for either to succeed. Though the practice of Kingdom business takes on

---

[11]Of course, not all jobs are society-building (e.g., drug trafficking, human trafficking, crime, prostitution, pornography and the gambling industries). Similarly, many society-building jobs can become society-destructive when polluted by such activities as degrading, abusive and unethical practices, corruption, greed, price gouging and negligent or inept service.

[12]Sharon Bentch Swarr and Dwight Nordstrom, *Transform the World: Biblical Vision and Purpose for Business* (Richmond, Va.: CEED, 1999), pp. 64-65.

many forms, what unites these efforts is a commitment to sustainable transformation.[13]

Societal transformation is high on God's agenda and the chief catalytic force to bring it about will be Christians ministering in the marketplace.[14]

Today millions of men and women are similarly called to full-time ministry in business, education and government—the marketplace. . . . [T]hey can do more than just witness; they can bring transformation to their jobs and then to their cities—as happened in the first century.[15]

We need to see this as a valid Christian ministry . . . *an holistic ministry, to see societies transformed by the power of the gospel displayed in the market place*, harnessing its power for God's kingdom.[16]

It is a global movement[17] that is having a global transformative impact: "There is a revival coming, revival that is returning us to our roots to understand what the early church understood—that work is a holy calling in which God moves to transform lives, cities and nations."[18]

A universal development strategy. While BAM started as a strategy for holistic mission to people in restricted and creative access nations, it quickly became apparent that it is a strategy that can go far beyond those nations. It is needed in every society in which there is rampant or endemic poverty or underdevelopment. In that sense, while BAM is a crosscultural strategy, it can also be used within the urban centers of the developed world. Within the United States alone, the inner cities of Los Angeles and Newark, Albuquerque and Detroit, and Seattle and New Orleans are ripe for BAM initiatives. The same can be said for Mexico City and São Paulo, Paris and London, Cairo and Johannesburg, Tokyo and Hong Kong, and Almaty and Moscow. Anyone who is familiar with any of these inner-city cultures knows that even when a local

---

[13]Eldred, *God Is at Work*, p. 60.

[14]C. Peter Wagner, preface to Ed Silvoso, *Anointed for Business: How Christians Can Use Their Influence in the Marketplace to Change the World* (Ventura, Calif.: Regal, 2002), p. 4. See also C. Peter Wagner, "The Church in the Workplace," *Global Prayer News* 4, no. 2 (2003): 1.

[15]Silvoso, *Anointed for Business*, p. 18.

[16]Tunehag, "Business as Mission," p. 4 (emphasis added).

[17]Os Hillman, *Faith and Work: Do They Mix?* (Alpharetta, Ga.: Aslan, 2000), p. 90.

[18]Os Hillman, "The Faith at Work Movement: Opening 'The 9 to 5 Window,'" *Regent Business Review* 1, no. 408 (2003): 8. See also, Os Hillman, *The 9 to 5 Window: How Faith can Transform the Workplace* (Ventura, Calif.: Regal, 2005).

citizen enters them with a BAM initiative, it will be as much a crosscultural experience as a Christian from Orange County, Southern California, going into Bangladesh. Regardless of locale, all poor, marginalized people have dreams, ambitions and families, and all want a better life, but they need jobs, they need hope, *and* they need Jesus. BAM can help meet all of these needs, virtually anywhere.

A STRATEGIC MISSION PARADIGM

Although BAM can be a powerful tool for effecting economic transformation of a community, it is so much more. At its heart it is a holistic mission strategy carrying the love and gospel of our Lord Jesus Christ to a lost and hurting world through the vehicle of business and the relationships created in that enterprise.

> [In BAM, the] emphasis is on mission as transforming community through business with an intentionality that Jesus is made known, encountered or followed. . . . This approach implies a holistic mission in which there is a conscious evangelistic engagement with the business world as a place where the Lordship of Christ and the Kingdom of God is hoped for and worked out in the decisions, culture, structures and systems of commercial life—the business of eternal living.[19]

Certainly, we can help people holistically through BAM without giving Jesus the credit or letting the people know who their true benefactor is. But in so doing we betray those people, leaving them without the living water they really need. Unwittingly, we even portray our Christ—by his apparent absence—as an unloving, invisible, insensitive, impotent god. After all, in the final analysis these people need Jesus and his saving gospel much more than improved living standards. As one BAM practitioner is reputed to have said, "Without Jesus, we are simply giving them fuller bellies on their way to hell."

Therein lies the key to BAM: It is so much more than a potentially powerful business-development and community economic-transformation strategy, because it brings eternal hope and healing along with temporal prosperity.

---

[19]Tunehag, "Business as Mission," pp. 4-5.

A MODERN MISSION PARADIGM

While BAM has significant historical roots within the broader church and its mission ventures, it is only in the recent past that it has assumed a life of its own as a specific mission strategy. The fact that its first appearance at a Lausanne Conference was not until 2004 attests loudly to its recent new visibility. In addition to the unique characteristics that define BAM in its modern state, six deserve special comment: BAM is a domestic and international, long-term, holistic, incarnational, contextually appropriate, empowering and real ministry to people in need.

Domestic and International. For the first time in human history, over half of the world's 6.7 billion people now live in urban areas. In 1990 the world's population was 5.3 billion people; by 2020 it is estimated to increase by 2.3 billion people, to 7.6 billion. Further, of the 7.6 billion, 84 percent, or 6.4 billion, will be in LDCs (lesser developed countries) and 1.2 billion in MDCs (more developed countries) with a growth rate of about 1 percent per year.[20] This is a dramatic demographic shift from only thirty years ago. The largest cities of the world now have multiple millions of residents, with all of the social, cultural, economic, political and infrastructure issues that go with such large numbers of people living in close proximity to one another. That is compounded by the massive migration and immigration that has occurred over the past few decades. The rates of migration in many Third World cities have been far in excess of the cities' capacities to absorb them. The resulting stress on city infrastructures alone has been debilitating. Health and welfare services, if any, are stretched to the maximum; law enforcement and educational systems are unable to cope; housing, utilities, garbage collection and sanitation services are wholly inadequate; and jobs, economic opportunity and social mobility are invisible dreams.

Further, and perhaps most significant in the long run, where most cities were once predominantly monocultural, today there is hardly a city of any size anywhere in the world that does not have numerous ethnic, nationality and language groups. A good example is the greater Los Angeles area, which is home to more than 14.5 million people of whom 27 percent are foreign born,

---

[20]"World Population at a Glance: 1996 and Beyond," U.S. Department of Commerce, Bureau of Census, September 1996, <www.census.gov/ipc/prod/ib96_03.pdf> and "World's Largest Cities," Mongabay.com <www.mongabay.com/cities_pop_01.htm>.

52 percent of whom arrived between 1980 to 1990. Los Angeles County has 224 languages (not including dialects) spoken by groups from across the face of the planet. Thirty-eight percent speak a language other than English at home, with 69 percent speaking Spanish.[21] Similar demographics can be found in almost every major city worldwide.

The point is that mission, which may be defined as crossing barriers (e.g., cultural, ethnic, geographic and religious) with the gospel, once was almost exclusively international. When a missionary spoke about going on the mission field it was invariably an international location distant from his homeland. It was *over there*—overseas, international, foreign. *Over here*, everyone was Christian (or Jewish), middle class and white. Over there, they were different. Over here and over there, the churches comprised ethnically similar worshipers, but in today's migrating, populous, pluralistic, globalized world, that is no longer true. Now, urban populations are an amalgam of dissimilar looking, speaking, thinking, acting and worshiping people—and so are the churches.

The implications of this for mission in general and BAM in particular are enormous. Quite simply it means, as Frecia Johnson has stated, that "mission is now next door as well as overseas; it is domestic as well as international."[22] Similarly, where BAM was once exclusively used as a strategy for reaching remote, inaccessible nations, it is now a strategy that can be implemented virtually anywhere the entrepreneur has access, start-up capital and sufficient infrastructure to support the proposed business venture.

Long term. In the days of William Carey (1793), the father of modern mission, missionaries were called to a particular foreign nation or people group and generally planned on being there for decades, if not for life.[23] In those days and in the two centuries since, missionaries were Christians who elected to spend their lives among foreign people, learning the local language and cul-

---

[21]Roger Waldinger and Mehdi Bozorgmehr, eds., *Ethnic Los Angeles* (New York: Russell Sage, 1996), p. 141, and "Language Spoken at Home by Individual Los Angeles Communities, Persons 5 Years and Over, City of Los Angeles, 2000 Census," Los Angeles Almanac <www.la almanac.com/LA/la10b.htm>.

[22]Personal conversation with Frecia Johnson, August 23, 2000.

[23]For excellent discussions of Carey and his business mission reforms, see Vishal Mangalwadi and Ruth Mangalwadi, *The Legacy of William Carey: A Model for the Transformation of a Culture* (Wheaton, Ill.: Crossway, 1999), and Timothy George, *The Life and Mission of William Carey* (Birmingham, Ala.: New Hope, 1991).

ture, bearing and rearing their children there, planting churches, shepherding their flock, and saving lost souls. Those were the days of wooden ships, long sea voyages and little or no contact with home for months or years at a time.

How different it is today! With modern technology, travel capabilities, instant global communications, pervasive media and Western affluence, the days of life-time mission commitments to one people group or community are quickly becoming a thing of the past. Thankfully, there are still many committed Christians who are willing and available for long-term, even life-time, mission service and who are actually so serving—and they are true children of the faith. However, in today's world the structure and strategy of missions by the sending agencies and churches has altered radically. Today a three-year commitment is a long-term commitment; today, many churches are as focused on short-term mission as on long-term mission, and today there is widespread recognition that short-term missions, while exceptionally valuable, tend to benefit the sending church more than the receiving church. In contrast, long-term missions were (and are) almost exclusively for the receiving church's benefit and the most effective means for propagating the gospel and winning lost souls to Jesus.

That is where BAM has an advantage. Like the missionaries of old, BAMers go to a country to establish a business and use it for mission purposes. By their very nature, businesses are designed to be long-lasting, even perpetual institutions that have a permanent presence in the community. As such a BAM entrepreneur is making a long-term if not a life-time commitment to live, work, play and minister among those people for years to come.

Holistic. BAM entrepreneurs are committed to using their businesses as *true platforms for holistic mission* in the Lausanne tradition: "The holistic mission of the Kingdom is to take the whole Gospel, to the whole man, by the whole church, to the whole world. This is our mandate and our task."[24]

In simplistic terms, *holistic mission* means showing the love of Jesus to people in need by ministering to each of them as a whole human being and trying to address all of their needs and pain. In that regard it means meeting their *spiritual needs* for eternal well-being through evangelism and loving witness. That requires understanding their worldview of god(s) and spirituality,

---

[24]Tunehag, "Business as Mission," pp. 2, 4.

the powers of darkness and agentive versus empirical causation. It means meeting their *emotional need* for inner well-being through Jesus-centered prayer counseling and inner healing ministries. Finally, it means meeting their *physical needs* for outer well-being through international and economic development. As Christians we minister to the outer person to help create environments—businesses, homes, neighborhoods and communities—in which people can live safe, decent, healthy, happy, prosperous, directed lives of purpose, growth and meaning. We minister to those in pain, not just for the sake of their immediate relief but to show them that Jesus the Christ loves them and that he knows of their suffering, grieves with them over it and has sent his faithful followers *to come alongside of them to help alleviate it—that is, to work with them, not dictate to them or do it for them.* In that way we hope to bring eternal relief as well as physical relief. This involves ministries in areas like

- *food,* by providing famine and malnourishment relief and by addressing nutrition, food supplies and agricultural needs

- *clean water,* by drilling needed water wells, as well as addressing purification, sanitation, quantity, access and quality issues

- *health and hygiene,* through education at personal, family and community levels

- *formal education,* by wrestling with such issues as teachers, materials, content, physical plants, gender, access and the like

- *economics,* by creating jobs and wealth, by helping to develop community and national infrastructures, and by providing market training, skills and opportunities at both the macro and the micro levels

- *politics,* by helping address issues of governmental institutions, processes and initiatives, as well as public policy formulation relating to civil rights, justice, oppression, religious freedom and persecution

- *power,* by identifying, advocating to, working with and perhaps confronting both the formal and informal institutional, extra-institutional and traditional power structures within a neighborhood, community, region, tribe or nation

In short, holistic ministry is the articulation of God's love and the good news of Jesus through actions and deeds, as well as words, in every aspect of a person's life.

While BAM companies unashamedly strive for profits, that is not their only or even primary measure of success. Indeed, one of BAM's key distinguishing precepts is its focus on holistic mission. As Steve Rundle and Tom Steffen assert, "The business itself is an integral part of a holistic mission strategy, one that meets physical as well as spiritual needs."[25]

BAM uses business to address the range of needs of people in a given locale. It does so both internally and externally, both within the business itself and through the business's community outreach efforts. It is a mission methodology that addresses the whole man, the whole woman, the whole child, the whole community. Of course, no one company can deal with all of a person's needs, but since so much of the dominant, nonspiritual needs in the world are economic or have economic roots, especially people's jobs, BAM is uniquely suited to minister to that specific need in crosscultural contexts. Beyond that, by taking a holistic approach (which includes but goes far beyond evangelism and discipleship), the BAM Company can choose to take actions much more broadly designed and from an infinitely broader, even overwhelming, range of needs that face its employees and the community it serves.

The later chapters on BAM models and BAM's multiple bottom lines speak directly to this, but there they are cast from the company's point of view. From the beneficiaries' point of view, BAM's holistic ministry takes on a much more personal aura. It is giving jobs to the marginalized, crippled, unemployed or underemployed with all that implies: wages, purpose, self-respect, self-esteem, personal identity, healthy pride and hope. It brings them unimaginable opportunity to work in clean, comfortable, safe and hospitable environments; learn marketable skills; receive training in health, nutrition, prenatal, sanitation, hygiene and parenting; be instructed in handling money, personal finances and conflict management; join Bible study and character development classes; receive counseling, mentoring, encouragement, support, day care for their babies, elder care for their aged parents, and summer school for their

---

[25]Steve Rundle and Tom Steffen, "Business as Mission: Globalization and the Emerging Role of Great Commission Companies," unpublished manuscript, La Mirada, California, 2003, p. 8. A later draft of this manuscript was published by Rundle and Steffen as *Great Commission Companies: The Emerging Role of Business in Missions* (Downers Grove, Ill.: InterVarsity Press, 2003), but without this particular quote.

children; participate in projects that improve the quality of their lives and their community; be empowered to make decisions and to take responsibility within their jobs and the business; have the freedom and opportunity to learn about the one, true living God, his Son Jesus Christ and the workings of the Holy Spirit; and to see the gospel lived out in the daily life of the BAM team and their families. That is holistic ministry/mission—and that is what BAM is all about.

Incarnational. If BAM's first dominant missiological theme is holistic mission, the second is incarnational mission/ministry. Christ demonstrated this to us in a power-packed, visible, tangible way that left no doubt of his commitment to and love for us. He did this by coming to us incarnationally. That is, being God, he took human form, came to us as a baby born of woman and lived among us. He did not come as an outsider or as a stranger visiting a strange land. He came as the ultimate insider, a Jewish boy who was reared in the Jewish culture and language, who made his living as a carpenter in the family business in Nazareth, who suffered, rejoiced, wept, laughed, loved and lived as a whole human being, and who embraced the whole human experience—with all the baggage that comes with life.

In the same way, the Jesus way, missionaries must become like insiders within the community they have been called to, living long-term and incarnationally in the midst of the people in need. It means *coming alongside* those people as paracletes (helpers and comforters), and meeting them as equals; it means ministering *with* them (reciprocally) and not *to* them or *for* them;[26] it means experiencing a mutual sense of learning, growing and healing together; it means participating with them (not vice versa) in genuine partnership to craft long-term strategies for dealing with their problems—strategies that they can own and are able to manage (without the missionary), and that can become integral to their community life.

In short, incarnational mission means being a witness to Christ's love for people by residing in their midst for the long term. Such commitment to others is rare in today's world, but it is the sacrificial road that Jesus modeled and calls us to.

Earlier missionaries, being long-term or lifetime residents of their adopted

---

[26]Frecia Johnson, "Reciprocal Contextualization," in *Appropriate Christianity*, ed. Charles H. Kraft (Pasadena, Calif.: William Carey Library, 2005), pp. 475-90.

country and city, were most successful when they followed Jesus' example and tried to become one of the people they served. Hudson Taylor is perhaps the most famous example. He broke with the prevailing mission tradition, lived among the people, adopted their language, dress, hairstyles and ways in order that he might relate to them incarnationally. In so doing he showed respect and deference to their God-given cultural experience and catered to their dignity as God's children. Taylor viewed this as the most effective way to reach people with the gospel and to help them overcome the view that Jesus is a foreign, Western God. In those and earlier times the arrogance of the Western ethnocentric worldview and the fear of *going native* regrettably made such true incarnational ministry rare.

BAM is the essence of incarnational mission, and BAMers are inherently long-term, incarnational missionaries. By definition, businesses are intended to have generational, even perpetual existence. As a practical, daily matter, for a business to survive and succeed the BAMer and his or her family must have local credibility and trust. That only comes from relating to the people to whom they are ministering, learning the language, living among the people long-term and embracing their ways—as long as the gospel is not compromised. Paul was a great example, saying he would be all things to all people to promote the cause of Christ, as long as his gospel was not compromised (1 Cor 9:22-23; Acts 17:16-28). As difficult as this is, the incarnational way is the Jesus way and makes BAM a strong, sustainable mission strategy.

Contextually appropriate. Contextualization, or *doing theology* in context, permeates every mission, including BAM.[27] Although far from simple, it means that all mission activities must remain sensitive to the mission setting: the people, their culture and their ways. It means that the missionary must bring Christ into the midst of a people in ways that are harmonious with and appropriate to that cultural context. Those ways must be designed to foster biblically sound relationships with Jesus and to effectively communicate not only the gospel but Jesus' profound love for those people in that place at that time. To do otherwise is to run the danger of destroying the God-ordained, God-blessed parts of their culture and of making God and Jesus seem like alien, hostile, foreign gods. It also prevents these people from finding a per-

---

[27]Dean S. Gilliland, ed., *The Word Among Us: Contextualizing Theology for Mission Today* (Dallas: Word, 1989), p. 11.

sonal relationship with Jesus. Equally tragic, it robs them of the opportunity to hear his call on their lives.

Having said this, it is important to note that "the meaning of contextualization is always open to interpretation."[28] David Hubbard, the former president of Fuller Theological Seminary, drawing on the stage play *Fiddler on the Roof*, expressed it poetically:

> "Without it," Tevye mused, "life would be as shaky as . . . as . . . as a fiddler on the roof." The *it*, for Anatevka's milkman, was tradition. For those who care about Christ's worldwide mission, the *it* is *contextualization*, a delicate enterprise if ever there was one. Like the fiddler, the evangelist and mission strategist stand on a razor's edge, aware that to fall off on either side has terrible consequences. . . . No word in the Christian lexicon is as fraught with difficulty, danger, and opportunity as contextualization. God's people cannot shy from it. Even though problem-laden to the hilt, not to attempt it would be the faultiest strategy and worst discipleship of all.[29]

This "commitment to understand mission with biblical clarity, cultural sensitivity, and spiritual wholeness" is the goal of contextualization, says Gilliland. He adds:

> The conviction . . . is that *contextualization, biblically based and Holy Spirit led, is a requirement for evangelical missions today. Contextualization is incarnational.* The Word which became flesh dwells among us. It clarifies for each nation or people the meaning of the confession, "Jesus is Lord." It liberates the church in every place to hear what the Spirit is saying. *Contextual theology will open up the way for communication of the gospel in ways that allow the hearer to understand and accept it.* It gives both freedom and facility for believers to build up one another in the faith. Contextualization clarifies what the Christian witness is in a sinful society and shows what obedience to the gospel requires. These are the components of a theology for mission that meets the needs of today's world.[30]

---

[28]Ibid., p. 3.
[29]David Allen Hubbard, foreword to ibid., pp. vii-viii.
[30]Gilliland, *Word Among Us*, pp. 3-4 (emphasis added).

Orlando E. Costas summarizes, "Contextual theologies are not the direct outgrowth of the traditional theological factories: the world of academia. They stem, rather, from the peculiar situation in which many Christians find themselves as they try to live their faith and fulfill their vocation in their respective life circumstances."[31] Of critical importance, however, contextualization must be appropriate to both Scripture and the people of a given culture.[32] While a detailed discussion of contextualization is beyond the scope of this book, it is a vital element of successful BAM. As such, it is worth emphasizing that the simplicity of the concept belies its complexity in practice:

> In order to give rise to an "appropriate Christianity" in a given context, Christians in that context need to construct a method of mission theologizing in such a way that the method itself is appropriate to Scripture, to the people of that context, and in relation to the world Church, yielding over time a contextually appropriate understanding of God's revelation to which the people of that culture may respond and by which they may be transformed (in truth, allegiance and power). This contextually appropriate methodology will need to be integrational, local, incarnational, praxeological and dialogical.[33]

Appropriate contextualization is even more essential in BAM since both the mission enterprise and the business itself are totally dependent on acceptance by the community. Without that acceptance, customers, sales and profits will diminish and the business will be in serious danger of collapse. It will almost invariably have failed to meet local needs and expectations, ceased to garner local respect, lost influence in the community, and may even have alienated it. With the business's demise, the opportunity for mission both within the business and within the community will also be lost—as will the hard work, dreams, morale, zeal, capital and time of the BAMers themselves.

An interesting feature of appropriate contextualization is that in the process of doing mission, the missionary is personally affected, often signifi-

---

[31]Orlando E. Costas, *Christ Outside the Gate: Mission Beyond Christendom* (Mary Knoll, N.Y.: Orbis, 1982), p. 3.

[32]Charles Van Engen, "Five Perspectives of Contextually Appropriate Mission Theology," and "Toward a Contextually Appropriate Methodology in Mission Theology," *Appropriate Christianity*, ed. Charles H. Kraft (Pasadena, Calif.: William Carey Library, 2005), pp.183-202, 203-26.

[33]Van Engen, "Toward a Contextually Appropriate Methodology," p. 203.

cantly, by the experience. He or she goes to the mission field to affect the indigenous people and in the process ends up being changed as profoundly (or more so) as they are. In describing this phenomenon—which is exceptionally pronounced in BAMers and their families—Frecia Johnson coined the term *reciprocal contextualization* in 1999.

> All of us who have worked cross-culturally return home as changed people. We have lived in what to us is a new world, with new rules of behavior based on assumptions [worldviews] we often don't understand. To the extent that we were able to adjust to that new world, then, *we become bicultural.* We become more than we were before we went into the other world and we were forever changed. As we became accustomed to that other world, we often began to assimilate some of the assumptions of the people among whom we worked and began to look at things from their point of view. . . . Upon returning home and sharing with our own people the insights that we had developed, we discovered that *we had changed in radically new and exciting ways that often startled those who sent us.*[34]

While reciprocal contextualization can either be constructive or destructive, good or bad, depending on the individuals affected, it is a very real, marked change that BAMers and their families can expect to experience. Not only will it affect their own behavior and worldview but their relationships with other BAM team members and with their own families. Further, this relational impact is highly individualized and will be significantly different for each person, both on the mission field and upon reentry into their own culture. As many returning missionaries know all too well, their new persona can have a profound, unexpected, disquieting impact on relationships with individuals, family and church back home.[35]

Biases. One astute commentator, Brad Smith, president of Bakke Graduate University, has voiced some strongly held opinions (what he calls "biases") about BAM.[36] "They are good biases," he says, "and the last one is a bit rare, but they come from many years of involvement in the field." I would add that

---

[34]Johnson, "Reciprocal Contextualization," pp. 475, 477, 481 (emphasis added).
[35]Ibid.
[36]Personal e-mail from Brad Smith, dated April 26, 2008.

these are also healthy biases in that they help define not so much *what* BAM is as *who* we are who practice and advocate it. Among Smith's biases are these critical points:

- *BAM is real ministry.* We frequently speak of BAM being real business and real mission, but we often gloss over the obvious: inside the BAM enterprise, whether it is business or mission, we are ministering to real people and their very real needs. "The call to business is not a call to second class ministry in God's view. And we don't have to be doing overt evangelism, closing our chicken stores on Sundays, or giving big money to 'real ministries' for God to be pleased with a business that is providing valuable good for society."[37]

- *BAM: Missions or mission?* There is a distinction between business as missions (plural) and business as mission (singular). "The former," Smith asserts, "emphasizes strategy; the latter emphasizes a genuine life call that results in transformed economies, societies, cultures as well as souls saved for eternity."[38] Stated in a different way, mission (singular) is a part of *missio Dei*, that is, God's grand, overarching, singularly integrated mission plan to see people of every tribe, nation and tongue reconciled to himself. Missions (plural) is humanity's strategic and tactical efforts to be a part of *missio Dei* through an infinite variety of methods and ventures. In that sense BAM (singular) is what we are all about, but we may engage in missions (plural) to fulfill our small but important part in God's grand scheme.

- *BAM empowers people.* "People made in the image of God are made to make decisions on behalf of God (Genesis 2:19-20). That means a business that is on God's mission is one that gives away decision-making authority to its employees and creates a culture to equip and empower them to make decentralized decisions. . . . [I]t reconnects people to what it means to be made in the image of God and opens their hearts to what God intended for them on earth, and for eternity."[39] Here, Smith is reflecting a major thesis of businessman Dennis Bakke, the former president and CEO of the world's

---

[37]Ibid.
[38]Ibid.
[39]Ibid.

second largest producer of electrical energy, AES, who says in his book, *Joy at Work*:

> Winning, especially winning financially, is a second-order goal at best. . . . A major point of this book is to suggest a broader definition of organizational performance and success, one that gives high priority to a workplace that is filled with joy for ordinary working people. Such a place gives all workers the opportunity to make important decisions and take significant actions using their gifts and skills to the utmost. Our experience at AES showed that this kind of workplace can be the cornerstone of an organization that is vibrant and economically robust.[40]

It almost goes without saying that every BAM practitioner and theorist has biases or opinions born out of his or her God-given experiences. Smith's biases are well-founded and important to absorb. Equally important, they help us realize that fulfilling both great commissions—stewardship (Gen 1:28-30; 2:5, 15, 19-20; see also Eph 2:10) and discipleship (Mt 28:18-20; Acts 1:8)—and doing missions in general, and perhaps especially doing BAM, is and always will be a work in progress. Clearly, if we as individuals are always *becoming*, we must realize (concede) that our BAM efforts always will be too. That realization commends each of us to approach this subject with a great deal of humility and grace—particularly when we consider the proposals on *how* to do BAM in part two of this book.

The Emic and Etic

Oddly enough, my concluding point in defining what BAM is must be a strange sounding pair of words: *emic* and *etic*. Quite simply, the emic are the *insiders* of the culture being targeted by mission; the etic are *outsiders* to the culture, such as expat missionaries or Western businessmen. Emic and etic are terms used by mission practitioners as shorthand for a very important mission concept: only insiders (emic) have the right to make fundamental changes within a given culture; conversely, outsiders (etic) have no right to make such changes, but they do

---

[40]Dennis Bakke, *Joy at Work: A CEO's Revolutionary Approach to Fun on the Job* (Seattle: Pearson Venture Group, 2005), p. 18.

have a right to advocate and model such change. And since the emic only see the trees and the etic see the forest, working in tandem they can see both and thereby effect better, healthier changes in the culture and society.[41]

God's etic. As the emic-etic distinction is applied to traditional missionaries, it is meant to show that (1) Jesus is the Lord of all peoples and all cultures, and he is not a foreign God but is rather their Lord and their God; (2) acceptance of Jesus and his gospel will demand major changes in the way the people think and live; (3) the missionary comes only as an advocate for Jesus and his gospel, not as the actual change agent; and (4) only the people themselves can actually incorporate Jesus and his teachings into their society. After all, the concept says, it is the insiders (the *emic*) who must live with the changes long-term. If they do not assimilate the changes into fundamental elements of their culture and way of life, the changes will not be sustainable. In fact, they will probably not survive the missionary's time in the country. Further, missionary-injected concepts can actually create long-term damage to the host culture if its members do not fully embrace and claim these concepts as their own. Working together, however, the emic and etic can lead the people to God-blessed changes that improve their lives *and* preserve the healthy aspects of their culture.

A legitimate question arises as to whether the emic-etic principle is applicable to BAM. As a traditional mission effort, certainly; but as a business and mission effort, it is far from clear. The BAM Company is, after all, seeking to introduce new (frequently Western and often international) business ideas, technologies, production concepts, management practices, marketing methods and money into a traditional, underdeveloped or impoverished setting. It is often expat (etic) led and globally connected, purposefully designed to bring the outside world into a culture, to remake it into a viable part of the world economic system.

Does BAM, by being a direct change agent in an alien culture, violate this basic modern mission cornerstone and thereby risk irreparable harm to the host culture, society and its people? This question begs for an answer. To help us find that answer, let's turn to a recent parallel in history: the fall of the Soviet Union.

---

[41]Paul G. Hiebert, *Cultural Anthropology* (Grand Rapids: Baker, 1983), pp. 50-54, and Charles H. Kraft, *Anthropology for Christian Witness* (Maryknoll, N.Y.: Orbis, 1996), pp. 76-79.

The Second World. When the Iron Curtain fell, Western business and governmental interests poured into the former Soviet Union's (FSU) sphere of influence. A predominant part of their mission was to bring this economically backward empire into the world market, to transition the states of the FSU from their command economy to a market economy. The process caused the FSU, as the former Second World (as opposed to the First World of developed nations and the Third World of underdeveloped nations), to be relabeled the *transitioning economies*. In simplistic terms the First World's mission was to bootstrap the FSU from an abacus society to a computer society overnight and to skip the intermediate steps that had burdened the rest of the world for decades.

That strategy flies in the face of the emic-etic principle. By its very nature the modern business-driven, market economy is not a respecter of cultures, except as may be necessary to increase sales. It is an ethnocentric, even paternalist philosophy that says, "You and your family will be better off, have higher living standards and enjoy the good things of life, if you become a part of the global market economy."

Al Capone and the robber barons. We unabashedly subscribe to the concept that global free trade is, in the long run, the only viable path for the world's economy if the grotesque poverty and growing chasm between haves and have-nots is to be eliminated. We note, however, that the wholesale, worldwide proselytizing of the market economy in the past two decades has raised four very important stumbling blocks. First, the new global free-market economy—in spite of such shibboleths as "think globally but act locally" or engage in "glocal" business—has launched an unrelenting attack on local cultures. We fear the long-term damage that will occur to the God-given, cultural diversity of the world. We see cultural diversity as being one of the most beautiful aspects of life on this planet and pray that humanity can find ways to preserve it in its best forms, while simultaneously helping people out of poverty.

Second, this new economic revival has been like a new religion, but without the moral values and foundational ethics that have caused it to prosper elsewhere. Raw capitalism, unchecked by these values and ethics, can lead to widespread economic inequality, class oppression and ruthless human rights abuses. The thing that made the United States the economic envy of the world was the combination of free-market capitalism and the Judeo-Christian ethic. That ethic was overlaid on the economic system to produce boundaries and constraints necessary to allow the nation and virtually its entire population to prosper and to enjoy higher living standards.

On the other hand, the capitalism exported to the FSU was raw capitalism, devoid of any such boundaries and restraints. The result was disastrous with its rampant cronyism, burgeoning oligarchy, monopolistic business practices, ruthless mafia and the suppression of individual initiative and freedom.

In short, the capitalistic proselytizing that has accompanied economic globalization has been without an underlying value system. Tragically, that has led to gross excesses, distorted social systems, corrupt political systems and rampant human-rights violations, including slavery, oppression and persecution (especially of women, youth and religious minorities).

Third, historically the American experiment in democracy and free-market economics was also seriously threatened by internal efforts to destroy both its political and its economic freedoms. The free-market system advocated by Adam Smith created a toxic environment that allowed organized crime and tyrannical dictators like Al Capone in Chicago to gain control of the local political processes. It allowed the rise of the robber barons and their powerful, monopolistic grip on the economic system. And it created excesses that led to catastrophic events like Black Tuesday (October 29, 1929) and the Great Depression.

Only through landmark legislative action and bold executive decisions was the nation able to survive this financial crisis. Congress passed laws that moderated the raw capitalist system and regulated commerce to keep it fair, competitive and consistent with the public good. They outlawed restraints on competition (monopolies), allowed collective bargaining, and created an independent central bank (the Federal Reserve Board) to protect our money supply, regulate our banks and monitor our economy. They also created the Federal Bureau of Investigation (FBI) and its G-men (Government Men) to destroy the criminal leviathans that were strangling our cities.

The nations of the FSU are facing similar threats today from the Russian mafia, the oligarchs and rampant corruption. Their heritage has been tsarist and communist for over a thousand years, with the public square being dominated by strongmen with virtually unlimited personal power. Ex-president and now Prime Minister Vladimir Putin is cut from that mold and can be expected to seek a way to combine free-market economics with tsarist power.

He sees the Chinese attempting that transition and may be encouraged by the short-term results of their bold experiment. Whether economic freedom can continue to flourish in the context of political oppression and authoritarian government remains an open question that is central to this new century.

Fourth, there is nothing attractive, admirable or God-ordained about the rampant sin that has accompanied raw capitalism and its aberrations. When these practices become intimately connected to the prevailing culture, they are abhorrent to basic humanity.

As other nations embrace the capitalist system they would do well to notice what made the American system so prosperous and to understand that we went through similar struggles in the decades following the industrial revolution and the Great Depression. If we are all to find our way in this new globalized market economy, we need to undergird it with value-laden, ethical boundaries and to moderate it with governmental actions that would maximize competition and preserve economic freedom.[42]

Perhaps nothing illustrates this better than the two most recent global failures of raw capitalism that plundered the world's wealth and devastated its economic stability. The 1997 financial crisis that started in Thailand and the 2008 financial tsunami or meltdown that started with the subprime housing debacle in the United States. Both originated with underregulated, loose banking and mortgage lending practices, looser government supervision (e.g., Fannie Mae) and unchecked human greed. The 2008 crisis was preceded by a decade of shameful corporate practices that made names like Enron (Kenneth Lay and Jeffrey Skilling), Tyco (Dennis Kozlowski), WorldCom (Bernard Ebbers), Arthur Anderson LLP (loss of 85,000 jobs) and Bernard Madoff (the $50 billion Ponzi scheme, which may be the greatest business fraud in history) iconic symbols for the dangers of raw capitalism. This sorry episode in capitalism disclosed massive regulatory failure on the part of government that matched these examples of massive corruption. Just as the United States was rocked by these scandals, so Europe was rocked by the Siemens bribery and corruption charges, which was perhaps the greatest corporate scandal in postwar Germany. Unfortunately, the list goes on, illustrating the simple fact that human nature is fallen and that systems

---

[42]This concept of value-driven capitalism is one of the foundational pillars of the new Bakke Graduate School of Business in Seattle. The author is privileged to serve as its founding dean.

must always be put in place to check power, whether in the public or the private sector.

Stumbling blocks. How is any of the foregoing discussion relevant to BAM? I suggest that it is not only relevant but is foundational, for BAM seeks to address all of these stumbling blocks. First, it respects the local culture and its people. It seeks to contextualize its presence within the bounds of that culture and to exist and operate in harmony with it. In so doing the BAM Company and the BAM team members are committed to becoming a part of the local economy, culture and society, while simultaneously creating global economic opportunities for the people to better their lives.

Second, BAM brings foundational values that were instrumental in American prosperity and made it the envy of the world. It brings the gospel of Jesus Christ to the people in a relational way that allows them to make his gospel their personal credo. The BAM Company itself witnesses to the gospel through its Christ-centered, Bible-based management practices, its management-style evangelism and its strategic master BAM plan. The BAM team members and their families, as residents in the local community, witness in their lifestyle evangelism. Through their friendships, community involvement, social interaction and demonstrated love, they show people what Jesus is about and why he and his message should be theirs for life.

Third, while BAM is not a governmental entity, it does promote the same values of competition, free trade and honest, noncoercive business practices as found in U.S. laws. This self-regulation among businesses is by far the best way to achieve the high ethical and fair-trade competitive standards so vital to a thriving free-market economy.

Fourth, the sin, corruption and social degradation that are produced by raw capitalism are directly in the crosshairs of BAM companies. They seek to eliminate them within their local business communities, their industries, and their products and services. They bring biblical values to the business table and attempt to operate in alignment with them in all of their business dealings. In so doing, they seek to reinstate within their part of the global market system those values and practices that destroy the sinful aspects of raw capitalism and promote a life-honoring, life-enhancing business paradigm.

Fifth, the BAM team's goal is to become an *insider* in the culture. By definition, that is impossible, but so is becoming like Christ. Nonetheless, the apostle Paul admonished all Christians to become more and more Christlike in all they do. BAMers and their families, in their quest to become insiders, not only seek this Christlikeness but also to become more and more like the indigenous people they serve.

Traditional civil service and early mission practice feared the concept of "going native" and did all they could to maintain their cultural identity in the midst of their foreign-duty stations. Even today, the U.S. State Department regularly rotates its diplomats to prevent them from identifying too closely with the local culture and thereby undermining U.S. national policy and interests.

The opposite is true with BAM. The BAMer seeks to go native to the extent that it is consistent with the gospel and to making disciples. As noted earlier, Paul insisted on being all things to all people to bring them the saving knowledge of Jesus the Christ, except where such actions would compromise the core gospel (1 Cor 9:21-23). That stance is so central to BAM's mission that it bears repeating here. Jesus engaged the people and their culture incarnationally, long-term and holistically. So does BAM.

Finally, BAM is designed to empower indigenous people to help themselves out of poverty their own way. To that end, BAM urges BAM businesses to bring local people into the management and even ownership of the BAM businesses, and through replication and peer groups (discussed later) to assist and mentor them into starting their own businesses. In this way BAM is outsiders advocating a better way of life economically and spiritually, but it leaves societal buy-in (or not) to those new ways solely up to the insider.

Based on this discussion I conclude that the emic-etic principle is directly applicable to sound BAM practice. As a respecter of culture, a purveyor of values and a counterweight to sin, and as a long-term incarnational mission strategy, BAM seeks to blend good market business practices into the local economy in ways that lead to an economically, ethically and spiritually improved society. It seeks to empower indigenous people and demonstrate, by example, the path to a more abundant life. Adoption of internal cultural change is strictly left up to those insiders whose lives are most directly affected. Any would-be BAMer—as an outsider (etic)—needs to understand this legitimate, self-imposed limitation and to adapt to it as one of the risks and costs of doing BAM God's way.

DISCUSSION QUESTIONS

1. The author defines BAM as "a for-profit commercial business venture that is Christian led, intentionally devoted to being used as an instrument of God's mission *(missio Dei)* to the world, and is operated in a crosscultural environment, either domestic or international." What could you add to (or take away from) the author's definition? Based on your reading so far, write your own definition of BAM.

2. Why is it important that BAM businesses are *real* businesses in every way, not just centers for ministry with a business name or component?

3. Expanding on an old adage, BAM says, "Teach a man (or a woman) how to start a fishing business that creates jobs and you feed the community for generations." Is job creation the primary answer to "community transformation"? Is there a difference? If so, what is it? How do these two concepts interrelate?

4. Why is job creation in economic development important? Explain how job creation can have a positive ripple effect throughout an entire community. What is meant by the "multiplier effect"?

5. What is holistic mission/ministry? What Scripture supports holistic mission/ministry? How can a BAM company engage in holistic mission through its regular business activities?

6. What is meant by "incarnational mission"? How is BAM incarnational? Does being incarnational improve the mission results? If so, how? If not, why?

7. Do you agree with Brad Smith that one way of empowering employees and respecting the image of God in them is to "give away decision-making authority to our employees"? Why or why not? What are the benefits of such a policy? What are the downsides or dangers? How can this translate into actual management policies and practices of real business? Give and discuss examples.

2

BAM MODELS

Model: A standard for imitation, comparison or emulation; a pattern.

"The way you know you are successful is when the powerless value the powerful and the powerful value the powerless. Without the powerless being valued, there is rebellion. Without the powerful being valued, there is domination.

"If God is there, He is in the powerless and the powerful, and seeks to see them connected. The marketplace is the vehicle that connects the two."

LOWELL BAKKE AND GWEN DEWEY

"We worked night and day, laboring and toiling so that
we would not be a burden to any of you.
We did this . . . to make ourselves a model for you to follow."

2 THESSALONIANS 3:8-9

IT IS SOMEWHAT PRESUMPTUOUS, if not wholly counterproductive, to attempt to corral the myriad expressions of BAM into a one-size-fits-all model or mold, or even to list the experiential best practices of companies that are engaged in this movement. Such attempts fly in the face of the critical importance of contextualization and work against the value of the emic and etic perspectives. There is no such thing as a ready-made BAM formula or kit— "BAM in a Box"—and any who would try to create such are arguably working against the primal forces of nature (and God) in at least four ways.

First, the essence of entrepreneurship is creative risk-taking, engaging a complex web of factors and attempting to create something productive and profitable where it did not previously exist. This aspect of business is nothing short of the finest artistic creativity of which humanity is capable. Those engaged in creating new businesses, new products, new processes, new markets and new technologies are usually type-A personalities who will find or invent totally unique, imaginative ways of leveraging business for mission and ministry. BAM is not about restricting those God-given creative capacities and gifts, but about releasing, harnessing and leveraging it to serve God and his kingdom through purposeful, beneficial service to humankind in the name and love of Jesus. Certainly BAM practitioners can and should learn from each other, but how they adapt those lessons to their own particular businesses, products, markets, communities and cultural contexts will be as individual and different as the businesses themselves.

Second, our Lord is creative and is continually showing us an infinite variety of ways to minister to our fellow humans on this planet. One has only to look at the countless forms of life found in nature, whether in the cosmos itself or in the more earthly geologic formations, the animal kingdom, aquatic life or the world of plants, insects, bacteria, germs, atomic particles, and subatomic particles. Consider the genius of human life and the creative intelligence at work in creating the human body. God is a God of variety who delights in creative expressions of his goodness and purpose. Surely, to fulfill the Great Commission (disciple the nations), the great commandment (love people) and the cultural mandate (steward the world), God expects his created beings to use every ounce of their creative abilities in pursuit of his kingdom's goals.

Third, having said that, it is also true that the Lord wants us to learn from each other and to build our lives and ministries on solid foundations gained from our individual and collective experiences. Etched over the library entrance to the University of Colorado library (where I spent many formative hours) are the words of Cicero, "He who knows only his own generation remains always a child." With sincere apologies to Cicero, it could just as easily be said of business in general and BAM in particular, that "He who knows only his own company and context remains always at a disadvantage." In that light, the following examples are company and contextual BAM experiences, a collage of human stories or, more academically, case studies. More to the point, they are examples of inspirational efforts that God's people (the church) have undertaken to see his love spread by and through the business community. They are definitely not presented as BAM molds into which a company must fit or a wooden formula that dictates what a true BAM Company looks like. Quite the opposite. They are presented for mutual edification and inspiration, and as spurs to creative adaptation and imaginative imitation.

Fourth, the following illustrations are not models. They are merely examples or stories of what various BAMers are doing in their contexts. Nonetheless, I unabashedly use the term *model* because each company I discuss is a concrete example of what has worked with those people in that place at that time. In that sense each company is a case study or, more to the point, a living laboratory that adds to our body of knowledge about BAM. These companies are, after all, God's pioneers in the BAM mission field—a first generation of intentional BAMers who will make all of the mistakes (and successes) that pave the way to more effective BAM and greater victory for Christ in the future.

GENERIC MODELS

Titling their book *Transform the World*, Sharon Swarr and Dwight Nordstrom cite the "unprecedented opportunities" and "limitless potential" of BAM. As they wrestled with defining generic BAM models, they saw the chief categories as being *functional* BAM missional opportunities: mentoring or coaching, venture capital and other types of investments, short-term teams to help new businesses, employment with a multinational firm, training entrepreneurial Great Commission teams to undertake "business planting in frontier nations," franchising a business by planting it "in new locations around the world," and working with microeconomic programs.[1]

This functional classification approach is quite valid for classifying BAM models. Another equally valid but quite different approach was enunciated by John Warton, international president of Business Professional Network. He sees "seven primary models of 'Doing Mission through Business' being employed in many parts of the world today." His models reflect the range of *venues* in which business can be carried out crossculturally and internationally. That is, he sees BAM as mission through Christian participation in transnational corporations, multinational corporations, new businesses or joint ven-

---

[1]Sharon Bentch Swarr and Dwight Nordstrom, *Transform the World: Biblical Vision and Purpose for Business* (Richmond, Va.: CEED, 1999), pp. 73-75, 96.

tures, training programs and consultancies, small and medium size enterprises, or microenterprises.[2]

Regardless of approach—by functions, venues or otherwise—it is clear that an almost endless variety of generic BAM models exists to implement mission opportunities. In order to understand these models and how they relate to each other (and to BAM) some working definitions are in order. Some will undoubtedly see these definitions or divisions (and those presented later in the book) as splitting hairs, since in today's multicultural, pluralistic world, all BAM is next door as well as overseas and in both small and large companies. Perhaps this criticism is right, but since the state of the movement and BAM are still embryonic, people are searching for labels to define both what they are today and where they will be tomorrow. Accordingly, the following definitions or divisions are useful, even though all aspects of business and mission are trending toward (and may eventually fall under) the single umbrella term Business as Mission.[3]

- Kingdom Companies. A KC is a Christian-led company, usually in a monocultural setting, whose CEO is intentionally integrating the Christian faith into his company's DNA and attempting to operate his company by biblical principles.

- BAM Companies. These are KCs that operate crossculturally, whose CEO engages the company in holistic community development projects that have kingdom impact. (See the discussion in chap. 1.)

- Great Commission Companies. GCCs are larger BAM companies that operate with sizable employee bases, greater resources and are often managed through executive leadership teams. The term was coined by Steve Rundle and Tom Steffen and is fully defined and developed in their seminal book *Great Commission Companies*.[4]

- Global outsourcing. BAM through global outsourcing was developed by

---

[2]John Warton, "Seven Models of Doing Missions Through Business: The New Stewardship of the Twenty-first Century," conference brochure of Business Professional Network, Chicago, 2001, p. 2.

[3]This is evident in the chapters that follow. Unless I pointedly distinguish them, when I use the term *BAM*, it necessarily includes Kingdom Companies and Great Commission Companies.

[4]Steve Rundle and Tom Steffen, *Great Commission Companies: The Emerging Role of Business in Missions* (Downers Grove, Ill.: InterVarsity Press, 2003).

Tom Sudyk through his Evangelistic Commerce Group (EC). It is a unique model that reflects a refreshing, creative BAM strategy for mission. Calling BAM "a new frontier," Sudyk and his EC Group utilize the outsourcing needs of U.S. firms to create BAM businesses overseas.[5] That is, EC approaches U.S. firms that have outsourcing needs and asks them to allow EC to meet those needs and simultaneously support Christian mission. He then sets up a BAM Company in a developing country to meet the new contractual requirements. For example, he contracts with U.S. hospitals to do transcription services from his BAM Company in India.

- Overseas private equity (OPE). This term is used to denote Christian businesspersons (would-be BAMers) going outside of their own nation, usually from developed to underdeveloped nations, and buying or investing heavily in a company or factory they find there and then using that as a ministry center and a mission outreach platform.[6] It should be noted that OPE is markedly different than the EC model. In OPE, BAMers actually start, buy or invest in overseas businesses and then leverage the existing product lines and sales channels to commercial and spiritual advantage. EC, on the other hand, first identifies the needed product lines and sales channels (i.e., the outsourcing needs and product or service demands of U.S. firms) and then leverages that demand to create a business.[7]

- Global enterprise development. This term describes the process by which Christian businesspeople or businesses (often through Christian NGOs) help indigenous people create new businesses or come alongside of existing indigenous business owners (as a paraclete) with various forms of support: providing capital investment, loans, equipment, expertise, prayer, encouragement, business training, one-on-one mentorship, hands-on business consulting and counseling, and perhaps partnerships or alliances. In this way successful businesspersons from developed countries are brought into

---

[5]Cover of "Business on a New Frontier: Fundament Principles of EC," Evangelistic Commerce Institute, Grand Rapids, 2002.

[6]For an excellent discussion of overseas private equity and OPE funds, see Ken Eldred, *God Is at Work: Transforming People and Nations through Business* (Ventura, Calif.: Regal, 2005), pp. 227-48.

[7]See Tom Sudyk, "Strategic Considerations in Business as Mission," in *On Kingdom Business: Transforming Missions Through Entrepreneurial Strategies*, ed. Tetsunao Yamamori and Kenneth A. Eldred (Wheaton, Ill.: Crossway, 2003), pp. 153-67.

creative, intimate partnership with budding entrepreneurs in lesser or underdeveloped countries across the globe or within the inner cities of their own countries.

Global enterprise development is distinguished from overseas private equity. In OPE the BAM companies have or acquire an equity position in the overseas business and manage the business as the center of their evangelistic, discipleship, and mission activities. In sharp contrast, those engaged in enterprise development do not usually acquire equity ownership in the overseas businesses. Neither do they assume management control of these businesses or use the business itself as an overt platform for ministry. Rather, the motive is simply to come alongside the new or struggling businesses in poor countries and assist them with making *their* businesses successful and prosperous. Such assistance may not even include an overt act of witnessing for Christ or seeking to obtain conversions. Instead, it may be built on a more holistic model of simply witnessing for Christ through deeds, character and relationships, thereby demonstrating the love of Christ for all people.

- Global enterprise leverage/outreach. This is a variation on global enterprise development. Here successful Christian businesspersons (frequently from developed nations) individually, corporately or in league with other businesses leverage their company's resources to holistically help people in need, internationally or domestically, long or short term, continuously or only once.

Three final points: First, these seven models often overlap within a single company (e.g., a GCC is also a KC and a BAM Company, and also may be an example of overseas private equity). Second, one priority common to all of these models (and to the ones discussed later) is that the first, primary function of the BAM Company is to maintain a healthy, profitable, sustainable business. Clearly, of necessity, evangelism, discipleship and community development must be secondary priorities. In BAM, without business there is no mission. Third, one major goal of all of these models is the utilization of the power, prestige, networks and resources of Christians in the marketplace to holistically help business entrepreneurs and others in the poorest parts of the world, domestically and internationally, and thereby, to visibly demonstrate Jesus' love for them.

THEIR STORIES

The stories that follow are arranged very roughly from the simplest to the more complex forms of BAM practice. BAM usually entails full-time paid work, but as the first example shows it can also be part-time and voluntary. It is usually focused on a single business, but as we will see with the Swiss job factory and the flying doctors, it can be a consortium of businesses, each leveraging their expertise and resources to accomplish kingdom impact that none of them could have achieved alone.

For the sake of brevity, sometimes I have ascribed certain BAM features to a single company when they actually come from one or more BAM companies. Further, for security or privacy, few real names, locations or identifying characteristics are given. The examples are, however, real companies doing real business as ministry in the world. As such they portray a breadth of options that illustrate how fertile this mission field is and the enormous potential it has for helping hurting people and having a major, transformative, kingdom impact on families, communities and nations.

The Flying Doctors. In a state bordering Mexico, a U.S. ophthalmologist (we will call him Ike) was fishing deep in Mexico. While at dinner in a Mexican café, he talked with a local missionary, Miguel, and learned that there were scores, if not hundreds, of people in that rural area who had eye cataracts. They were unable to obtain the needed eye surgeries because there were no eye doctors within the district, and even if there were, these people could not afford the operations.

On returning to the United States, Ike continued thinking about the conversation and was deeply moved to act. He was not only a committed Christian, but his own eye clinic specialized in cataract surgeries. He shared his concern with other Christians in the local business community and ultimately put together a consortium of business owners and a workable plan. One weekend a month Ike flies into this Mexican village to perform cataract surgeries. He takes all of the needed equipment, plus a nurse. In addition, since there is no local dentist there, he is usually joined by a dentist, Dean, who brings a hygienist and a field dental unit. The local fixed-base operator at the airport agreed to furnish two airplanes for the trips and the local bank president, Barbara, agreed to cover the costs of aviation gasoline. Other expenses such as lodging, meals and in-country transportation were pledged by local churches and their mission committees. The churches also furnish Bibles and other Christian literature (particularly children's works) in Spanish. While the group does not include a community-development specialist or church workers, it could easily be expanded in that way to meet the other needs of the people and churches in the village.

These arrangements took care of the supply side of the mission. For the demand side, IKE contacted the missionary, Miguel, who agreed to use his contacts, influence and staff to arrange visas at the airport, customs clearances for the team and their equipment, local transportation, hotel accommodations, a suitable site for their medical procedures, local publicity of the doctors' planned visits and other logistic support as needed.

On the first trip into Mexico the plane made a pass over the small town, and to their delight and astonishment Ike and Dean saw a line of people several hundred yards long. They quickly cleared customs, dropped their luggage at the hotel and went to the new, makeshift clinic. To their amazement they were greeted by the mayor, church leaders and a gaggle of laughing, playful children. The women from the church had caught the vision as well and had prepared food and water for everyone, but especially for the patiently queued people in need of care. Throughout the weekend, Ike removed cataract after cataract, while Dean and the hygienist addressed the people's dental needs.

Businesspeople acting together in partnership with the local missionaries and churches can accomplish holistic mission in a way that none could accomplish alone. It not only met the real needs of hurting people but gave them a sense of hope and a tangible understanding of the universal brotherhood of Christ. In this simple act of BAM mercy, the blind were given sight and the sick were healed—all in the name and love of Jesus, which was made clear to the entire village.

El Salvador. Business Professional Network (BPN) under the leadership of John Warton has been a major player in the Marketplace Mission Movement for years. High on BPN's agenda is their small- and medium-sized enterprise (SME) program to assist start-up businesses in underdeveloped nations. This is done by making loans in the $1,000 to $10,0000 range to prequalified, indigenous entrepreneurs to launch their businesses. The loan proceeds are used for a number of start-up purposes, including obtaining shop space, equipment, inventory and working capital. In El Salvador BPN contracts with World

Vision to administer the loan payments, monitor the businesses, and mentor and nurture the business owners. During a trip to El Salvador with Warton, I interacted with several of BPN's client companies. All but one were current on their loan payments, and all understood that this program was being carried out by Christians to help them and their families improve their standards of living and to come to know the living Christ. The following businesses are among BPN's El Salvador clients.

Rollo: The baker. Perhaps the most successful was a baker, Rollo, who was previously unemployed and barely able to feed his family. With his loan application, Rollo presented a business plan for opening a wholesale bakery. He was awarded the funds necessary to purchase a large oven. With the oven Rollo was able to produce sufficient daily quantities of bread and rolls to meet the demand of local restaurants. The geographic spread of his customers was such that Rollo needed to augment his business with a reliable delivery system. With his profits he purchased several bicycles and contracted with a local weaver to make large, flat, covered baskets that were designed to be mounted between the handlebars of each bike. He then attracted local unemployed young men and boys to use the bikes to deliver his bread on a commission basis.

Rollo's business was so successful that he was able to pay off his BPN loan ahead of schedule and then applied for another loan to buy two more ovens. With these, he expanded his wholesale customer base and his fleet of delivery bikes. He also repaid the new loan and with internally generated funds was able to build a home for his family on top of the bakery. He is now a productive citizen of El Salvador, providing a much-needed, healthy, consumable product, employing over thirty people and generating additional business income for his suppliers, the building contractors, the bicycle shop and the weaver. The beautiful part of the story is that Rollo is totally deaf, and prior to this loan was unable to obtain long-term meaningful work. Now, because of Christ's love for him and BPN's faithfulness, he is a successful business owner and able to provide for himself, his family and a host of employees and their families for generations.

Fernando: The furniture maker. A long drive out of the capital city took us down winding dirt roads amid thick jungle foliage and past sparse thatch huts on rickety stilts. Half-naked children and scrawny chickens ran wild in the bare, dusty yards, and pigs wallowed in their troughs trying to stay cool in the unbearable heat. Arriving at one of these homes, we were ushered into a make-shift workshop with stacks of lumber at one end, deep sawdust on the dirt floor and an antiquated crosscut saw, jigsaw and lathe scattered amid half-finished tables, chairs and wardrobes. The owner, a young man in a sweat-stained pair of coveralls, met us with a broad grin and a huge *embrazo* (embrace). He was excited by our interest in his business and eagerly showed off the various pieces of furniture that he was working on.

During the interview we learned that Fernando had started his business by making beautifully finished, high-end pieces of furniture. He proudly showed us pictures of many of the pieces, and we were definitely impressed with his skills. He was indeed a gifted young man with an eye for taking a rough log, stripping it into lumber and creating a practical yet stunning work of art. The problem was that he had to put so much time into each piece that his prices were out of reach of most of his targeted clientele. Accordingly, after much thought and consultation with World Vision and BPN, Fernando changed his product from finished to unfinished furniture. Now he builds the furniture but leaves it up to the purchaser to finish it as he or she pleases. This allows him to complete more furniture faster at lower prices and to substantially increase his sales and his ability to repay the BPN loan. Further, rather than sell his furniture through his own local store, he contracted with several stores in the area to take his products on consignment. That eliminated each store's risk and allowed Fernando access to a broader market. The increased volume of production and sales also allowed him to expand his work force and spread the benefits to other families.

During the visit we heard about the many challenges Fernando faced in growing his business, but we did not leave without praying with him over his business and his family. We also discussed the strong possibilities of inviting a retired U.S. cabinetmaker who was in BPN's circle of contacts to come to El Salvador for further mentoring and to help him obtain newer, more sophisticated woodworking equipment.

Maria: The dry-goods merchant. Returning to town we went to the local market, an exciting, active, grimy place teeming with people, noise, smells and clutter. We walked past outdoor kiosks, sidewalk vendors and women hawking their wares in one hand while holding babies in the other. Our destination was the main market shed, a covered area with dozens of stalls that formed a maze of corridors in the interior. It was there that we found BPN's next client, Maria, and her stall store *(tienda)*, which held an impressive inventory of items for the kitchen: pots, pans, rice, beans, flour, sugar, spices, odd canned goods and candy for the children. Maria was delighted to see us and proudly pulled out her general ledger to show us her basic bookkeeping system. As she described her expenses, it was clear that she knew the profit margins on every item in her store and was carefully monitoring her cash flow to keep pace with the demand.

Maria had begun her business as a single mother trying to earn enough money to feed her family. In those days she would come to the market, find a place on the sidewalk, spread her wares on a piece of clean newspaper and transform that patch of concrete into her storefront and counter. She longed for the day when she could go inside the covered market and open a real store as others had. The opportunity for that transition came with a small loan from BPN. With that money Maria obtained a lease on a stall that was about five feet deep and seven feet across, with a waist-high counter and plenty of shelving against the back wall.

Knowing the neighborhood and her clients' needs, Maria purchased her inventory wisely and limited her markup to attract and maintain customers. Soon her store was so successful that she was able to make her loan payments to BPN and expand her inventory. While her store only supports herself and her family at this point, Maria—ever the entrepreneur—sees a day when she will be able to lease the stall next to hers to double the size of her *tienda*, to employ clerks and possibly open a second store within the market. She was profuse in her thanks to BPN, World Vision and Jesus for giving her this opportunity, and welcomed our team laying hands on her in the open market and praying over her and her shop.

Javier: The electronic repairman. Outside of the market we made our way slowly through the crowds of busy people and entered another, large, corrugated steel building that resembled a block-long, block-wide barn. Inside was a jungle of merchants, each claiming a space on the floor. The pathway among them was almost unintelligible, but the larger sections were divided by ten-foot corrugated walls, with stalls built against them that also reduced the light to a dim, dirty tone. In one such stall, about three feet deep and five feet wide with a three-foot counter and a small door accessing the restricted area behind the counter, we found BPN's next client, Javier.

Javier repairs electronic goods, especially television sets. Every square inch of his small, cluttered space was covered with tools, guts of TV sets in various states of repair, cannibalized spare parts and butt-filled ashtrays. For protection the stall had a metal screen that could be pulled down at night, a lockable door and an old .45 caliber handgun under the counter. These observations brought home the sobering reality of the rough, crime-infested, corrupt, uncertain world in which these people seek to survive and to build their lives.

In contrast, Javier was a gentle man with a warm smile, a big laugh and a decency that reflected his determination to forge a better life for himself and his family. He also understood the role that Jesus played in giving him the opportunity to own his business and welcomed our questions, suggestions and prayers as empowering manna.

Muñoz: The biker. A short drive from the market brought us to another repair shop, this time motorcycles. We wandered through the dozen bikes parked at various angles in front and entered a truly bleak concrete building with about 300 square feet of space divided into three rooms and a bathroom. Each room was dark and greasy, one filled with parts, another with four disassembled bikes and motors, a third was a makeshift office.

The owner, Muñoz, was busy working over one of the bikes while two other men labored over another. They were all glad for the break in routine caused by our unexpected arrival. Muñoz was especially happy to meet his patron from the United States, Señor Warton, and to thank him personally for the BPN loan that had allowed him the opportunity to have his own business and pursue his passion for motorbikes. As with the others, we discussed the various aspects of his business, his progress in meeting his goals and the challenges that threatened that progress. The business was steady and growing with good prospects for the future. Muñoz recognized and appreciated the financial and spiritual help that BPN had given him. In affirming and praying for him, we hastened to hope that one day soon his passion for Jesus would outshine his passion for motorbikes.

THE 10/40 WINDOW

Hopefully the stories given above will help the reader understand the realities of many Third World businesses, realities that are far different from the business models we in the West are accustomed to and consider the norm. What is true of Latin America is equally true of the cultural and economic realities of the Far East, the Middle East, Africa and the 10/40 Window. BAM is gaining a foothold in these areas, but with the 10/40 Window's population exceeding three billion people, mostly unreached with the gospel and largely impoverished, BAM's efforts at this point are a drop in the proverbial bucket. Today, out of the literally millions of businesses in this region, we can count only a relatively few businesses that are kingdom or BAM companies, or that are being positively impacted by BAM and the movement. Yet God started with only two people, and our Lord Jesus started with only twelve disciples and the power of the Holy Spirit. BAM, in his image and example, is sowing holistic seeds on fertile soil. Through the power of the Holy Spirit and the faithfulness of his followers, we can pray that the long-term effect will be a bountiful harvest. The rest is up to the Lord of the harvest.

Examples of BAM businesses operating in a wide range of countries within the 10/40 Window today include: companies in publishing, television production and distribution, management training, computer training, software design, high-tech consulting, engineering, air freight, construction, radio stations, tourist hotels, pig and fish farms; and in the manufacture and export of electronics, pottery, cardboard boxes, cut glass, leather goods and wrought iron.

This list isn't glamorous or complete, but it speaks to both the ordinary and extraordinarily creative nature of BAM businesses. The citizenship list of those setting up these businesses reads like the membership of the United Nations. It represents Christians from virtually every country on earth reaching out to their own people domestically and to those of other nations, all within the 10/40 Window and all in the name of the Lord.

These examples are a small sampling of Christ's faithful followers working in and through the marketplace. Needless to say, the story behind each one is poignant, filled with dreams and prayers, faith-stretching and faith-testing experiences, victories and defeats, suffering and rejoicing. They are the stories of BAM missionaries on the mission field in different businesses, different contexts, different challenges, but one God and one faith. So too the type of mission and community outreach each has will be different depending on the needs they discover, but all will have two commonalities.

First, they will seek to run their companies as Kingdom Companies, to manage by biblical principles and to model servant leadership. The object will be to have a positive internal kingdom impact on their employees and all who deal with the company. Second, they will seek to reach outside of their companies and have a positive external kingdom impact within the community through their informed initiatives and projects. As I have said, BAM does not come in a box, but it does seek both an internal and an external kingdom impact to build the kingdom of God in that context at that time among those people.

ELSEWHERE, EVERYWHERE

The story is the same outside of the 10/40 Window. God is seen working within and through the marketplace virtually everywhere on earth. Some additional examples may be helpful to see that there is no one method or place for doing BAM. As noted earlier, the names are masked for security and privacy, but the companies are as real as the Lord they serve.

- A company in a large metropolitan area provides vehicles, money and doctors to conduct a mobile heath clinic in its inner city.

- An IT company provides technical computer support to mission agencies, churches and start-up businesses.

- An automobile repair shop in California sends one of its officers to the former Soviet Union (FSU) on a long-term assignment to engage in urban relief work.

- A farm-implement dealer in Tennessee provides farm equipment and agricultural expertise to Central Asian farmers.

- A Dallas banker helps Asian entrepreneurs start a Western-style bank.

- A Korean merchant underwrites a Bolivian micro-loan program.

- A German toy manufacturer hires the mentally challenged within his community.

- A Swiss business consortium sets up a "job factory" to train unemployed youth.

- A Mississippi Christian business consortium starts both a call center and a truck import business in Ukraine.

- A seminary in the FSU establishes a business-development center, involving its faculty, students and church members, with capital, mentoring and business acumen furnished by American Christian partners in Georgia and Alabama.

- A weight-loss clinic is established in Asia Minor by U.S. businessmen in partnership with expat BAM entrepreneurs already in the country.

- A hotel and restaurant are organized in the Philippines by an American NGO.

The possibilities—and needs—are limitless.

I will finish with four examples that are particularly noteworthy as they give a greater roadmap for other would-be BAMers at home and abroad.

An Asian BAM Company. First, we will examine an Asian company founded and run by American entrepreneurs that has tried to exemplify the best of BAM. Internally, they specifically purposed their company for Christ and kingdom impact. They then entered into a business that can manufacture an exportable product so as not to adversely affect any other businesses in the given vicinity. Next, they intentionally searched out and hired the physically handicapped members of their community—those who could not obtain employment because of their physical condition. These employees were then trained in meaningful jobs, paid well by the local standard, given safe, well-maintained, attractive working conditions and taught excellence in all things—from quality control over the product to their personal lives.

Specifically, these employees experienced growth

- *professionally,* through skills training and gift identification and development

- *personally,* through courses on character development, integrity, money management, literacy, nutrition, health, hygiene and parenting, and through company-provided counseling, meals, inoculations, and Sunday rest

- *spiritually,* through Bible studies, devotionals, choir and Bible verses pasted around the work and cafeteria areas; BAM team testimonies, management-style and lifestyle witnessing; summer school for employee children; and support of employees and families during times of personal crisis and celebration

- *financially*, through fair wages, good benefits, family assistance and housing improvement and construction projects

The host company has also incubated another company from the United States, allowing it to co-locate within the company for the first few months, helping it get started and learn the local context, and mentoring its leaders in developing its own unique BAM model.

Externally, the company has entered into a number of projects in partnership with local officials, community leaders, local churches, Christian NGOs and their own employees. These include hiring the handicapped (employ the unemployable); placing branch factories in slum areas (job creation); helping clean up those areas (litter removal and beautification); paving streets to curb air pollution and asthma (environmental and health benefits); developing potable water supplies (disease prevention and hygiene promotion); finding foster homes for abandoned babies; assisting local orphanages with money, manpower and children's programs; helping handicapped children find assistance, like surgery for cleft palates and training for blind children; and housing renovation projects, especially for their employees.

A Canadian BAM Company. A second company is in the heavy equipment business and is owned and operated by Canadians. The CEO first made sure that his home operation in Canada was specifically and clearly committed to BAM through its mission statement, policies and practices, and all internal functions. He led his management team to develop an integrated strategic business-and-faith plan, with clearly identifiable goals, objections, actions and accountability in each functional area of the company. The team then made every effort to lead their company for Christ, to manage by biblical principles, and to set and achieve multiple bottom lines.

As the company expanded overseas into South America, they were struck by the large numbers of homeless children and their desperate plight. That caused the company to partner with local churches and orphanages to develop plans and programs for helping these children come in from the cold and find needed shelter, nurture, sustenance, counseling, job training, family placement, spiritual renewal and a better life. Hand in glove with this, they developed a rehabilitation plan in partnership with a local hospital for people (especially youth) addicted to drugs and alcohol.

As the company moved into India, it deliberately located within a slum area predominantly inhabited by *Dalits* (the untouchable caste). The company helped with community development, but gave the Dalits jobs, employee and family care, nurturing and spiritual comfort, and training in job and life skills. Universally, these were blessings that the local culture would never have afforded them. Taking a cue from the company's South American operation, they also worked with local churches on programs for street children.

In all of these activities this company invited their indigenous employees to take the leadership, especially in identifying the needs, defining and communicating with their partners, and carrying out the hands-on work required to accomplish the mission they had chosen. Not only did this build a highly motivated workforce and team spirit, but it gave them a sense of the higher purpose of their business and jobs. It also made the company a desirable, admired place to work and helped attract and retain good people. While the company did not proselytize Christianity, its values, mission and Savior were all publicly and prominently displayed through the loving, caring example of the company's leaders—known throughout the community to be Christians.

U.S. inner-city BAM enterprises. The third and fourth companies are quite different. They involve the inner cities of Chicago and Jackson, Mississippi, which are as crosscultural, foreboding and in need of BAM as sections of the 10/40 Window. While there are many examples of corporate efforts to reclaim the cities and help their poor, these two bear special mention.

1. *Being legit.* In the first, I learned up-close and personal about the importance of business in penetrating the inner city of Chicago with the gospel. That came from my friendship with an urban missionary, Mark. Married to a teacher of urban studies, Mark and his bride could have taken up residence in the suburbs and commuted to their mission field daily. Instead, they chose to obtain an apartment in the heart of the city's poorest area, to drive a vintage car and to keep their home on a par with the local residents. They made friends with their neighbors and joined the local church. Through a relationship-evangelizing approach that was both incarnational and holistic, they brought a strong witness to the community for Christ.

Nonetheless, it quickly became apparent to Mark, who spent all of his time in the heart of the city, that to be accepted as an insider he had to be "legit" (i.e., legitimate) within the local parlance. Part of being legit was to "have your own economy" (i.e., a means of earning a living that is compatible with and observable by the local community). Donor-supported missionaries and church professionals were always suspect and always remained outsiders. They lacked their own economy, had no real stake in the local economy (no "skin in the game") and had a ticket out anytime they chose. Real insiders are permanent—some may say "trapped"—and have little or no hope of ever leaving or bettering their circumstances by legal means.

Accordingly, Mark fished around for different "economies" he might adopt. He needed a business that would give him the mobility to move about the community and to meet and interact with a large number of people, and yet would be (and appear to be) legit. His ultimate selection was to be a sidewalk vendor who carried his wares on a tray slung about his neck and hawked them to passersby. With this portable business Mark blended into the scenery. It also gave him an excuse to be anywhere and everywhere, to talk to anyone and everyone about anything. It worked well and actually generated sufficient income to support himself and to earn him a place in the life of the community as an insider. More recently Mark has been looking at start-up business opportunities that will not only help those he has led to the Lord and befriended, but give himself an increased presence and influence in the community, and will increase his ministry's kingdom impact.[8]

It is worth noting that the lessons Mark has learned and the stories he can tell have also added greatly to the relevance and effectiveness of his wife's classes on urban development. Not only does she bring a personal expertise to the class but she is also able to bring in Mark and others from the community as guest speakers—and to take her classes into the inner city to places they would never otherwise experience.

2. *Being involved.* Doug Wilson is the head of a second-generation, highly respected and profitable car dealership in Jackson, Mississippi. Doug, a devout Christian and an active member of a Southern Baptist Church, has personally seen the steady erosion and degradation of Jackson's urban center over the past decade, and it has sickened him. Sometime in 2007 I had the privilege of attending an Atlanta seminar with Doug and several others from his church, including their pastor. That seminar focused on the crying need for Christian-

---

[8]While some purists might reject this as BAM since the bulk of the family's income came from his wife's college salary, he is the owner of a real business (albeit small) that adds value to the community, and is intentional, incarnational and holistic.

led city transformation throughout the United States and internationally—
and the important role that business plays in making that happen. It emphasized that over the past few years the world has made a cosmic, demographic
shift from which it will never retreat. It moved from a rural-dominated planet
to an urban-dominated one. With this shift, which has been coming at increased speed globally, the problems facing the cities have escalated geometri-
cally. The challenge is clear: What will we, as Christians and as businesspersons, do about it?

Deeply moved, Wilson returned from the conference and did not waste
any time. Within two weeks he assembled a group of community and
church leaders, black and white, to pray over the city and seek divine guidance as to what could be done. In the years since that initial prayer meeting,
Wilson's group has launched a "Transform Jackson" initiative to reclaim
and permanently transform Jackson into a healthy, law-abiding, God-fearing, civil society. It has brought together God-fearing people of good will
from every area of the city, every economic level, every denomination, and
every ethnic and racial group. These people included innumerable organizations that have labored for years in isolated, virtually fruitless, niche
urban-relief ministries in Jackson. It is an awe-inspiring movement that for
perhaps the first time in Jackson's beleaguered history has unified the radically diverse elements of the community into a common, God-sized cause.
As is relevant here, they all recognized that business is a key element to the
recovery of the city and that the unflagging, long-term commitment of the
business community is an absolutely essential element to success. Wilson,
an influential business leader who is devoted to Christ, was perhaps one of
the few people who had the clout and resources to inspire and lead the way.
That too is BAM.

Similar transformational efforts are currently underway in dozens of cities
around the United States. Equally important and virtually unknown is the
fact that city and national transformation initiatives have been launched in
hundreds of cities worldwide by world evangelical leaders like Luis Bush, Ed
Silvoso and other committed evangelicals. All participants have recognized
that (1) business leadership *and* participation are key elements of these initiatives and (2) city and national redemption and transformation are the logical
extensions of our God-ordained goals to disciple the nations (Great Commis-

sion), to love the people (great commandment) and to steward the Earth (cultural mandate).[9]

SUMMARY

God is definitely working in and through the marketplace. There are no ready-made models for would-be BAMers to follow, only inspiring stories, ideas and examples that we can draw upon. At this point, however, BAM seems to be a key strategy that has attracted Christian businessmen and women around the globe to find in BAM a genuine convergence of their passions for Christ, for business and for mission. These men and women and their businesses come in every form imaginable, and they are going into every country that their business opportunities permit and their callings dictate. They witness to a hurting world through every internal aspect of their company and every point of influence that they have. They also witness through their demonstrated love for the city in which they operate and through their ability—and willingness, even eagerness—to make an intentional, tangible difference in the life of that community and its citizens in the name and love of Jesus through their businesses. In fact, *BAM's infinite potential and variety is its genius*. It is like a wildfire that, once lit, moves on the wind in unpredictable directions with formidable speed, driven by God's holy breath and his Holy Spirit—with unforeseeable consequences and unfathomable kingdom impact.

DISCUSSION QUESTIONS

1. The author provides BAM models for the reader but suggests that there is no replicable "BAM in a Box." What does he mean by "BAM in a Box"? What are the strengths and weakness of models generally? Do you agree with the author about the limited ability of BAM to find a replicable model? Why?

2. In the community in which you live, identify one major problem and describe various ways or steps that could be taken through a BAM model to address it.

---

[9]See Doug Wilson's website at <www.transformationjackson.org/mission.php>, Luis Bush's websites at <http://gbo.faithsite.com/content.asp?CID=78746> and <www.joshuaproject.net>, and Ed Silvoso's website at <www.harvestevan.org/international-transformation-network.html>.

3. In what ways can a BAM Company influence a community directly and indirectly within the inner city of the United States? Within the slums of Mombasa (that you may have seen in the movie *Slumdog Millionaire*)? Or within Smokey Mountain in Manila, Philippines? What is Smokey Mountain?

4. What is the 10/40 Window? From what was its name derived? What nations does it include? What are the dominant characteristics of the nations within the 10/40 Window? How has BAM been especially helpful for ministry in the 10/40 Window?

5. What is meant by being "legit"? Is that only applicable within U.S. inner cities? Why or why not? What are some perks for being "legit" as a missionary in a foreign country?

6. BAM engagement: What are some ways that you—with your current gifts, skills, resources, contacts and experience—could engage in BAM where you are, as you are?

3

BAM's Place in the Sun

"This market is yours, I dedicate it to you, and may it prove a benefit to you and your children. It is for you to defend, to protect and to uphold. It is for you to see that those who occupy it treat you fairly, that no extortion be permitted and that the purpose for which it was created be religiously adhered to. This is one of the greatest days in the history of Seattle, but is only a beginning, for soon this city will have one of the greatest markets in the world. It is here to stay and there is no influence, no power, no combination and no set of either political or commercial grafters that will destroy it."

THOMAS PLUMMER REVELLE,
DEDICATION OF THE PIKE PLACE MARKET, SEATTLE

As will soon be apparent, BAM is not alone in the universe of Christians focused on the marketplace. Instead, BAM is only part—albeit a significant part—of a much broader movement of God across the face of the earth. The next three chapters will attempt to shed some light on how this movement has developed, how it is manifesting itself, how it is affecting Christian outreach, and BAM's unique place in it.

Marketplace Defined

Up to this point I have used the term *marketplace* generically. However, there is a problem of definition in much of the business literature. Many books have *marketplace* in their title but never define the term.[1] Bill Hybels, senior pastor

---

[1]For example, Randy Kilgore, *Talking About God in the Twenty-First Century Marketplace* (Boston: Marketplace Network, 2003); Bill Hybels, *Christian in the Marketplace: Practical*

of Willow Creek Community Church, is much more specific, using *market-place* synonymously with *workplace* or *job site,* that is, the place and the location one does God-given work, earns a living, obtains dignity and produces value for society. He explains the role of the Christian in that marketplace:

> I assumed . . . that Christians actually believe that if God has called them to work in the marketplace, He has also called them to be *mission-aries in the marketplace.* Without that assumption, there is no reason to talk about bringing "the light of Christ" to the marketplace; there is no need to concern ourselves with Christian credibility; and there is surely no need to learn to articulate our faith.[2]

Ed Silvoso defines the term *marketplace* with a poignant metaphor that resonates with the core of my own definition:

> The marketplace—the combination of business, education and government—is to a metropolis what the heart is to the human body. Through these three arteries flows the life of a city. A city cannot exist without a marketplace in the same fashion that a body cannot live without a heart.[3]

I define *marketplace* in a similar way. My definition includes two active venues and a third, passive, reflective venue.[4] Each of these venues reflects a

---

Help for the Workaday Christian in a Materialistic Society (Wheaton, Ill.: Victor, 1982); Jack Serra, *Marketplace Marriage and Revival: The Spiritual Connection* (Orlando: Longwood, 2001); Foy Valentine, *The Cross in the Marketplace* (Waco, Tex.: Word, 1966); Pete Hammond, R. Paul Stevens, and Todd Svanoe, *The Marketplace Annotated Bibliography: A Christian Guide to Books on Work, Business and Vocation* (Downers Grove, Ill.: InterVarsity Press, 2002). Though each of these books has a different approach to the term (and they do not define it), the implicit assumption is that it equates to work, workplace, job and vocation. In fact, many others readily use those terms instead of *marketplace*. For example, Mark Greene, *Thank God It's Monday: Ministry in the Workplace* (Bechley, U.K.: Scripture Union, 2001); Doug Sherman and William Hendricks, *Your Work Matters to God* (Colorado Springs: NavPress, 1987); Larry Burkett, *Business by the Book: The Complete Guide of Biblical Principles for the Workplace* (Nashville: Thomas Nelson, 1998); Verla Gillmor, *Reality Check: A Survival Manual for Christians in the Workplace* (Camp Hill, Penn.: Horizon, 2001); and the classic by R. Paul Stevens, *The Other Six Days: Vocation, Work, and Ministry in Biblical Perspective* (Grand Rapids: Eerdmans, 1999).

[2]Hybels, *Christians in the Marketplace,* pp. 32-33 (emphasis added).

[3]Ed Silvoso, *Anointed for Business: How Christians Can Use Their Influence in the Marketplace to Change the World* (Ventura, Calif.: Regal, 2002), p. 16.

[4]Of course, real life is not as tidy as these categories suggest since each venue has its own workplace and is, therefore, part of the marketplace as I define it. For example, governmental offices and schools often face the same mission issues as the commercial business workplace and, as a result, are included. That is, when I speak of marketplace ministries (MMs) taking faith to the

power center within a given society or nation that has a major economic impact on that society and its people, and on mission, especially BAM. The two active venues include the commercial business community (private sector) and the governmental, quasi-governmental, and political institutions that (1) regulate national and transnational economic policy and practices, and (2) set the legal climate and noneconomic, business laws, regulations, policies and practices (public sector).

The third venue is the educational community, which studies each of the other venues, attempts to impose a disciplined approach to understanding them and then teaches that discipline to new generations. Viewed missionally, it is in this third venue that the policies, practices, impact and symbiotic relationship of the other two marketplace venues can be best understood, thoughtfully reflected upon and translated into effective action agendas for mission. In essence the educational arena is the ultimate place of praxeological reflection and as such is a vital venue for influencing marketplace mission.

In summary, all three venues that constitute the broader marketplace—business, government/politics and education—are major nuclei of power in any society and hence in any mission effort to touch the lives of a people for Christ, especially BAM. They are vital components of every people group's real world experience and are intimately, inexorably entwined. The marketplace is, as Silvoso says, as essential to the life of a people and a society as blood is to the human body. It is, quite simply, the *sine qua non* of virtually every society everywhere throughout history. The point is that the marketplace is more than simply the commercial business world. For purposes of this book, it is important to understand two points: first, this broader view of the marketplace, and second, as used in this book, the term *marketplace* focuses almost exclusively on the business component of the marketplace and the specific niche of BAM.

In that regard, to comprehend what the term *marketplace* personally means to me, at both a mental and a visceral level, it is fundamental to visualize some of the world's marketplaces: see the people there; hear the sounds; smell the odors; taste the food; soak in the ambiance; sense the importance of these places to the daily lives of every person there; discern the embedded, often

workplace, it would include a business, a governmental office and a school classroom. In that sense, tidiness sacrifices for mission reality.

invisible, power centers that control both the markets and the lives of all who buy, sell and trade there; and grasp the complex task of mission to, within, and through that context—the marketplace.

The marketplaces of the world are part of the essence of my life and shape my view of humanity, in all of its diversity and universality. Often I have vis-

Markets of the World

My experience includes traveling, working and living in over seventy countries on five continents. I have spent my life traveling the globe, experiencing firsthand the wide variety of foreign cultures, customs, mores and practices resident on this small planet. And it is always to the local markets—be they local flea markets, daily food or flower markets, or global commodity and financial markets—that I turn for a sense of who the people are. I have been to the markets in the teeming cities of Europe, the Middle East and Asia, and in the steaming jungles of the Amazon and plains of Africa. I have trod the Great Silk Trade Route of Marco Polo, sipped ouzo in the Plaka of ancient Athens, eaten tandoori and curried rice in the cafes of Old Delhi and Agra, placed my chop on a roasting pig's flank in Taipei's open-air market, bargained for cloth in the shadows of Mount Kilimanjaro, haggled with street merchants over Soviet military caps in the shadows of the Kremlin, eaten exotic sea creatures in Hong Kong's backwater fish markets, pondered Paul's imprisonment amid the ruins of Rome's Forum, worked in the sheep-shearing stations and bid at the wool auction in the remote hills of New Mexico. I have traded stocks and bonds on the international markets, witnessed this massive flow of currency globally and stood in the pit on the floor of the Commodities Market at the World Trade Center in New York City amid the deafening storm of active trading. I am well acquainted with the bazaar of Istanbul, the Ponte Vecchio of Florence, Piccadilly Circus in London, the plaza in Santa Fe, the Ginza in Tokyo, the old city of Jerusalem, the cannery in San Francisco, the glorious flower markets of Almaty and the spice markets of Tashkent. From the mountains of Cuzco and Machu Picchu to the castle on Mont Saint-Michele to the river market in Bangkok, people everywhere find their lives revolving around bustling markets where the goods of life, survival and pleasure are traded.

ited them with a camera, because it is in these markets that I acquire the most candid, honest images of people's characters, what they eat and wear, how they interact, what they hold cheap or dear, who serves and who is served, and how they treat their children, their elderly, their peers and their customers. It reveals their true nature, virtues and weaknesses, and their worldview with all of its assumptions, values and allegiances. It is in this place that I not only witness the uniqueness of the people group that I am observing, but also where I come to appreciate the universalities and the commonalities of humankind.

The global, aggregate marketplace is equally enlightening. I have integrated my lifetime experience in business, banking and government into the globalization, macroeconomics, and international business courses that I teach. As I read the local newspapers and see the impact of the World Trade Organization, the International Monetary Fund, the World Bank, the Group of Seven and various regional development banks, both positively and negatively, on the economic lives of nations and the very survival of indigenous peoples, I wonder at the naiveté of Christian missions in not addressing these marketplace venues.

Whether it is encountered in the individual or the aggregate, the marketplace ultimately bears witness to the economic, political, religious or cultural power struggles that a people group faces. Accordingly, the term *marketplace* as used in this book, denotes the larger, more expansive, innovative image of a living commercial organism rather than the narrow, restrictive meaning ordinarily associated with it. If mission—especially BAM—is to be truly holistic and contextual, it must deal with the entire marketplace in all of its drudgery and glory.

THE MARKETPLACE AND THE CHURCH

The marketplace and the church are finding a common ground in the context of what I call the Marketplace Mission Movement. Historically, that has not always been so. A great historic, cultural divide has existed for centuries—and still remains—between the pulpit and the business community. This divide, in many instances, manifests itself not only in mutual antipathy but often in outright hostility and suspicion. An eye-opening research project on the relationship between the business community and church leaders was conducted by Harvard Business School senior research fellow Laura Nash and Stanford dean for religious life, Scotty McLennan, both committed Christians, in their book, *Church on Sunday, Work on Monday: The Challenge of Fusing Christian Values with Business Life.* They found that there is a "new collision of [the] spiritual and business," that "many people's faith suffers a bifurcation when set in a business context," and that the church is "anticapitalist" and "antibusiness." Furthermore, they see a "self-destructive pattern" emerging that generates counterproductive, even "syncretistic approaches to faith," among baby boomers, Christian businesspeople and professionals:

> One of the most disturbing findings in our interviews was the pervasive lack of awareness or interest among ecclesiastics on how deeply anticapitalist the message continues to be among many liberal and conservative clergy, however much they cultivate a warm relationship with members of their congregations. . . . [E]ven deeply faithful Christians in business tend to feel a strong disconnect between their experience of the church or private faith, and the spirit-challenging conditions of the workplace.[5]

Nash and McLellan do not simply point their fingers at the church. Rather, they see the matter as one of mutual misperceptions, mistrust and misunderstanding, with plenty of blame on both sides:

> We were also struck by how the business and religious professional mirrored each other's strategies, despite their differing economic ideologies. The patterns do indeed run deep. Both groups are turning capitalism and Christianity into an either-or proposition, an exclusive choice between two distinct realms.[6]

Hybels takes a more gracious approach but ends up at the same place: an open recognition that there is a mutual, marked lack of understanding, empathy and cooperation between the business community and the church. He writes:

> *Why is a minister [speaking of himself] talking about the "marketplace?"* Shouldn't he be speaking to religious issues as ministers of the Gospel

---

[5]Laura Nash and Scotty McLennan, *Church on Sunday, Work on Monday* (San Francisco: Jossey-Bass, 2001), pp. xxvii, xxx, xxxi, 5.
[6]Ibid., p. 66.

have been doing for hundreds of years? What interest, if any, does God have in the marketplace? Does He really know that it exists? Does He know what goes on there? Does He care? Didn't He design the church as a refuge from the marketplace?

These questions are typical, and because of them many Christian leaders have avoided the subject of the marketplace. And yet, one of the greatest challenges facing the true follower of Jesus Christ lies in determining how he or she should fit into the marketplace of the world. Should not the church address itself to this subject?[7]

This observation is particularly poignant when we consider the enormous outreach potential of marketplace missions. Christ@Work (also known as the Fellowship of Companies for Christ International or FCCI) has an exercise for its member CEOs. First, they count the number of employees and their families, investors and their families, creditors, suppliers, vendors, and tradespeople with whom their business deals. They add to that the number of clients or customers served, as well as the competitors and trade associations with whom the business interacts. If the average size of the local church in America is one to two hundred people, as is popularly thought, it is apparent (1) that the number of people that even the smallest business can directly touch is far higher than the average church size, and (2) that many, if not most, of these are people who would not ordinarily darken the door of a church.

The marketplace has a huge potential for taking holistic mission to needy areas of the world, both domestically and internationally. The enormous economic and political power of the marketplace is a matter of common knowledge. If that secular power were aligned with God's Holy Spirit—that is, if the church and the marketplace were fully aligned, and unleashed around the world in the name, the love and the gospel of Jesus of Nazareth—it could be completely transformational to the people of the entire world, whether they claimed Jesus as their personal Savior or not. Biblically, it could also result in the fulfillment of Jesus' Great Commission in our time. Unfortunately, given the current and historic tensions between the church and marketplace, that is a very big if—at least for us, but not for our Lord.

Thankfully, the hostility between church and business is changing. An

---

[7]Hybels, *Christians in the Marketplace*, p. 7.

emerging, powerful movement of God's mission, *missio Dei*, is being seen globally in and through the marketplace. Van Engen has noted, "The commercial business marketplace may well be the primary mission field of the twenty-first century."[8] Nash and McLennan are quick to concur: "Support for this book came at a critical time. It allowed us to follow *the spirituality and business movement as it exploded in the latter part of the 1990s*, and to keep a Christian focus despite cultural pressure to secularize the business ethics questions."[9] In support of this view, over twelve hundred organizations, most of whom have only emerged in the past few years, are now actively engaged in ministry to, within or through the global marketplace.[10]

THE MARKETPLACE MISSION MOVEMENT

To fully understand BAM it is necessary to understand how it fits into the larger picture of Christian missions to, within and through the marketplace. That is no small task, as God has been working in very powerful ways below the radar for over two decades vis-à-vis the marketplace. His hand has been seen among Christian businesspeople around the world who have come to the same vision of Christ in the marketplace, and they have done so independently, spontaneously and globally. In fact, the phenomenon has engendered such massive global momentum that it is being called a movement that may well be *the* dominant Christian mission movement of the twenty-first century and, if developed, may become one of the great mission movements in Christian history. That is why I call it the Marketplace Mission Movement—and BAM is a major part of it.

The marketplace: A new mission movement. It has been said that "the marketplace is the last mission frontier" and that "Christianity in the marketplace is salt and light in a dark world. . . . the greatest possibility of revival is corporate America."[11] Leading mission experts, theologians, church leaders and evangelists have seen it.[12] So has the secular and evangelical press.

---

[8]Charles Van Engen, personal conversation with the author, January 12, 2002.

[9]Nash and McLennan, *Church on Sunday*, p. xiii (emphasis added).

[10]Mike McLoughlin et al., eds. *International Faith and Work Directory 2003-2004* (Cumming, Ga.: Aslan, 2003).

[11]Ed Silvoso, personal telephone conversation with the author, April 10, 2002; and Henry T. Blackaby, "Experiencing God in Business," Fellowship of Companies for Christ International conference, Kapalua, Maui, Hawaii, September 24 and 26, 2001.

[12]This book focuses only on the Christian Marketplace Mission Movement and any discussion

As early as July 16, 2001, the cover story for *Fortune* magazine was titled "God and Business: The Surprising Quest for Spiritual Renewal in the American Workplace." It stated:

> Bringing spirituality into the workplace violates the old idea that faith and fortune don't mix. But a groundswell of believers is breaching the last taboo in corporate America. . . .
>
> These executives are in the vanguard of a diverse, mostly unorganized mass of believers—a counterculture bubbling up all over corporate America—who want to bridge the traditional divide between spirituality and work. Historically, such folk operated below the radar, on their own or in small workplace groups where they prayed or studied the Bible. But now they are getting organized and going public to agitate for change.[13]

Soon after, on January 11, 2002, the *Washington Post* "Style" section headline read: "Prayer and Profits: These Business Leaders Seek Regular Counsel from Their Silent Partner—God."[14] Similar articles appeared in a variety of newspapers, business magazines and industry trade journals with cover stories in *Business Week, U.S. News and World Report, Time* and *Industry Week.*[15]

---

about non-Christian marketplace mission activities is beyond its scope. It should be noted, however, that spiritual activities may also be occurring in the marketplace among Jews, Muslims, Buddhists and other non-Christians. Although most news articles speak to a Christian context, many articles use the term *spirituality* to denote the broader scope of marketplace religious activities. As John Leland says, "[There is] a growing faith-at-work movement: an assortment of programs and groups, often unconnected to churches, that seek to increase the presence of religion in the workplace. . . . Some are office prayer or Bible study groups; other programs are presented at conferences attended by executives. Other groups form in local churches, *mosques or synagogues* to apply religious principles to the business world. Some emphasize ethical conduct, others evangelism or proselytizing. Most do not involve formal services or clergy. . . . Several groups, such as Spirit at Work and Spirit in Business, avoid doctrine in order to bring together *Christians, Jews, Muslims, Buddhists and others* ("Thou Shalt Not Call in Sick," *New York Times*, March 17, 2004, pp. 1-2 [emphasis added] <www.nytimes .com/2004/03/17/nyregion/17work.html>).

[13]Marc Gunther, "God and Business: The Surprising Quest for Spiritual Renewal in the American Workplace," *Fortune* 144, no. 1 (2001): 59, 61.

[14]Lonnae O'Neal Parker, "Prayer and Profits: These Business Leaders Seek Regular Counsel from Their Silent Partner—God," *The Washington Post*, January 11, 2002, p. C-1.

[15]A sampling of such articles includes the following: Leland, "Thou Shalt Not Call in Sick," pp. 1-2, on the "growing faith-at-work movement"; Victor Godinez, "Some Corporate Execs Follow Spiritual Beliefs: Displays of Faith Can Be Beneficial to Companies, Advocates Say," *Dallas Morning News*, December 25, 2001; Frank Green, "Mission Statement: Some Christian-Owned Businesses Reach Out to a Like-Minded, Faithful Market," *San Diego Union Tribune*, Novem-

In the years following, this phenomenon also gained the attention of the evangelical press with *Christianity Today* having featured it in five issues and three covers.[16]

Nash and McLennan cited their research as being in the forefront of a massive movement toward the integration of faith into the workplace and noted the growing body of literature addressing this subject: "In all, we reviewed *more than 125 books* in the areas of new spirituality, science, and religion, or management and religion . . . from which we drew our main conclusions about the content, underlying assumptions, and techniques of the new spirituality and business movement."[17] A year later, an annotated bibliography for marketplace ministries was published listing over seven

---

ber 24, 2002, secs. H-1, H-10, the business section lead story; Jane Lampman, "A New Spirit at Work: Leaders Moving to Transform the Business World with Spiritual Values," *Christian Science Monitor*, November 19, 2003; Michelle Conlin, "Religion in the Workplace: The Growing Presence of Spirituality in Corporate America," *Business Week*, November 1, 1999; Marci McDonald, "Shush—The Guy in the Cubicle Is Meditating. Spirituality Is the Latest Corporate Buzzword," *U.S. News and World Report*, May 3, 1999; Jeffery L. Sheler, "Faith in America: In Troubled Times, How Americans' Views of Religion are Changing," *U.S. News and World Report* 132, no. 15 (2002): 40-44; "A Spiritual Approach to Success," *Inc.*, January 1, 2000, which features Ian I. Mitroff and Elizabeth A. Denton, *A Spiritual Audit of Corporate America* (San Francisco: Jossey-Bass, 1999); Susan Hansen, "Let Us Now Pray . . . For Accu-Fab," *Inc.*, February 3, 2003, which features the Fellowship of Companies for Christ International; David Van Biema, "Missionaries Undercover," *Time*, June 30, 2003, pp. 36-44, cover story featuring tentmaking or "tunneling" mission through business; Ian I. Mitroff, "A Study of Spirituality in the Workplace," *Sloan Management Review* 40, no. 4 (1999); Jim Braham, "God and the CEO: The Spiritual Side—CEOs Speak Up About How Spirituality Helps Their Companies, Employees, Customers—and Themselves," *Industry Week* 148, no. 3 (1999): 48-51; John O. Enander, "Prayer Groups on Company Time," *Industrial Distribution* 89, no. 2 (2000): 78; even *The American Legion Journal* commented on the phenomenon, but in a different context: the governmental workplace of Washington, D.C.: Wesley G. Pippert, "The Other City of Angels: Faith Finds a Home Inside the Beltway," *The American Legion Journal* 154, no. 2 (2003): 20-23.

[16]For example, Tony Carnes, "The Silicon Valley Saints," *Christianity Today*, August 6, 2001; Ken Walker, "Prayer, Incorporated," *Christianity Today*, July 2003), pp. 20-21; *Christianity Today*, February 2003 cover and associated stories: Jeff M. Sellers, "The Higher Self Gets Down to Business," *Christianity Today*, February 2003, p. 34; Tim Dearborn, "Bad Company Corrupts," *Christianity Today*, February 2003, p. 41; Jeff Van Duzer and Tim Dearborn, "The Profit of God," *Christianity Today*, February 2003, p. 42; Mark Galli, "Glocal Church Ministry," *Christianity Today*, July 2007, pp. 42-46; *Christianity Today*, November 2007 cover story, "Heeding the Profits—How Entrepreneurs Are Building the Kingdom by Building Businesses" and associated stories: Joe Maxwell, "The Mission of Business," *Christianity Today*, November 2007, pp. 24-28; Uwe Siemon-Netto, "Work *Is* Our Mission," *Christianity Today*, November 2007, pp. 30-32; Collin Hansen, "Scripture and the *Wall Street Journal*," *Christianity Today*, November 2007, pp. 33, 38-39; Tim Stafford, "The Evangelical Elite," *Christianity Today*, November 2007, pp. 34-37.

[17]Nash and McLennan, *Church on Sunday*, pp. 289-90 (emphasis added).

hundred titles, and a year after its release, one of its authors, Pete Hammond, known as the father of marketplace ministries, said that the "InterVarsity marketplace faith-and-work book collection now numbers over 1,500 English language titles" and admitted that the incredible growth of books is both "encouraging" and "overwhelming."[18] He then candidly assesses a major problem with many of them:

> Some of the works are not good additions to this church renewal and mobilization movement. Some are even embarrassing, in that they are shallow, less than biblically accurate, poorly written, ego-centric, or just confusing. But even these are a symptom of the church recovering the calling, privilege and responsibility of every believer to be an agent of the kingdom of God in their work on the job.[19]

Many business owners and CEOs are actively seeking effective ways to integrate their faith into the lifeblood of their companies and into their daily business practices. Hundreds of church-based, parachurch and independent marketplace ministries are sprouting up worldwide. Scores of faith-in-the-workplace websites are now on the Internet. Christian business schools are starting to add faith integration discussions and courses into their curricula. One magazine, *Life@Work*, made an open (albeit unsuccessful) bid to be the trade journal for the emerging faith-in-work phenomenon.[20] Another, *Business Reform* magazine, is endeavoring to become the Christian think-tank journal that "can be used as a tool for Christians being discipled, to seriously think through how God's work specifically applies to all areas of business."[21]

Noted evangelical, business and marketplace-ministry leaders alike speak out and declare that the new faith-in-the-workplace, ministry-in-the-marketplace phenomenon is the cutting edge of a major mission movement and cannot be ignored (see appendix 1). Billy Graham said, "I believe one of the next

---

[18]Pete Hammond, R. Paul Stevens, and Todd Svanoe, *The Marketplace Annotated Bibliography: A Christian Guide to Books on Work, Business and Vocation* (Downers Grove, Ill.: InterVarsity Press, 2002); Pete Hammond, "The Best Marketplace Ministry Books of the Twentieth Century," *Marketplace Bibliography* 1 (2008): 1.

[19]Hammond, "Best Marketplace Ministry Books," p. 1.

[20]John W. Styll, publisher and editor, *Life@Work*, personal interview with the author, January 17, 2002.

[21]Ralph Cochran, steward of marketing, *Business Reform* magazine, personal interview with the author, March 1, 2002.

great moves of God is going to be through the believers in the workplace."[22]
Tetsunao Yamamori prophesied, "Kingdom business will be a strategy of
choice for missions in the twenty-first century."[23] Henry Blackaby affirmed
this by stating, "God is moving in a powerful way in the marketplace."[24] John
Warton sums up the collective view when he says, "The business community
is the most potent mission force for this century."[25]

Christian pollsters George Barna and Mark Hatch state that one of the core
future "innovations in 'doing church' " will be "Marketplace Ministry."[26] Ed
Silvoso, founder of Harvest Evangelism, takes it a step further and explains his
ideas more fully:

> Today millions of men and women are similarly called to fulltime min-
> istry in business, education and government—the marketplace. These
> men and women work as stockbrokers, lawyers, entrepreneurs, farmers,
> chief operating officers, news reporters, teachers, police officers, plumb-
> ers, factory foremen, receptionists, cooks and much more. Some of them
> have great influence on mainstream society, others are unsung heroes
> with low profiles, but each of them has been divinely called to bring the
> kingdom of God to the heart of the city. . . . God has explicitly *called*
> them and *anointed* them for it. . . . [T]hey can do more than just witness;
> they can bring transformation to their jobs and then to their cities—as
> happened in the first century.[27]

Bill McCartney, the founder of Promise Keepers, looked at this movement
of God from a historical perspective and stated:

> It is frequently acknowledged that the Second Great Awakening, the re-
> vival that swept America in the early nineteenth century . . . was at least
> partly initiated by businessmen praying together in the city of New
> York. Is it possible that a third great awakening could take place in our

---

[22]Billy Graham, preface in Os Hillman, *His Presence in the Workplace Conference Manual*
(Asheville, N.C.: Billy Graham Training Center, 2003), p. 1.
[23]Tetsunao Yamamori and Ken Eldred, *On Kingdom Business* (Wheaton, Ill.: Crossway, 2003),
p. 10.
[24]Blackaby, "Experiencing God in Business."
[25]John Warton, personal interview with the author, March 23, 2002, transcript, p. 24.
[26]George Barna and Mark Hatch, *Boiling Point: How Coming Cultural Shifts Will Change Your
Life* (Ventura, Calif.: Regal, 2001), pp. 249-50, 253.
[27]Silvoso, *Anointed for Business*, p. 18.

times, also led by believers in business? . . . In God's economy there is really no distinction between ministry and business.[28]

As these and other sources underscore, the faith-in-the-workplace phenomenon and its crosscultural partner BAM began taking on the shape and dynamic of a new, powerful, global mission movement in the early 2000s.

This emerging form of Christian mission to, within and through the marketplace is related to other emerging global phenomena. Though at first glance these other developments would appear to be unrelated to the earlier discussion, in reality they forge a remarkable convergence that has broad implications for missiology and missions. It is important to consider the following examples from a virtually inexhaustible list: the enormous technological advances in communications, travel and computerization in science, medicine and agriculture, and in digitalization, robotics, and miniaturization; the emerging threats to the earth's fragile, interdependent ecosystems; the ballooning competition for the earth's limited natural resources and fossil fuels; the growing power of transnational governing and regulatory institutions and regimes/constructs; the massive and growing underground global economy (and power structures) with its drug lords, arms dealers, mafias, and epidemic human slave and sex trafficking; the rise of global terrorism, its identification with Islamic extremism, and the warrior cries of Jihad heard during and since the attacks of September 11, 2001; the subsequent unprecedented use of anthrax and other biological weapons; the militant cries of defiance heard in the proclamation of the war on terrorism and the associate invasions of Afghanistan and Iraq launched in retaliation; the resulting sectarian (and worldwide political) bitterness, hatred and violence that erupted during the prolonged struggle with nation building in both countries and in neighboring Pakistan; the likely prospect of nuclear weapons falling into terrorists' hands; the frightening new levels of political and military interdependence, and the concomitant assault on individual liberties and social freedoms in even the most advanced Western nations; the rapid, complex economic integration of the world and the resulting global economic tsunami (or meltdown) being experienced in every corner of the world; and the frightening scenarios all of this portends for the future.

---

[28]Bill McCartney, foreword to ibid., p. 13.

In addition, consider the global human condition and its undeniable effect on mission. Three primary examples are the plague of grotesque poverty that is sweeping major portions of the globe; the increasingly pluralistic and polarizing nature of human society (ethnic, culture and religious) in virtually every nation on the face of the planet; and the growing visibility of horrendous human-rights abuses, especially against children, women and ethnic minorities, of ethnic cleansing efforts, and of widespread religious persecution all too often occurring in the name of one god or another.

When we consider these earth-changing matters and realize the profound direct and indirect nexus between each of them and the commercial business community with its global economic interests, we are nearly overwhelmed with the radical implications this has for global Christian mission. Is it any wonder that in the midst of today's globalized world, God might move in a dynamic, fresh and powerful way in the world? Is it any wonder that leading pastors, missiologists and marketplace-ministry activists might be speaking openly about a new global, God-initiated movement, *missio Dei*, into, within and through the marketplace?

Often referred to simply as the *movement* by insiders, the Marketplace Mission Movement is considered to be the leading edge of a God-driven tidal wave that may sweep the planet and see the final realization of the Great Commission mandated by Jesus. It is thought to be one of the truly great Christian movements of history that is emerging here and now, through people in this present time. Jesus told his people to study the signs of the times (Mt 16:2-3; 24:3-31) and to know that God is moving among us. In *Experiencing God*, Blackaby and King said, "Watch to see where God is working and go join Him!"[29] That is what this book is really about.

Major Christian movements. God has moved in powerful ways in human history throughout the ages. When the history of the Protestant church since the Reformation is examined, even the most casual observer cannot fail to see God's hand at work in various ways for different times and in distinct contexts.[30] For instance, there was the strong, dedicated movement among the

---

[29]Henry T. Blackaby and Claude V. King, *Experiencing God: Knowing and Doing the Will of God* (Nashville: Southern Baptist Sunday School Board, 1990), p. 15.

[30]See Stephen Neill, *A History of Christian Missions* (London: Penguin, 1990); Andrew F. Wall, *The Missionary Movement in Christian History: Studies in the Transmission of Faith* (Maryknoll, N.Y.: Orbis, 1996); and Paul E. Pierson, "Historical Development of the Christian Move-

Anabaptists rising out of the sixteenth century; the movements of Puritanism and Pietism in the late seventeenth and early eighteenth centuries; the advent of Moravianism, Methodism/Wesleyanism and the American Great Awakening in the eighteenth century; the modern mission movement birthed by William Carey sailing to India in 1793 at the dawn of the nineteenth century; the China Inland Mission, the Student Volunteer Movement, the Women's Missionary Movement, and the Edinburgh and Ecumenical Movements that dominated the mission agenda during the nineteenth century; Pentecostalism ushered in during the twentieth century; and the assortment of new mission and church movements throughout the twentieth century.

> There have been eight renewal movements over the last generation that
> have changed our understanding of the Christian life, of ministry, and
> of the character of the church. These are
> • Charismatic Movement
> • Small Group Movement
> • Worship Renewal Movement
> • Spiritual Gifts Movement
> • Ecumenical Movement
> • Church Growth Movement
> • Seeker Church Movement
> • New Paradigm Church Movement[31]

God will undoubtedly continue to move among his people just as he has in the past. While he can be expected to move in unexpected ways, as has been his pattern, he can also be expected to move globally in ways that tap into the needs, resources and realities of today's world. In short, he will move contextually in ways that are appropriate to the times and to his character. We firmly believe that is what he is doing today through the Marketplace Mission Movement and, more specifically, through BAM.

Characteristics of Christian movements. Before proceeding, it is appropriate to ask, What constitutes a major Christian mission movement? Paul Pierson, the Christian historian and former dean of Fuller Seminary's School

---

ment," MH520/620 class syllabus, Fuller Theological Seminary, Pasadena, Calif., 1998.
[31]Greg Ogden, *Unfinished Business: Returning the Ministry to the People of God* (Grand Rapids: Zondervan, 2003), p. 19.

of World Mission, says that each major mission movement of the past needed the following essential components:

1. A theology which informs and guides mission implicitly or explicitly [that is, a missiology]

2. A spiritual dynamic which motivates mission and moves people out of their comfort zones

3. Structures that enable people to carry out mission

4. Leadership which communicates vision and mobilizes people[32]

In addition to these four factors, Pierson identifies eleven elements that seem to be present in each new movement or revival. He does not suggest that this is a litmus test or a formula, but rather that these are elements which the major church movements of history have had in common.

First, a mission movement usually arises from a "sense of crisis." Things do not work for a large number of people, and this causes them to begin questioning many of the presuppositions of the particular group or culture. In that sense, they begin to reexamine the foundational elements of their worldview relative to that context and to search either for new meaning or for old meanings in new places or novel ways. In short, the historic and contextual conditions are ripe for change.[33]

Second, movements usually arise on the periphery of the larger church and often "in surprising ways through surprising people."[34] Pierson says firmly, "Movements come out of the fringe, rather than out of the center," but notes that "as the fringe edge acquires structure, they move toward the center."[35] This latter point is no small matter, he continues, because movements are like orbiting spheres around a sun. They either move centrifugally (tending outward, into orbit and away from the center) or centripetally (tending inward, toward the center). If they move outward there is always "the danger of flying out of the Christian orbit . . . [beyond] acceptable historic Christianity."[36]

Third, a "new concept or new way of defining reality . . . a new worldview"

---

[32]Paul E. Pierson, "Historical Development of the Christian Movement," MH520/620, class syllabus (Pasadena, Calif.: Fuller Theological Seminary, School of World Mission, 1998), p. 136.
[33]Ibid., 187, 218; and Paul E. Pierson, personal interview by the author, February 4, 2003.
[34]Pierson, "Historical Development of the Christian Movement," p. 165.
[35]Pierson, interview.
[36]Ibid.

emerges and is articulated by the leadership. This new concept finds favor with a "sufficient number of people" who begin to grasp it and to spread the word "somewhat spontaneously."[37]

The next few elements deal with leadership and those who follow the new movement's leaders. According to Pierson, a fourth element is that the new movement frequently will be triggered by a key person.[38] Fifth, there is usually a spontaneous, grass-roots leadership that emerges from the bottom, rather than from the elitist top. Pierson defines these "non-elitists" as "people who don't come up through the normal ecclesiastical, defined channels."[39] Sixth, and as a corollary, the new leadership is often broadly based, with "new people formerly excluded" coming into leadership.[40] Seventh, similarly, the leadership either has no control over the movement, or only loose control, and new leadership patterns often emerge.[41] Eighth, there is also a spontaneity and a contagious spirit among the followers. Pierson compares a movement to bamboo and notes wryly: "It grows into the ground, and then suddenly pops up everywhere."[42] Ninth, both with the leadership and the followers, "barriers of race, social class, gender, clergy-laity, are lowered."[43]

His last two elements deal with thought and theology. Tenth, there is "some theological re-discovery" involved, which is often a theological breakthrough.[44] Finally, there is always a "significant re-contextualization," in which the new theology is being communicated by new people, to new people, in new ways, new places, along with a new spiritual dynamic.[45]

Sustainability of mission movements. Once those elements are in place, it is likely that a movement is starting to form. Usually, Pierson says, a Spirit-filled movement invariably "predates its visibility," especially its visibility to the established church.[46]

On the other hand, formation and sustainability are quite different things.

---

[37]Ibid.
[38]Pierson, "Historical Development of the Christian Movement," pp. 165, 187.
[39]Ibid., and Pierson, interview.
[40]Pierson, "Historical Development of the Christian Movement," p. 165.
[41]Ibid., pp. 165, 187.
[42]Pierson, interview.
[43]Pierson, "Historical Development of the Christian Movement," p. 165.
[44]Ibid., pp. 167, 187.
[45]Ibid.
[46]Pierson, interview.

Without getting into the many issues surrounding sustainability, Pierson was quite adamant on one point: if the movement is to have long-term viability and survivability, it must find a significant relationship with the church. Pierson does, however, define "church" broadly and emphasizes that church is not an organization or hierarchy but is the "people of God. The people who come together to worship and serve Jesus Christ. Nurture each other. Seek to glorify God in their lives, in their vocations. And who see themselves as part of a larger, universal Church."[47] He pays homage to the importance of Scripture, preaching and the sacraments, but says, "While those are important, what about the people of God? Where the people of God are attempting to glorify God, serve God, nurture each other—that is Church."[48]

Another major point impacting a movement's sustainability involves a historical dilemma. "What are the compelling values, motif and energy of the movement? And to what extent is the second generation's and third generation's understanding—or are they simply born into a movement?"[49] Pierson notes that first generation adherents are invariably called to make a "countercultural u-turn, usually at some cost."[50] On the other hand, the second and third generations are born into the movement, have little or no worldview change, and often do not carry a sustaining passion for the movement.

A variation on this problem is frequently seen in immigrants who attempt to maintain the old ways in the context of a new society. In all such situations, intergenerational differences inevitably arise, leading to a lax in commitment to the movement or to pressure for significant changes in the original vision. Such changes can either be good or bad and can introduce improvements, revitalization and envisioning, or distortions, heresies and syncretism. In this situation, the foundational issue in the debate becomes the movement's sustainability and survivability.

The Marketplace Mission Movement. Without belaboring the point, it is helpful to note how Pierson's movement criteria fit the Marketplace Mission Movement. While a deeper analysis and exegesis is needed (and encouraged), for present purposes a cursory review will suffice to demonstrate its potential

---

[47]Ibid.
[48]Ibid.
[49]Ibid.
[50]Ibid.

to be one of the great movements of Christian history.

First, Pierson says that each new movement involves a new theology. It only takes a brief appraisal of the new books and articles being published on marketplace mission to see that a new theology of work, faith and mission is being propounded in this movement. Any participant in the frequent, worldwide faith-and-work and BAM conferences can verify this, but sadly, will also attest that much of the scriptural exegesis and lay theologizing is painfully shallow, dangerously misleading or wholly in error. Nonetheless, serious attempts are being made to craft a new way of looking at Scripture. Silvoso calls it "reading the Scriptures through marketplace glasses."[51] A. R. Bernard, the founder and pastor of the Christian Cultural Center, a church of seventeen thousand members in Brooklyn, New York, simply says, "God is trying to teach us how to read the Bible from a marketplace perspective."[52] I agree with both men, but from a missiological perspective. I prefer to think of a new marketplace theology in terms that include both an economic hermeneutic and a political hermeneutic. Since this is so key to all that follows, let me explain.

1. *Fundamental concerns of life.* J. Andrew Kirk notes that theology of mission is very difficult to define, but "by its nature, [mission theology is] about fundamental concerns which affect life at all levels."[53] Accordingly, in Kirk's view, any theology of mission that addresses these "fundamental concerns" of life must "incite to action."[54] This requires the following elements: (1) an analysis of reality that examines the "ideological commitments that *underlie political and economic strategies*"; (2) actions that empower the poor; (3) actions that help Christians "arrive at a 'Christian mind' on how to relate their faith to *the contemporary world*"; and (4) special training for leaders within Christian communities for "all kinds of ministry done on behalf of the community by Christians working *in secular occupations* as well as voluntary agencies."[55] He summarizes his position by saying that "theology can best be assessed by seeing it in action."[56]

---

[51]Ed Silvoso, "The Redemption of the Marketplace," His Presence in the Workplace Conference, platform speaker (Asheville, N.C.: April 2-3, 2003).

[52]A. R. Bernard, "Grow the Church from a Marketplace Perspective," His Presence in the Marketplace Conference platform speaker (Asheville, N.C.: April 1, 2003).

[53]J. Andrew Kirk, *What is Mission? Theological Explorations* (Minneapolis: Fortress, 2000), p. 11.

[54]Ibid., pp. 11, 12.

[55]Ibid., pp. 12, 13 (emphasis added).

[56]Ibid., p. 16.

2. *Political hermeneutic of the gospel.* Defining hermeneutics as "the discipline of interpreting and applying the [biblical] message . . . within the contemporary context into which the text is to be brought," Kirk endorses the necessity of a "political hermeneutic of the gospel. . . . [which is] a way of weaving together the biblical text, history, an understanding of social systems and actions to bring about God's liberating plan for human beings."[57]

3. *Economic hermeneutic of the gospel.* My broad definition of marketplace encompasses not only private, commercial and business sectors, but also public policy formulation by governments that define the business and economic processes by which we feed, clothe and prosper ourselves. Therefore, the marketplace incorporates not only a "political hermeneutic of the gospel" but also an "economic hermeneutic of the gospel." With the rise of American-style capitalism as both a new world secular religion and an economic system, and with the overwhelming reality of globalization, especially economic globalization, there is a definite need for an economic hermeneutic as part of the biblical theology of mission and hence of missiology.

The Puerto Rican theologian Orlando Costas agrees. He says that he speaks as an outsider *(etic)*, from outside the gates of the holy city where Jesus was crucified, "outside the gate of a comfortable and secure ecclesiastical compound."[58] He sees the need for a new theology of mission, a "theology of the crossroads," which he defines as "a critical reflection at the point where cultures, ideologies, religious traditions, and *social, economic, and political systems* confront each other, and where the gospel seeks to cross the frontiers of unbelief."[59]

All of this is highly pertinent to the Marketplace Mission Movement, as it not only begins the process of defining a new marketplace theology, but vividly illustrates the fact that a new theology is being formed in modern society as it seeks to put Christ's gospel into practice in and through today's global and local marketplaces.

Pierson's second factor involves a spiritual dynamic that moves people out of their comfort zones.[60] If there is anything most observers of the current move-

---

[57]Ibid., pp. 16, 18.
[58]Orlando E. Costas, *Christ Outside the Gate: Mission Beyond Christendom* (Maryknoll, N.Y.: Orbis, 1982), p. 194.
[59]Ibid., p. xiv (emphasis added).
[60]Pierson, "Historical Development of the Christian Movement," p. 136.

ment agree upon, it is that God is doing something powerful on a global scale. There is a new spirit moving within the worldwide business communities, workplaces, Christian organizations and the church that is casting a fresh vision for mission and generating new, exciting, creative mission methodologies.

Pierson's third factor addresses structures for people to carry out the new vision.[61] The survey of marketplace ministries (MMs), especially the large number that have entered the mission field in the last few years alone, illustrates that God's people are seeking, even experimenting with, a wide variety of new structures through which to carry out their marketplace mission calling. Although the organizational situation is more than a little confused, perhaps even chaotic at times, this is frequently true of any new mission movement.

The final Pierson factor is the existence of vision-casting leadership.[62] Without a doubt, a loosely defined leadership group has emerged within the Marketplace Mission Movement, largely through these new structures—that is, through the MMs, BAM companies, associations and the Christian academy. This group of men and women fills a wide variety of roles by casting the movement's vision through conference speeches, workshop presentations, sermons, books and articles, mobilizing marketplace participants and providing the needed support services that both the marketplace participants and the movement need at this stage.

The first of Pierson's eleven elements entails a sense of crisis.[63] Under that criteria the historic and contextual conditions are definitely ripe for the emergence of a Marketplace Mission Movement. To a large degree, the church and the Christian missiological communities have seen the marketplace as virtually off-limits. To many clerics it is a place of evil to be tolerated and tapped into only for financial resources, committee leadership and church business issues. They reject it as a place in which to minister or frequent, and as a place to find partners in mission or ministry.

This historic, documented antipathy between the business community and the church has led to a modern crisis in which literally thousands of business believers are seeking spiritual meaning in their daily lives outside of traditional ecclesiastical institutions, outside of the church and on the periphery.

---

[61]Ibid.
[62]Ibid.
[63]Pierson, interview.

Often they do so through hundreds (perhaps thousands) of parachurch organizations, marketplace ministries and BAM conferences that now exist to fill the void and meet their needs.

The second element is that new movements arise and initially exist on the periphery of society, outside or on the edge of the traditional church.[64] As noted above, most mission/ministry to, within and through the marketplace is currently being performed outside the established ecclesiastical church. In fact, until the last few years, one of the movement's weaknesses has been the absence of any meaningful connection with the church. I am pleased to report that after years of wandering in the ecclesiastical wilderness, the movement is now experiencing a definite centripetal force pulling it back toward the center and toward rapprochement with the church. While this is exceptionally encouraging, there is still a long way to go and, for the moment, it is fair to say that the movement still remains on the periphery of most churches' radar screens.

The third element is the emergence of a new worldview.[65] Currently, a major paradigm shift for thousands of faithful marketplace participants is definitely underway. For the first time in most of their lives, these men and women are seeing their secular vocation as a calling from the Lord and realizing that it is as valid, meaningful and spiritual as the calling of a traditional pastor to the pulpit or a traditional missionary to foreign lands. This startling realization is causing these business people to reexamine their lives, to redefine their reality and, for many, to radically adjust their life choices.

The fourth element notes that a key leader frequently emerges to help focus the movement's direction.[66] That has not happened in the Marketplace Mission Movement. No central figure has triggered this movement. Rather, a handful of leaders from a variety of organizations are gradually coalescing into an informal leadership network that seeks to bring structure to the movement. This is in keeping with Pierson's fifth element, which notes the rise of spontaneous, grass roots leadership,[67] and his sixth element which sees the rise of new leaders that were formerly excluded from meaningful leadership

---

[64]Ibid.; and Pierson, "Historical Development of the Christian Movement," p. 165.
[65]Pierson, interview.
[66]Ibid.
[67]Ibid

roles within the church.[68] As noted above, this leadership network comes from a wide variety of organizations located around the globe and incorporates a wide assortment of vocational callings and experience. In this sense, it is very ecumenical, which Bosch prophesied,[69] almost entirely consists of church laity, which Ogden foresaw,[70] and has emerged spontaneously, completely outside the walls of the ecclesiastical church.

The seventh element highlights the absence of leadership control.[71] Clearly that exists within the movement today and into the foreseeable future. By their very nature these businessmen and women are independent creatures who prefer to work in loose relationship with others based on personal friendships, cooperative coalitions and some strategic alliances.

Pierson's eighth element identifies followers' spontaneity and contagion.[72] The same unplanned, contagious spirit that infects this movement's leaders is found within the members of their organizations. One finds an excitement, an expectation and an eagerness wherever the message of the movement is shared. People in the marketplace and in the pews are highly stimulated by the concept, want to know how it applies in their lives and workplaces, and are eager to turn their often dull or sour jobs into meaningful ministry/mission opportunities for Christ.

The ninth element involves the assault on and the falling of various social and faith barriers.[73] Without a doubt, bringing down barriers is one of the Marketplace Mission Movement's major impact areas. The doctrine of the priesthood of all believers stands foundational to the movement's theology (see chapter seven) and is an unabashed call to obliterate clergy-laity barriers and the secular-sacred divide. Many movement leaders also have a strong desire to see other barriers dropped as well. Unfortunately, to date, gender barriers remain formalized but softening in certain marketplace ministries. Ironically, racial and ethnic barriers have also proven difficult to overcome primarily because minorities outside the MMs have been slow and reluctant to

---

[68]Pierson, "Historical Development of the Christian Movement," p. 165.

[69]David J. Bosch, *Transforming Mission: Paradigm Shifts in Theology of Mission* (Maryknoll, N.Y.: Orbis, 1991), p. 467.

[70]Ogden, *Unfinished Business,* p. 19.

[71]Pierson, "Historical Development of the Christian Movement," pp. 165, 187.

[72]Pierson, interview.

[73]Pierson, "Historical Development of the Christian Movement," p. 165.

join. Although social class barriers are also being attacked by many MMs, little progress has been made. These class barriers remain particularly difficult, due to the nature of the marketplace and the fact that many MMs and BAM initiatives focus primarily, if not exclusively, upon CEOs, business owners, executives and top-level leaders. Only a few major MMs and BAM initiatives currently address lower-level Christian marketplace participants directly. The long-term goal, however, even of those initiatives that focus solely on business leaders, is to cause them to radically transform their company's cultures so that all such barriers fall to Christ's gospel.

The tenth element addresses theological breakthroughs.[74] At least three major theological rediscoveries or breakthroughs have influenced the Marketplace Mission Movement. First, being laity led, driven and focused, it emphasizes making the doctrine of the priesthood of all believers a reality. Second, its participants are intent upon rereading Scripture with marketplace eyes and understanding which scriptural principles are applicable to the marketplace. Third, as discussed above and perhaps most exciting, the movement's participants are actively seeking and developing new ways of "doing" theology in and through the marketplace, i.e., defining new ways in which the gospel can truly be lived out within the marketplace context.

Pierson names the final element as re-contextualization, communicating this new theology to new people in new places.[75] As seen above, re-contextualization is a major, even foundational, component of the movement. By definition, the movement contextualizes mission vis-à-vis the marketplace. In other words, the marketplace serves as the new context for gospel application, missional penetration, evangelization, discipleship and empowerment for Christ. The movement then—through a "new" theology that is laity-defined and peer-communicated—is the gospel being heard outside the church walls, in the marketplace, where people live their daily lives. It is the same message with a new messenger for its new context.

Sustainability of the Marketplace Mission Movement. When considering the sustainability of the movement and its newly shaped theology, two dynamics must be highlighted: the movement's nexus to the church, and intergenerational momentum. Both are important to the future life of the move-

---

[74]Ibid., pp. 165, 187.
[75]Ibid.

ment. Pierson offers the following caution regarding the first dynamic:

> The marketplace has something very important to contribute, but the movement, if it is a Christian missionary movement, is not going to last if it doesn't result in the formation of . . . worshipping, nurturing, on-going communities of believers. That doesn't presuppose any particular structure of Church, but it presupposes an on-going, worshipping group of believers.[76]

Without a doubt, the movement's estrangement from the church is one of the major obstacles in the road ahead. That has, however, visibly changed during the past few years as the trendsetting, influential churches like Saddleback, Willow Creek, North Point, Perimeter and the like are institutionalizing programs focused on the marketplace. While a solid relationship is still missing between the church and the movement, bridges are being built and signs of progress are emerging.

The second dynamic, intergenerational momentum, is critical—it asks, Can the movement survive beyond the first generation? To many movement insiders today, the values, motif and energy of the movement are so deeply compelling that they believe the next generation (defined as both the young, future businessmen and women, and the "half-timers" who are seeking to re-define their careers) will be highly energized to take the message and the practice to entirely new heights and to directly impact everyone in the marketplace. At least that is their hope, their prayer and their challenge. The current movement is, however, so embryonic, vast and wide-ranging, and has so many obstacles to overcome, that it may take several generations to achieve meaningful levels of success. Nonetheless, if the relationship with the church becomes secure and solidifies, and if the structures of the movement strengthen, the generational appeal of this movement should emulate the transgenerational appeal of the gospel.

A caveat. This chapter has presented a foundation for understanding whether the signs of the times point to the Marketplace Mission Movement being a major twenty-first century mission movement, as many surmise, or whether it exists simply as a spiritual revival whose light will quickly fade. Such an inquiry, especially with the movement in its current formative state,

---

[76]Pierson, interview.

not only sheds light on what God is actually doing, but posits a warning for its leaders. They can easily, albeit unintentionally, distort and derail the movement if they do not keep their focus on Jesus and his gospel, intentionally nurture the movement's intimate connection to the ecclesiastical church, and become a firm "part of the whole" body of Christ.[77]

In that regard, it is appropriate to end this discussion with a stern, almost foreboding warning that may well serve as a "reality check" to the movement's leaders. Rebecca Avery, in her study of spiritual movements, has examined the Marketplace Mission Movement. She warns that the sustainability of the current momentum, both in the church nexus and in aspects of the intergenerational momentum, is vulnerable to erosion if the movement does not see itself as part of the larger, whole body of Christ. Avery begins by noting the eight-step cycle of most spiritual movements:[78]

1. Realization of spiritual limitations. This step is very close to the sense of crisis that Pierson addresses. During this period, the participants experience considerable "unhappiness with current spiritual status/outreach/ holiness/vision of the religious movement" in which they are involved. They feel very much like second-class citizens and are engaged in questioning why they are a part of the group and what role, if any, they have in it.

2. Period of development of faith and vision. This step finds those people gaining insight into the possibilities of the movement and sharing their vision with others. They have total trust in God and are filled with great excitement and a strong desire to reach the world and society in some meaningful way.

3. Great acts of courage. During this phase the adherents show a great willingness to sacrifice for the movement, set their sights on goals higher than themselves, feel highly motivated by the Spirit, yet feel quite overwhelmed with the challenges they face. They do, however, see their priority as the social change engendered by the movement and "persevere for the prize," as Paul urges.

4. Abundance. During this phase, the movement's goals and vision have been

---

[77]The following discussion, points and quotations are from Rebecca L. Avery, e-mail to the author, August 23, 2003; see also, Rebecca L. Avery, "Cycle of a Movement," *The Weaver Curriculum* 5 (1995): 55.
[78]Ibid.

largely realized. The members are pleased, feel that they have been faithful to God's calling, realize that there is still much work to be done, but are generally satisfied with their progress, and "'Good old boy' feelings abound, kudos to all."

5. Turning inward. The movement then begins turning inward, focusing on structure, finances and training, "rather than on the mission field of the World. Fissures begin to appear in the group as whole. There is considerable intent on issues of control. Members begin to feel under pressure to succeed, and legalism replaces the Spirit."

6. Complacency. At this stage, the movement begins to feel content, satisfied with the status quo, and no new vision emerges. Those born into the movement "are raised on the manna of previous accomplishments." There is an emphasis on the past, the leadership divides, resources diminish, the movement's impact on the outside world shrinks, and it begins losing touch with the real needs of the society it is serving.

7. Apathy. The tendencies in step six expand and become more intense. The total focus is inward; resources are drying up; leadership is closed to new ideas for growth and change; "members, while possibly going through the routine, simply don't care"; the impact on society is minimal; and "no one bothers to divide anymore and multiplication is out of the question."

8. Final decline. At this point, "the Movement, for all practical purposes, is dead. A few hollow shells of practicing membership remain, but there is zero effect on either society or the mission field." The movement is simply not taken seriously any longer; resources dry up; the second and third generations move on to their own causes; and "upon the death of the original leadership, the Movement perishes." The remaining members scatter and eventually find themselves back at step one.

Avery says, "This eventually applies to all movements, given enough time. Which is why Christianity in and of itself is not a movement. *Like a musical composition, movements are part of a bigger whole.*"[79] She then bluntly addresses the Marketplace Mission Movement and concludes, "I believe the movement you are writing about is in trouble, headed for a serious decline,

---

[79]Ibid. (emphasis added).

unless they understand that they are part of the whole."[80] In this, she and Pierson are in complete accord.

Avery and Pierson sound a warning worth heeding. It is my contention that at this point in the movement's development, the leaders understand this and are actively seeking to bring the movement into proper spiritual alignment as an integral part of the larger church, the larger body of Christ. They are doing this in a variety of ways, including prayer, scriptural guidance, theological understanding, purposeful dialogue, focused discussions and negotiated alliances. They seem to realize that it is important to be connected with the ecclesiastical part of the body, but whether the movement will maintain this focus and momentum remains to be seen. It is, after all, still a young movement. That, too, is one of the reasons for this book—to do what I can to help the movement's forward momentum and to train the next generation on the meaning, importance and exciting potential of BAM.

MISSION AND THE MARKETPLACE

What is God doing with the Marketplace Mission Movement? It is nothing short of awe-inspiring in its breadth, depth and complexity. It not only radically affects our view of Scripture but our view of the church, mission, stewardship, obedience and the respective roles of those in the pulpit and the pews. Indeed, if we have ears to hear, it has eternal implications for the nature of our calling from Christ and what he expects of each of us during our earthly sojourn. At the same time, it is emphatically simplistic in its profundity: Jesus wants each of us to honor, obey and worship him in *all* aspects of our lives— our actions, feelings, thoughts, words, gestures, countenance, time, resources, relationships, play, study, work and worship. Everywhere, always, in everything, with everyone. That includes the marketplace and who we are and what we do there. As the caustic proverb says, "What part of 'all' don't you understand?"

That being the case, it is important for the BAM practitioner or would-be BAMer to understand how he or she fits into the movement. Accordingly, before we launch into *how* to do BAM, we need to see the big picture. It is the forest and trees dilemma: before we become absorbed (lost?) by the trees, let us

---

[80]Ibid.

see an aerial view of the forest to gain perspective. One way to do that is to think of the movement as *a giant, divine, global jigsaw puzzle.* As any good puzzle buff knows, the first step toward solving a puzzle is to look at the picture on the box. We will do the same here, albeit ever so humbly and modestly, remembering that no matter how clear we try to make it, we can never truly grasp God's infinite, mysterious plans, ways and puzzles. In this life, as mere humans, we "see through a mirror dimly," but being made "in his image," we are creative problem-solvers who continually seek to understand the unexplained mysteries of our existence.

To understand the big picture, we will take two approaches. First, we will look at each of the movement's three different components: mission *to* the marketplace, mission *within* the marketplace, and mission *through* the marketplace. Second, in chapters four and five, we will see how the movement has self-divided functionally into at least four major camps.

Mission **to** *the marketplace.* This component of the movement, mission *to* the marketplace, is where God's people who are outside of the marketplace see it as a legitimate mission field to be penetrated with the gospel. It is marketplace outsiders seeking to evangelize and disciple marketplace insiders. This can take many forms, such as conducting Bible studies for the insiders, holding prayer walks around and through the business and commercial sections of the city, developing relationships with insiders and evangelizing them indirectly or through open witness and even loving, personal confrontation. Figure 3.1 is a simplistic, even childlike illustration of mission to the marketplace. All of them, insiders and outsiders, come in a wide variety of shapes to emphasize the uniqueness of all of God's people and, as a result, their very different needs and approaches to life.

Mission **within** *the marketplace.* The second component, mission *within* the marketplace, is a bit more complex. As might be suspected, it is about marketplace insiders who are Christians reaching out to other marketplace insiders with the gospel. This occurs in two ways. First, marketplace Christian to marketplace Christian, and second, marketplace Christian to marketplace non-Christian. As to the first of these, several active ministries exist, called marketplace ministries (discussed in greater detail later), in which Christian marketplace insiders reach out to other Christians marketplace insiders with systematic encouragement, discipling and coaching.

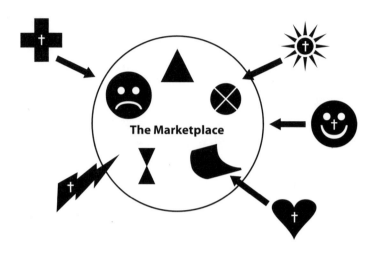

Figure 3.1. Mission to the marketplace

Often these marketplace ministries focus on Christian business CEOs and executives, equipping them to lead their companies for Christ and to manage by biblical principles. They usually minister through small peer groups that meet periodically, often weekly, to discuss real business problems and pending business and personal decisions, and to seek Christ-honoring, Bible-based solutions. In that sense, they use each other as a spiritual board of directors.

The second function of mission *within* the marketplace involves marketplace insiders championing the gospel within the marketplace, actively witnessing to marketplace nonbelievers and leading them to a saving knowledge of Jesus Christ. This evangelistic role—often through relationship evangelism as opposed to overt proselytizing—is very natural in the business world. It involves both evangelism and follow-up discipleship to the broad range of people with whom a business has direct contact: employees and their families, clients and customers, suppliers and vendors, creditors and investors, trade unions, trade associations, and competitors. Once a person becomes a new believer within the marketplace, he or she can be directed both to a church and to a marketplace ministry for continued daily growth in Christ. (Figure 3.2 illustrates this dual challenge.)

Personally, this is how I came to know Jesus as my Lord and Savior—

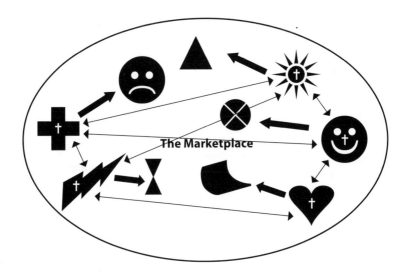

The Marketplace

Figure 3.2. Mission within the marketplace

through my bank executive officer, Bob Runyan, and our bank director, Tom Sivley. Even though I was an active church member, it was within the marketplace that I encountered God and changed my life forever.

Mission **through** *the marketplace.* The third component, mission *through* the marketplace, is quite different than the other two components. Here, Christian marketplace insiders seek to leverage the resources, power and networks that God has placed into their hands for kingdom impact—but in other parts of the world. Christian businesspeople reach outside of their immediate marketplace to holistically help people globally. Their actions may be directed toward distant or foreign marketplaces, to people in impoverished nations who have no marketplace, or to needy people outside of the mainstream of commerce in the inner city, barrio or ghetto of their hometown. At its essence it is Christian businesspeople harnessing their God-given resources to holistically help people outside of their immediate spheres of influence and is almost always crosscultural if not international (see fig. 3.3).

Since BAM falls within the mission *through* the marketplace framework, the examples in chapter two on BAM models illustrate the almost infinite ways this type of outreach can be effected.

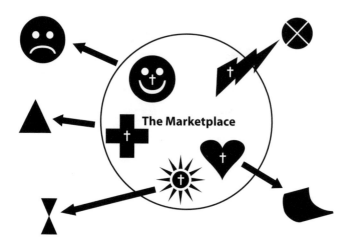

Figure 3.3. Mission through the marketplace

DISCUSSION QUESTIONS

1. Various Christians have said that the Marketplace Mission Movement may be the next great movement in Christian history. Do you agree? Why or why not? What evidence is there for the truth of these statements?

2. What are some characteristics of the major movements in Christian history? What movements illustrate these characteristics? Which, if any, of these characteristics do you see in the Marketplace Mission Movement?

3. What is your definition of the marketplace?

4. What evidence, if any, have you seen that church and business are at odds? What are some of the consequences of this conflict? What should be done about it? By whom?

5. How could God transform the cities through Christians in the marketplace? What would a transformed city look like? How does that differ from what you see in your city? Discuss, contrast and describe what realistic steps need to be taken (by whom) to bridge this gap.

6. What are some beliefs Christians have that prevent them from embracing business as a form of ministry? As a form of mission? What are these beliefs

based on? Are these beliefs well-founded? Why or why not?

7. What changes are needed to help the church and its members embrace the Marketplace Mission Movement, marketplace ministries and BAM? What is needed to help Christians in the marketplace personally and actively engage in faith integration?

8. BAM engagement: According to your vocational position at this moment, which of the three models of marketplace mission/ministry presented in this chapter do you see yourself engaged in? In what way?

4

Four Camps

SECTION 1

*"Jesus knew their thoughts and said to them, 'Every
kingdom divided against itself will be ruined, and every
city or household divided against itself will not stand.'"*
MATTHEW 12:25

*"May the God who gives endurance and encouragement give you
a spirit of unity among yourselves as you follow Christ Jesus."*
ROMANS 15:5

*May "we all reach unity in the faith and in the knowledge
of the Son of God and become mature, attaining to
the whole measure of the fullness of Christ."*
EPHESIANS 4:13

*"There is neither Jew nor Greek, slave nor free, male
nor female, for you are all one in Christ Jesus."*
GALATIANS 3:28

THE FIRST APPROACH TO OUR DIVINE jigsaw puzzle was to see mission *to*, *within* and *through* the marketplace. The second approach is to see how the movement has compartmentalized itself in actual practice. Although the contemporary Marketplace Mission Movement is quite young and ill-defined, it seems to be dividing into four distinct, self-selected camps: tentmaking, marketplace ministries, enterprise development and Business as Mission.[1]

---

[1]For further discussion on these four camps, see Neal Johnson and Steve Rundle, "Distinctives and

The next two chapters will address these four camps and attempt to shed some light on the fast-paced, ever-changing movement. In this regard the 2004 Forum for World Evangelism, hosted by the Lausanne Committee for World Evangelization (LCWE), held in fall 2004 in Thailand, boasted the addition of these four camps as individual tracks for the conference. It also had two other tracks, "Globalization" and "The Diaspora," both of which have significant bearings on each of the four camps. Apparently, pressure from disaffected movement activists led to the late inclusion of three of these tracks.[2] As Rundle explains, this is an evolving process in which these activists are attempting to discern their own place in *missio Dei:*

> The upcoming Lausanne conference is revealing an important shift within evangelicalism as a whole. . . . Specifically, there are separate issue groups for (1) marketplace ministries, (2) tentmaking, and (3) business as mission. . . . [T]he definitions that appear to be emerging, and solidifying, are, respectively, (1) workplace witness in a near-neighbor context, (2) workplace witness in a cross-cultural context, and (3) combining personal, cross-cultural witness with the fact that the business itself can be a witness for Christ.[3]

Rundle's comments refer to the theory of missions advanced by Ralph D. Winter at the 1974 Lausanne Conference. Since it is key to a future understanding of the camps, a short explanation of Winter's theory is appropriate before we briefly examine each camp to help distinguish BAM.

Winter's E-Scale

In a 1974 address to the Lausanne Congress, Ralph D. Winter announced a set of mission and evangelistic measures that have become part of the missiological lexicon. He notes that Jesus, as part of the Acts 1:8 crosscultural, evangelistic, mission mandate, described the task in geographic terms, "You will receive power when the Holy Spirit comes on you; and you will be my witnesses in Jerusalem, and in all Judea and Samaria, and to the ends of the earth" (Acts 1:8).

Challenges of Business as Mission," in *Business as Mission: From Impoverished to Empowered*, eds. Tom Steffen and Mike Barnett (Pasadena, Calif.: William Carey Library, 2006), pp. 19-36.

[2]It is heartening to see that the 2010 Lausanne Congress to be held in Cape Town, South Africa, October 16-25, 2010, will also include these four camps as issue-groups.

[3]Steve Rundle, e-mail to the author December 5, 2003.

Once empowered by the Holy Spirit, Winter says, Jesus "distinguishes between different parts of that world and does so according to the relative distance of those people from his hearers." In other words, Jesus sees different phases and perhaps different methods of mission based on distance. Winter is quick to point out that this distance is not just geographic but cultural as well. That is, Winter sees each of the geographic references in Acts 1:8 as also referring to a different cultural context, stating: "It seems clear that he [Jesus] is not talking merely about *geographical* distance, but about *cultural* distance. The clue is the appearance of the word *Samaria* in this sequence."[4]

From this analysis, Winter defines three different kinds of evangelism. First, he labels evangelism in Jerusalem and Judea (among one's own people and involving the same language and the same culture) as "E-1 Evangelism" or as " 'near neighbor' evangelism." In this type of evangelism, a person crosses only one frontier, the boundary between the Christian community and the non-Christian community, "between the church and the world." The culture and language remain the same.

On the other hand, evangelism in Samaria involves crossing a second frontier that is "constituted by significant (but not monumental) differences of language and culture." He labels this "E-2 Evangelism." As might be expected, Winter then uses the tag "E-3 Evangelism" to describe witnessing across even greater frontiers and cultural differences. That is, E-3 evangelism is mission into the remotest parts of the earth. In this mission context the people "live, work, talk, and think in languages and cultural patterns utterly different from those native to the evangelist. . . . [They are a] totally different people." He sees E-1 evangelism as the most powerful, but E-2 and E-3 as absolutely essential for the fulfillment of the Great Commission.

In a later article published with Bruce A. Koch, Winter added a fourth category, "E-0 Evangelism" in which one evangelizes "church-going Christians" within one's own culture. They note that while E-0 and E-1 consist of monocultural evangelism, E-2 and E-3 are crosscultural. They also expand their scale by mirroring Winter's "E-Scale: Evangelist's Cultural Distance from Po-

---

[4]This quote and the following discussion are taken from Ralph D. Winter, "The New Macedonia: A Revolutionary New Era in Mission Begins," *Perspectives on the World Christian Movement*, 3rd ed., ed. R. D. Winter and S. C. Hawthorne (Pasadena, Calif.: William Carey Library, 1999), pp. 342-44.

tential Convert" with a "P-Scale: People Group's Cultural Distance from Nearest Church."[5] As might be expected, an "M-Scale" ("M" for mission) quickly developed as well, also mirroring both the E-Scale and the P-Scale.[6]

When assessing both mission strategy and business strategy, any potential tentmaker or BAMer must take these scales and the geographic and cultural differences that they represent into account. Failure to do so will almost assuredly prove fatal to the enterprise or result in flawed, futile, frustrated activity and quite possibly attrition from the mission field altogether.

CAMP 1: TENTMAKING

Paul understood the vital importance of the marketplace to himself, to the gospel and to mission. It not only helped him to make a living but, in so doing, illustrated the reality and relevance of Jesus and his message in the real world. By trade, Paul made tents. It was a good profession. During the era in which he lived, tents were a primary place of residence, storage and shelter. His product was in high demand and his trade was imminently mobile. No matter where he went, it helped him financially while he preached the gospel.

During his mission trips, Paul used the money received from his professional tentmaking to support himself financially. He even boasted that his message contained greater credibility because he did not rely on others to support him and was not paid to bring the gospel to his audiences (1 Cor 9:12, 15, 18). As other missionaries followed in Paul's footsteps, pursuing their professions while preaching the good news, this practice became known as *tentmaking*. In the popular mind it quite simply means making your money in your business so that you can afford to do ministry outside of the business. In short, they see tentmaking as earning money in one place, so that a person can minister in another, that is, making money *here* so that he or she can preach the gospel *out there*.

The modern tentmaking movement. In 1979, J. Christy Wilson Jr., a twenty-three-year veteran missionary to Afghanistan and Iran, and until his death, the Emeritus Professor of World Evangelization at Gordon-Conwell

[5]Ralph D. Winter and Bruce A. Koch, "Finishing the Task: The Unreached Peoples Challenge," *Perspectives on the World Christian Movement*, 3rd ed., ed. R. D. Winter and S.C. Hawthorne (Pasadena, Calif.: William Carey Library, 1999), pp. 510-11.
[6]Patrick Lai, "Tentmaking: In Search of a Workable Definition," e-mail, November 5, 2001, p. 2.

Theological Seminary, wrote a seminal book, *Today's Tentmakers*.[7] Wilson's book traced Paul's tentmaking and, through a series of contemporary tentmaker stories, challenged marketplace Christians everywhere to use the expertise of their secular calling for the Lord's work. Wilson's challenge struck a responsive chord worldwide. The book was translated into several languages and became the launching pad for countless tentmakers as well as for several tentmaking organizations and associations. Wilson became the leading spokesman for an emerging modern tentmaking movement that continues to affect the lives of countless business missionaries and many thousands who have been reached for the gospel by their efforts.

Wilson became known as the "father of the modern tentmaking movement," "a senior statesman of the modern tentmaking movement," and "Mr. Tentmaker."[8] Don Hamilton, one of the true pioneers in modern tentmaking practice and research even dedicated his book *Tentmakers Speak* to Wilson, calling him "the tentmaker *par excellence*," a term Hamilton reserves for only one other man, William Carey.[9]

TENTMAKING TERMINOLOGY

One of the major problems facing the uninitiated in the tentmaking world is the endless confusion over the label *tentmaker*, the definition of a tentmaker and the variables that comprise its essence. Let us briefly examine these issues.

The term **tentmaker.** Even within tentmaking circles, there is widespread dissatisfaction, great confusion and seemingly endless wrangling over the term *tentmaker* and its meaning. Many ask, How can we readily accept the anachronistic label "tentmaker" in the modern and postmodern context? Many alternatives have been put forth, but none has found universal appeal. For examples see figure 4.1.[10]

---

[7]J. Christy Wilson Jr., *Today's Tentmakers: Self Support: An Alternative Model for Worldwide Witness* (Wheaton, Ill.: Tyndale House, 1979).

[8]John Cox, "The Tentmaking Movement in Historical Perspective," *International Journal of Frontier Missions* 14, no. 3 (1997): 116; Derek Christensen, "Training: Endurance Food for Serious Tentmakers," *International Journal of Frontier Missions* 14, no. 3 (1997): 133; and Cox, "Tentmaking Movement," p. 112.

[9]Don Hamilton, *Tentmakers Speak: Practical Advice from Over 400 Missionary Tentmakers* (Duarte, Calif.: TMQ Research, 1987), pp. iii, 10.

[10]For definitions on each of these terms, see "lay missionaries" from Hamilton, *Tentmakers Speak*; "non-professional missionaries" from Wilson, *Today's Tentmakers*, pp. 15, 146, attributed to Roland Allen, Kenneth Grubb and J. Herbert Kane; "the lay apostolate" (ibid., pp. 15,

Tentmaking Terms

- Lay Missionaries
- Non-professional Missionaries
- The Lay Apostolate
- Lay Pastors
- Self-Supporting Witnesses
- Self-Supporting Missionaries
- Bi-vocational Missionaries
- Bi-vocational Pastors
- Lay Professionals

- Kingdom Professionals
- Christian Professionals
- Great Commission Companies
- Global Christians
- God's Envoys
- Holistic Entrepreneurs
- Kingdom Entrepreneurs
- Bussionaries

Figure 4.1. Tentmaking terms

The reasons for seeking a new term to replace *tentmaking* are many, but one predominant reason is its intrinsic ambiguity. This ambiguity was vividly illustrated at a mission conference in India when local Christians ignored the tentmaker sessions, because they thought that tentmakers were "a group who put up tents (temporary shelters) for new churches."[11]

What is a tentmaker? Dictionaries do not recognize the religious or mis-

---

146, attributed to R. Pierce Beaver); "lay pastor" (ibid., attributed to Emmett McKowen); "Self-Supporting Witness" (ibid., attributed to usage at Urbana 73); "Self-Supporting Missionary" (ibid., p. 16); "Bi-Vocational Missionaries" from Lai, *Tentmaking*, p. 1; "Bi-Vocational Pastors" from Luther M. Dorr, *The Bivocational Pastor* (Nashville: B&H Publishing Group, 1988); "Lay Professionals" from Hau-Ming Lewis Chau, "Serving in China Today: Do Hong Kong Lay Professionals Have a Unique Contribution to Make?" Ph.D. diss. (Pasadena, Calif.: Fuller Theological Seminary, 2001); "Kingdom Professionals" from Gary Ginter, ed., *Kingdom Professional Resource Guide*, 3rd ed. (Chicago: Intent, 1999), and from Steve Rundle and Tom Steffen, *Great Commission Companies* (Downers Grove, Ill.: InterVarsity Press, 2003), p. 36; "Christian professionals" from Wilson, *Today's Tentmakers*, p. 142, and from Dwight Nordstrom and Jim Neilsen, "How Business Is Integral to Tentmaking," *International Journal of Frontier Missions* 15, no. 1 (1998): 15; "Great Commission Companies" from Rundle and Steffen, *Great Commission Companies*, p. 41; "Global Christians" from Steve Rundle, e-mail to author, April 6, 2003, p. 1; "God's Envoys" from Tetsunao Yamamori, *God's New Envoys* (Portland, Ore.: Multnomah, 1987), and from Wilson, *Today's Tentmakers*, p. 142; "Holistic Entrepreneurs" from "Consultation for Holistic Entrepreneurs," conference brochure (Regent University, Virginia Beach, Va., 2002); "Kingdom Entrepreneurs" from Tetsunao Yamamori and Ken Eldred, *On Kingdom Business* (Wheaton, Ill.: Crossway, 2003), pp. 8; and even "Bussionaries" from Lai, *Tentmaking*, p. 1.

[11]E. David Chaldran, "Tentmaking in India," *Kingdom Professional Resource Guide*, 3rd ed., ed. Gary Ginter (Chicago: Intent, 1999), p. 3.01.03.

siological use of the term *tentmaking*, yet for centuries this "nonword" has garnered major attention and controversy within many Christian circles. The debate is especially prevalent within Christian tentmaking circles, where the term is defined in an infinite variety of ways. Here are a few examples:

- J. Herbert Kane: "[A tentmaker is] any dedicated Christian who lives and works overseas . . . and who uses his secular calling as an opportunity to give his personal witness to Jesus Christ."[12]

- Andrew Dymond: "The tentmaker is a missionary in terms of commitment, but is self-supporting."[13]

- Lynn Buzzard: "Because of the special context of our commitment to world evangelization, and the special character of the ministry of laity in cross-cultural contexts, we are here reserving the term 'tentmaking' to refer to a subspecies of the larger ministry of the laity. We refer to persons whose particular sense of God's calling is marked by two emphases: one having to do with *purpose* and the other with *place*."[14]

- Global Consultation on World Evangelization 1995: "[Tentmakers are] believers from all nations who use their professional and working skills in response to God's call to proclaim Christ cross-culturally."[15]

- Ruth Siemens: "I will use the term *tentmaker* to mean mission-committed Christians who support themselves abroad, and make Jesus Christ known on the job and in their free time. They are in full-time ministry even when they have full-time jobs, because they integrate work and witness."[16]

- Don Hamilton: "The term 'tentmaker' refers to a Christian who works in a cross-cultural situation, is recognized by members of the host culture as

[12]Herbert J. Kane, *Winds of Change in the Christian Mission* (Chicago: Moody, 1973), p. 177; see also Wilson, *Today's Tentmakers*, pp. 16, 146.

[13]Andrew Dymond, cited in Wilson, *Today's Tentmakers*, p. 16.

[14]Lynn Buzzard, "Tentmaking: A Biblical and Contextual Apologia," *Kingdom Professional Resource Guild*, ed. Gary Ginter, 3rd ed. (Chicago: Intent, 1999), p. 3.01.03.

[15]Global Consultation on World Evangelization 1995, "The Seoul Statement on Tentmaking," *Kingdom Professional Resource Guide*, ed. Gary Ginter, 3rd ed. (Chicago: Intent, 1999), p. 3.02.01.

[16]Ruth E. Siemens, "The Vital Role of Tentmaking in Paul's Mission Strategy," *International Journal of Frontier Missions* 14, no. 3 (1997): 121, 128; see also Ruth E. Siemens, "GO Paper A-1: Why Did Paul Make Tents? A Biblical Basis for Tentmaking," *Global Entrepreneurship and Tentmaking*, ed. S. Rundle (La Mirada, Calif.: Biola University, 1998), p. 96, for a slight variation.

something other than a 'religious professional,' and yet, in terms of his or her commitment, calling, motivation, and training, is a 'missionary' in every way." As to the "cross-cultural barriers" that must be crossed by the tentmaker, Hamilton notes, "They may be found in their home countries or 'overseas,' but wherever they may be geographically, in terms of culture they are far from home."[17]

The one thing all agree upon is that the term almost defies definition. Buzzard observes, "Defining the term *[tentmaking]* is not without hazards."[18] Siemens is more direct: "Everyone uses a different definition," many of which are often contradictory.[19] Lai laughs at this internal "identity crisis," noting sarcastically but cryptically, "Tentmakers tentmaking tents! Sound confusing? You ought to try being one. . . . What's all the talk about anyway? Sending sojourners off to some surreal situation to reach the unreachable—or is this simply the unreached? Does anybody know who we are?"[20]

Another point that they all agree upon is succinctly stated by Hamilton:

> What's the consensus of tentmakers? *Tentmaking is not for everyone.* Certainly, it is no easy alternative to being a conventional missionary. Being a successful tentmaker is one of the hardest jobs ever, but the rewards that come from being used by God to help others know him is worth all the effort, pain, and frustration.[21]

WHO ARE THE TENTMAKERS?

In *Today's Tentmakers*, Wilson lists the variety of tentmaking professions that he encountered during his long tenure overseas, including an army doctor in India; a Mennonite English teacher in Central Asia; a Christian engineer also in Central Asia; a U.S. Air Force Colonel in Peshawar, Pakistan; a nurse in Tehran, Iran; an American lawyer in the Middle East; a Texas oil engineer in Iran; a cattleman and government teacher in Zambia; an educator in Peru, Brazil, Portugal and Spain; a mining engineer couple in Bolivia, Colombia and Surinam; and in Wilson's own mission station, Afghanistan,

---

[17]Hamilton, *Tentmakers Speak*, pp. 7-8.
[18]Buzzard, "Tentmaking," p. 3.01.02.
[19]Siemens, "The Vital Role," p. 127.
[20]Lai, e-mail, November 5, 2001.
[21]Hamilton, *Tentmakers Speak*, p. 89 (emphasis added).

an embassy secretary, a medical couple, a teacher of the blind and a Peace Corps volunteer.[22]

Teaching English as a second language (ESL) has been perhaps the most popular form of tentmaking. Kitty Barnhouse Purgason comments:

> The English language is an important commodity in today's world. From Tunis to Tashkent, from Harbin to Hanoi, people are studying English. . . . [D]emands for English language teachers are great in the least evangelized world. . . . In limited access countries where missionaries would not be welcome, the English teacher is often welcome.[23]

Sabrina Wong confirms this for Central Asia: "English as a Second Language has become a popular avenue of service for many tentmakers in Muslim Central Asia and, for that matter, many developing countries."[24]

ESL is but one of many tentmaking avenues. Phill Butler, international director of Interdev and chair of the AD 2000 Task Force on Partnership Development, has spent many years dealing with mission and development in the Hindu, Buddhist and Islamic worlds. He has observed, "This world, with rare exception, [is] inaccessible to individuals who apply for visas as 'missionaries.' Therefore, those doing Kingdom work almost always function in some type of tentmaking role." Specifically, he notes that in eleven years he has dealt with "missionaries playing every conceivable role. Scripture translators, literacy workers, literature production, radio programming, health and medical work people, environmental and business personnel, and those engaged as teachers or academics would be just some categories of tentmaking activities we have regularly seen."[25]

A tentmaker in her own right (as an educator in Peru, Brazil, Portugal and Spain), Siemens speaks as founder of Global Opportunities (GO)—an organization supporting tentmakers worldwide—more specifically about the vocations needed and utilized as tentmakers. "G.O. works with 3000+ vocations and many job titles." She elaborates:

---

[22]Wilson, *Today's Tentmakers*, pp. 58-64.

[23]Kitty Barnhouse Purgason, "Teaching English to the World: Options and Opportunities," *International Journal of Frontier Missions* 15, no. 1 (1998): 33.

[24]Sabrina Wong, "Teaching, Tents and Telling the Good News," *International Journal of Frontier Missions* 15, no. 1 (1998): 20.

[25]Phill Butler, "Tentmaking and Partnership for Church Planting Among the Unreached," *International Journal of Frontier Missions* 15, no. 1 (1998): 3, 4.

Governments issue work permits only to foreigners with expertise their country needs. *About half* of all positions open to Americans are in *education* at some level, from elementary school to university, and for most subjects. . . . Other large categories are health care of every kind, *engineering and technology, the sciences, agriculture* and related rural specialties, *business and finance, computer science,* and *transportation and tourism.* There are fewer openings in the *social sciences, athletics* and the *fine arts,* etc. . . . There are even jobs in *scuba diving!*[26]

Hamilton is quick to point out, however (and Siemens would agree), that tentmaking is far more than simply being a Christian in the workplace, whether at home or overseas. He emphasizes the following with disapproval:

Originally applied to Christians who live and work overseas, it has now become possible for some people to suggest that all Christians who work at secular jobs are tentmakers. "You don't have to be an evangelist, and you certainly don't have to live overseas," they say. "As long as you're living for Christ, you're a witness, and if you are earning your own living rather than being supported, then you're a tentmaker." . . . I don't want to detract from the need for people who live for Christ on the job. But a person who "lives for Christ" here or overseas is not a tentmaker in the sense we mean in this book![27]

LAI'S T-SCALE

Patrick Lai (a pseudonym for security purposes), a long-term tentmaker in Southeast Asia and author of *Tentmaking: Business as Missions* (2005), took Winter's E and P Scales as his cue and developed a corresponding tentmaking scale, the "T-Scale." In this scale Lai suggests that tentmakers can identify themselves in one of five different ways and said, somewhat self-deprecatingly, that "to sound missiological, I call them: T-1, T-2, T-3, T-4, T-5. (The 'T' is for tentmaker.)"[28]

---

[26]Ruth Siemens, "G.O. Paper A-5," *Kingdom Professional Resource Guide,* ed. Gary Ginter, 3rd ed. (Chicago: Intent, 1999), pp. 3.12.03-04.

[27]Hamilton, *Tentmakers Speak,* p. 7.

[28]This quote, those that follow and this discussion are all taken from Patrick Lai, "Problems and Solutions for Enhancing the Effectiveness of Tentmakers Doing Church Planting in the 10/40 Window," Ph.D. diss. draft (Manila, Philippines: Asia Graduate School of Theology, 2003),

Under Lai's scale, T-1 tentmakers are Christians who are hired in their own countries for their unique professional skills to be sent to the company's overseas offices with significant incentive packages in salary and benefits. Their primary motive for going overseas is their work. They are fully supported by the company, usually do not know nor become fluent in the local language, have no special call from the Lord for overseas mission, have no mission or evangelistic training, and have no special evangelistic plan or design. "In other words, their life and outreach is much the same as it was in their home country. The majority of T-1s work and witness in an E-2 (near cultural) situation, though some have an E-3 (distant cross-cultural) ministry."

T-2 tentmakers are similar to T-1s in that they are fully supported by the company sending them. Their primary motive for going overseas is to serve the Lord and they have sought the work as a means of accessing a particular people group. They frequently know some of the local language but are rarely fluent in it, usually have a call of the Lord to this people group, have some mission experience and training, have a definite plan for evangelism on the field, and may be associated with a mission agency or church for emotional support and counsel. "T-2s take a job primarily, if not solely, to facilitate their getting into the country to plant a church among their people. For the T-2, ministry is their job and their job is their ministry."

T-3 tentmakers are quite different than T-1s, but similar to T-2s. Their interest in the job is first as a vehicle to gain access to the targeted people group, second an outreach platform and third as a means of earning a living. They usually have extensive (often three years or more) missiological and business training, and have a definite strategy for evangelism, discipleship and church planting. They enter a country with a specific, desirable secular skill that not only allows them to open their own business or to work for a team member, but gives them flexibility and control over their time. It also gives them a source of income, although their salaries are frequently supplemented by sending agencies with whom they associate, their home church or by raising partial or full support from donors back home. To their home church they are seen as missionaries, but to the local authorities they have a nonreligious identity.

---

p. 15, which was later revised and published as Patrick Lai, *Tentmaking: Business as Mission* (Waynesboro, Ga.: Authentic, 2005), pp. 21-29.

T-4 tentmakers are a hybrid that is neither a full-time businessperson nor a missionary. "T-4s have real jobs and do real work, but unlike a T-3 who is involved in a purely secular position, T-4s usually work for a charity or nongovernmental organization (NGO) and often among the poor." Examples would be dentists, doctors, nurses, social workers, economic development workers and expatriate students studying in local universities. They are not paid for their work but raise their own support back home and are associated with a sending agency or home church for emotional support, guidance and accountability. Their home church recognizes them as missionaries, but like T-3s, the local authorities see them as having a nonreligious identity.

T-5s are not tentmakers at all. They are traditional missionaries who use business as a *cover* to obtain an entry visa into a RAN. They are there covertly, often through an arrangement with a local company, but with the tacit understanding that they will not do any work for the company. Alternatively, some will gain access to a country by creating a shell or paper company but do little or nothing to make the company into a real, viable business that benefits the people. They raise their own salary back home or are supported by a sending mission agency or home church.

In a departure from his earlier classifications, Lai later expanded his T-Scale to include T-6 workers, whom he defines as "married women," some with children. Lai candidly admits, "This was not intended to be a category from the beginning of this research; however, it evolved out of the process of assigning roles to each of the workers." He discovered that many tentmakers' wives supported the tentmaking enterprise in at least two ways: First in "their roles as wives," and second in their roles within "their own ministries or the ministry of their husbands. . . . Clearly each woman, as a homemaker, is a primary support to her husband and likely to other workers as well."

In closing his discussion of the T-Scale, Lai notes that there are definite advantages and disadvantages to each T model. He is quick to clarify, however, that "I am not proposing that one is better, or more spiritual than the other."[29] The choice, he explains, is a matter of one's calling, skills, background and comfort zone. Regardless of the choice, "each person is needed and all have a place." He then adds, almost sardonically, "And now that we know who we are,

---

[29]Lai, e-mail, November 5, 2001.

let's get on with what God has commanded us to do."[30]

David English, executive director of GO, gives special praise to Lai's categorizations, calling his concept of applying Winter's scales to tentmaking "brilliant" and noting that Lai "has done us a service by clarifying today's tentmaking conception."[31] English does, however, take minor issue with Lai's T-1 category, saying, "T-1's are not 'tentmaking' at all because they have no cross-cultural evangelism purpose. . . . I appreciate the desire to affirm all [overseas] Christians as witnesses to Christ, but if every Christian is a 'missionary,' then the term no longer means anything. Relative to tentmaking, T-1s are not even in the same ballpark with T-2s, T-3s, and T-4s."[32]

Hamilton wholeheartedly agrees with English and debunks the idea that every Christian in the workplace is a missionary or tentmaker.[33]

While English embraces Lai's T-Scale, his primary response focuses more on Lai's seven tentmaking variables than on his tentmaker types. Those variables are motive for taking their secular job, mission intentionality, the degree of missionary vocation, the degree of secular vocation, their mission agency accountability, mission training and income source.[34]

TENTMAKING GOALS AND PURPOSES

As basic as this issue is, the question of tentmakers' goals and purposes goes largely undiscussed in the literature. Agreement on the goal(s) seems to be assumed, yet from reading the discussions on other elements this assumption is highly suspect. Customarily the goal is stated in terms of the Great Commission or generalities about reaching the lost. As David J. Price sees it:

> Paul's passion to preach the Gospel where Christ has not been named, burns on in the tentmaker's heart. (See Rom. 10:12-15 and 15:17-20.) . . .
>
> Paul's ambition was *to share the Gospel* with unreached people and *to strengthen young churches.* This is the particular goal of the modern tentmaker also, and it is no peripheral goal, but central to his vocational faithfulness. . . . Like his biblical predecessor Paul, . . . the tentmaker is

---

[30]Ibid.
[31]David English, "A Workable Definition? A Response to Lai's Search," missiology forum at the U.S. Center for World Mission, Pasadena, Calif., April 24, 2001, p. 1.
[32]Ibid., p. 100.
[33]Hamilton, *Tentmakers Speak*, p. 7.
[34]English, "A Workable Definition?" p. 1.

constantly looking for opportunities for spoken witness at every level of his involvement with another people. His purpose in living amongst them is to proclaim and persuade so that they might be brought into relationship with Jesus Christ as His disciples. Neither is this any shallow engagement. Like the Master, the tentmaker is concerned to make disciples by fellowship through initial contacts and investing quality time with individual people.[35]

Many think that the goal of tentmaking is the same as that of regular missionaries. They find support for this proposition in the writings of Winter and Koch, who explicitly declare the goal of any crosscultural mission to be church planting:

> The essential missionary task is to establish *a viable indigenous church planting movement* that carries the potential to renew whole extended families and transform whole societies. It is *viable* in that it can grow on its own, *indigenous* meaning that it is not seen as foreign, and a *church planting movement* that continues to reproduce intergenerational fellowships that are able to evangelize the rest of the people group. Many refer to this achievement of an indigenous church planting movement as a *missiological breakthrough*.[36]

Robertson McQuilkin, former missionary to Japan and former president of Columbia International University, takes serious issue with this, making a sharp distinction between two types of tentmaking, Pauline and Priscilline. He notes that while both Paul and Priscilla (with her husband, Aquila) made tents as part of their mission activities, the similarity ends there. In McQuilkin's view, Paul's vocation was planting churches and he used his tentmaking trade only as a necessary means to reach his goal of church planting. Priscilla, on the other hand, was a tentmaker by vocation who witnessed through her job and taught, preached and helped with mission in her free time.[37]

---

[35]David J. Price, "The Tentmaker's Mandate," *International Journal of Frontier Missions* 14, no. 3 (1997): 108, 110 (emphasis added).

[36]Winter and Koch, "Finishing the Task," p. 517.

[37]Robert McQuilkin, "Six Inflammatory Questions: Part 2," *Global Entrepreneurship and Tentmaking*, ed. S. Rundle (La Mirada, Calif.: Biola University, 1998), p. 83.

English agrees that there is a significant difference between the tentmaking ministries of Paul and Priscilla, but sees the tentmaker's purpose, in both the Pauline and the Priscilline roles, as "extending the church" through evangelism and discipleship, relational support and church planting.[38] Whereas most tentmakers generally speak of bearing witness, spreading the gospel and the like, English's definition of tentmaking strikes at the heart of the tentmaker's primary goal: "Tentmaking is going as an ordinary, everyday, working Christian, totally committed to the Great Commission, for the deliberate, conscious purpose of reaching another people group with the gospel and extending the church."[39] He goes on to address the issue of the great commandment that seems to be at the forefront of most discussions about goals:

> Jesus called us not to make converts, but to make disciples. In my mind, real biblical evangelism always continues into biblical . . . discipleship. The core thing is the making of disciples, which requires that evangelism is a part of it, but the end goal is making disciples. And when you make disciples, you cannot make isolated disciples. They inevitably must be folded into healthy functional churches. . . . And it's the nature of healthy churches to reproduce, so that healthy churches will be, I think, based by the four Ss: . . . self-governing, self-supporting, self-replicating, self-nurturing.[40]

Lai strongly agrees and sees "an increasing need for tentmakers to plant churches among the least reached people groups." He further declares, "The possibilities and opportunities for church planting via tentmaking entry strategies and work are limitless so it's time we bring clarity and reality into our views of tentmaking."[41] In that regard, both Lai and English are in harmony with Winter.

Tentmaking Summary

As simple as the commandment to *go to the nations* is, accomplishing that in today's complex, globalized, geopolitically interdependent, terror-ridden, war-torn world is no easy task. With so many nations now becoming RANs,

---

[38]David English, personal interview by the author, April 25, 2002.
[39]Ibid.
[40]Ibid., p. 8.
[41]Lai, e-mail, November 5, 2001.

with Islam sweeping aside enlightened notions of modern civilization, human rights and religious freedom, and with so many lost souls who cannot be approached through traditional mission methods, tentmaking emerges as a shining star against a dark, foreboding sky. Its only aim is to help people with their physical and spiritual conditions. Ari Rocklin, a veteran tentmaking spokesman and advocate with GO, states:

> Tentmaking is not intrusive; it allows seekers to learn about Jesus without demanding a conversion. Our mandate as Christians is to make the Gospel available in such a way that people can either accept or reject it. We can do no more! When the message is accepted, the tentmaker is in an ideal position to model a work ethic and to plan a self-supporting, self-reproducing church and then leave, or at least move to another location.[42]

Rocklin's GO co-laborer English sees the enormous potential in tentmaking for carrying the gospel to the uttermost parts of the earth. He believes that God has shown the way for Christians everywhere to become involved in this process, but notes sadly that the popular, from-the-pulpit and in-the-pew view of tentmaking falls short of its shining potential. Due to that unrealized potential, he pleads:

> This is why we cannot settle for defining tentmaking by simply describing tentmaking as it exists today. We lose too much. We are simply not talking about the same thing Paul did. If we are to recapture the power that Paul engaged through tentmaking, we must realign our paradigm with his. As we do, we will release enormous resources and power for world evangelism.[43]

Regardless of the controversies, Paul's model was well-suited to the times in which he lived and continues to be well-suited, even preferred, as a methodology for many mission efforts today. But just as the times have changed and evolved, so have the methods for reaching the lost for Jesus. That is true of the Church with its great, diverse movements of God through the centuries; its extensive changes in worship styles, congregational expectations, musical

---

[42]Ari Rocklin, personal e-mail to the author, March 26, 2003.
[43]Ibid., p. 4.

trends and pastoral roles, and the unprecedented explosion of parachurch organizations. That is also true of the Marketplace Mission Movement with the dramatic emergence of large numbers of marketplace ministries, conferences, events, articles, books, websites and resources—all going far beyond the traditional, Pauline and Priscilline concepts of tentmaking.

Discussion Questions

1. Of the three models of mission *to, within* and *through* the marketplace, which would you most naturally become involved in? Why? How? What role, if any, should the church have in this form of mission? Why?

2. In your opinion, what are the positives and negatives of tentmaking?

3. Explain your understanding of Winter's E-Scale and Lai's T-Scale, giving examples of each. What is the difference between them? Are these scales realistic and useful for people actually thinking of going onto the mission field? Why?

4. The author suggests several terms that have been unsuccessfully offered to replace *tentmaking*. Which of these is more attractive to you, and why? What is one major drawback of using *tentmaking*? What term would be more useful?

5. BAM engagement: Would you ever consider being a tentmaker? Why? How could you be an effective tentmaker where you are in your own workplace? Is that really tentmaking or something else? Why?

5

Four Camps

SECTION 2

"Keep the main thing, the main thing, or suffer mission creep."
DICK WYNN

"The greatest temptation at work is self-reliance:
doing what we do well without Jesus
and bringing no glory in it to God."
MARK GREENE

"Capitalism has improved the lives of billions of people . . .
[but] we need a more creative capitalism. . . .
We need new ways to bring far more people into the system—
capitalism—that has done so much good in the world."
BILL GATES

WE HAVE LOOKED AT THE FIRST CAMP, tentmaking, now we will look at three more camps: marketplace ministries, enterprise development and BAM.

Camp 2: Marketplace Ministries

Marketplace ministry (MM) organizations are essentially those described in chapter three as mission *within* the marketplace. They are also known widely as faith-at-work organizations. Regardless of name, they involve groups of Christian businesspersons who band together for mutual support, evangelistic outreach and workplace discipleship. One prominent example and perhaps the dominant MM is Christ@Work. It focuses on business leaders and divides them into three categories: owners, CEOs and top executives ("Company Leaders"); retired executives ("Legacy Leaders"); and Christian business students ("Future Leaders"). Christ@Work's purpose is to equip these men and women to lead their companies for Christ and to manage by biblical principles. The ministry has a wide variety of resources available for its members, including a major annual conference. Most of its members meet in small groups, usually weekly, for mutual support, edification and equipping. They bring their business issues to the group seeking Christ-centered, Bible-based advice and guidance. Christ@Work has had over fifteen hundred companies among its American members and now has a presence in over twenty countries.

The emergence of marketplace ministries as an alternative, parachurch outreach to the business community is not new. Over one hundred years ago Charles Shelton wrote the classic *In His Steps*, which challenged each business CEO to make every business and personal decision by the single standard, "What would Jesus do? Or WWJD."[1] About that same time, a group of German Christian businessmen decided to do what they could to penetrate the Berlin business community for Christ. They organized a group known as CiW or *Christen in der Wirtschaft* (Christians in the Workplace), which was devoted to evangelizing and discipling their brothers in the workplace.[2] CiW is still a strong Christian force in the German-speaking nations of Europe. A few of CiW's international counterparts are: Europartners; IVCG *(Internationale Vereinigung Christlicher Geschaftsleute*, International Association of Christian Businessmen) headquartered in Switzerland; FGBMI (Full Gospel Businessmen's International) in Asia; and *La Red* (Spanish for "The Net" as in "business network") in Latin America and Central Asia.

Today, there are over twelve hundred examples of MMs in ninety-six countries and virtually all states of the United States. Many are simply known by their initials, but all have one thing in common: they are efforts by businesspeople to reach other businesspeople in and through the marketplace for

---

[1]Charles M. Sheldon, *In His Steps: "What Would Jesus Do?"* (1897; reprint, Nashville: Thomas Nelson, 1999).

[2]Jorg W. Knoblauch and Juerg Opprecht, *Kingdom Companies: How 24 Executives Around the Globe Serve Jesus Through Their Business* (Holzgerlingern, Germany: Hanssler Verlag, 2003), pp. 219-22.

Christ, and until recently they have generally had virtually no connection to the church or other MMs.

Marketplace ministry motivations. There are many motives that drive the MM effort: to evangelize and disciple the lost within the marketplace; to provide mutual encouragement, mentoring and support for Christians within the marketplace; to equip marketplace leaders to lead their companies for Christ; to discern how to apply Scripture to the rough-and-tumble, work-a-day world with its own particular business ethic and credo; to learn how to live out one's faith on a 24/7 basis; and to discover ways that they can balance work with home, family, recreation, and church. The motives can be listed, but in the end they are as individualistic as the men and women who make up the MM membership.

While there are many worthwhile motivations for Christians engaging in MM activities, one perhaps deserves special comment. Those of us who have been in the movement for several years have a strong, compelling desire to reach lonely, needy Christians in the marketplace. As a result of our own personal life experiences, we have come to realize that there are many isolated Christians in the marketplace who, like us, have not heard the faith integration message. No one has told them it is possible to be an obedient follower of Jesus Christ and a successful businessperson—Christ's emissary in the workplace—all at the same time in the same context.

In fact, many marketplaces have significant numbers of wholehearted believers in Jesus Christ within their ranks. They may be Christian business owners, CEOs, executives, managers, sales people, clerics or workers. They may be in the private or public sector, in businesses, classrooms or government offices. Since no one has told them that they may have been called to that place and time for God's purposes, they have been denied the fellowship and encouragement of associating with fellow believers in their marketplace niche. They have been denied the privilege of seeing how important their jobs can be in the lives of those around them from God's point of view.

This is tragic. It is in the workplace, the marketplace, that most people spend the bulk of their waking hours, the prime of their lives. Think of the increased meaning their lives would have to themselves, to others, to the lost and to God's kingdom if they reenvisioned their roles in life from God's perspective.

These marketplace Christians are a major focus of the movement and a continual reminder that our marketplace service to God is to help hurting people find that abundant life Jesus spoke about, both in this life and the hereafter. It is about serving them, whether they are lost or just lonely.

Marketplace ministry functions. Marketplace ministries come in a variety of forms with many agendas and perform a multitude of diverse ministerial/missional functions. The primary functions include:

- *Equipping.* Helping Christian marketplace insiders understand how to be more effective for Christ in their workplace and to have a greater kingdom impact through their companies.

- *Fellowshiping.* Spending quality time with fellow marketplace Christians to relieve the stress and anxiety that often come from business and to add joy to their work.

- *Motivating.* Lifting up brothers and sisters in Christ in the marketplace to be more Christlike in their work environment and to see their role, no matter how menial or tedious, as a useful tool for kingdom impact.

- *Encouraging.* Being a Christian in the marketplace is often a lonely, isolated, intimidating experience. Christians, like everyone, need encouragement in difficult situations and it can often best come from the Barnabases in their midst.

- *Mentoring.* Receiving systematic guidance, instruction and wisdom from fellow marketplace believers, especially where older, more experienced Christians help younger, greener Christians in the marketplace.

- *Coaching.* Like mentoring, coaching focuses on providing guidance and instruction, but whereas mentoring often focuses on the holistic life needs of the individual, coaching focuses more on performance-related activities in such contexts as work, the family or play. A mentor comes alongside the individual in his or her life journey; a coach is in a more directive, instructive role.

- *Discipling.* Bringing to the Christian marketplace insider the instruction necessary to help him or her grow in Christ, increase in scriptural knowledge and life application skills, and generally mature in all ways in the gospel.

- *Advising.* Serving as a spiritual board of advisors for business and personal issues and decisions; bringing wise counsel and helping to analyze and resolve these from a Christian-values perspective.

Other functions were suggested by a group of MM leaders who were convened in Atlanta by the Business Professional Network:

The following activities fall to Christians who are called to serve God within business and professions:

1. evangelism, especially among business and professional people

2. discipleship, especially among these groups

3. training in how to manage businesses biblically and according to Christian ethics

4. stimulating new businesses and creating new jobs in economically depressed regions of the world

5. giving generously, especially for disaster relief and urgently needed social programs

6. helping the poor

7. coaching men and women facing business crises and mediating business disputes outside of court

8. guarding the health and security of the business community

9. referring people in business and the professions to other marketplace ministries that can serve them best[3]

Let's briefly examine three of these functions—evangelizing, discipling and coaching—and then nine categories into which the MMs fall. Hopefully this will help us grasp the breadth and depth of God's movement within the marketplace.

Evangelism. Whereas BAM focuses heavily on the RANs/CANs and on crosscultural, E-2 and E-3 ("uttermost parts of the earth") evangelistic mission, MMs are largely monocultural, E-1, near-neighbor ministry outreach. Marketplace ministries are also one of the hottest areas of ministry globally.

---

[3]Business Professional Network, "The Mission of Marketplace Ministries," *Connect* 6, no. 4 (2001): 1.

But, as previously noted, they are not new. Europartners boasts a broad membership of indigenous Christian MMs that date back over one hundred years and focus on both evangelizing within the marketplace throughout Europe and discipling their own Christian business participants. Similarly, Christian Businessmen's Committees (CBMC) focuses on having members, Christian marketplace insiders, evangelize non-Christian marketplace insiders, with discipleship its natural but secondary goal, and its third goal being Christ in the workplace.[4]

Discipleship. Groups like Christ@Work have taken a different tack than Europartners and CBMC. Rather than focus on evangelizing nonbelievers within the marketplace, Christ@Work has seen the need to disciple those business CEOs, owners and executive leaders who have made the salvation decision and are already Christians. Christ@Work seeks to teach these executives how to lead their companies for Christ, to be priests in their own businesses, to run their companies by biblical principles and to use their businesses as platforms for ministry. It still believes strongly in evangelizing, but its first emphasis is on discipleship. Where CBMC starts with evangelism and lets discipleship follow, Christ@Work starts with discipleship and lets evangelism flow from the changed lives and transformed company environments.

Coaching. Ron Jenson, who calls himself "America's Life Coach," and his Future Achievement International is a fertile example of a ministry that is focused on providing frequent, intimate, one-on-one coaching and mentoring to marketplace leaders in professional, personal and spiritual life skills. Other such ministries include Kingdom Way Ministries, Ft. Collins, Colorado; HIS Business of Laguna Beach, California; Building His Champions, Bend, Oregon; C-12, Apollo Beach, Florida; Business Proverbs, Tucson, Arizona; Life-Chasers, Chicago, Illinois; InsideOut Impact, Vancouver, Washington; Wise Counsel, Jacksonville, Florida; and Henry Blackaby Ministries, Atlanta, Georgia. Some of these ministries charge a fee; many are national in scope. At this point there seems to be little international outreach among these coaching ministries, with Jenson's organization being a notable exception.

Marketplace ministry categories. If you are having a problem sorting out

---

[4]CBMC was originally known as the Christian Businessmen's Committees, but now goes by various names such as Connecting Businessmen in the Marketplace to Christ, Connecting Businessmen to Christ and Concerned Businessmen for Christ.

the various types of MMs, you are not alone. In an earlier MM study, I discovered that a large number and variety of MMs were literally springing up overnight and that they fit into eight loosely defined categories. These are not presented here as the definitive types of MMs but rather to show their diversity and variant niches. God calls people to his work in myriad ways, but the overview leaves no doubt that he is at work and has chosen the business community as a major tour de force in his dynamic *missio Dei.*

1. *General marketplace ministries.* By "general marketplace ministries" I refer to Christian, not-for-profit, nonchurch-based ministries that are primarily focused on mission to, within or through the marketplace. The following examples are illustrative of the size and diversity of the general MMs:

- *Christen in der Wirtschaft* (CiW) (Christians in the Workplace) was founded in Berlin in 1902 and focuses on evangelizing within the marketplace of approximately 40 cities and regions of Germany.[5]

- Christ@Work (also known as FCCI) is a niche ministry founded over twenty-five years ago in Atlanta to serve Christian business leaders who want to be intentional about integrating their faith into their business and using it as a platform for ministry.

- Christian Businessmen's Committees (CBMC), out of Chattanooga, is an established international ministry with a variety of program-delivery methods to reach virtually every Christian man in the marketplace.

- *Internationale Vereinigung Christlicher Geschaftsleute* (IVCG, International Association of Christian Businessmen) is a Swiss-based evangelistic outreach ministry founded in 1957 in Zurich, Switzerland, and Karlsruhe, Germany, to evangelize to the German-speaking business communities of Europe, as well as leaders in politics, the military, science and culture.[6]

- *La Red* Business Network (*La Red,* The Net/Network) is a microenterprise and small-business ministry based in Berlin, Ohio, that trains and equips entrepreneurs in the poor business communities of Latin America, Central Asia, New Zealand, East Africa and South Africa.

---

[5]Jorg Knoblauch and Jurg Opprecht, *Kingdom Companies* (Manawatu-Wanganui, New Zealand: River City Press, 2004), pp. 219-20.
[6]Ibid., pp. 222-23.

- Wise Counsel for Christian Entrepreneurs (WC or Wise Counsel) is a Jacksonville-based national ministry focused on larger companies that involves monthly peer-group meetings and a high degree of personal coaching.

- Full Gospel Business Men's Fellowship International (FGBMFI), founded in 1952 in Los Angeles by Demus Shakarian, a California dairyman, and led by his son Richard Shakarian, is now taking the gospel to businessmen and women in approximately 150 countries.

- HIS Business Ltd., a coaching marketplace ministry in Laguna Beach, California, is oriented toward personal spiritual formation in business leaders and bringing God's kingdom into business through faith integration.

2. *Associations of marketplace ministries.* As the MMs developed, their leaders increasingly felt the need to associate for mutual support, encouragement, information, idea exchange and cooperative joint ventures. These cooperative efforts are still happening in many different forms. Some are formal associations that bring together MM leaders as members of the association. Others are informal, even ad hoc or one-time organizational efforts such as jointly sponsored conferences, symposia or meetings. Still others are strategic alliances where two or more MMs come together for a specific purpose or goal, long or short term. Although some of these alliances are informal, others are based on formal written agreements. The variety and tenure of these associations is like the movement itself, dynamic and ever-changing to meet the needs of the moment. The following four are examples of these types of associations:

- The International Coalition of Workplace Ministries in Cummings, Georgia

- Europartners, a formal association of European-based MMs in Wetzidon, Switzerland

- The International Christian Chamber of Commerce (ICCC), a network of Christians in business with members in over one hundred nations

- Business Professional Network (BPN), an informal association of member-based MMs that grew out of the AD 2000 movement.

3. *For-profit marketplace ministry entrepreneurs.* To this point we have been very specific in stating that the term *marketplace ministries* refers to

those Christian, *not-for-profit* ministries that are primarily focused on mission to, within or through the marketplace. Now, however, it is appropriate to introduce a hybrid form of MM that has grown out of a convergence of diverse factors:

- The unique U.S. tax structure: To gain both state and federal approval to become a not-for-profit Christian ministry within the United States and to accept tax-fee donations, U.S. tax laws require that a ministry go through an arduous, time-consuming process. As a result, and for varying strategic and even theological reasons, a new breed of U.S. entrepreneurs has avoided this legal maze by adopting a *for-profit* model for their ministries.

- The business mindset: Being private sector entrepreneurs, they often have a disdain for governmental intervention and involvement in their affairs. They simply prefer to render unto Caesar than to navigate the often nightmarish, bureaucratic process necessary to avoid taxation. The profit motive is high on most Christian businesspeople's agenda. When it comes to establishing their own MM, however, the primary motivation of most is simply to have a successful, sustainable MM free of administrative and policy control by any established church, parachurch or other nonprofit ministry.

- The public perception: Although most MMs depend on charitable gifts to cover their expenses, many have found that the public is seldom motivated with a charitable, donation-driven spirit toward MMs, no matter how noble. This is because the public's misconception of businesspeople, as well as their ministries, is almost as simple as the prevailing myth, "Everyone knows that all businesspeople are 'rich' and don't need any outside funding."

- The members' perception: Unfortunately, a version of this common folklore is even present within the MMs themselves. Many of their own members fail to recognize the MM's need for sustaining financial support or simply refuse to provide it, while still wanting to avail themselves of its benefits. While denouncing the secular-sacred divide, these same members will generously support their church's ministry but are not yet attuned to supporting their own business ministry. They will unhesitatingly support a secular trade association that lobbies the legislature about secular business laws, but will not readily support their spiritual trade association (MM) that lobbies members about following God's business laws.

These realities face virtually all MMs, but like any organization, they must have financial support to be viable and effective for the kingdom. Accordingly, with no public and little member support, these ministries have been driven to look elsewhere for their daily bread. This brought these ministry entrepreneurs back to the very skills on which they built their professional lives. Seeing the need to be independent of the public's charity, they have focused on generating ministry income from the activities and products of the ministry itself. In other words, they have sought ways for the ministry to be self-funded and financially self-sufficient.

This situation leaves the MMs with a dilemma. They need to develop a new funding model that will be both a ministry provider and a revenue generator. They need a model that will be consistent with Christian outreach principles and simultaneously provide support for the founder and staff, cover all ministry expenses and capitalize the ministry's future growth and expansion. Resolving that dilemma has fostered a new type of ministry, unique perhaps to the marketplace and the church, and it may alter the entire face of mission over the coming decades. Illustrations of this new breed of for-profit MMs are some of those coaching ministries mentioned previously: Building His Champions, C-12 and Future Achievements International, as well as Convene (formerly known as Beyond the Bottom Line Forums or BBL) of Placentia, California, which specializes in formal peer groups for business CEOs, presidents and owners. Convene business leaders meet monthly to discuss issues surrounding the integration of faith, family and business, and to receive personalized coaching from trained facilitators.

4. *Christian professional associations, affinity groups and guilds.* One of the truly exciting areas of MMs is that of Christian professional associations, affinity groups and guilds. These occur when Christians who share a common affinity or profession band together for mutual support, encouragement, information, mentoring, fellowship and spiritual protection. In so doing they hope to discern how to best live out their faith within their common context and to honor Christ in their vocation and industry. Since the format and structure for each affinity ministry is unique, no generalized overview will be attempted. The nature of these groups is, however, fairly evident from their

names. The following is a sampling of these ministries, past and present:

- Artists in Christian Testimony, Brentwood, Tennessee
- Associates in Media, Burbank, California, a Campus Crusade for Christ (CCC) ministry that is led by members of the acting and screenwriting profession to the Hollywood film industry
- Association of Christian Hairdressers, Altena, Germany
- Association of Protestant Bookstores, Stuttgart, Germany
- Athletes in Action, a CCC ministry, Xenia, Ohio
- Catholics in Media, Studio City, California
- Christian Association of German Train Employees, Remchingen, Germany
- Christian Bakers Association, Stuttgart, Germany
- Christian Legal Society, Pasadena, California
- Christian Mail Association, Radevormwald, Germany
- Christian Medical and Dental Association, Bristol, Tennessee
- Christian Police Association, Winterlingen, Germany
- Fellowship of Christian Peace Officers, Chattanooga, Tennessee
- International Fellowship of Christian Airline Personnel

5. *Church- and parachurch-based marketplace ministries.* The previous discussion relates to those nonchurch-based MMs that are primarily focused on mission to, within or through the marketplace. As might be expected and hoped for, the church has started taking notice of the movement of God within the marketplace. No longer is the marketplace off-limits to churches or clerics. In fact, many churches have served notice that they now see the marketplace as a legitimate mission field and are already engaging it or intending to do so. In fact, several large churches now devote major staff, space and budget resources to their marketplace ministries. Since these churches see their marketplace ministries as only one segment, one niche, of their broader mission, I have included them in this category, along with those parachurch organizations that also minister to concerns that are broader than the marketplace. The following examples are illustrative of the more visible category six ministries to the marketplace:

- Saddleback Community Church, Lake Forest, California (Rick Warren)

- Willow Creek Community Church, South Barrington, Illinois (Bill Hybels)

- Christian Cultural Center, Brooklyn, New York (A. R. Bernard)

- Harvest Evangelism, San Jose, California, but with significant marketplace campaigns in both North and South America (Ed Silvoso)

- Campus Crusade for Christ through (1) Athletes in Action to the sports world (category four), (2) Christian Embassy to the international governmental community in Washington, D.C., and at the United Nations, (3) Executive Ministries to highly successful business leaders, and (4) Priority Associates to young creative and corporate professionals (the late Bill Bright)

- The Billy Graham Evangelistic Association (BGEA), working through the Billy Graham Training Center, first moved dramatically into the MM arena with "His Presence in the Workplace" conferences at The Cove, Ashville, North Carolina, April 2003, and in Atlanta, March 2004, and has held several similar conferences since.

6. *Academic institutions and academicians.* As the hand of God has moved through the marketplace, various ministries both within and outside the church have been formed. The Marketplace Mission Movement's outreach has extended globally and, in so doing, has brought a new face to *missio Dei.* As with many historical Christian movements, the leading edge has come from the mission field—from the periphery—with the church and finally the academic community lagging behind. The new arena of MMs is no exception.

The Marketplace Mission Movement's visibility is causing some Christian (and even some non-Christian) academic communities to begin assessing and engaging the movement and, in so doing, to expand and legitimize it. Not only are colleges and scholars addressing the new phenomenon, but specific MMs are now attracting both faculty members and students to the cause. The following examples are illustrative:

- Yale University has, for the past few years, operated its Center for Faith and Culture led by Miroslav Volf "to promote the practice of faith in the spheres of life through theological research and leadership development . . . [and to explore] Ethics and Spirituality in the Workplace."[7]

- Princeton University's department of religion has established the "Faith and Work Initiatives" under the direction of David Miller to generate intellectual frameworks and practical resources for the issues and opportunities surrounding faith and work . . . as people live out their faith in an increasingly diverse and pluralistic world.[8]

- Bakke Graduate University in Seattle, Washington, has established a new school of business specifically based on BAM to offer a values-driven, Christian executive M.B.A. and an M.A. in social and civic entrepreneurship both in the United States and in developing countries.[9]

- The Biola University Crowell School of Business in La Mirada, California, has launched a dynamic M.B.A. program specifically focused on the integration of faith and business. Dr. Steven Rundle, leader of that effort, also sponsors an intercollegiate BAM trip to China each summer.

- The Regent University Graduate School of Global Leadership and Entrepreneurship in Virginia Beach, Virginia, is aggressively claiming the high ground through its Center for Entrepreneurs founded by Dr. John Mulford.

- Leadership Development International (LDi) of Tianjin, China, with U.S. offices in Atlanta, has initiated a bold program of business education in China with business training and consulting offices in Tianjin, Qingdao and Shenyang, and an experiential learning center in Jixian County between Beijing and Tianjin. LDi presents both a business curriculum and consulting services from an overtly Christian ethical base with a value-driven, evangelical agenda.

- InterVarsity Christian Fellowship has expanded its Ministry in Daily Life division, originally organized under the leadership of the late Pete Hammond (known as the father of marketplace ministries), for students to address the growing movement of God in the marketplace. Urbana 06 featured a separate BAM conference within the conference called "Open for

---

[7]<http://www.yale.edu/faith/>.
[8]<http://www.Princeton.edu/csr/current-research/faith-and-work/>.
[9]In the interests of full disclosure, I am the founding dean of this school.

Business," which was limited to (and drew) fifteen hundred participant college students from all over the United States. Even larger crowds are expected for the BAM section of Urbana 09.

- Calvin College of Grand Rapids, Michigan, hosts a two-week summer program on BAM, presented by Steve Rundle and me, specifically designed for Christian business school faculty and church leaders.

- Various organizations are partnering with graduate and undergraduate business schools to develop faith-based business curricula and to provide international business summer internships for students.

This list is only a sample, but it illustrates how God is moving to address the multiple, often divergent facets of the marketplace and the Christian academy. These events are also highlighting many new challenges currently facing the academic missiological community since the advent of the Marketplace Mission Movement as part of God's *missio Dei*.

7. *Marketplace ministry activists.* Another colorful vestige of the new Marketplace Mission Movement is a group I call the marketplace ministry activists. These are Christian entrepreneurs who have gone beyond the guild associations and through their own nonprofit businesses are proactively engaging the enemies of Christ within the marketplace. They are organizations of Christian businesspersons, often lawyers, who use the tools of their marketplace professions to "fight the good fight" (1 Tim 1:18; 6:12; 2 Tim 4:7) on a daily basis within the marketplace. The following examples are illustrative:

- Alliance Defense Fund, Scottsdale, Arizona, is a legal advocacy group supported by "an alliance with more than 300 ministries and organizations . . . [that serves in] ongoing battles . . . to preserve and defend religious freedom . . . the sanctity of human life, and marriage and family" through its staff of attorneys in six regional service centers throughout the United States.[10] One of ADF's primary concerns is the dramatic loss of religious freedom and the ability of people of faith to live and share the gospel.[11]

- Amen, Inc., Atlanta, Georgia, attempts to plan and start new, profitable, independent businesses for Atlanta Union Mission alumni in the inner city.

---

[10]Alliance Defense Fund <www.alliancedefensefund.org>.
[11]Ibid.

- Christian Community Credit Union, Covina, California, serves the financial needs of Christians and a variety of churches, denominations and parachurch organizations.

- Counseling for Circus Employees, Feuchtwangen, Germany, does "evangelism, counseling, and social welfare work among circus members and families."[12]

- Faithworks Worldwide, Miami, Florida, seeks restorative justice for women.

- Pacific Justice Institute, Citrus Heights, California, is a legal advocacy group focused on the "defense of religious freedom, parental rights, and other civil liberties" without charging the clients.[13]

- *Institut Koinonia*, Oberweningen, Switzerland, operates The Job Factory Basel AG and *Stiftung* Job Training, both in Basel. These are on-the-job training centers for young people in what they call "hand work" (e.g., carpentry or contracting), "time work" (temporary work in companies) and "shop work" (retail, clothing, etc.). The object is to help their students earn a temporary living and develop employment skills for finding permanent employment.

- *Weizenkorn*, Basel, Switzerland, trains and employs the mentally and physically handicapped in productive jobs manufacturing and marketing candles and toys.

8. *Organizations supporting marketplace ministries.* Finally, the MMs have attracted a host of other organizations, some for-profit and others not-for-profit, that provide ancillary services to the movement. Some examples are

- *Business Reform* magazine, Ashland, Ohio, has an online bimonthly circulation of over seventy-five thousand and is geared primarily to small- and medium-sized Christian business owners. It recently converted to *Christian Business Daily* for news and events and www.ChristianBusiness.net for advertising by self-proclaimed Christian businesses.

- *Faith Works* magazine, Jacksonville, Florida, started in 2007, but stopped

---

[12]Mike McLoughlin, C. Neal Johnson, Os Hillman, and David W. Miller, eds., *International Faith and Work Directory 2003-2004* (Cumming, Ga.: 2003), p. 62.

[13]Pacific Justice website <http://pacificjustice.org>, accessed May 23, 2009.

publishing in September 2009 for lack of circulation.

- The *Life@Work Journal* suffered a similar fate to *Faith Works*.
- Global Opportunities supports tentmakers worldwide.
- London Institute for Contemporary Christianity, London, England.

Marketplace ministry summary. From all of the evidence it appears that the number and diversity of MMs and their mission methodology is high and growing. In addition, each ministry examined seems to be continually undergoing an ever-deepening search for identity, not only among its particular stakeholders but also within the context of the broader Marketplace Mission Movement.

It is important to note that while *missio Dei* to, within and through the marketplace has taken on many different hues and facets, that is as it should be. I suggest that nothing less will be successful or sustainable in a mission context as broad and as varied as the marketplace. The marketplace is by its very nature a complex, pluralistic, often incomprehensible environment. It is also a constantly changing, evolving environment. Accordingly, any effective marketplace mission strategy must contend with these realities and can only be carried out with continuous creative diversity and a highly flexible, even mobile, mission approach that learns from its experience.

CAMP 3: ENTERPRISE DEVELOPMENT

Private sector Christian enterprise development generally occurs under the auspices of Christian nonprofit organizations (NPOs), known internationally as nongovernmental organizations (NGOs), dedicated to holistic community development and poverty alleviation. These NGOs are full-time ministries, in poverty stricken areas of the world, that attempt to help indigenous people improve their lives by starting and developing businesses. As a general rule the NGOs work with the poor and the poorest of the poor to help them bootstrap themselves out of poverty. Their methods are known as MED (microenterprise development), SME (small and medium enterprise development), and MFI (microfinance institutions or microloan programs) that are essentially village banks for the poor.

The concept of enterprise development may at times be confused with the more generic term *economic development* or the emergency services called *relief.* To clarify the matter, *disaster relief* is short-term aid to meet a genuine human need caused by some tragic event like an earthquake, typhoon, tsunami, famine, war or refugee crisis. It is not intended to provide long-time support, but rather to be a stopgap measure to stabilize the society and to help the people return to a normal life—whatever that might have been. *Urban relief* is also short-term, immediate relief for people in need within the heart of the city. Examples would be meals and shelter for the homeless and derelicts; half-way houses, rehabilitation and emergency aid clinics; and jail work-release and job-training programs. Unlike disaster relief, which has a beginning and a termination date, urban relief is as perpetual as the problems it seeks to address.

Economic development, on the other hand, tries to take the normal life of people living in poverty, often grotesque poverty, and help them create physical infrastructures, social and health services, environmental projects, and economic opportunities that will improve the quality and longevity of their lives. *Enterprise* or *business development* focuses on a specific aspect of economic development: helping create businesses that generate jobs that create wealth that, through the multiplier concept, raise the economic level of the community or nation. In that sense, *economic* development customarily works with a top-down strategy with large, expensive projects, whereas *enterprise* development works with a bottom-up strategy with small and medium businesses. The goals of enterprise development are to improve the general economy and living standards of the society by (1) creating jobs that turn the unemployed and underemployed into productive, self-supporting citizens, and (2) creating valuable goods and services that bring a better life to the community. Given their focus on poverty, many NGOs primarily concentrate on the 10/40 Window.

Some suggest that enterprise development mission efforts are not legitimately part of the Marketplace Mission Movement. Their objections are that most Christian development groups are NGOs and not businesses; they are not managed or operated as a business by businesspeople; they are not structured to generate profits; the sources of their funds are not from investors or internally generated income; they do not manufacture, produce, distribute or sell valuable goods and services of their own; and they generally do not relate their activities to the local or foreign business community.

I disagree and include enterprise development as one of the distinct, prominent camps of the movement. Regardless of its structure these NGOs are dedicated to helping men and women develop profit-making businesses that will help lift them out of poverty. Successful Christian-led businesses are the endgame. These efforts will help the entrepreneurs create businesses, jobs and wealth, boost the community's economy, and provide valuable goods and services to its people. Any quibbling about who is *in* or *out* of the movement misses the point: it is not about us. We are all ministering holistically through business to hurting people in the name and love of Jesus so that our Lord will be glorified. Examples are

- Business Professional Network, Portland, Oregon, promotes business development groups (BDGs) in churches, schools, colleges, and professional and civic organizations. BPN assists these organizations to form, sponsor and participate in both MED and SME in a variety of foreign countries.

- The Alliance of Philippine Partners in Enterprise Development (known as APPEND), Pasig City, Philippines, is the first network of Christian development NGOs in the Philippines and has over two million microfinance clients nationwide.

- The Center for Community Transformation, Manila, another microfinance provider for the Philippines.

- World Vision, Monrovia, California, has an aggressive Christian worldwide enterprise development program, including microfinance.

- HOPE International of Lancaster, Pennsylvania, is a network of microfinance institutions that works with fourteen countries "to empower men, women, and families to break the cycles of physical and spiritual poverty through the provision of loans, savings services, basic business training, mentoring and discipleship."[14]

CAMP 4: BUSINESS AS MISSION

The fourth camp, BAM, has been discussed at length in chapters one and two. It is, however, a unique camp in that it combines aspects of all of the other camps. In a very real sense BAM is an outgrowth of tentmaking and it incor-

---

[14]HOPE website <www.hopeinternational.org>.

porates holistic enterprise development. And once the BAM business is launched within a given country, the internal issues of running the company by biblical principles are largely the same as those addressed by the marketplace ministries. The MM's practice of employing weekly meetings of peers in small groups to look for biblical, Christ-honoring approaches to their business problems is directly applicable to BAM and will be discussed later. The point here is that each camp, but especially BAM, has much it can learn from the other camps about how to have a kingdom impact with the business resources God has placed at their disposal in the crosscultural mission setting.

A generalized summary of key differences among these various groups is reflected in figure 5.1, which is a slight modification of the excellent work of Dr. Steven Rundle of Biola University:

Camp	Vocation	Focus	Context	Vision
Tentmakers	any professional skill	job-takers; any level	crosscultural	"uttermost parts of the earth" E-2 and E3
Marketplace Ministries	business specific	job-makers; primarily CEOs and execs	monocultural	Jerusalem E-1
Enterprise Development	business specific	microjob-making; primarily jobless people	crosscultural	"uttermost parts of the earth" E-3
Business as Mission	business specific	job-makers; almost exclusively CEOs and owners	crosscultural	"uttermost parts of the earth" E-2 and E3

Figure 5.1. Key differences among the four camps

The practice of BAM raises a host of issues that the BAMer must deal with, such as discerning one's call; the true ownership of the business; the role and uses of profits; Christian values in business, especially the complex issues surrounding integrity and maintaining holiness; how one integrates faith and work; time usage; styles of evangelism in the business context; appropriate lifestyles; the complexities of bribery; the role and theology of work; accountability, especially in relationship to sending agencies, teams and "lone rangers"; business competence; the relationship and impact on the culture; and spiritual warfare. While some of these issues are explored in this book, exploring all of them (and others like them) is beyond its scope. They are, however, areas of considerable importance, both spiritually and professionally, from both a business and a mission perspective. They are mentioned here to simply remind the would-be BAMer that while the practice of BAM, if done correctly, is far from easy, it is exceptionally stimulating and seldom boring.

■   ■   ■

This presentation on the four camps has been necessarily, woefully inadequate. Excellent books have been written on each topic and anything more than a survey or cursory explanation of the topics is beyond the scope of this book. The object here is not to fully explore each camp, but to give enough of an overview that all readers can have a general understanding of the larger picture (the jigsaw puzzle box picture), that those with a specific interest in BAM can see its (and their) legitimate place in the movement and that those who want to delve more deeply can be stimulated to do so.

Closing Observations: A Reality Check

Before closing, there are four points about the camps and their place in the movement that deserve special comment. These points are intended to help bring a touch of reality to the theory of BAM and how it is practiced. In that sense, they set the stage for the discussion that follows and the remainder of this book.

The laborers are few. To date the Marketplace Mission Movement has been largely characterized by awareness-building events like conferences, workshops, websites, sermons, articles and books. A large number of organizations have also sprung up to meet the various needs of the movement and to answer individuals' calls to specific camps. Unfortunately, far more businesspeople and companies have expressed a strong interest in the movement than have actually begun engaging it. Admittedly, the movement is embryonic and in its formative stages. In that regard it is chaotic and confusing, and long on talk, theory and concepts, but short on action. As long as the movement has been in play, however, there should be a vastly greater number of companies signing on to its concepts, especially when so many companies are led by well-intentioned, committed Christians. Sudyk enthusiastically agrees with BAM but asks, with a sense of profound sadness:

> With all of the enthusiasm about using the marketplace to reach lost people, why are so few people doing it? Remarkably, very few people are moving from theory to action. . . . These Holistic Entrepreneurs have little time to teach or mentor, and therefore the movement is stagnated by its very success. But the fundamental reason that business is not being effectively used for missions runs much deeper. So deep in fact, that there is *a vast chasm between the world of business and the mission community.*[15]

Hopefully, this book will help stimulate Christian business leaders and students to become BAM *doers* and practitioners, rather than mere observers. Unless we actually field a strong team of BAMers, we will have few victories for Christ.

Isolation. Until recently the businesspeople serving within each camp have been operating in isolation, with little or no awareness of the other camps, little or no communication among the camps, and little or no connection with the ecclesiastical church. Each camp has had its own distinct associations and conferences, literature, informational and teaching resources, ministry methods and models, advocates, practitioners, goals and leadership. Niche ministries are the rule, and many are totally isolated from others within their own camp, not to mention those in other camps. That is a shame. A great deal of wasteful duplication is occurring and there are distinct lessons that each can learn from the other.

On the bright side, things are beginning to change. The ice is being broken between and among the camps by mutual conferences and workshops. Simi-

---

[15]Thomas Sudyk, "Strategic Considerations in Business as Mission," paper presented at the Consultation for Holistic Entrepreneurs, Regent University Graduate School of Business, October 3-5, 2002, p. 1 (emphasis added). A revised version of this paper was later published as Thomas Sudyk, "Strategic Considerations in Business as Mission," *On Kingdom Business: Transforming Missions Through Entrepreneurial Strategies*, ed. Tetsunao Yamamori and Kenneth A. Eldred (Wheaton, Ill.: Crossway, 2003), pp. 153, 161.

larly, marketplace ministries and mission is now an integral part of the outreach by role model megachurches like Willow Creek, Northpoint, Perimeter and Saddleback. These influential churches—and many others—are finally beginning to see the powerful potential of the movement and of this new, exciting form of business-church liaison. We pray that interest continues, grows and matures, for we firmly believe that a strong nexus among the camps and between the laity-driven movement and the ecclesiastical church is essential. Without it we have serious concerns about the movement's sustainability, the realization of its mission potential and its continued favor with God.

Competition. In some ways, we would expect nothing less than a highly cooperative spirit from a group of practical, bottom-line, results-oriented businesspeople committed to penetrating the marketplace for Christ. They will generally do whatever it takes to get the job done. On the other hand, these same people, whose lives are centered on business realities, are naturally and professionally very competitive and self-protective. We would also expect to see a great deal of rivalry, jockeying for position, advantage, primacy and status for the benefit of themselves and their ministries.

Surprisingly, cooperation is currently dominating competition. In fact, MM leaders are frequently heard to discuss putting individual differences aside and acknowledging, as Crown's chairman, Larry Burkett, said, "There are no competitors in Christ's work!"[16] Christ@Work's (FCCI) past-president Kent Humphreys concurs, "This is about the Kingdom, not about FCCI. I will not fight with other Christian organizations. I will work with them whether they work with me or not. We will not hold anything close to the vest."[17]

Occasionally there are signs of rivalry, territoriality and competitiveness, but on the whole I have found that these businessmen and women are sold out to Christ and are currently displaying an amazing, God-ordained unity in Christ within the Marketplace Mission Movement. Notwithstanding the apostle Paul's repeated calls for unity within the body of Christ, this MM unity is, in my experience, very rare—and is something that the church of our Lord Jesus Christ has seldom seen and would do well to emulate.

This unity is so striking and wondrous to experience, in fact, that I can only

---

[16]Larry Burkett, "Ministry Update," platform speech, FCCI Execute with Excellence Conference, Cancun, Mexico, September 30, 2002.

[17]Kent Humphreys, personal telephone conversation with the author, January 3, 2003.

hope and pray that it can be maintained and will continue as the movement grows. If it does, in addition to being a mission outreach to the marketplace, the movement's unity could forge an infectious example of selfless servant leadership that could manifest itself in the church at large, especially at the heart of its ecclesiastical and denominational strongholds. Since all of the movement's leaders are also active members of their local churches and often of their denominations, there is bound to be some contagion effect. Let us pray so!

War. At this point, an important caveat must be given: as followers of Jesus the Christ we are an invading army moving with force and power into Satan's territory. He does not like it and will resist. And he plays hardball.

Moreover, the marketplace is a spiritually dark maze that Christ's warriors are now venturing into with ever-increasing troop strength and with innovative strategies and organizational approaches. To be successful for Christ, however, it is vital that these warriors also be bathed in prayer, clothed in the armor of God, armed with the power of the Holy Spirit and alert to the dangerous road ahead.

More specifically, BAM is engaged in spiritual combat with God's enemies, and BAMers will be resisted and obstructed at every turn if not properly covered in prayer. Spiritual warfare is not a popular concept in the West, but it is as real as good and evil, and as God's angels (which many Christians readily believe in) and fallen angels, Satan and his demons (which many Christians disparage). Scripture tells us that God and his army will ultimately win back the earth, but not before there is a bitter, bloody battle. Warfare language is not currently politically correct or theologically popular in mission and church circles, but anyone who has been effective on the mission field will tell you that it *is* war; it is very real and has significant casualties. Further, these mission veterans know and proclaim, often to deaf ears, that to ignore this reality is the purest form of self-destructive folly—especially for missionaries, whether traditional or nontraditional, such as BAM.

Perhaps foremost among the dangers to all four camps is the absolute fact that Satan will attempt to attack each business leader and his or her mission through the very business worldview that is so ingrained within each of them. He will tempt them to go down a secular path of mission, to do mission in their own strength, using their own strategies, structured through their own business acumen and relying on their own resources. Satan knows that their very strength as marketplace leaders, business people and entrepreneurs is also their greatest weakness and vulnerability. He also knows just how easily their sense of spiritual dependence on God can be lost when they succumb to their sinful natures and forsake the ways of the Spirit. It is a dangerous and proverbially slippery slope, and we must never forget this ever-present, looming danger in the midst of our mission efforts.

In short, the marketplace is Satan's giant leviathan, but our God is stronger. The marketplace is dynamic, ever changing, ever shape-shifting, but our God is an ever-constant, omnipresent, omnipotent power. Paradoxically, because of who God is, his mission-purposed companies can and should have both continuous, dynamic mission flexibility and simultaneously remain firmly rooted in cosmic reality. Anything less will not produce the abundant harvest that awaits.

Discussion Questions

1. Do you see the eight categories of marketplace ministries discussed by the author (see pp. 135-44) as a sign that the MM camp is fragmented and under-organized, or do you think that the many models reflect the complex nature of the needs of the marketplace? Explain. Are these categories useful to a person considering involvement in the movement? Why or why not?

2. Define the different forms of relief work, economic development, and enterprise or business development. Explain the differences and give examples of each. What is the goal or goals of each? How, if at all, does each of these contribute to the goal of reaching the marketplace for Christ internationally? Is enterprise development a legitimate part (camp) of the Marketplace Mission Movement? Explain.

3. How does the BAM model relate to all the other models?

4. Are the author's warnings about attacks from Satan realistic or obsolete thinking? Why? Is spiritual warfare real or an anachronistic view from pre-enlightenment days? Is Satan real or merely symbolic or mythical? What is your scriptural basis for these views?

5. BAM engagement: The author names four camps in the Marketplace Mission Movement: tentmaking, marketplace ministries, enterprise development and BAM. What are their differences? Which one, if any, do you see yourself being most actively involved in? Why?

6

BAM's Basic Beliefs

"Beliefs and values are the footings on which we build answers
to the questions 'Who matters?' and 'What matters?' The promises
we make as leaders must resonate with our beliefs and values."
MAX DEPREE

"Values are not a 'management tool.' . . . Nor are they bits of ethereal
matter. . . . [They are] beliefs, aims, and assumptions that undergird the
enterprise and guide its management in developing strategies, structures,
processes, and policies. They constitute an organizational 'infrastructure' that
gives a company its distinctive character and ethos—its moral personality."
LYNN SHARP PAINE

"I think you missed a most important point. . . . We are trying to
live these values because they are right, not because they work."
DENNIS W. BAKKE

WE HAVE INVESTIGATED THE Marketplace Mission Movement and BAM's place within it from two complimentary vantage points: (1) seeing the movement in each of its three different components—mission to, within and through the marketplace; and (2) seeing the movement functionally in each of its four camps—tentmaking, marketplace ministries, enterprise development and BAM. It is now time to ask two important questions, *Why* do these camps (and the movement) exist? and *Why* would someone want to be a BAMer?

The answer to these questions, paradoxically, is both profoundly simple and profoundly complex. It is as simple as a child's unconditional love; it is as complex as the universe, infinity and God. And it is only found by examining the movement's basic beliefs (this chapter), the biblical challenges they present and the biblical foundations that undergird them (chap. 7). After that, we will focus the remainder of the book specifically on BAM, to see *how* to do it and to count the potential personal and family costs of engaging in it.

But unless we understand *why* we do BAM, *how* we do it is irrelevant.

Understanding this point is critical to every mission enterprise, but perhaps more so to BAM, which is admittedly on the margins of current mainstream mission practice and missiology. If it is to attain greater visibility and acceptance within the ecclesiastical church and the Christian academy, not to mention the laity in business, it must be biblically sound. If it is not, it has no rightful place in the mission field and should not expect God's continued blessings.

BASIC BELIEFS

We may rightly ask, What are the beliefs of the Marketplace Mission Movement and BAM? This is not an easy question to answer, since there is no formal belief structure and definitely no creed or doctrine to which business Christians are asked to subscribe—or to which they probably would subscribe. There are, however, certain common, general biblical beliefs among most Christians who are being intentional about faith-work integration and about using business as a vehicle for missions. These commonalities are not denominational or doctrinaire, with possibly one exception: the priesthood of all believers, which will be addressed later.

Fundamental truths. First, the most basic, fundamental truths for most BAM practitioners include the following:

- BAMers are trinitarian followers of Jesus Christ who believe that the Bible is God's holy Word, that the gospel is to be lived 24/7 in every aspect of life, including business, and that businesses are to be managed by biblical principles consistent with the gospel.

- BAMers firmly believe that: work was ordained by God before the Fall; work after the Fall can and should be redemptive for his followers; there is intrinsic good and value in work; work can (and should) be a form and vehicle of ministry/mission; and through our vocations we are fellow workers with God, being allowed by him to help humanity be reconciled to him and to help him redeem the world.

- BAMers find that God gave his followers four distinctive commandments:

1. The *cultural* or the *stewardship mandate* (Gen 1:28-30; 2:5, 15, 19-20; see also Eph 2:10). In the beginning, before the Fall, God made humans to be fruitful and multiply; to fill, subdue, rule over, and steward the earth and its resources; and to work and care for all God's creation. To this end the Lord gave away his power and authorized Adam to name the animals. In so doing God immediately made his power-sharing principle a cosmic reality by giving humans decision-making authority over all of creation.

2. The *great commandments* (Mt 22:37-40). Jesus commanded us to love God with all of our heart, soul, and mind and to love our neighbors as ourselves. BAM practitioners understand that God mandated, allowed and privileged us to love our neighbors through our work by providing the products, services, encouragement and support they need to live life, even abundant life.

3. The *holistic commitment* (Mt 25:31-46). In these verses Jesus tells us unequivocally that God will separate the sheep (his righteous) from the goats (the unfaithful), sending the goats to "eternal punishment" and the sheep to "eternal life" (Mt 25:46). One of the primary tests God will use to determine the difference between the sheep and the goats is how well they cared for their neighbors in distress and thereby loved them—holistically. In that sense, it is a further explanation of the extent to which the Lord wants us to love our neighbors (the second great commandment).

   By way of illustration, Jesus cites such actions as feeding the hungry (or not), giving drink to the thirsty (or not), providing shelter to the stranger (or not), giving clothes to the naked (or not), and visiting the sick and imprisoned (or not). Jesus says to the sheep, "Whatever you did for one of the least of these brothers of mine, you did for me," but also warns the goats, "whatever you did not do for one of the least of these, you did not do for me."

   This is a vivid illustration of two major points: God calls us to love people *holistically* in their real needs and God holds us *personally accountable* for our actions wherever we are and whatever our circumstances. BAMers understand this and by doing BAM are committing themselves to obey our Lord's call.

4. The *Great Commission* (Mt 28:18-20; Acts 1:8; Lk 24:47-48; Jn 15:26-27; see also what has been called the Old Testament Great Commission, Is 49:6): Here Jesus charged each of his followers to "go and make disciples of all nations," baptizing, teaching and loving them where they are, as they are, as children of God. As we have seen, BAM is about going, long-term and incarnationally, to minister holistically to hurting people in the name and love of Jesus, bringing them the gospel by word and deed, witnessing for and showing them Jesus and his heart in real, tangible, meaningful ways and discipling them in the faith.

- BAMers affirm the doctrine of the priesthood of all believers, which will be discussed in chapter seven.

- BAMers reject the *secular-sacred divide*, which says that work and vocation in the secular sphere are somehow less worthy and esteemed by God than work in the ecclesiastical sphere.

- BAMers reject the so-called *holy hierarchy*, a corollary to the secular-sacred divide, which says there is a hierarchy of work in terms of holiness, that is, that certain work to which believers have been called is more worthy in God's eyes than other work.

- BAMers reject what I call the *serf complex*, which occurs when the clergy view the members of the business community as serfs, only to be used or co-opted (some would say manipulated) by the church in ways that tend to benefit the church alone. The church all too often only wants the capitalist's money and help with church business and some committee positions, but it rejects this vocation as a God-ordained way of earning that money. In so doing, the church makes less than the highest and best use of the business Christians' gifts, skills and calling—and shows little concern for meeting their real spiritual needs.

- BAMers emphatically embrace the belief that, contrary to popular notion and church tradition, you can be both a good, successful businessperson *and* an obedient follower of Jesus Christ.

- BAMers affirm that we are all to be (and can be) salt and light to the entire world through our work.

- BAMers affirm that the Bible is God's holy Word and, as such, is the best business and mission guidebook for BAMers and their families.

Corollary principles. There are an infinite number of business truths that flow directly from BAMers' reliance on Scripture. As Eldred says, "Biblical principles are the basis for successful capitalism."[1] Larry Burkett agrees, but warns:

> God's principles of business are not offered "cafeteria style." In other words, you can't simply pick and choose those you like and ignore those you don't. God's Word sets up a whole structure by which a business is to operate: a foundation. You can build a business (or a house) without a solid foundation. But when the wind blows and the waves come, it will collapse. God's Word is the Rock upon which a business must be built.
>
> Do the biblical principles of business work? Without question they do—over the long run. If you're looking just for quick profit, don't choose God's way; but, if you desire long-term growth and stability, God's way is the only way.[2]

Some of the more prominently mentioned principles within marketplace mission circles are

- *Business ownership.* God owns everything, including the business the BAMer starts or works for (e.g., Job 41:11; Ps 24:1; 50:10, 12; Is 66:2).[3]

- *Business practices.* All business practices should reflect Christ and his gospel. That includes such basic character traits as total honesty (Prov 3:32; 4:24), integrity (Lk 16:10), morality, keeping your word and your vows (Mt 5:33-37), grace, forgiveness, fairness, humility and dignity.[4]

- *Accountability.* Each business owner, CEO, manager and employee must be

---

[1]Ken Eldred, *God Is at Work: Transforming People and Nations through Business* (Ventura, Calif.: Regal Books, 2005), p. 74. An excellent book that specifically speaks to these principles is Henry Blackaby and Richard Blackaby, *God in the Marketplace* (Nashville: B & H Publishing, 2008), which looks at a wide variety of biblical issues through forty-five questions asked by Fortune 500 executives and arranged in six categories: the businessperson's personal life, business life, devotional life, family life, church and community life, and kingdom life.

[2]Larry Burkett, *Business by the Book: The Complete Guide of Biblical Principles for the Workplace* (Nashville: Thomas Nelson, 1998), pp. 10-22.

[3]See Wayne Grudem, *Business for the Glory of God: The Bible's Teaching on the Moral Goodness of Business* (Wheaton, Ill.: Crossway, 2003), pp. 19-24. The opening chapter is on "ownership" of business as seen from Scripture.

[4]Ibid., pp. 10, 19; Eldred, *God Is at Work*, pp. 88-89.

held to a high standard of accountability, with "a system of checks and balances" to keep everyone from "eventually drifting off course."[5]

- *Productivity.* God has called each of us to be productive both personally and within our businesses, but always within his ethic, values and precepts (e.g., Gen 1:28). Grudem speaks to the complex nature of this issue:

> God did not have to create us with a need for material things or a need for the services of other people (think of the angels, who apparently do not have such needs), but in his wisdom he chose to do so. It may be that God created us with such needs because he knew that *in the process of productive work* we would have many opportunities to glorify him. When we work to produce (for example) pairs of shoes from the earth's resources, God sees us imitating his attributes of wisdom, knowledge, skill, strength, creativity, appreciation of beauty, sovereignty, planning for the future, and the use of language to communicate. In addition, when we produce pairs of shoes to be used by others, we demonstrate love for others, wisdom in understanding their needs, and interdependence and interpersonal cooperation (which are reflections of God's Trinitarian existence).[6]

- *Quality products.* Each business must provide quality products and services at a fair price that provide value to both the customer and the community.[7]

- *Creditors.* Christians in business are to honor their creditors, suppliers and investors, and to pay their just debts in a timely manner (e.g., Prov 3:27-28).[8]

- *Employees.* Each business creates jobs and helps people live better, but the business has both a responsibility and an opportunity to witness by deed to its employees. This requires a concerted effort to treat all employees fairly, whether it is through pay, benefits, working conditions, empowerment, attitudes or relationships, and to honor all of them as children of God by showing no favoritism, partiality, bias, abuse or neglect (e.g., Jas 2:9).[9]

---

[5]Burkett, *Business by the Book*, p. 11.
[6]Grudem, *Business for the Glory of God*, p. 27, and more generally chap. 2 on productivity, pp. 25-29.
[7]Ibid., p. 16.
[8]Ibid., p. 17.
[9]Ibid., pp. 19-21.

- *Customers.* The people a business serves are its lifeblood. Without customers who are willing to pay the asking price for a product or service, there is no viable, sustainable business. More than that, for the Christian-led business the way the customer is treated is a witness as to the values and integrity of our Lord. Fairness, courtesy, cheerful service, going the extra mile, making good on sales promises, warranties and service expectations, valuing the person of the customer (not just his value to the company) even in collection or debt-recovery situations, and meeting real needs are all part of Christian service through business (e.g., Phil 2:3).[10]

- *Money and profits.* Scripture does not say that money is the root of all evil. Paul, a businessman himself, clearly recognized that money is essential to the straightforward, uncomplicated exchange of goods, services, labor and resources, but warned that it is "the love of money," not the money itself, that "is a root of all kinds of evil" (1 Tim 6:10). Just as many godly people in the church misunderstand this today—and have for decades—they have also misunderstood the role, necessity and potential godliness of that major form of money called profits. Profits are the lifeblood of any business and its sustainability. If a business is to continue to deliver useful, needed services and products to people, and thereby show God-commanded love for them, it must stay in business. That requires profits. Money and profits, however, also raise universally recognized, special temptations. As Richard J. Foster warns, "According to Jesus and all the writers of the New Testament, behind money are very real spiritual powers that energize it and give it a life of its own. Hence, money is an active agent; it is a law unto itself; and it is capable of inspiring devotion" that can "win our hearts" and lead us away from God and his paths.[11] "And in point of fact, money has many of the characteristics of deity. It gives us security, can induce guilt, gives us freedom, gives us power and seems to be omnipresent. Most sinister of all, however, is its bid for omnipotence."[12]

- *Balance.* Balancing the business with other obligations to family, church, community and God is also part of the biblical approach to business. Bur-

---

[10]Ibid., p. 21.
[11]Richard J. Foster, *Money, Sex and Power: The Challenge of the Disciplined Life* (San Francisco: Harper & Row, 1985), p. 26.
[12]Ibid., p. 28.

kett sees the danger of losing balance because of what he calls "business bondage," which is characterized by arrogance (the belief that "I am a self-made person!"), overwork, excessive use of credit, bad time-management, disorganization, laziness and focus on money and getting rich quickly (e.g., Prov 28:20).[13]

- *Planning.* One of the key ways to avoid the "core problem of business bondage is to do realistic planning both in business and in personal life."[14] Planning is not an option to a business, it is essential to its survival and to its intentionality of witness for the Lord.

- *Morality.* In biblical, ethical business practices, the question is not legal or illegal, but right or wrong. Businesses, to be Christian witnesses, must be engaged in products and services that are neither immoral nor amoral.

  > *Immoral* business is that which operates contrary to the established laws of God and the nation. Illegal drug trafficking, organized crime and child pornography fit this category of business activity. Fraud, violence, bribes and extortion are the byproducts of immorality. . . . *Amorality* is an attitude often found in modern Western business. Its mantra may be summed up as follows: maximize profits. While staying within the law, amoral business remains unconcerned with moral principles. The question is not "right or wrong?" but "legal or illegal?"[15]

- *Evil powers.* One of the key realities of Scripture is the demonic powers that will confront and challenge the Christian in the marketplace. This is a very real issue, requiring considerable, serious scriptural maturity to address successfully.[16]

■ ■ ■

This is only a sampling of the Scriptures available to help guide a Christian businessperson. Some business practices and decisions can be addressed in a

---

[13]Burkett, *Business by the Book*, pp. 23-39.
[14]Ibid., p. 39.
[15]Eldred, *God Is at Work*, p. 80.
[16]R. Paul Stevens addresses this issue under the heading of "Resistance—Grappling with the Powers" in his iconic book *The Other Six Days* (Vancouver, B.C.: Regent College Publishing, 1999). Stevens takes his cue from Scripture and, among other books, Walter Wink's *Naming the Powers* (Philadelphia: Fortress, 1984), which is a powerful exposition of the demonic, especially in institutions, including businesses.

black and white scriptural litmus-test way, but those instances are few and far between. More often the issues are subtle, complex and require mature scriptural discernment. In such situations we must often seek guidance through a case-by-case examination of God's Word and advice from godly counsel.

There is, however, an urgent need to reach the church, pastors in the pulpit, seminary students and businesspeople alike to evoke a dialogue about these basic beliefs and corollary principles. This is especially so in three areas where most marketplace mission practitioners firmly believe the church is perpetuating misguided and unbiblical perceptions: the secular-sacred divide, the holy hierarchy and the serf complex.[17]

The secular-sacred divide. The secular-sacred divide essentially says that wholly committed Christians should enter full-time ministry by going to seminary and becoming pastors or missionaries. All other vocations are secondary to this clerical calling. This view divides the working world into two camps: the secular business community and the sacred ecclesiastical/missionary community. This clergy-laity bifurcation is the result of centuries of church history and, in Robert Munger's words, has been called the "greatest single bottleneck to the renewal and outreach of the church."[18] Further, it is not biblical and flies in the face of the doctrine of the priesthood of all believers. Its continued propagation by the church does great harm to the entire body of Christ and is a direct challenge to the movement and BAM.[19] Stevens speaks of this secular-sacred divide as "the tragic separation of the Great Commission (Mt 28:18-20) from the Cultural Commission (Gen 1:26-28) . . . [that] has led Christians to disagree about which type of work is most sacred."[20] Dallas Willard concurs and speaks plainly about this travesty:

There truly is no division between sacred and secular except what we

---

[17]These three perceptions deserve greater discussion, but that effort is far beyond the scope of this book. They are listed here because they are highly motivational to the movement and need to be the subject of extensive intrafaith and interfaith dialogue.

[18]Greg Ogden, *Unfinished Business: Returning the Ministry to the People of God* (Grand Rapids: Zondervan, 2003), p. 96.

[19]This matter has received a great deal of attention from within the movement. See, for example, Lesslie Newbigin, *The Gospel in a Pluralistic Society* (Grand Rapids; Eerdmans, 1989); Os Hillman, *Faith and Work* (Alpharetta, Ga.: Aslan, 2000), pp. 7-15; John D. Beckett, *Loving Monday* (Downers Grove, Ill.: InterVarsity Press, 1998), pp. 70-75; and Steve Rundle and Tom Steffen, *Great Commission Companies* (Downers Grove, Ill.: InterVarsity Press, 2003), p. 12.

[20]R. Paul Stevens, *Doing God's Business* (Grand Rapids: Eerdmans, 2006), p. 82.

have created. And that is why the division of the legitimate roles and functions of human life into the sacred and secular does incalculable damage to our individual lives and the cause of Christ. Holy people must stop going into "church work" as their natural course of action and take up holy orders in farming, industry, law, education, banking, and journalism with the same zeal previously given to evangelism or to pastoral and missionary work.[21]

The holy hierarchy. Another misconception is the *holy hierarchy* in which certain vocations (callings) are ranked in order of holiness and righteousness, with overseas missionaries and clergy at the top of the ladder and wealthy Christians and business leaders at the bottom. This is exposed in two classic works in the BAM literature: Stevens's *The Other Six Days* and Steve Rundle and Tom Steffen's *Great Commission Companies*.[22] Mark Greene, a former advertising executive, calls this an "unholy hierarchy" and says with stinging satire:

This overall marginalization of work is further reflected in a belief within the church which goes something like this: All Christians are born equal, but "full-time" Christians are more equal than others.

In turn, there is an unspoken hierarchy that goes something like this:

Pastor
Overseas missionary
Full-time Christian worker
Tent-maker (as long as it is abroad)
Elder
Deacon
Poor Christian
Christian
Rich Christian
Former advertising executives[23]

The serf complex. Another common attitude among pastors is what I call the serf complex: like serfs, the relationship between the members of the busi-

---

[21]Dallas Willard, *The Spirit of the Disciplines* (San Francisco: HarperCollins, 1990), p. 214.
[22]Stevens, *The Other Six Days*, pp. 109, 174-176; Rundle and Steffen, *Great Commission Companies*, p. 12.
[23]Mark Greene, *Thank God It's Monday* (Bletchley, U.K.: Scripture Union, 2001), p 18.

ness community and the Church is a one-way street in which the business-people exist solely to serve the church (rather than the Lord), and the business community is useful to the church for money, building campaigns, committee assignments and the business of the church but for little else. Nash and McLennan note that there seems to be little or no understanding by pastors on (1) how (whether and why) to minister to those in the business community in real, tangible ways that have meaning on Monday morning, and (2) how to mobilize this potential ministry and missionary force within the pews to help achieve the goals of the local church and the kingdom.[24] Simon Phipps, a canon of the Church of England, noted these tendencies over forty years ago:

> The laity, for instance are welcomed in the performance of all sorts of ecclesiastical chores, from sitting in church Assembly to counting the collection. But they tend not to be taken seriously, either by the clergy or by themselves, as secular men and women in secular employ, with professional commitments and professional knowledge and skills, strategically placed where God is speaking, and where He is calling for insight and action. The "church work" they do is often necessary and valuable, and not without its element of sacrifice in time and energy. But the implication is that *that is their Christian work,* while the rest of the time, as an accountant or a parent or a shop steward or an artist or a national assistance board officer is something else.[25]

Affirming Phipps and my own personal experience, Sudyk laments this failure of the business community and the church to engage each other in the context of the businessperson's gifts, skills and experience as well as in mission. To Sudyk this is largely because the church has yet to catch the vision of how businesspeople can be utilized in mission. Instead, the church directs these businesspeople to such ecclesiastical tasks as full-time church business managers or youth ministers. Saying that this trend "makes no sense," Sudyk eloquently indicts the current system and calls for a revisioning of the cleric-laity relationship. In so doing he highlights one major reason for their differences: their vastly different worldviews and workplace cultures.

---

[24]Laura Nash and Scotty McLennan, *Church on Sunday, Work on Monday* (San Francisco: Jossey-Bass, 2001).

[25]Simon Phipps, *God on Monday* (London: Hodder & Stoughton, 1966), p. 49 (emphasis added).

It makes no sense to move a business professional away from his/her talents and calling just so the work can be labeled "spiritual." . . .

A business person relocated from the rigor and risk of a business into the culture of the typical church suffers a tremendous shock [and vice versa]. Gone is the discipline of the marketplace, which keeps business people constantly accountable for their decisions. Gone is aggressive pursuit of easily measured goals. Gone also is the healthy insistence that employees consistently contribute some tangible value to the organization. Often, "feelings" and "spiritual revelations" seem to replace analysis and strategy as the guideposts for decisions. Methods of successful businesspeople are suddenly considered harsh, insensitive or, at a minimum, out of place. A new vocabulary must be mastered, different expectations adopted and varying results tolerated.[26]

These shortcomings are not necessarily the pastors' fault. Understanding how to minister to the business community, grasping how to mobilize the entrepreneurial and organizational marketplace power within their own pews, and seeing business as a vehicle for mission are generally not part of their paradigm. In most cases it is also not part of their pastoral seminary training, personal experience, calling or gifts. If it were, they would probably have gone into business. Nonetheless, where it exists, it is a major flaw in the model of church that is a lose-lose-lose situation for the clergy, the laity and the kingdom of God.

BEYOND TENTMAKING: A BIBLICAL PERSPECTIVE

Marketplace mission has gone far beyond tentmaking in modern and postmodern times. God has spawned a Marketplace Mission Movement that is sweeping the globe and causing many Christians to see that "The business world is the most exciting 'mission field' that exists today."[27] In that regard, there seem to be an endless assortment of Scriptures that today's marketplace mission activists are claiming in support of their ministries and their BAM callings.

---

[26]Tom Sudyk, "Strategic Considerations in Business as Mission," in *On Kingdom Business: Transforming Missions through Entrepreneurial Strategies*, ed. Tetsunao Yamamori and Kenneth A. Eldred (Wheaton, Ill.: Crossway, 2003), p. 153.

[27]Jones, *Jesus Inc.*, p. xxv.

The number of books on the subject has grown dramatically. Early pioneering books like Larry Burkett's *Business by the Book* (1990) paved the way and were followed by a host of others proclaiming, "The Bible is still the best business book!"[28]

In plain fact, the workplace itself is so pervasive in human life and Scripture—addressing virtually every area of human existence on earth and beyond—that any attempt to cite chapter and verse would be woefully inadequate. The applicable Scripture depends on the context, the spiritual maturity of the person seeking guidance, the nature of the problem to be addressed and an endless string of other variables.[29]

Having said that, it may be helpful to list some of the more basic Bible verses that speak about a Christian's role in the marketplace, especially in the BAM arena. Each one speaks loudly and eloquently to the theme of mission and ministry in and through the marketplace, but collectively they are deeply moving and instructive. These Scriptures unequivocally impress on all business believers that they are to honor Jesus Christ with their work, to encourage humankind—especially their brothers and sisters in the faith—to do likewise, and to use the marketplace as a ministry or mission platform:

> You also, like living stones, are being built into a spiritual house to be a holy priesthood, offering spiritual sacrifices acceptable to God through Jesus Christ. . . . But you are a chosen people, a royal priesthood, a holy nation, a people belonging to God, that you may declare the praises of him who called you out of darkness into his wonderful light. (1 Pet 2:5, 9)

> You are the salt of the earth. . . you are the light of the world. A city on a hill cannot be hidden. Neither do people light a lamp and put it under a bowl. Instead they put it on its stand, and it gives light to everyone in the house. In the same way, let your light shine before men, that they may

---

[28]Steve Marr, *Business Proverbs* (Grand Rapids: Baker, 2001), p. 3.

[29]Consider, for instance, the Christian CEO who opens a business on Monday morning only to discover that he or she has major cash flow problems, is overdrawn at the bank and has a payroll to meet. The CEO further learns of an argument between the plant superintendent and the human resource director, of a regulatory audit later in the week, of defects in the latest product shipment which has caused the company to lose a major account, and of his or her most trusted employees being suspected of embezzlement. How, the CEO asks, thinking of the sermon heard the previous day, does he or she honor Christ in each of these situations? Which Bible verses speak most directly and poignantly to this situation? How and with whom does he or she interpret them?

see your good deeds and praise your Father in heaven. (Mt 5:13-16)

Therefore, I urge you, brothers, in view of God's mercy, to offer your bodies as living sacrifices, holy and pleasing to God—this is your spiritual act of worship. (Rom 12:1)

Whatever you do, work at it with all your heart, as working for the Lord, not for men. . . . It is the Lord Christ you are serving. (Col 3:23-24; see also 1 Cor 9:23; 10:31; 16:14; 1 Pet 4:11)

Whatever your hand finds to do, do it with all your might. (Eccles 9:10)

Whoever wants to become great among you must be your servant, and whoever wants to be first must be your slave—just as the Son of Man did not come to be served, but to serve, and to give his life as a ransom for many. (Mt 20:26-28)

Each person's list will differ, depending on how God speaks to him or her. Regardless of the circumstances, however, humanity has always dealt in and through various sorts of marketplaces as part of its survival strategy. Jesus' coming did not change that. Quite the contrary, he embraced the marketplace personally and made it a vivid context for his parables and gospel message. Down through the ages, from the apostles and early disciples to today's tentmakers, BAMers and business managers, Christians have recognized the vital relationship between Scripture, the marketplace and mission. This relationship is foundational, it is life-giving, it is energizing, and it brings purpose, meaning and joy to our daily lives.

DISCUSSION QUESTIONS

1. The author speaks of the fundamental truths (pp. 154-57) and corollary principles (pp. 157-60) of BAM. Which of these resonate with you, and why? Are there any that you do not agree with? What others should be included? Why?

2. What does Larry Burkett mean when he says that we cannot take the biblical principles about business "cafeteria style"? Do you agree? Why or why not?

3. The text says that money has spiritual powers that "inspire devotion," that

it has "many characteristics of deity" and that it drives peoples' decision and lives (p. 159). Do you agree? Why? Give personal or business examples and discuss.

4. BAM engagement: The author speaks against a supposed "secular-sacred divide," a "holy hierarchy" and a "serf complex." Define each and explain their differences. In your experience, are these three conditions real? Explain, giving personal examples if possible. What should the church do about them? What, if anything, can you personally do in your church to assist the pastor and congregation to overcome these harmful thought patterns?

7

BAM's Biblical Roots

"Jesus replied, 'You are in error because you do not
know the Scriptures or the power of God.'"
MATTHEW 22:29

"From infancy you have known the holy Scriptures, which are
able to make you wise for salvation through faith in Christ Jesus.
All Scripture is God-breathed and is useful . . . so that the man
of God may be thoroughly equipped for every good work."
2 TIMOTHY 3:15-17

"Do not merely listen to the word, and so deceive yourselves.
Do what it says. . . . [T]he man who looks intently into
the perfect law that gives freedom, and continues to
do this, . . . he will be blessed in what he does."
JAMES 1:22, 25

TO THIS POINT WE HAVE DISCUSSED the personal beliefs of many in the Marketplace Mission Movement, including the biblical passages that speak loudly to various individual participants. There is, however, another more objective view that must be taken: Scripture itself.

BIBLICAL FOUNDATIONS

Are marketplace mission and BAM biblically sanctioned and spiritually anointed by God? This subject can be approached in a wide variety of ways—and has been in several books already on the market. Accordingly, a detailed exegesis of Scripture on marketplace mission and BAM is not called for and is also beyond the purpose of this book. Here I only want to touch briefly on some key defining biblical points about the movement in general and BAM in particular. When Scripture is read with "marketplace eyes" (i.e., examining the Bible to see its use of marketplace examples, language and applicable principles), support for the proposition that Christ wants and needs to be in the marketplace is overwhelming.

To support this statement, let's briefly examine Jesus in the marketplace, biblical foundations of Paul's tentmaking practice, Old and New Testament examples of marketplace mission/ministry, and a suggestive review of New Testament texts that call all believers in the marketplace to be a holy priesthood, living stones, and salt and light. Finally, we will briefly review the foundational doctrine of the priesthood of all believers.

Jesus in the marketplace. The Bible is replete with stories of Jesus' ministry to, within and through the marketplace. He was in the marketplace continually, both literally and metaphorically. He was a businessman himself, he worked in the marketplace, called his disciples from the marketplace and during his ministry actively and repeatedly engaged the marketplace: he taught there, set many of his parables there and abhorred its desecration of God's holy temple through crass commercialization and the unabashed commoditization of God. Ed Silvoso notes:

> Traditionally we picture Jesus more as a monk than as a manager. However, He was a businessman much longer than He was a preacher. He was also born in the marketplace—in a stable at an inn—and later identified with the marketplace—when He became a carpenter. His teachings dealt extensively with the marketplace. . . . Because of the roles He embodied—ruler, teacher and businessman—He belongs in the marketplace even more than in a monastery.[1]

In support of this position Silvoso recounts the miracles that Jesus performed in the marketplace, calling many of them "business wonders," and provides an interesting list of Jesus' parables, showing that Jesus "was thoroughly familiar with the marketplace and its operations." Set in today's language, Silvoso cites these examples:

---

[1]Ed Silvoso, *Anointed for Business* (Ventura, Calif.: Regal, 2002), pp. 9, 37.

- construction (Mt 7:24-27)

- winemaking (Lk 5:37-38)

- farming (Mk 4:2-20)

- treasure hunting (Mt 13:44)

- ranching (Mt 18:12-14)

- management and labor (Mt 20:1-16)

- family-owned business (Mt 21:28-31)

- hostile takeovers (Lk 20:9-19)

- return on investments (Mt 25:14-30)

- futures markets (Lk 12:16-21)

- crop yield (Mk 13:27-32)

- management criteria (Lk 12:35-48)

- the need for observation and research (Lk 14:24-35)

- misuse of money; bankruptcy (Lk 15:11-16)

- the advantage of leverage (Lk 16:1-13)

- venture capital in high-risk situations (Lk 19:11-27)[2]

Others have recognized Jesus' involvement with the marketplace and the applicability of his management style to today's marketplace. For example, consider these titles: *Jesus CEO* and *Jesus Inc.* by Laura Beth Jones and *The Management Methods of Jesus* by Bob Briner, who says that Jesus was the "all-time greatest management entrepreneur." He adds, somewhat whimsically:

> Just look at what Jesus accomplished. By any measurement standard, the empirical evidence bears witness that the organization founded by Jesus is the most successful of all time. Longevity? Two thousand years and counting. Wealth? Beyond calculation. Numbers? Beyond counting. Loyalty of adherents? Many gave their lives for it. Distribution? World-wide, in every country. Diversification? Successfully integrated into all kinds of enterprises. Ergo, Jesus Christ reigns supreme as the greatest manager the world has ever known. . . . Don't get me wrong. None of this

---

²Ibid., p. 41.

is to say that Jesus is some twentieth-century management guru—replete with formulas, slogans, and seminars for revolutionizing business life. For one thing, he is so much more than that. . . . [His] life and teaching . . . [are] packed full of wisdom highly relevant to my world and yours—the world of business.[3]

This is a mere sampling of the relationship people have seen between business and Jesus. Regardless of marketing labels, it is clear from Scripture that Jesus recognized that the marketplace is where people actively engage life, earn their livings, conduct their daily lives, feed their families and receive the bread and wine that graces their tables. He understood that the marketplace, in one form or another, is a thriving part of every human community and transcends all cultures, national borders and ethnic differences. Everyone is affected, directly or indirectly, by the marketplace and its commerce, and all humans encounter the marketplace in their daily lives, either as a participant or as a consumer. Jesus knew this. In order to identify with the people, to speak to their needs and their pain, to save them as they were and where they were, he met them there, in the marketplace.

As a businessman—a carpenter by trade—Jesus was intimately familiar with the necessities of running a business and making a living. Granted, when he commenced his ministry Jesus put his trowel aside for a towel and replaced his saw with Scripture. The hand-carved basin and a wooden cross became the new tools of his trade. Through them he worked his wonders and brought life and love to a needy people. In so doing, when he calls to each of us *in* the marketplace, he does not necessarily call us *out* of the marketplace, that is, to leave our workplaces. Quite the opposite, he calls us to be salt and light in the very place that God planted us and to conduct ourselves in that setting so as to cause people to "see your good deeds and praise your Father in heaven" (Mt 5:16).

Furthermore, Jesus was a practical man. He recognized that people live in the midst of the marketplace and must meet their needs through the structures of that world. His preaching was equally pragmatic. His gospel gave people not only hope for living but the practical, useful tools to meet the daily challenges of life. He called them to a new way, to a higher standard, to be all

---

[3]Bob Briner, *The Management Methods of Jesus* (Nashville: Thomas Nelson, 1996), pp. xi-xii.

that God intended them to be. Further, he laid out practical guidelines for doing that, even though they were often counterintuitive to the traditional ways of the world. He challenged people to live by his new way and thereby walk the high road.

Jesus' challenge was met with skepticism, ridicule, mockery, violence and hatred. However, in the two thousand years since, humanity has continued to be challenged, asking, "Can we live in the marketplace and still be an obedient follower of Jesus?"

It was in this context that Charles Sheldon in 1897 first wrote *In His Steps*, asking whether every decision, personal and business, large and small, could be based on a single standard: What would Jesus do? The resulting acronym, WWJD, continues to be seen to this day in all parts of the world, frequently as a bracelet or as a placard in offices. It effectively keeps Jesus' challenge before us and reminds us that *if the good news Jesus brought is truly from God, truly relevant to the way humans live and genuinely transcultural, then it must work in the marketplace. If it does not work there, it does not work at all and is virtually useless to humans.*

Paul in the marketplace. The apostle Paul understood the vital importance of the marketplace to himself, to the gospel and to his mission. In fact, Paul's tentmaking was the first methodology of Christian mission, the first tangible nexus both between mission and the marketplace and the emerging church and the marketplace. "The central affirmation and vision of . . . 'tentmaking' . . . [is that it] reflects a biblically sound, historically affirmed, and contextually powerful model of witness and ministry in world mission."[4]

This observation is critical to the church's understanding of the biblical basis of tentmaking (and by analogy, BAM), for *tentmaking is not a theological doctrine.* Rather, it is an evangelistic and missiological (mission) methodology, *a means of carrying the gospel to the world.* As such, its biblical basis is found in the history of the Bible and the story of God's people. No Bible passage gives a command to be a tentmaker. No clear theological proof-text exists. Scriptural examples illustrate the way tentmaking was done two thousand years ago and, through the Holy Spirit, help us discern what works in this day and this time.

---

[4]Lynn Buzzard, "Tentmaking: A Biblical and Contextual Apologia," in *Kingdom Professional Resource Guide*, 3rd ed. (Chicago: Intent, 1999), p. 2.

Was tentmaking used to carry God's banner? Was the use of this method blessed of God? Is this methodology applicable in today's globalized, high-tech world?

Christy Wilson unhesitatingly answers these questions in the affirmative, saying tentmaking has the "imprimatur of Scripture,"[5] that is, Scripture approves and sanctions this method of delivering the gospel, both then and now. In support of this, both Wilson and Ruth Siemens give a comprehensive review of the biblical and historical support for tentmaking.[6] In particular, Siemens leaves no doubt that propagating the gospel through business is not only an effective mission method but because of the ever-present nature of the marketplace, it is part of the mission message itself.

A missionary herself to Peru, Brazil, Portugal and Spain, and a prolific biblical scholar, Siemens examines a considerable body of Scripture that she believes supports tentmaking as a biblically sanctioned mission method. For example, Paul's relationship to tentmaking, and Priscilla and Aquila and their tentmaking activities (Acts 18); Paul's testimony that he and his team supported themselves by their own hands (Acts 20:33-35); Paul's statements about his team's poor, homeless condition and his protestations, "We work hard with our own hands" (1 Cor 4:12); Paul's vigorous defense of his manual labor (1 Cor 9); Paul's recollections of the incidents in Corinth during the first mission journey and his protestations of regret that he caused that church any pain (2 Cor 1:8–2:13); Paul's boast, "Unlike so many, we do not peddle the word of God for profit. On the contrary, in Christ we speak before God with sincerity, like men sent from God" (2 Cor 2:17); Paul's insistence that no one can dispute the fact that he preaches the gospel free of charge (2 Cor 11–12, esp. 11:7-9; 12:14-18); Paul's appreciation for the donor support he received from the church at Philippi (Phil 4:10, 14-18); and Paul's reminders of his labor and hardship, working day and night not to be a burden to them but to proclaim the gospel (1 Thess 2:9; 2 Thess 3:7-12).[7]

---

[5]J. Christy Wilson, Jr., *Today's Tentmaker* (Wheaton, Ill.: Tyndale House, 1979), p. 19.

[6]Ruth Siemens, the founder of Global Opportunities (GO), an influential tentmaking support organization, addressed this issue several times, but particularly in Ruth Siemens, "GO Paper A-1: Why Did Paul Make Tents? A Biblical Basis for Tentmaking," in *Global Entrepreneurship and Tentmaking*, ed. Steve Rundle (La Mirada, Calif.: Biola University, 1998); and Wilson, *Today's Tentmaker*, pp. 19-25.

[7]Siemens, "Why Did Paul Make Tents?"

Old Testament figures in the marketplace. The principles of BAM "ante-date Paul by eighteen centuries."[8] Hundreds of years before Paul, men and women carried the messages of God to the corners of the known world, supporting themselves as they went and using their businesses or trade as a vehicle for mission. Many others served God where he placed them, earning their living through their professional gifts and skills, plying their trade to God's benefit and glory in their hometowns and villages. Some notable examples include:

- *Adam.* A farmer both inside and outside of the Garden of Eden, fathered the human race as God's creation.

- *Abel.* A shepherd, called by God to give a righteous offering that split God's family.

- *Abraham.* Called by God from Ur of Chaldeans to move his family and his business to a land that God would show him.

- *Isaac* and *Jacob.* Both sheep ranchers who became the patriarchs of God's chosen people, the nation of Israel.

- *Joseph.* Sold into slavery in Egypt and rose to serve God through his extraordinary administrative skills as prime minister over all of Egypt.

- *Moses.* A Hebrew slave, then a prince of Egypt and then a shepherd who became the political leader of Israel, leading God's people out of Egyptian bondage and into the Holy Land.

- *Daniel.* Carried into slavery in Babylon and rose in rank and power to serve God through his own extraordinary administrative skills as prime minister of Babylon and later of Medo-Persia.

- *Amos.* An "agri-businessman . . . [who] was a tree surgeon and a specialist in a certain kind of long-haired sheep, who was in Israel on a marketing trip" and served God as a prophet.

- *Other Old Testament notables*: Gideon (military leader), Samson (judge), and David (shepherd and king), among others.[9]

---

[8]Ruth Siemens, "GO Paper A-2: Tentmaking and the 1990's Global Job Market," in *Kingdom Professional Resource Guide*, 3rd ed. (Chicago: Intent, 1995), p. 2.

[9]These references are primarily from Siemens, "GO Paper A-2," p. 2, and Wilson, *Today's Tentmaker*, pp. 12, 20, 21.

New Testament Christians in the marketplace. Besides Jesus, Paul, Priscilla and Aquila, many other New Testament notables were active in the marketplace. A small sample includes Zacchaeus, a tax collector, who used his role in the marketplace to right many wrongs; Nicodemus and Joseph of Arimathea, both Sanhedrin officials; Barnabas, a landowner; Cornelius, a military officer; Luke, a doctor; Lydia, a merchant; Erastus, a city treasurer; Joseph, both a carpenter and Jesus' stepfather; and, Jesus' disciples, all of whom were in the crafts, various trades, the fishing industry or the government before and at times during their ministry.

Christian missionaries and activists in the marketplace. The postbiblical history of the church and mission is filled with the faithful who saw the intimate, biblically sound relationship between mission and the marketplace. For centuries after Paul's mission journeys, men and women carried the gospel around the world, not based on donor support but on their own ability to work and earn their way. Notable examples include the controversial Nestorians who entered China, perhaps as early as the fifth century, as traders more than missionaries; Marco Polo (1254-1323), a Roman Catholic explorer and tradesman who established the Silk Road and, as one of his primary motives, carried the gospel to Cathay (China); Christopher Columbus (1451-1506), a Roman Catholic explorer, cartographer and sailing master who, moved greatly by a desire to extend the faith to the people of India, discovered the New World and carried the gospel to its shores; Francis Xavier (1506-1552), a self-supported Roman Catholic, the first Jesuit missionary, known as both "The Apostle of the Indies" and "The Apostle of Japan";[10] Jesuit missionaries to Japan who supported themselves by the silk trade; Roman Catholic missionaries to the New World who supported their missions by agriculture and ranching; Hans Nielson Hauge, an eighteenth-century Norwegian entrepreneur who practiced both church planting and what we now think of as BAM, having "started 30 businesses, including fishing industries, brickyards, spinning mills, salt and mineral mines, paper mills, and printing plants";[11] William Wilberforce (1759-1833), a British statesman and devout Christian, who abolished his nation's

---

[10]Jack Wintz, "St. Francis Xavier (1506-1552)," *Friar Jack's E-spirations*, November 29, 2006 <www.americancatholic.org/e-News/FriarJack/fj112906.asp>.

[11]Mats Tunehag, "God Means Business! An Introduction to Business as Mission, BAM," unpublished monograph, 2008, p. 5.

slave trade; and the Moravians (from 1727), under the leadership of Count von Zinzendorf (1700-1760), who took the gospel and holistic ministry from Germany to the West Indies, Labrador, Surinam, Africa and America through a variety of businesses ranging from shipping and trading posts to artisans such as potters, carpenters, tailors, bakers and watchmakers.[12]

Wilson notes that in addition to the gospel being preached through self-supporting businesses and trades, the new believers were being helped to holistically improve their lives and living standards by teaching them useful skills and modeling the dignity of work in God's scheme of life.[13] William J. Danker, who wrote the classic study of the Moravians, *Profit for the Lord*, comments:

> The most important contribution of the Moravians was their emphasis that *every Christian is a missionary* and should witness through his daily vocation. If the example of the Moravians had been studied more carefully by other Christians, it is possible that the businessman might have retained his honored place within the expanding Christian world mission beside the preacher, teacher, and physician. . . . Mission strategy was as decisive as economic considerations in choosing a vocation.[14]

This impressive list must be topped by two other business-missionary enterprises. First, William Carey (1761-1834), a simple shoe cobbler, is known as the father of the modern mission movement. Carey was sent from England to India as a self-supporting missionary businessman. He served there his entire life and made enormous inroads for the cause of Christ. Carey was joined in his business mission by Joshua Marshman, a schoolteacher, and William Ward, a printer, both of whom practiced their trades to support themselves and the mission.[15]

Second, the Swiss Basel Mission (from 1815) under the leadership of Christian Friedrich Spittler (1792-1867) and John Haller, a master weaver, established missionary trading companies in Africa and India.

---

[12]These references are from Wilson, *Today's Tentmaker*, pp. 26-37.
[13]Ibid., p. 30.
[14]William J. Danker, *Profit for the Lord* (Grand Rapids: Eerdmans, 1971), p. 73 (emphasis added).
[15]See Timothy George, *The Life and Mission of William Carey* (Birmingham, Ala.: New Hope, 1991), and Vishal Mangalwadi and Ruth Mangalwadi, *The Legacy of William Carey: A Model for the Transformation of a Culture* (Wheaton, Ill.: Crossway, 1999).

No other mission society exhibits such an extensive and developed economic activity [as the Basel Mission Society]. . . . The general theory was that every man of good character and sincere Christian purpose could be utilized somewhere, and it was the business of the Society to find out where. The first two groups trained in a new mission school at Basel comprised . . . [of stocking weavers, a factory worker, a glove maker, a shoe maker, rope maker and] a scrivener, the only white collar worker in the lot.[16]

An interesting side note is that the Student Volunteer Movement of the late nineteenth century, under the leadership of Dwight L. Moody, Robert Speer and John R. Mott, sent over twenty thousand student volunteers into the mission field. While these students were not tentmaking, the Christian business community made their efforts possible. Roberta H. Winter, Ralph Winter's wife, noted, "It was these businessmen and their wives in thousands of women's missionary societies . . . which provide the much needed money to send the youth who were on fire to go."[17]

Finally, I include myself (banker and lawyer) and my wife, Frecia (commercial real estate broker), in this category, along with Ross King (agriculturalist) and Martha King (teacher), Richard Hale (Certified Public Accountant) and Kelly Hale (homemaker, mother and teacher), and Ellis Bush and Becky Bush (both teachers and musicians). All of us were tentmakers in the newly formed Republic of Kazakhstan. We were sent to found a graduate school of business, create an MBA program, teach free-market economics to communist leaders, plant churches and through our professions reach the people for Christ.

PRIESTHOOD OF ALL BELIEVERS

Any discussion of the biblical roots of the Marketplace Mission Movement and BAM would be incomplete without a brief reference to the doctrine of the priesthood of all believers or, as it is sometimes called, the doctrine of universal priesthood. In fact, the doctrine is so critical to the entire Reformation and its theology, to the Protestant church and its beliefs, to the evangelical believers and their callings, to marketplace mission and its cause, that I would be

---

[16]Danker, *Profit for the Lord,* p. 80.
[17]Roberta H. Winter, *Once More Around Jericho* (Pasadena, Calif.: William Carey Library, 1978), p. 194.

remiss in not giving the reader a taste of this critical doctrine before moving on.[18] After all, at its heart the Marketplace Mission Movement is a God-inspired, laity-led, laity-organized, laity-implemented and laity-driven ministry (i.e., of, by, to and through the laity of the marketplace). In fact, the movement has prospered to date in spite of the noticeable absence of the church, its priests and its pastors.

Definition. For centuries, the doctrine of the priesthood of all believers has been variously defined, seriously debated and the subject of countless volumes of books. It is highly complex in all of its nuances and has persisted as a perennial topic of theological discussion in every era. Herschel Hobbs complains that "Even in those churches that accept the doctrine of the priesthood of the believer there are diverse understandings of its exact meaning. . . . Reduced to its simplest form, the principle of the priesthood of all believers means that all believers in Christ are priests. . . . In short, it means that every person, or soul, is competent to stand before God without any need for a human or human-made 'go-between.' "[19]

Eastwood says it somewhat more lyrically. He attempts to bring the discussion back to a simpler, all-encompassing root, saying that God has conferred on all of his people the "right of entrance into God's very presence. . . . [T]he priesthood of all believers—the right of every believing man and woman whether lay or cleric, to go to God directly with confession seeking pardon, with ignorance seeking enlightenment, with solitary loneliness seeking fellowship, with frailty and weakness seeking strength for daily holy living."[20]

History of the doctrine. As Eastman and Hobbs convincingly demonstrate, the doctrine of universal priesthood has developed over the centuries in ways

---

[18]This discussion is set in an evangelical context, but it is certainly not limited to a Protestant perspective, as Edgar J. Elliston noted in an e-mail to the author, November 23, 2003, p. 1: "The Catholic church through its monastic movement in the Middle Ages used this method to preserve the church, extend the economy [and] preserve learning. . . . While this kind of movement may be more apparent in contemporary evangelical circles and evangelical publications, I would suggest caution about excluding Catholics or Orthodox. Egyptian Orthodox traders brought the gospel to Ethiopia in the beginning of the 4th century. . . . While they may not have been so focused on the priesthood of all believers in their theology, they were clearly not among the 'ordained' clergy/priesthood."

[19]Herschel H. Hobbs, *You Are Chosen: The Priesthood of All Believers* (San Francisco: Harper & Row, 1990), preface and p. 1.

[20]Charles Cyril Eastwood, *The Priesthood of All Believers* (London: Epworth, 1960), p. 72, and Thomas M. Lindsay, *History of the Reformation*, vol. 1, 2nd ed. (Edinburgh: T & T Clark, 1907), pp. 239-41, 435-44.

that have profoundly shaped not only the doctrine but the church itself and its relationship to the faithful. This has profound implications for the laity-driven Marketplace Mission Movement and BAM, since the doctrine and its history provide key scriptural authority for laity missions to, within and through the marketplace.

Old Testament covenant. Exodus 19:5-6 records God's covenant with his people through Moses. In this Mosaic Covenant, God said: "Now if you obey me fully and keep my covenant, then out of all the nations you will be my treasured possession. Although the whole earth is mine, you will be for me a kingdom of priests and a holy nation." Hobbs notes that the word *priests* is in the plural, indicating not only a collective priesthood but also an individual priesthood of every citizen of Israel. Israel agreed to this covenant but never fulfilled it. "Instead of evangelizing the pagan Canaanites, they were paganized by them,"[21] causing God to make the Levites a tribe of priests for the people.

> The whole nation of Israel failed in its priesthood, so God set aside one of the twelve tribes, the Levites, as a tribe of priests. Aaron, Moses' brother, assumed the role of High Priest and led the people in the rituals of worship and sacrifice. Here, too, God's people and His priests failed Him, setting up the "sad story" of prophets being sent to reclaim the people of God.[22]

New Testament covenant. In the fullness of time, God entered into a new covenant with his people: God sent his Son, Jesus Christ, the Messiah, to be the new sacrificial lamb and to offer his blood as atonement for the sins of Israel and for all believers. Jesus was to be both the guarantor and new mediator of the new covenant between God and his people, and to be the new high priest, replacing the former Levitical priesthood for all times (Heb 9:11-12, 15-28).

Jesus' ministry was marked with great controversy among the Jewish people and their leaders. So much so that they plotted his death and executed him on the cross. On Tuesday of Passion Week, after Jesus' triumphal Palm Sunday entrance into Jerusalem and after he had personally driven the money chang-

---

[21]Hobbs, *You Are Chosen*, p. 6.
[22]Ibid.

ers from the temple, Jesus was directly confronted by the chief priests and elders in the temple (Mt 21:23-46). Hobbs says:

> In this encounter on that fateful Tuesday Jesus definitely sounded the death knell to Israel's covenant relationship with the Lord God. Because Israel failed to meet the condition, God was not bound by the promise (cf. Exod. 19:5-6). And while God still loves the Jewish people and longs to save them in Jesus Christ, that is quite separate from the old Mosaic Covenant.[23]

This not only heralded the end of the old priesthood but the beginning of the new one, with Jesus as the high priest. As such it is foundational to the New Testament (the new covenant). As John portrays, Jesus went further and conferred priestly status on all believers; he *"has made us to be a kingdom and priests to serve his God and Father"* (Rev 1:6, emphasis added; see also Rev 5:9-10; 20:6). Peter is equally clear:

> You also, like living stones, are being built into a spiritual house to be a holy priesthood. . . . But you are a chosen people, a royal priesthood, a holy nation, a people belonging to God, that you may declare the praises of him who called you out of darkness into his wonderful light. (1 Pet 2:5, 9)

Jesus, the new high priest "has become the guarantee of a better covenant" that is permanent, a new covenant that "has made the first one obsolete" (Heb 7:22, 24; 8:13; see also Heb 7–10). Hobbs says, "In Christ we have a *better* revelation, a *better* high priest, a *better* tabernacle, a *better* covenant, and a *better* sacrifice."[24] Eastwood adds that under the old Mosaic Covenant the priests functioned primarily as the intermediary, the mediator, between God and his people. "All such notions were abolished by the Incarnation."[25]

The Protestant Reformation. "In the writings of the Early Fathers the doctrine of the universal priesthood has a central place."[26] Nonetheless, during the centuries that followed, the

Roman church developed an ecclesiastical system that centered power

---

[23]Ibid., p. 9.
[24]Ibid., p. 11.
[25]Eastwood, *Priesthood of All Believers*, p. x.
[26]Ibid., p. xi.

in the clergy. . . . A complex hierarchical system of church orders emerged in which deacons, pastors, and bishops—priests—assumed control. The autonomy of the local church disappeared and the principle of the priesthood of believers gave way to the priestly order and functions.[27]

This situation, particularly prevalent during the two centuries preceding the Reformation, continued to escalate with clear abuses of authority, great unrest within the church and strong pressure for reform. Although many names are associated with the Protestant Reformation, none is more synonymous with it than Martin Luther. Timothy George says that "Luther's greatest contribution to the Protestant ecclesiology was his doctrine of the priesthood of the believers. . . . The essence of his doctrine can be put in one sentence: Every Christian is someone else's priest, and we are all priests to one another."[28] Hobbs mildly protests, noting that Luther did not create the doctrine but simply "rediscovered" it in the New Testament, where it had been "from the beginning."[29] Nonetheless, Hobbs implicitly agrees with Eastwood: "The doctrine of the Priesthood of all Believers is the basic doctrine which underlies Luther's teachings on the seven outward 'marks' of the true Church."[30]

At this point the church was faced with "two widely divergent views: 1) The Roman Catholic view which places the Hierarch *above* the congregation and regards it as a special state or caste; and 2) the Lutheran view which sets the Ministry *in* the congregation and maintains that it may adequately fulfill its functions there."[31] Eastwood portrays Luther as "bewildered" about the church's restrictions on believers' freedom of religion, both in thought and in action. To Luther, "the Priest should ensure the freedom of the believer and not his bondage."[32]

The doctrine of the marketplace. The previous discussion begs us to ask whether the laity—those in the pews, those in the workplace, those in the marketplace—can serve our Lord Jesus Christ as faithfully and meaningfully in their positions as those in the pulpits, those in ecclesiastical robes

---

[27]Hobbs, *You Are Chosen*, pp. 12-13.

[28]Timothy George, *Theology of the Reformers* (New York: Random House, 1987), pp. 95-96.

[29]Hobbs, *You Are Chosen*, pp. 13-14.

[30]Ibid., p. vii; see also George, *Theology of the Reformers*, p. 96, who concurs with Hobbs and Eastwood.

[31]Eastwood, *Priesthood of All Believers*, p. 4.

[32]Ibid., p. 9.

and those on the traditional, church-sanctioned mission field? That is, is the call to the marketplace by Christ the same as the call to be a pastor or a missionary? The doctrine of the priesthood of all believers as found in Scripture, as practiced by the early church and as envisioned by the leaders of the Reformation, says Yes!

The recovered role of the laity. The biblical use of the term *laity* is synonymous with being chosen of God, a full partner in the ministry, special, respected and *filled with dignity and honor in Scripture.* Regrettably, the traditional and popular ecclesiastical meaning is just the opposite. "In common speech 'layperson' and 'laity' have largely negative connotations."[33] In common parlance the laity is a negative, pejorative term that is synonymous with such terms as amateur, unqualified, unprofessional and passive. It is almost always mentally contrasted with the clergy, who are considered to be qualified, trained and active professionals. Ogden notes the sad irony: "The Reformers . . . all agree that the doctrine of the priesthood of all believers obliterates the caste distinction between clergy and laity. There is no qualitative difference between the two. Yet the gulf between clergy and laity remains."[34]

This reality has led the Marketplace Mission Movement to arise from the laity and to be led by the laity, for the laity, accountable only to the laity and God. For the reasons already cited, until recently it had virtually no connection with the institutional church and its clergy. There has, however, been a growing realization within the movement that it may not be sustainable and retain God's blessings apart from rapprochement with the church. The same realization has been coming to the church, which sees the Holy Spirit's stirrings within the business community and realizes how this movement has been marginalized by the church. Both are seeing that long-term sustainability will require a definite nexus between the church and the business community for both ministry and mission, locally and internationally.

Since those in the movement are part of the larger church—the people of God—the first step is the simple recognition by the church of the movement's existence and its affirmation that it is a valid movement of God among his people. Following that, the church needs to embrace the movement (without absorbing or suffocating it) and commission its participants into the market-

---

[33]Ogden, *Unfinished Business*, p. 91.
[34]Ibid., p. 96.

place as holy ministers and support them in that setting.

Beyond that, the movement is coming to realize that it needs something more from the church and its pastors that it has been unable to give: a new, equipping role for the clergy, an integrated dialogue between the clergy and the laity in business, a meaningful reconciliation, and a genuine partnership in mission.

This will require a bold but necessary new paradigm shift for the church. It will also require a high degree of patience from the business community and a healthy portion of forgiveness and grace all around. But the end result is so filled with promise that the risks are worth taking and should not be delayed. *The stakes are also incredibly high for both parties: the business community risks losing God's blessings by not seeking unity through reconciliation and forgiveness; the institutional church risks becoming irrelevant and increasingly impotent in its efforts to further the gospel in today's society.* The future of both the movement and the church, as vital forces in society for the kingdom, is virtually assured *if* (and perhaps, only if) they can work together with a common vision.

The changed role of the clergy. This tension between the clergy and the laity continues today in many different contexts, both Roman and Protestant, in denominations, local churches, on the mission field, in marketplace ministries and in BAM. Ogden sees the tension that arises from the doctrine of the priesthood of all believers as heralding the start of a new reformation. "It has been broadly observed," he says, "that the first Reformation of the early 1500s *placed the Bible in the hands of the people* and that the Second Reformation will *place the ministry in the hands of the people.*"[35] Ogden says that for sixteen hundred years, from the time of Constantine to the 1960s, the pastor was seen primarily as a "teacher/caregiver" with four major roles: the teacher of doctrinal tradition, a caregiver, a public symbol of the sacred, and a presider over rites of passage. Since that time, however, the church has been "largely marginalized and rendered powerless. We no longer enjoy a respected and favored position in Western culture." Although this change has been gradual during the past three hundred years, Ogden notes that only "in the last decade has it dawned on church leaders and Christian academics that we are now in a new missional environment."[36]

---

[35]Ibid., p. 9 (emphasis added). This book is a revised, retitled edition of his earlier work bearing the title *The New Reformation* (1990).
[36]Ibid.

Ogden sees the church of the future as being a much-changed institution, both pastorally and missionally, with the ministry itself no longer being on the shoulders of the clergy, but shifting instead to become "the province of the people of God." Similarly, theology will shift from clergy-given and clergy-driven, to being "written in a style I like to call 'accessible,' or popular theology." This, Ogden believes, will give ministry a new, fresh appeal and a new credibility because it "comes out of real-life community."[37]

In this view, the clergy would move from the role of "teacher/caregiver" to that of an "equipping leader," from a "Dependency Model" to an "Equipping Model," and from "pastor-centered" to "people-centered" ministry. The role of the laity would also be drastically altered as it moves boldly toward the empowered, servant leadership advocated and modeled by Jesus.[38]

The dignity of work. Ogden notes that "one of the great legacies of the Reformation was the rediscovery of the dignity of work."[39] To Luther, "There is simply no special religious vocation . . . since the call of God comes to each man at the common tasks. . . . As [Luther] had extended the priesthood of all believers, so likewise he extended the concept of divine calling, vocation, to all worthy occupations."[40] Luther is quite clear on this point:

> A shoemaker, a smith, a farmer, each has his manual occupation and work; and yet, at the same time, all are eligible to act as priests and bishops. Every one of them in his occupation or handicraft ought to be useful to his fellows, and serve them in such a way that the various trades are all directed to the best advantage of the community, and promote the well-being of body and soul, just as organs serve each other.[41]

Calvin also viewed a person's priesthood as rooted in a person's calling.[42]

---

[37]Ibid., pp. 9-13.

[38]Ibid., pp. 211-12.

[39]Ibid., p. 255.

[40]Roland H. Brainton, *The Reformation of the Sixteenth Century* (Boston: Beacon, 1952), pp. 201, 233. See also Martin Luther, *Reform Writings of Martin Luther*, vol. 1, trans. Bertram Lee Woolf (New York: Philosophical Library, 1953), pp. 115-16; and *The Joshua Victor Theory: Calvin and Luther on Universal Salvation*, ed. Hilton C. Oswald, trans. Richard J. Dinka of Luther, *Works*, vol. 28 (St. Louis: Concordia, 1973), pp. 41, 43-44.

[41]Luther, *Reform Writings*, p. 116; see also Eastwood, *Priesthood of All Believers*, p. 12.

[42]John Calvin, *Commentary on the Epistles of Paul the Apostle to the Corinthians*, vol. 1, trans. John Pringle (Grand Rapids: Eerdmans, 1948), p. 248; see also John Calvin, *Institutes of Christian Re-*

Dakin summarizes this prevailing New Reformation attitude:

> All men are priests in their daily vocation. All are priests though their duties vary according to their calling. The only real farmer is a Christian farmer; the only real doctor is a Christian doctor; the only real mother is a Christian mother; the only real man is a Christian man; the only real woman is a Christian woman; and so on covering every detail and aspect and station in life. Apart from Christ we are not who we ought to be.[43]

According to Dakin, Calvin was cognizant of the reality of God's call on a person's life and implicitly understood that callings are not easy and in fact, often (usually) bear special burdens, fears and sufferings:

> Every man's mode of life is a sort of station assigned to him by the Lord that he may not always be driven about at random. . . . And everyone, from magistrate to the father of a family, will bear the inconvenience of his calling, its cares, uneasiness, and anxiety, persuaded that God and no other has laid the burden on him.[44]

Noting that Calvin speaks of our calling as "life duties that govern our life action," Ogden concludes:

> The important rediscovery of both Luther and Calvin for our purposes is simply, "Work is a place to serve God." Our life situation is the locale of responsible calling. Therefore, work is not merely the way we earn a living, but the way we give expression to our Christian life. . . . In other words, *vocations are not hierarchically graded on a religious-secular continuum.* . . . The workplace is not just the locale for Christians to witness to the gospel or minister to human need but also an avenue to express our unique abilities. Work is an expression of being. Being good stewards of the abilities God has placed in us is also a fulfillment of the call

---

ligion, vol. 2, 7th ed., trans. John Allen (Philadelphia: Presbyterian Board of Education, 1921), pp. 227-31; Eastwood, *Priesthood of All Believers*, pp. 72, 74; and Ogden, *Unfinished Business*, p. 257.

[43]John M. Barkley, quoted in Eastwood, *Priesthood of All Believers*, pp. 72-73.

[44]A. Dakin, *Calvinism* (Philadelphia: Westminster, 1946), pp. 221-222, as quoted in Eastwood, *The Priesthood of All Believers*, p. 72. Please note: Eastwood cites Dakin as his source, yet when I went to Dakin's *Calvinism* to confirm this, the quotes and information cited were not there. Regardless of this apparent error in scholarship, I believe the statement makes a point worthy of mention in this discussion.

to work. This is often referred to as the *cultural mandate*. In other words, we are free to seek a vocation that expresses the inner design God has given to us.[45]

Closing Observations

While theologians will continue to discuss and debate this topic for centuries to come, it is clear that Scripture fully supports the Marketplace Mission Movement, that the cultural mandate and the doctrine of the priesthood of all believers form its biblical and theological foundations, and that God is moving within and through the laity of the marketplace in powerful new ways. Charles H. Spurgeon perhaps summarized it best:

> Some persons have the foolish notion that the only way in which they can live for God is by becoming ministers, missionaries, or Bible women. Alas! How many would be shut out from any opportunity of magnifying the Most High if this were the case. Beloved . . . God is most surely glorified in that cobbler's stall. . . . Nay, glorified far more than in many a . . . stall where official religiousness performs its scanty duties. The name of Jesus is glorified by the poor unlearned carter as he drives his horse . . . as much as by the popular divine who throughout the country . . . is thundering out the gospel. God is glorified by our serving Him in our proper vocations. . . . Every lawful trade may be sanctified by the gospel to noblest ends. . . . Whatever God has made your position, or your work, abide in that, unless you are quite sure that he calls you to something else. Let your first care be to glorify God to the utmost of your power where you are.[46]

Discussion Questions

1. Share a new insight that you have gained about Jesus' connection to the marketplace.

2. Danker believes that "The most important contribution of the Moravians was their emphasis that every Christian is a missionary and should witness

---

[45]Ogden, *Unfinished Business*, pp. 256-57 (emphasis added).
[46]Charles H. Spurgeon, *Morning and Evening* (Peabody, Mass.: Hendrickson, 1991), p. 359.

through his daily vocation." Do you agree with this statement? Why? If you agree and endeavored to fully live your life consistent with this view, what change(s) would you make in your approach to your daily vocation and workplace?

3. This chapter gives many examples of people throughout history who used business as a form of ministry or mission. Among them, who has the most meaning for you? Why, and to what extent? How, if at all, does this rich history of Christian businesspeople inform the way you intend to use your gifts, talents and profession to be involved in mission to the world?

4. In reading the section on the priesthood of all believers, what new insight did you gain? Given the active MM and BAM involvement by many committed Roman Catholics, is this doctrine as vital as the text suggests? Why?

5. What is the original meaning of the word *laity* and how is it misrepresented in our common use of the word today in the church?

6. Do you agree with Ogden's statements "that the first Reformation of the early 1500s placed the Bible in the hands of the people" and that "the Second Reformation will place the ministry in the hands of the people"? Explain. If this statement is true, do the clergy have a role in this new paradigm? Should church clerics alter their role as Ogden suggests? If so, what is their new role? What would church look like, given this new role? Should someone replace them in their old role? Is that even important or necessary?

7. Ogden states, "Every lawful trade may be sanctified by the gospel to noblest ends. . . . Whatever God has made your position, or your work, abide in that, unless you are quite sure that he calls you to something else. Let your first care be to glorify God to the utmost of your power where you are." If all Christians throughout the world put this statement into practice in their lives, how would that affect the church? The world? You?

8. BAM engagement: Are you fully serving Christ in your vocation? What could you do to serve him more fully through it? Will you? If yes, why and when? If not, why not?

PART TWO

BUSINESS AS MISSION

How to Do It

"Between the idea and mission defined,
between the mission defined and the mission accomplished,
between the promises made and the promises kept,
there is the 'How.' And that makes all the difference."

LOCKHEED-MARTIN TV COMMERCIAL

UP TO THIS POINT WE HAVE DISCUSSED *what* BAM is and *why* it is done. From this point forward we will address the nagging question of *how* to do BAM. Without question the first step is one that is critical to the rest of the BAM effort: making a commitment to actually do mission through business. In practical terms this means that after learning what BAM is, the CEO and leadership team or counselors need to give careful thought to *whether* to do BAM. That involves an in-depth consideration of this part two, as well as part three, "Counting the Cost."

WHETHER TO DO BAM

Whether to do BAM is the first step in how to do BAM. Discerning that commitment, both conceptually and practically, is a complex issue that varies with the CEO's spiritual maturity, business experience and relationship with the Lord. Clearly, the question is whether the CEO will seek to be all that God would have him or her (and the company) to become—and is BAM it? Acting without that commitment would be foolish and premature, inevitably leading to disappointment, discouragement and probable failure.

Beyond prayer, Scripture and wise Christian business counsel, a part of discerning that commitment is, of course, to read as widely as possible from the dozens of books on the market that address faith-at-work management practices and BAM, and where possible attend BAM conferences and consult with BAM leaders and practitioners.

On the other hand, regardless of how much commitment, passion and resourcefulness the would-be BAMer brings, BAM will often be unsuccessful without the convergence of four other forces: (1) the power, resources and creativity of the Holy Spirit working within us; (2) the God-instilled gifts, the experiential business and trade skills, and the human and financial capital necessary to launch the selected business; (3) an understanding of the cultural, political and economic context in which the business is conducted, the context's mission history, and the mission methods best suited for that setting; and (4) proper and adequate preparation, training and planning for the many demands, roles and functions required by BAM.

Further problems arise when many good Christian businesspeople see the theory and love it conceptually, but are quickly frustrated in two ways. First, many have attended conferences or workshops where they first learn about BAM. These attendees are well-meaning, committed Christians in business, but they are also busy men and women who, in the press of daily business and in spite of their best intentions, more often than not, never quite get started, much less get it done. Too many are full of faith-words and good-faith intentions, but little or no faith in action. This phenomenon is so prevalent that many leaders in the movement are frustrated with the seemingly endless conferences, workshops and meetings on BAM that never quite have a direct, identifiable impact within the executive suites, much less on the plant floors and in the mission field. It is almost as if some see BAM as a new Christian fad or this year's "in" thing, but never connect it with the serious need to literally *go and do it*. People are dying, and no one seems to be listening. Words are spoken, concepts communicated, buy-in is apparent, and yet little tangible impact for God's kingdom is seen.

Second, those who actually try to put BAM into action are equally frustrated in their attempts. Not only are they not sure how to approach it, but they are fearful that their attempts may have significant adverse effects on their business, their client support and their financial bottom line. In addition, the task of going out of country (if applicable), planning, doing, taking action and running risks is not only time-consuming and resource-draining, but often difficult to the point of intimidation and spiritual paralysis.

Both obstacles are inherent in the faith integration process, but as Jesus' brother James quite plainly said:

> What good is it, my brothers, if a man claims to have faith but has no deeds? . . . Suppose a brother or sister is without clothes and daily food. If one of you says to him, "Go, I wish you well; keep warm and well fed," but does nothing about his physical needs, what good is it? In the same way, faith by itself, if it is not accompanied by action, is dead. . . .
>
> Show me your faith without deeds, and I will show you my faith by what I do. . . .
>
> [F]aith without deeds is useless. (Jas 2:14-17, 18, 20)

The message could not be clearer. No matter how busy we are, how fearful or intimidated we become, because of our inaction the adverse consequences to our own testimony and to the lives of those *not* being served are even more troublesome and perhaps even damning. After all, Jesus said that when we feed the hungry, give water to the thirsty and clothe the naked, we are serving Jesus himself. "I tell you the truth, whatever you did for one of the least of these brothers of mine, you did for me" (Mt 25:40). But equally important, he immediately gave us a stern, even ominous warning, "I tell you the truth, whatever you did *not* do for one of the least of these, you did *not* do for me" (Mt 25:45, emphasis added).

For true followers of Jesus, *whether* to do BAM is a matter of individual calling and discernment. *Whether* to integrate faith into the business aspect of a believer's life is not. Any fair reading of Scripture leads to only one conclusion: we are expected to live the gospel 24/7 in every venue of our lives. We are expected to be people of *integrity*, that is, people whose lives visibly integrate our faith into the DNA of our person and of our interaction with the world. Even in business—and even if we choose not to be a kingdom company or a BAM Company.

The How Factor

Once the would-be BAMer has crossed the *whether* threshold, doing BAM can be a challenging adventure. Usually, the next question is, How do I do it? The matter is a bit troublesome, however, since the meaning of *how* may be as varied as those who ask it. Often, what they are seeking is a detailed list of *best practices*. Others, though, are looking for more generic *big picture* answers, and still others want a step-by-step, systematic path to BAM. Let's briefly look at each.

First, best practices are techniques, methods and activities that specific BAM practitioners have developed to bring Christ and the Holy Spirit into the workplace. Ideally, they will promote Christ and his gospel in very real, meaningful ways for the employees, their families and those who deal with the company. Best practices may be as simple as praying for the employees, holding Bible studies, hiring a corporate chaplain, putting Scripture on product labels or paying bills on time. Or it may be as complex and intentional as relocating the business in the inner city, hiring the handicapped, literacy training or distributing water-purification systems to rural villages.

Of the two hundred companies I counseled in Christ@Work, I found that the CEOs had been moved by the Holy Spirit in different ways, each appropriate to his or her particular circumstances, context and calling. At some point a survey of BAM and MM companies will start cataloging these ideas and inspirations. This will be most helpful to struggling CEOs who want to think more broadly and creatively about how they can bring Christ into the workplace and into their communities. And, of course, they need to do so in meaningful yet inoffensive ways that respect the religious freedom and diversity of their workforce and are culturally sensitive to their external context. I wholeheartedly support this research and the dissemination of its findings.

Second, rather than address best practices, this book attempts to address the more systemic, generic, *big picture*, macroview, listing the prerequisites for doing BAM (chaps. 8-9), the stages of BAM development in the faith integration process (chap. 10), the levels of faith integration (chap. 11) and the corresponding levels of accountability (chap. 11), the multiple bottom lines of BAM (chap. 12) and how to achieve and measure kingdom impact (chap. 13).

Each of these is a part of how BAM is done. In combination they form a mosaic that is foundational to forming and managing a BAM Company. Especially important in those chapters is the list of prerequisites about calling, intentionality, buy-in at the top, walking with Christ and participating in peer groups. Each of these is particularly relevant to Christ-honoring management. So too is the discussion on creating a culture of relationships, defining and adhering to a set of biblically sound core values, leading in Christ's way (servant leadership) and being acutely aware of the spiritual warfare that one is entering as a BAMer.

Stated differently, the would-be BAMer, whether a new entrepreneur, seasoned business owner and CEO, or business student, must understand where to start (prerequisites), what stages will be encountered as he or she moves ahead, how to approach different types and levels of faith integration, what his or her accountability is for undertaking the BAM journey, and the key to doing BAM: understanding the different types of bottom lines that must be defined, managed and measured for different levels of kingdom impact.

Third, we will drill down to the more business-specific, microview of BAM. That can be approached in several ways, but most commentators, including myself, favor a systematic, faith-planning approach. This approach is highly intentional, purpose-driven and structured, yet it is undergirded and guided by focused prayer and Scripture, and allows flexibility for the spontaneous, unforeseen workings of the Holy Spirit. The faith-planning approach described in this book is focused on the budding entrepreneurial, would-be BAMers and business students, because they need the most guidance. Seasoned businesspeople who want to re-envision their companies into Kingdom Companies or BAM companies will find that this faith-planning approach also serves their needs, even though they may be able to skip steps they have already taken in their own pilgrimage.

The faith-planning approach advocated here demonstrates how to write a strategic master BAM plan for the new or existing company (chap. 14). It is also designed to show how to achieve different depths of planning and faith integration over time through the functional analysis approach (chaps. 15-16). It then takes the would-be BAMer through a step-by-step process from desire to decision to delivery (chaps. 17-19). Hopefully, in so doing, it will bring convergence to our discussions and a synthesis that helps would-be or new BAMers gain a better understanding of how to proceed. As Proverbs 14:15 says, "A prudent man gives thought to his steps."

DISCUSSION QUESTIONS

1. The author queries whether to do BAM, and offers four necessary forces that must find convergence before attempting to do BAM. What are they? Do you agree? Why or why not? What other elements, if any, should be added to this list? Why? Do you sense that any of these elements are coming together in your life? Explain.

2. This author strongly urges the would-be BAMer to have "proper and adequate...training" before doing BAM. What areas of training might he be referring to? What areas of expertise/training would be most beneficial for doing BAM successfully? Which are critical and which are not? Discuss.

3. BAM engagement: Are you being called to BAM? Why or why not? Either way, set aside a time of silent listening before God, and ask what you would or should do with the knowledge you are gaining from this book.

8

BAM: Personal Prerequisites

"The road of life twists and turns and no two directions are ever the same.
Yet our lessons come from the journey, not the destination."
DON WILLIAMS JR.

"For the pagans run after all these things,
and your heavenly Father knows that you need them.
But seek first his kingdom and his righteousness, and
all these things will be given to you as well."
MATTHEW 6:32-33

"Joshua told the people, 'Consecrate yourselves, for tomorrow
the Lord will do amazing things among you.'...
'Consecrate yourselves in preparation for tomorrow.'"
JOSHUA 3:5; 7:13

To integrate faith into a company, there are certain prerequisites that need to be considered—both personal and corporate. This chapter will explore the personal prerequisites for the CEO and the would-be BAMer.[1] The next chapter will consider the corporate prerequisites for the company's leadership team.

---

[1]While much can be accomplished by Christians within a company that is not Christian-led or is not intentional about faith-integration, this book is focused on those leaders who want to understand and be a part of the BAM movement. Accordingly, this discussion of prerequisites is addressed to the CEO and business owner (collectively the "CEO"), because these persons provide the leadership for and set the culture of the company. Nonetheless, this and the action plans discussed in later chapters may prove equally applicable to whatever level of leadership is actually charged with developing and implementing a faith-integration and mission plan for the company.

Nothing is more important to the CEO than his or her calling from the Lord to engage in BAM. Once that is received, the CEO needs to understand that he or she is called to a holy quest, not just a job, and that will require major spiritual growth, including internalizing Jesus' servant leadership style. As with all great quests, the CEO must also prepare for the unique roles that he or she will assume as a businessperson, business missionary and family member, including not trying to go it alone. This mandates both a BAM team to work with and a peer group of other kingdom oriented CEOs to associate with on a regular basis.

CALLING

The *calling* of God on a person's life can be a difficult subject to grasp, both theologically and personally. Nonetheless, three types of callings are quite important to the CEO who would engage in BAM: God's universal call, God's call to business as a vocation and God's call to mission through business— BAM.

God's universal call. Perhaps the foremost modern discussion of God's call is Os Guinness's 1998 classic, *The Call: Finding and Fulfilling the Central Purpose of Your Life*. Guinness states his thesis quite plainly:

> This book is for all who long to find and fulfill the purpose of their lives. It argues that this purpose can be found only when we discover the specific purpose for which we were created and to which we are called. Answering the call of our Creator is "the ultimate why" for living, the highest sources of purpose in human existence. Apart from such a calling, all hope of discovering purpose (as in the current talk of shifting "from success to significance") will end in disappointment. To be sure, calling is not what it is commonly thought to be. It has to be dug out from under the rubble of ignorance and confusion. And, uncomfortably, it often flies directly in the face of our human inclinations. But nothing short of God's call can ground and fulfill the truest human desire for purpose. ... The inadequacy of other answers is growing clearer by the day.[2]

Guinness defines calling as *"the truth that God calls us to himself so decisively that everything we are, everything we do, and everything we have is in-*

---

[2]Os Guinness, *The Call* (Nashville: Word, 1998), p. 4.

vested with a special devotion and dynamism lived out as a response to his sum-mons and service."[3] He distinguishes two types of callings. The first and primary calling is "to Someone" (God) and not to some cause or work, nor to some geographic place. We are called to salvation, to be a disciple and follower of Jesus "by him, to him, and for him." The secondary calling, says Guinness, is "do something," that is,

> everyone, everywhere, and in everything should think, speak, live, and act entirely for him. We can therefore properly say as a matter of second-ary calling that we are called to homemaking or to the practice of law or to art history. But these and other things are always the secondary, never the primary calling.[4]

Charles Stanley, senior pastor of the First Baptist Church of Atlanta, Geor-gia, agrees that the primary calling is to salvation, which is a once-in-a-lifetime event. After that, Stanley believes that Scripture calls us to a lifelong process of sanctification (to live holy, godly lives) and service (Eph 2:8-10; Col 3:23-24) for which we will be held accountable (Rom 14:12). We are, Stanley says, called to a life of service and good works according to our gifts. To that end, we are each gifted by God for special service which will generally be through a job or vocation. In that capacity, however, we must always "reflect him no matter what. If [you are] a painter or plumber . . . [then] give the best paint or plumbing job you can possibly do."[5]

Calling to business. Clearly, both Guinness and Stanley see God's calling to business as a secondary calling—an important, even vital calling, but sec-ondary to our call to the person of Jesus. Gene Edward Veith Jr. puts it this way, "'The priesthood of all believers' did not make everyone into church workers; rather, it turned every kind of work into a sacred calling."[6]

Leading missiologists, biblical scholars and theologians, as well as mature Christian businessmen and women, note that Jesus, most of the apostles (in-cluding Paul) and undoubtedly many of Jesus' followers were businesspeople and that there is ample scriptural support for three propositions: (1) that a person can be both a good, successful businessperson *and* a faithful follower

---

[3]Ibid.
[4]Ibid., p. 31.
[5]Charles Stanley, "In Touch Ministries," sermon heard on KTTV 11, Los Angeles, July 7, 2002.
[6]Gene Edward Veith Jr., *God at Work* (Wheaton, Ill.: Crossway, 2002), p. 19.

of Jesus Christ; (2) that God is working in today's world in a powerful way, reaching out to, within and through the marketplace in general and business in particular; and (3) a person can be called to business as surely as a person can be called to preach, pastor or serve on the traditional mission field.

> Today millions of men and women are similarly called to fulltime ministry in business, education and government—the marketplace.... Some of them have great influence on mainstream society, others are unsung heroes with low profiles, but each of them has been divinely called to bring the kingdom of God to the heart of the city.... God has explicitly *called* them and *anointed* them for it.[7]

R. Paul Stevens agrees that a calling to any type of work is a part of a much larger call, but sees it as a corollary to the cultural mandate of stewardship. Those called through business have a unique opportunity, Stevens says, as they are specifically called

- "to develop the potential of creation"
- "to improve and embellish human life"
- "to build community on Earth"
- "to [participate in] global enrichment and unity"
- "to create wealth and alleviate poverty"
- "to invest in Heaven" (i.e., to partner with God to help build a new earth and a new heaven; the "Doctrine of the Return to the Pristine Beginning")[8]

Vocational discernment. Being called to vocational service is exciting, but are we called to a specific vocation? The fairly unanimous conclusion of biblical scholars seems to be *no.* On the other hand, we are each given specific gifts and talents from God and are intended to use those for the kingdom. In that sense, our gifts are an important part of what Stevens calls our vocational discernment. It is clear that as we exercise our free will, yield to the Spirit's leading and embrace our ever-increasing age and experience, our specific *job* or *profession* may well change through the seasons of life.

Stevens notes that "vocational discernment is a life-long process. Many fac-

---

[7]Ed Silvoso, *Anointed for Business* (Ventura, Calif.: Regal, 2002), p. 18.
[8]R. Paul Stevens, *Doing God's Business* (Grand Rapids: Eerdmans, 2006), pp. 22-33.

tors contribute to a life direction—personal passion, motivation, gifts and talents, circumstances, compulsions and dysfunctions, and sometimes, a direct word from God."[9] Over and above all of these factors, however, and perhaps even guiding it, is our God-given hard-wiring: the way we have been fashioned by him for his purposes. Some call this our *central motivational thrust.* Steven says that in navigating the discernment process, "we start with motivation and passion because it is through the heart that God mainly guides." Stevens also distinguishes between gifts and talents, saying that gifts are "temporary empowerment by the Spirit for service and talents are abilities we are endowed with."[10]

Ultimately, we must realize that life is a dynamic series of events that lead us into a multitude of decisions. Each decision closes off other avenues of life experience and leads us away from paths we can never travel again. Economists call it the *opportunity cost* of a decision. Robert Frost, writing in 1920, simply calls it "The Road Not Taken."

> Two roads diverged in a yellow wood,
> And sorry I could not travel both
> And be one traveler, long I stood
> And looked down one as far as I could
> To where it bent in the undergrowth;
>
> Then took the other, as just as fair,
> And having perhaps the better claim . . .
> Oh, I kept the first for another day!
> Yet knowing how way leads on to way,
> I doubted if I should ever come back.
>
> I shall be telling this with a sigh
> Somewhere ages and ages hence:
> Two roads diverged in the wood, and I—
> I took the one less traveled by,
> And that has made all of the difference.[11]

---

[9]Ibid., p. 204.
[10]Ibid., pp. 204-6.
[11]Robert Frost, "The Road Not Taken."

Vocational holiness. The real concern, Stevens says, is that in exercising our chosen profession, whatever that might be, we should continually seek "vocational holiness." In his view this has three dimensions, "the first dealing with the work, the second and third with the worker. Each dimension involves dedication to God and a beautiful fruitfulness."[12]

The first of these three dimensions is "God-Sent-ness." Here, vocational discernment with all of its facets and nuances leads to a particular vocation at a particular juncture in life. Stevens is quick to note that discernment is infinitely different than guidance, as in "God's guidance" toward a specific vocation, position, job or decision.

> Significantly, the bible never uses the word "guidance." Guidance is essentially a pagan idea. The Bible reveals a guide, not a system for determining the will of the gods, which is called "divination" and involves reading "signs" or using mechanical means such as casting lots and reading the entrails of birds.[13]

The second dimension of vocational holiness is "God-Ward-ness." By this Stevens means that our vocational choices and performance should always be God-oriented and God-directed.

> What makes a type of work holy is not the religious character of the work but first, the character of the work itself (God-sent-ness) and second, the character of the worker. . . . Therefore we can speak of virtuous work because time and again the New Testament apostles spoke of working with faith, hope, and love.[14]

The third dimension of vocational holiness, Stevens says, is "God-Like-ness," that is, that the character of the worker "is increasingly being conformed to the image of Christ." The result of this growing Christlikeness is to have our lives exhibit the entire range of fruits of the Spirit—"love, joy, peace, patience, kindness, goodness, faithfulness, gentleness, and self-control"—which will, by design, tend to make us more fruitful for the kingdom in every way, particularly through our vocations (Gal 5:22-23).[15]

---

[12]Stevens, *Doing God's Business*, p. 203.
[13]Ibid., p. 204.
[14]Ibid., p. 209.
[15]Ibid., pp. 215, 218.

Calling to BAM. Being called to business is quite different than being called to BAM. True, the calling to business must be dominant in a BAMer's life, but it alone is not sufficient. One must also be called to mission, then to mission as business. As we saw earlier, in the discussion of the Marketplace Mission Movement's four camps, BAM is far different than marketplace ministries and their domestic, monocultural businesses. BAM is also different than tentmaking which, though crosscultural, is essentially for job takers who frequently separate their ministry from their work. So too BAM is unlike enterprise development primarily because BAM is business-led, not NGO-led, and it is about larger, job-creating businesses, rather than small or microbusinesses.

A call to BAM is a call to a very specific, unique type of mission. It is a call to create or own a job-making business that will be capital intensive, skill specific, resource dependent, market sensitive and culturally challenged. The BAM business will be conducted in a crosscultural context and usually (but not necessarily) in a foreign country with a different culture, language, traditions, currency, foods, working and living conditions, and political, economic, and legal systems and stability.

This is not a life for everyone, especially when the businessperson considering BAM is married or has dependents and chooses to engage in BAM internationally. Often the overseas context, while initially fascinating, even exotic and stimulating, can be quite harsh. Over time, it has been known to seriously wear on the missionary and his or her family, dangerously eroding the mission, the marriage, their faith and their joy. It can also cause serious health, emotional and stability problems. These issues are explored in detail in part three, because the costs of following Jesus onto the mission field are frequently quite high, and they must be faced realistically. Properly assessing them also speaks to the legitimacy and intensity of the BAM calling.[16]

Discerning a BAM calling is no simple matter. It is axiomatic, of course, that one must be a mature Christian. On the other hand, being Christian is not sufficient to engage in BAM. BAM, like other forms of mission, requires a specific calling from God to utilize one's business gifts, skills, experience and resources on the mission field through business. Michael Novak put it this

---

[16]It should be noted that the costs of BAM are not confined to those who do BAM in a country not their own. Regardless of where it is performed, all mission for our Lord carries a cost.

way, "To identify [callings], two things are normally required: the God-given ability to do the job, and (equally God-given) enjoyment in doing it because of your desire to do it."[17] He then turns to the calling of business and highlights one of BAM's priority goals: relieving global poverty.

> In particular, business has a special role to play in bringing hope—and not only hope, but actual economic progress—to the billion or so truly indigent people on this planet. *Business is, bar none, the best real hope of the poor.* And that is one of the noblest callings inherent in business activities: to raise up the poor.[18]

In short, BAM is a noble but not an easy task. In fact, it may well be among the most difficult, albeit effective, forms of mission ever. No one should consider entering into it without first having a deep conversation with the Lord, a genuine sense of his blessing and calling to this mission endeavor, the wholehearted support and commitment of one's spouse and dependent children, significant prayer support, a faith body (church, sending agency, NGO, board of directors) that is willing to hold him or her accountable, preferably a BAM team, and (as will be discussed at length later) as Jesus admonished, a willingness to pay the price of saying *yes* to a BAM calling.

A HOLY QUEST

Once the CEO feels called to lead a BAM Company, he or she must come to a basic understanding of what this implicitly means, both personally and professionally. Without these basics, the CEO's efforts are in jeopardy from the beginning.

Leading for Christ. Leading a company for Christ is a demanding challenge. BAM CEOs must mentally step down from their position and recognize that *it isn't about them*, that they are no longer *the boss*, that from now on they will be leading their company for Christ and in accordance with biblical principles. CEOs must further recognize that their company is owned by God, that God is the ultimate boss to whom they are accountable, and that their effort to manage for the Boss is a holy quest. This holy quest, while sounding a bit like Camelot, will actually require unflagging commitment, great effort and the

---

[17]Michael Novak, *Business as a Calling* (New York: Free, 1996), p. 19.
[18]Ibid., p. 37 (emphasis added).

possibility of considerable suffering. It can also be expected, however, to bring both temporal and eternal rewards (but not necessarily *success* as business traditionally defines it), unparalleled spiritual growth and maturity, and increasing intimacy with Christ. In addition, the CEO's main focus must be to provide a continual, positive, Christian witness through word and deed to the BAM team and their families, to all who associate or interact with the business, both internally and externally, and to the community the company will serve.

Walking with Christ. The primary method by which CEOs lead their company for Christ is not simple. First, it involves personally walking with Christ on an intimate basis: having an abiding, deep personal relationship with Christ. Accordingly, since CEOs set the culture of their company, their personal relationship with Jesus is critical. CEOs can *say* they are leading the company for Christ, but if their actions on the plant floor, in their management style, in their relationships with the many stakeholders in the company, and in their personal lives do not reflect that commitment, their efforts will become counterproductive. Quite simply, each will be seen as a hypocrite who says one thing and does another, totally lacking integrity. That is the reason why so many marketplace ministries focus on the CEO, business owner and executive team. These executives have to walk with Christ before they can lead for Christ.

What does it mean to *walk with Christ?* That is a subject of countless books, articles, sermons and discussions. To us, quite simply, it means *abiding with Jesus* as he called for in John 15. It means deliberately seeking to develop a deep, personal relationship with Jesus the man (the Son of Man) as well as Jesus the Christ (the Son of God). That requires, as most mature Christians know, a series of disciplines whose bottom line is spending regular, quality time with God the Father and Jesus his Son: church attendance, involvement and leadership; Bible study (both taking and leading, both individual and corporate); prayer (continual; reflective and listening; individual, group and intercessory); quiet time; living by biblical standards and in a manner worthy of the gospel; and an active life of service and good works for others. It also requires attitudes of humility, generosity, genuine concern for others, and those fruits of the Spirit found in Galatians 5:22-23: "love, joy, peace, patience, kindness, goodness, faithfulness, gentleness, [and] self-control."

Conversely, it means abandoning the ways of the world, leaving the old life and putting on the clothes of a new man or woman. In that regard, Scripture speaks at length about the ways of the Spirit versus the ways of the sinful nature; it admonishes those who would be Jesus followers to adopt the former and forsake the latter (see, e.g., Rom 8:1-17; Gal 5:1, 13-21; Eph 4:25-32; 5:1-20). Scripture also notes, however, that the man or woman of God who adopts the new lifestyle and gives up the ways of flesh does so not as a sacrifice but as a joyful, free, privileged choice. Those who follow Jesus deeply desire, as Paul says, to become more Christlike, to live their lives and to walk in ways that are "worthy of the gospel" of Jesus (Phil 1:27-28).

Servant Leadership

A part of the CEO's quest to find a right relationship with the Lord vis-à-vis his or her personal and professional walk is his leadership style. There are many styles for managing people and the organization, but for the BAM CEO one stands out: Jesus' leadership style, now called servant leadership. The biblical discussion on this style was part of Jesus' efforts to teach his disciples how to lead. The disciples were quarreling among themselves about who would be greatest in the kingdom of God. Jesus rebuked them:

> You know that the rulers of the Gentiles lord it over them, and their high officials exercise authority over them. Not so with you. Instead, whoever wants to become great among you must be your servant, and whoever wants to be first must be your slave—just as the Son of Man did not come to be served, but to serve, and to give his life as a ransom for many. (Mt 20:25-28)

The apostle Paul embraced this theme when he said,

> Do nothing out of selfish ambition or vain conceit, but in humility consider others better than yourselves. Each of you should look not only to your own interests, but also to the interests of others.
>
> Your attitude should be the same as that of Christ Jesus. (Phil 2:3-5)

> For by the grace given me I say to every one of you: Do not think of yourself more highly than you ought, but rather think of yourself with sober judgment. (Rom 12:3)

Nobody should seek his own good, but the good of others. (1 Cor 10:24)

Do not let any unwholesome talk come out of your mouths, but only what is helpful for building others up according to their needs. (Eph 4:29)

The apostle Peter was equally direct: "Each one should use whatever gift he has received to serve others, faithfully administering God's grace in its various forms. . . . If anyone serves, he should do it with the strength God provides, so that in all things God may be praised through Jesus Christ" (1 Pet 4:10-11).

Undoubtedly the classic modern work on the subject is Robert K. Greenleaf's *Servant Leadership: A Journey into the Nature of Legitimate Power and Greatness*. Greenleaf coined the term *servant leadership,* which at first blush seems to be an oxymoron, from his reflections on a story in Hermann Hesse's *Journey to the East.*

> In this story we see a band of men on a mythical journey. . . . The central figure of the story is Leo, who accompanies the party as the servant who does their menial chores, but who also sustains them with his spirit and his song. He is a person of extraordinary presence. All goes well until Leo disappears. Then the group falls into disarray and the journey is abandoned. They cannot make it without the servant Leo. The narrator, one of the party, after some years of wandering finds Leo and is taken into the Order that had sponsored the journey. There he discovers that Leo, whom he had known first as servant, was in fact the titular head of the Order, its guiding spirit, a great and noble leader.[19]

Greenleaf opens his own book with the bold statement "*the great leader is seen as servant first . . . deep down inside . . .* and that simple fact is the key to his greatness." His leadership grows out of his heart for serving, rather than his service coming out of his leadership role. Greenleaf recognizes that his thesis turns traditional leadership concepts upside down and is plainly not

---

[19]Robert K. Greenleaf, *Servant Leadership* (New York: Paulist, 1991). See also Grace Preedy Barnes, ed., *Servant First: Readings and Reflections on the Practice of Servant Leadership* (Indianapolis: Precedent, 2006), for an excellent collection of essays on servant leadership.

popular. Nonetheless, he sees it as "a new moral principle" that is emerging by which those who are led (the followers) will only pledge their allegiance to a servant leader. *"They* [the led] *will freely respond only to individuals who are chosen as leaders because they are proven and trusted as servants."*[20]

To Greenleaf the best test of whether a person is a servant first is found in the answers to questions like "Do those served grow as persons; do they, while being served, become healthier, wise, freer, more autonomous, more likely themselves to become servants? And what is the effect on the least privileged in society? Will they benefit, or at least, not be further deprived?"[21] Judy Gomoll, of the Navigators, also asks, "Is a Christian called to be a leader who serves, or to be a servant who leads? . . . What impact will genuine servant leadership have on the servant leader herself? . . . on others? . . . What is it about a servant leader that attracts followers?"[22]

Taking the matter one step further, Markus Melliger notes that "the model of servant leadership is not a leadership philosophy that has been theoretically analyzed down to the last detail. Rather, it is to be 'fleshed out' on a day-to-day basis in the community with others." He then lists the characteristics that he has gleaned from his readings and experience that capture "the essence of servant leadership":

A servant leader . . .

- puts others first

- builds others up

- is committed to the growth of people

- encourages people

- empowers people

- is a listener

- facilitates dialogue

- develops genuine empathy

- builds community

---

[20]Greenleaf, *Servant Leadership*, pp. 7, 10.

[21]Ibid., p. 7.

[22]Judy Gomoll, "The Dance of Servant Leadership," in *Servant First*, ed. Grace Preedy Barnes (Indianapolis: Precedent, 2006), pp. 54-56.

- works for the good of society

- keeps the well-being of others in mind

- admits mistakes

- is a faithful steward

- leads by example[23]

"The serving leader—a paradox in and of itself!" says Ken Jennings and John Stahl-Wert, who boldly call on servant leaders to "Run to Great Purpose . . . Upend the Pyramid . . . Raise the Bar . . . Blaze the Trail . . . Build on Strength."[24]

Greenleaf, a businessman, specifically addresses servant leadership in the context of business. While it is well known that the best, most successful businesses are those that *actually* put their customers first, sadly this is the exception rather than the rule in today's commerce. Greenleaf sees the "problem of not servicing well" as an epidemic-sized malady of modern business, as well as "schools, churches, hospitals, philanthropies and government," but optimistically prophesies that "in the next few years" servant leadership through business, "more than any other field" will become "a major social force."[25]

CEOs who aspire to lead a BAM Company should take note of this leadership style before starting a BAM initiative. They need an honest, critical assessment of whether they are truly a servant leader "deep down inside." One thing is certain, this characteristic cannot be faked for long, and, if missing, it can seriously erode and unwittingly sabotage the BAM efforts. In fact, a would-be BAMer may expect shallow blessings to come from a leadership style that does not reflect Jesus' own practices and commandment to "love one another" (Jn 13:34).

Preparation

William Carey, the acknowledged father of modern Christian mission and an earlier business missionary, set sail for India in 1793 as an accomplished busi-

---

[23]Markus Melliger, "Choosing a Leadership Model: Servant Leadership at a Glance," in *Servant First*, ed. Grace Preedy Barnes (Indianapolis: Precedent, 2006), p. 19.

[24]Ken Jennings and John Stahl-Wert, *The Serving Leader: 5 Powerful Actions That Will Transform Your Team, Your Business, and Your Community* (San Francisco: Berrett-Koehler, 2003), pp. 101-2.

[25]Greenleaf, *Servant Leadership*, pp. 134-35.

nessman (cobbler), but with virtually no mission training. Almost every mission agency since has become increasingly aware of the need for preparatory training before going to the field. Much of this awareness, sadly, has been the result of countless, tragic mistakes made by well-intentioned missionaries who were ill-equipped to meet the significant, often overwhelming challenges of foreign service. Their failures, as well as the successes of other missionaries over the past two hundred years, have led to the establishment of numerous mission-training programs within churches, sending agencies, societies, ministries, Bible colleges, seminaries and missiological schools. Fuller Seminary's School of World Mission (now the School of Intercultural Studies), arguably the premier mission-training institution for decades, is a primary example.

It is naive to think that going to the field under a BAM banner would require anything less. In fact, the training requirements are even more onerous for BAMers. They must be knowledgeable in at least five areas: (1) Scripture, the church, missiology and mission history; (2) the entire range of business management, operational and relational practices in an international or crosscultural context (e.g., administration, human resources, finances, accounting, marketing, sales, business law and import-export requirements); (3) their chosen business enterprise (e.g., their product's manufacturing, assembly and distribution, its local and international markets, sources of raw materials, parts or inventory, industry supply chains, etc.); (4) the contextual issues relevant to doing business and living in their particular foreign country (or domestic crosscultural context) with its own peculiar culture, traditions, religions, language, power centers, markets, government, laws, corruption, security issues and infrastructure; and (5) community development, a complex mission specialty unto itself that requires skill and competence to undertake within the crosscultural settings with which BAM is faced.

Lai underscores this and gives a wise admonition to would-be BAMers:

Tentmaking missionary preparation covers many disciplines and requires much time and energy. *Those who think tentmaking is an easy alternative to regular missionary work need to think again.* Having been a regular missionary and a tentmaker, I have found that, if anything, tentmaking is more difficult and stressful than regular missionary service. Tentmaking requires more thorough preparation, *not less.* Tentmakers are fully business people and fully missionary, thus we need to be fully trained in both areas. It requires time, commitment, and discipline to become adequately equipped for service as a tentmaker. Too often we are in too big of a hurry to get overseas. Those who view tentmaking as a quick path to overseas service will be disappointed. There are not shortcuts.[26] ·

Lai notes further that "it is not uncommon for tentmakers to invest four to six years in preparation after graduating from university. Wise tentmakers invest their time and effort to be adequately equipped for every good work."[27] He endorses Yamamori's list of training objectives of God's business envoys or ambassadors as

1. physically, emotionally, and spiritually self-reliant

2. adaptable

3. biblically literate

4. alert to the emerging mission context

5. trained in meeting needs vital to the people group they seek to penetrate

6. trained in long-term and low-profile evangelistic skills

7. equipped with broad new strategic thinking, and prepared with a special strategy for responding to opportunities by need[28]

Major corporations that do business overseas understand this fully and prepare extensively for their direct foreign investments by extensive planning, site inspections, market studies, financial analysis, cultural assessment and engagement, and training for their personnel, both U.S. and indigenous. BAM companies can do no less if they are to have long-term viability, stability, growth and success in both their secular and kingdom effects. The CEO and the BAM leadership team must adequately prepare for their own crosscultural business and mission venture. Failure to do so can have tragic consequences and, as Lai says, there are no shortcuts.

---

[26]Lai, *Tentmaking*, p. 52 (emphasis added).
[27]Ibid., p. 18.
[28]Tetsunao Yamamori, foreword to *Working Your Way to the Nations: A Guide to Effective Tentmaking*, ed. Jonathan Lewis, 2nd ed. (Downers Grove, Ill.: InterVarsity Press, 1996), p. vi.

PEER GROUPS

Being a CEO is a lonely, frustrating, isolated job; being a Christian CEO who wants to be intentional about honoring Jesus is even more demanding. Such desires not only increase the time and energy required to do the job in a godly manner, but also raise the CEO's personal and corporate bar of accountability. Further, if this load (no matter how eagerly it is carried) is not shared with others, it can add layers of vulnerability and anxiety to an otherwise demanding endeavor. Experience has shown that in order to be successful, these kingdom-oriented CEOs need similarly oriented peers around them on a regular basis. Many CEOs meet formally in organized peer groups, or less formally at conferences and workshops, at church or on the golf course.

A growing number of marketplace ministries now exist to support CEOs in their kingdom quest. They specialize in forming different types of Christian peer groups for CEOs and executives that afford their members mutual nurture, solace, encouragement, edification, mentoring, inspiration, fellowship and, perhaps most importantly, accountability. They also receive scriptural mentoring and wise counsel on daily decisions, share experiences, successes and mistakes, and explore ideas and biblical truths—all designed to increase their wisdom and options in approaching the BAM task.

In addition, these groups provide a forum for assessing new and better kingdom practices within the company, they strengthen the member's resolve to sustain the company's focus on kingdom goals, and they provide a refuge and a safe haven for the embattled CEO. Perhaps the ultimate benefit, however, is that by participating in such peer groups the leader builds into his or her business model an essential element for maximizing both personal life-time growth in Christ and the long-term sustainability of the enterprise as a KC or BAM Company. The benefits of these organizations to the growing CEO and his or her company are as enormous as they are essential. In fact, given the power and structure of the enemy, Satan—who will forcefully endeavor to undermine a CEO's kingdom efforts—it is exceptionally difficult to sustain a BAM Company's kingdom momentum without this type of support.

One of the largest and arguably the most influential marketplace ministries is Christ@Work (FCCI). With a presence in over twenty countries and approximately 850 companies among its members, this twenty-five-year-old ministry focuses on equipping, mentoring and encouraging business executives on how to lead their companies biblically. They do this through a wide array of videos, tapes, CDs and written materials, but their primary method is to bring Christian business leaders together on a periodic basis, usually weekly, to sit with their peers in small groups of eight to twelve. At these meetings the CEOs share their business issues and seek Christ-honoring, Bible-based counsel on how to apply Christ's gospel and the Bible to their business decisions and to discern *what Jesus would do*. Those CEOs who regularly participate in such groups testify to the importance of their group in keeping themselves focused, grounded, encouraged and accountable.

The peer groups are composed of business owners, CEOs and executives who are bound by their love of Christ, their commitment to integrating faith into the DNA of their companies, their shared common experience at the highest levels of corporate management, and their mutual covenants of confidentiality and transparency. In essence, they act as a spiritual board of advisors for each other. In this setting they are only accountable to the degree that they agree to be held accountable. Accordingly, one of the covenants that they tacitly make is that if a member lays a problem on the table and seeks godly counsel on how to handle it, he or she agrees to be held accountable by that group for how the advice is used and the problem is resolved.

There are several such Christian business leader peer groups within the United States and internationally; for example, Convene (formerly Beyond the Bottom Line Forums or BBL), C12 (Colossians 12) and Christian Businessmen's Committees Forums (CBMC-F).[29] Each has different formats and slightly different rules, but they exist for the same equipping, accountability, advisory and fellowship reasons. For example, Convene and CBMC-F groups meet once a month for six to eight hours and rotate their meetings among the businesses represented in the group. At the meetings the host usually offers a tour of his or her business to give the members a better understanding of this particular business environment and even shares detailed financial statements of the business.

This same type of accountability can be found in affinity groups, where a company or professional leader meets with other leaders within this industry

---

[29]See "Camp 2: Marketplace Ministry" categories in chap. 5.

or profession on a regular basis and uses them as a spiritual board of advisors. The two rules that must be kept in both this and the traditional peer groups are (1) these groups should not include people who are competitors in business, and (2) absolute and inviolate confidentiality—what is said within the group stays there. The presence of a competitor tends to stifle the transparency and openness that is essential if these groups are to be effective. Similarly, the confidentiality covenant is critical on both a personal and corporate level. The mere potential for inadvertent or unintentional disclosure will sharply smother the open, vulnerable discussion that is at the heart of the group's integrity, can result in actual harm to a member's company and can corrupt and irreparably damage an otherwise exceptionally healthy tool for helping the Christian CEO.

The ultimate object of the peer group members is, of course, to grow in Christ, to mature in Jesus-modeled leadership styles and to manage their companies in ways that bring glory to God, give honor and credit to Jesus, and have positive, long-term kingdom impact. In our view, membership in one of these peer groups is not only highly useful in reaching those goals, but is virtually indispensable to the CEO who would make the company into a KC or a BAM Company. Those CEOs in foreign or remote settings, or in places where no such groups exist, should consider forming their own. Most of these marketplace ministries will welcome the opportunity to assist any CEO in starting a group. Through today's communications technologies, making that connection and obtaining the necessary information, materials and directions is no longer difficult, regardless of where the CEO and the company reside. While this is an extra effort, it is well worth the time and energy invested.

DISCUSSION QUESTIONS

1. What is a "calling"? The author speaks of a first/primary calling and of a secondary/vocational calling. What is the difference between them? Do you agree with this distinction? Why? What other types of callings might one have? Are callings permanent or temporary?

2. Have you ever experienced a calling in the sense used in this chapter? If so, describe it. What makes you think it was a calling from God? If not, how do you react to the concept that God calls us?

3. What do you see as your secondary or vocational call at this point in your life? How can that vocational call be used by God? What are you doing to answer it? Do you feel that it is a lifetime call? Why? What steps, if any, might you take to answer it?

4. What does R. Paul Stevens mean by God-sentness, Godwardness, God-likeness? How are they different? How are they relevant to your life?

5. Does God call his people away from the world or into the world? How does this relate to your life?

6. The author suggests that a calling to BAM is more of a quest than a job. What is the difference? Do you agree? Why or why not?

7. Define *servant leadership*. What are its characteristics? Is it a realistic leadership style in the non-Christian business world? Why or why not? How does servant leadership relate to faith integration? What if faith integration and this leadership style cause you to lose your best client, causing your business to fail?

8. Name and define at least five types of leadership styles and the professions with which they may be most closely associated. Describe the settings in which you are a leader. What is your leadership style? How successful is it? What makes you think so? How do others respond to your leadership?

9. What is a *peer group*? Do you have a personal peer group with whom you meet regularly? Describe it. Why do you meet with the group? What need does it fulfill in your life? What need do you fulfill in the members' lives by being a part of the group?

10. BAM engagement: Do you meet with a group of business or nonprofit peers? If so, describe the group, how often you meet and why. If not, would it be good for you to do so? Why or why not? What steps do you need to take to locate and join one?

9

BAM: Corporate Prerequisites

Prepare. To make oneself ready.

"[Preparation] is the be-all of good trial work.
Everything else . . . is a satellite around the sun.
Thorough preparation is that sun."
LOUIS NIZER

"I have every confidence in the ultimate success of our joint cause;
but success in modern war requires something more than courage
and a willingness to die: it requires careful preparation."
GENERAL DOUGLAS MACARTHUR

"In peace, as a wise man, he should make suitable preparation for war."
HORACE

"Be Prepared."
BOY SCOUT MOTTO

"Who can speak and have it happen
if the Lord has not decreed it?"
LAMENTATIONS 3:37

ALTHOUGH PERSONAL PREREQUISITES are a must for the BAM CEO, so are corporate prerequisites. Perhaps the first thing for the CEO to understand is that becoming a BAM Company is seeking to become a Kingdom Company. A company can be a KC without being a BAM Company, but it cannot be a BAM Company without first being a KC. Quite simply, a KC is a Christian-led company, usually in a monocultural setting, whose CEO is intentionally integrating the Christian faith into the company's DNA. In terms of the camps described earlier, the KC is ministry *within the marketplace*, and the CEO generally obtains primary support, encouragement and equipping from a marketplace ministry, rather than from the church. As we will see, achieving KC status is no small task. On the other hand, being a BAM Company is about reaching crossculturally with business and mission, as well as intentionally engaging in community development.

Corporate BAM prerequisites include: intentionality of faith engagement on both a personal and corporate level; obtaining complete, conscious, conspicuous buy-in at the top of the organization to the business's BAM emphasis; creating an in-depth culture of relationships within the company; and developing corporate, faith-based core values. This chapter will examine each, as well as four warnings about dangers inherent in doing BAM.

BUY-IN AT THE TOP

John Beckett, a practicing Christian CEO, is emphatic about one point in the faith integration process: "I believe it is imperative for those in leadership to follow and model corporate values. (Otherwise leaders would be hypocritical in expecting others to observe them.) Senior executives, department heads and managers all represent management. They must 'buy-into' and 'walk-out' their organization's values."[1] I could not agree more. I also recognize that as valid as this principle is, it is far more difficult to achieve in many remote, crosscultural or international settings than it is within the United States with its vast pool of skilled, Christian workers. I say this in spite of the relatively severe U.S. legal and governmental restrictions on exercising faith in the workplace, particularly where some employees are not Christians.

Regardless, in determining whether to make the considerable, intentional effort to be a Kingdom Company, a BAM Company or even a Great Commission Company, the CEO and his or her team should not move forward until they receive the ringing endorsement, enthusiastic encouragement and active support of those with plenary power and authority over the company. Where that power resides will vary from company to company. While such power is usually with the CEO or business owner, that is not always true; frequently

---

[1]John D. Beckett, *Mastering Monday: A Guide to Integrating Faith and Work* (Downers Grove, Ill.: InterVarsity Press, 2006), p. 143.

other stakeholders such as investors, shareholders, creditors or members of the senior management team or the board of directors must also be considered.

If the company is to be successful with its faith-integrating BAM initiatives, all of these players must be on board. Otherwise, that initiative is likely to sow discord, create division and be used by Satan to render the company, its kingdom efforts and its witness ineffective, even counterproductive.

Obtaining alignment with BAM initiatives may not be easy or come quickly. It will often require focused individual and group education to explain BAM, its biblical basis, the reasons for moving the company (or starting it) in this direction, the reasonable expectations and process of becoming a BAM Company, and the anticipated risks, rewards and impact for the business, its stakeholders and God's kingdom.

A warning is in order here: ironically, often the greatest resistance and open opposition may come from committed Christians in the company who do not grasp the BAM concept and its kingdom potential. They are the members of the company whose preconceptions of mission come from a lifetime of being steeped in traditional mission paradigms. Their faith, denominational preferences and practices, mission experience, and stereotypes all come into play. Their buy-in is critical, however, not only because of their institutional power, but because a quarrel among the company's Christians will most assuredly be observed by nonbelieving company stakeholders. Predictably, any dissention within the Christian ranks can have an adverse, deleterious effect on the company's BAM efforts. On the other hand, resolving this conflict requires great patience, discernment, dialogue—and continual prayer—to keep from stifling or snuffing the BAM initiative at its conception.

In the end, formal endorsement by the board (and perhaps, by major shareholders) is also advised to prevent subsequent shareholder challenges or to burden senior management with mixed signals. This hurdle must be cleared before moving to the next steps. Here too, patience, prayer and waiting on the Lord are required before everyone is singing in harmony.

INTENTIONALITY

A corollary to having complete buy-in at the top of the organization conceptually is the intentionality of leadership's actions at the company's working level. It is no understatement to say that the degree to which the BAM Company's faith integration is effective will be in direct proportion to the priority it is given by the CEO and senior staff. Or, stated differently, the speed with which a CEO will take the company from one stage of spiritual development to another is in direct relationship to the intentionality with which he or she pursues the agreed-upon kingdom goals.

Continuum of personal intentionality. Unlike measles, intentionality is not a condition you do or don't have; it comes in shades and degrees, and can vary over time. Gary Ginter recognized this in his 1999 discussion of intentionality in the mission context of tentmaking. He categorically rejected the dichotomous, either-or approach taken by many. Instead, he suggested that there are a myriad of current mission practices that are, to one degree or another, tentmaking or a variation on that theme. All are characterized by different degrees and types of intentionality and effectiveness, but all seem to honor our Lord and promote the cause of Christ. Accordingly, Ginter proposed that we think of tentmaking, not in terms of one or two models, but rather in terms of a continuum of business mindedness or focus.[2]

Rundle and Steffen acknowledge Ginter's basic focus in their 2003 landmark book, *Great Commission Companies*, but propose a significant modification to Ginter's model. Whereas Ginter sees the continuum as having Christian professionals (traditional missionaries) on one end and kingdom professionals (tentmakers) on the other, Rundle and Steffen focus on the intentionality of the person witnessing for Christ. They propose a "continuum of intentionality." On one end of this continuum are those who are bent on giving "highly intentional witness" and on the other end are those who give "less-intentional witness." This approach places both of the Christian "professionals" at the same end of the continuum (rather than opposite ends as Ginter does), because both are totally dedicated to mission and both share as their primary, driving motivation the desire to witness for Christ.[3]

Rundle and Steffen's continuum would be anchored at the opposite end by those ordinary Christians who simply experience unintentional or "serendipitous" witnessing opportunities by "happenstance." In between these polar

---

[2]Gary Ginter, "Overcoming Resistance Through Tentmaking," in *Kingdom Professional Resource Guild*, ed. Gary Ginter, 3rd ed. (Chicago: Intent, 1999), p. 3.05.06.

[3]Steve Rundle and Tom Steffen, *Great Commission Companies* (Downers Grove, Ill.: InterVarsity Press, 2003), pp. 37-40.

extremes the business professionals would be rated by the degree to which they are being intentional about their witness, regardless of whether it is on the job or on their personal time. Key factors in assessing the intentionality of tentmakers and BAMers was discussed by Patrick Lai in *Tentmaking*. He categorized tentmakers in five different categories, each with different defining characteristics, which included:

1. living and working in a crosscultural setting

2. living in a closed country, that is, a CAN or RAN

3. having a legal resident visa

4. residing among the people

5. degree and extent of religious ministry

6. defined ministry goals

7. calling or clarity of leading

8. intentionality of witnessing activity

9. secular job or identity

10. number of hours worked each day on the job

11. source of financial support, that is, job, church home, raised support and so on

12. missiological and secular training

13. local language training

14. sending agency, if any

15. accountability structure[4]

These characteristics, and perhaps others, are all indicia of the intentionality of a person who is engaging in business on the mission field. The degree to which the person embraces the local culture, language, business system and people as a life calling becomes a measure of the genuine sincerity of that person to utilize his business skills for kingdom impact outside of his own home sphere of influence. The same can be said for companies, especially BAM companies.

---

[4]Patrick Lai, *Tentmaking* (Waynesboro, Ga.: Authentic, 2005), p. 28.

Continuum of corporate intentionality. The Christian business professionals just discussed, according to Rundle and Steffen, are businesspeople

> who are called and gifted for service in the marketplace . . . [who] see
> their profession not as a distraction from ministry but rather as the *nec-*
> *essary context* through which relationships can be built and Christ can
> be revealed. . . . [Their] work itself is an integral part of God's holistic,
> redemptive plan for the world.[5]

They note, however, that among these committed Christian business professionals, there is also "a continuum of *corporate* intentionality." On one end
of this continuum are Great Commission Companies and on the other end are
those companies that they apologetically call "Christian companies." Apolo-
getic because, they say, "Obviously companies cannot be 'saved' . . . but to the
degree that they reflect biblical values and behave 'Christianly' in other ways,
this can be a useful term."[6]

Of critical importance to their definition of a Christian company is the
observation that such companies "can and quite often do have a positive impact in their communities. But the process is usually more serendipitous than
intentional. It is not centrally coordinated or the result of planning, equipping
or accountability." They go on to explain, "By comparison, GCCs are characterized by a higher level of intentionality and accountability" that represents
the best of BAM practices.[7]

The corporate continuum itself represents a movement from being a good
Christian-led, Bible-based business toward increasingly becoming a fully
committed GCC. The authors hasten to add, however, that this is not a new
hierarchy of faith in which one is better or holier than the other. Quite the
contrary, the continuum of corporate intentionality is merely a tool to determine how intentional a company is being about (1) its faith integration in relationship to other Christian-led companies, (2) its willingness to use the
company and its resources as a vehicle for Christian mission, and ultimately
(3) its potential usefulness to God and (4) its potential kingdom impact.

By making these distinctions it is not our desire to introduce a new spir-

---

[5]Rundle and Steffen, *Great Commission Companies*, p. 37.
[6]Ibid., p. 39.
[7]Ibid., pp. 37-40.

itual hierarchy but rather to point out the obvious fact that some Christians give more thought to ministry and missions than others. Those who are not as intentional can, and quite often do, have a meaningful, positive impact on people's lives. But their efforts are guided more by happenstance than by planning, prayer and accountability. Moreover, because of their uneven experience and training, their impact is usually limited to people of similar language and cultures (also known as near-neighbor outreach).[8]

A CULTURE OF RELATIONSHIPS

Kent Humphreys, former CEO and president of Christ@Work and a lifetime business owner/CEO, makes a compelling case that the Christian CEO's primary job is to create a "culture of relationships."[9] By this, he means that all executive decisions affect the people of an organization, and that all interactions with people communicate impressions, attitudes and values. By its very nature, communication is dynamic, and, as such, its impact is seldom neutral. Each interaction either builds or diminishes relationships.

Accordingly, if a CEO is to build a healthy, loving, God-honoring company, it must be accomplished by focusing on building healthy, loving, God-honoring relationships. If the CEO wants to lead for Christ and become a KC or BAM Company, it is especially critical that his or her actions bring credit to the gospel and person of Jesus Christ. This is also required scripturally. After all, when our Lord said the greatest commandments were to love God and to love people, those commandments were all about relationship building.[10]

Under this approach to creating a Christ-honoring corporate culture, Humphreys' business model is to do business well and, in the midst of all of the business decisions and interactions, to look for every opportunity to minister to his people. He cites a litany of practical, daily practices such as praying for and with employees and customers, sending year-long grief packages to those who have lost a loved one, and planning week-long celebrations of Mother's Day for the mothers in his workforce. Although not spectacular programs, Humphreys

---

[8]Ibid., p. 38.
[9]Kent Humphreys, "Building Relationally: Practices and Hard Work," Christ@Work audiobook, Oklahoma City, 2005.
[10]Ibid.

says, they have had enormous kingdom impact on his employees, bringing them comfort in times of stress or illness, celebrating with them in their good times and grieving with them in their hard times. That sounds much like the program Jesus modeled and called each of his followers to emulate.

Other suggestions for ministering to the workforce are found in the literally thousands of *best practices* that Christians in business leadership are performing every day. To date, no concerted effort has been made to catalog such practices, but that will come in future research, hopefully stimulated, at least in part, by this book. Two suggestions, however, for building a culture of relationships bear special mention. First, the CEO and his or her team should consciously pray over every worker and workstation every day. It can be as simple as walking through the office or plant floor, praying silently over the empty chairs before people arrive for the day. Second, set aside a time weekly for the senior staff to meet, pray, share specific problems, concerns, joys, victories and defeats that arise from both their corporate and personal activities. The team should also feel free to make themselves into a peer group to brainstorm and give mutual advice and counsel from a kingdom perspective.

CORE VALUES

Beckett sees the starting place in any search to become a KC or a BAM Company as succinctly defining the company's core values and then living by them. He defines core values as those non-negotiables that drive the company, its goals, objectives, decisions and practices. Like the U.S. Constitution, they establish the underlying principles by which all company rules and activities must be judged. They become the gyroscope that keeps the company properly motivated and, at the same time, lays down the rules and expectations that define and govern the company's "playing field." In short, Beckett says, they

- define the "organization's *distinctive*"
- become "a powerful driver for *change*"
- create "a proper *constraint*" and impose needed boundaries
- help "shape the *corporate culture*"
- "point us toward what is noble, good and sustainable"[11]

---

[11]Beckett, *Mastering Monday*, pp. 137, 116.

"Core values needn't be trendy," Beckett says, but they give a strong impetus to top leaders to "shape the character of the organizations they lead. If they don't, their companies will fall victim to the inherent gravitational pull toward society's lowest common denominator."[12]

Defining these core values is challenging and time-consuming, but in the end they define the character of the company and its leaders. In that sense, Beckett advises, "They need to reflect the hearts of the people in senior leadership, for they will be their primary advocates."[13] He then looks at various companies and summarizes their core values: *integrity* (Alaska Airlines), *growth* (Cass Bank and Trust Company), *diversity* (Eastman Chemical), *profit* (A. G. Edwards and Sons, Inc.), *continuous improvement* (Emerson Motor Company), *personal balance* (Fresh Express), *change* (Gordon Food Services), *respect for people* (Graphic Packaging Corporation), *responsibility* (GuideOne Insurance), and moral and ethical absolutes grounded in "'*God's unchanging laws and directions* from which there is no compromise'" (Metokote Corporation).[14]

Beckett's own company embraced three values that the employees proudly proclaim on their company T-shirts: "Let Beckett employees be known throughout the world by a commitment to living their values: Integrity, Excellence, and A Profound Respect for the Individual."[15]

A Hong Kong affinity peer group, the Association of Christian Accountants (ACA), defines their core values with the acrostic "FAITH": fairness, accountability, integrity, thoughtfulness and holiness. These core values support ACA's 4-S goals: sharing, support, study and serve.[16] Another company builds its core values on 2 Peter 1:5-8's (NASB) themes: faith, excellence, knowledge, self-control, perseverance, godliness, brotherly kindness, love and useful productivity. Christian Resource Ministries' BAM arm, Enterprise International, cites its core values in both personal and corporate terms:

- Calling: discovering how God's kingdom purposes intersect with the talents and skills I possess

---

[12]Ibid., pp. 137-38.
[13]Ibid., p. 139.
[14]Ibid., pp. 139, 141-42 (emphasis added).
[15]Ibid., pp. 147-48.
[16]Patrick Yuen, ACA chaplain, interview with the author, November 16, 2008, in Hong Kong.

- Integration: connecting calling, commerce and character to transform culture
- Excellence: committing the best people and practices in order to create transformation in the business communities we serve
- Passion: linking desire and sacrifice to follow God
- Servanthood: offering God and others all that we have and are[17]

Bill Wimberley, a CEO and BAM activist from Austin, Texas, defines his company's core values in four categories:

- Kingdom centered

  1. eternity focused/sense of urgency

  2. prayerful decision-making that is not presumptive

  3. Spirit-led . . . yielded to the Holy Spirit/radical faith

  4. kingdom building/purpose driven/no spiritual mediocrity

  5. corporate "tithe" (first fruits) for kingdom investment, development and advancement

  6. excellence in business + excellence in mission/ministry = excellence in business for mission/ministry

- Investor centered

  1. partners in mission/ministry/business

  2. fiscal responsibility and accountability

  3. financial ROI with a kingdom ROI (KROI) perspective

  4. Spirit-directed advisory and accountability in all aspects of the business

- Customer centered

  1. strive for customer "delight"

  2. high quality, high-value solutions

  3. partnership for mutual success

---

[17]Enterprise International, "Business as Mission" (Anaheim: Christian Resource Ministries, n.d.), p. 3.

4. do what is right by God's definition—no situational ethics

5. commitment to innovation and continual improvement

6. healing and responding to customer feedback

- Employee centered

  1. executive management—model servant leadership

  2. invest in, mentor and develop entry-level people

  3. truth, honesty and integrity in all business dealings

  4. community/ministry active, engaged and invested

  5. respect for personal beliefs—equal opportunity employer[18]

A prerequisite to becoming a BAM Company is to lay a solid foundation. Core values are one of the most important ingredients in that foundation. *What are they for you and your company? Do you measure* everything *in the company by them or are they just pious words to place on a plaque, in advertising or on annual reports?* Failure to adhere to cited core values likely reveals the presence of a silent, toxic core value that may actually define the company's true reality.

FOUR WARNINGS

It may seem unnecessary to give the following warnings or caveats to those who are contemplating becoming BAMers, but that feeling is itself an indicator of dangerous complacency. The dangers cited below can invade a ministry almost unnoticed, and once inside, they can devastate the BAM mission. They are as dangerous to BAMers as any slow-acting poison and are like the proverbial lobster that is not aware that it is slowly being boiled alive. The first danger is the tendency to put BAM before Christ; the second, to put the needs of people before Christ; the third, to put the needs of the BAM Company before family; and the fourth is unabashed spiritual warfare. Each of these threats is very real and can test a BAMer's faith to the limits.

BAM before Christ. In the midst of the struggle to launch, operate or expand a BAM Company, an insidious danger can be incubating in the bowels

---

[18]William S. Wimberley, "XYZ International, Inc. Business Plan," Austin, Texas, 2007, pp. 10-11.

of the enterprise. The danger is in pursuing BAM (initially or eventually) for BAM's sake, rather than for Christ's sake; for its own sake rather than for Jesus. It is slowly letting the unrelenting daily pressure of simultaneously doing mission and business—especially in a strange land—overwhelm the BAMer's sense of why he or she is doing it in the first place. It is the malady suffered by the church at Ephesus that garnered Jesus' sharp rebuke, "I know your deeds, your hard work and your perseverance. . . . You have persevered and have endured hardships for my name, and have not grown weary. Yet I hold this against you: You have forsaken your first love. Remember the height from which you have fallen! Repent and do the things you did at first" (Rev 2:2-5).

BAM is a *means* to an end, not an *end* in itself. The endgame is bringing God glory and effecting kingdom impact by introducing lost people to Jesus and by making their lives better—because Jesus loves them.

Regrettably, even the most committed Christian tends to become so caught up in ministry—whether it involves leading a church, serving as a missionary, helping the poor or wrestling with the survivability of a BAM business—that the ministry business and its good works become the objects of affection and action. This demotes Jesus from first to second (or lower) priority. In so doing it distorts the BAMer's service, diminishes and even dishonors Jesus, grieves the Holy Spirit, encourages Satan, compromises the company's kingdom impact and hinders its usefulness to God.

Oswald Chambers addressed this danger in his 1935 devotional classic, *My Utmost for His Highest*. In the October 26 entry Chambers asks, "What is a Missionary?" and then thoughtfully answers:

> A missionary is one sent by Jesus Christ as He was sent by God. The great dominant note is not the needs of men, but the command of Jesus. The source of our inspiration in work for God is behind, not before. The tendency to-day is to put the inspiration ahead, to sweep everything in front of us and bring it all out to our conception of success. In the New Testament the inspiration is put behind us, the Lord Jesus. The ideal is to be true to Him, to carry out His enterprises.[19]

In the December 2 devotional Chambers shows a tinge of rare humor when

---

[19]Oswald Chambers, *My Utmost for His Highest* (1935; reprint, Westwood, N.J.: Barbour, 1963), p. 300.

he likens such reprioritizing to substituting personal holiness for God's holiness. He reminds us that our true BAM ministry is to glorify God, not to glorify our ministries—or ourselves.

> It is a snare to imagine that God wants to make us perfect specimens of what He can do; God's purpose is to make us one with Himself. The emphasis of holiness movements [like BAM] is apt to be that God is producing specimens of holiness [e.g., BAM businesses] to put in His museum. If you go off on this idea of personal holiness, the dead-set of your life will not be for God, but for what you call the manifestations of God in your life.[20]

Third, Chambers's June 19 devotional turns more serious:

> "Lovest thou Me? . . . Feed My sheep." John xxi.16. We count as service what we do in the way of Christian work; *Jesus Christ calls service what we are to Him, not what we do for Him.* . . . To-day . . . so many are devoted to causes and so few devoted to Jesus Christ. *People do not want to be devoted to Jesus, but only to the causes He started.* . . . Our Lord's first obedience was to the will of His Father, not to the needs of men; the saving of men was the natural outcome of His obedience to the Father.[21]

People before Christ. Another danger also lurks. It is not born of placing the business mission before God, but rather becoming totally committed to the mission and meeting the needs of the people whom you came to serve. Again, Chambers, in his inimitable style, speaks to this in his October 26 devotional:

> In missionary enterprise the great danger is that God's call is effaced by the needs of the people until human sympathy absolutely overwhelms the meaning of being sent by Jesus. The needs are so enormous, the conditions so perplexing, that every power of mind falters and fails. We forget that the one great reason underneath all missionary enterprise is not first the elevation of the people, nor the education of the people, nor their needs; but first and foremost the command of Jesus Christ, "Go ye therefore, and teach all nations."[22]

---

[20]Ibid., p. 337.
[21]Ibid., p. 171 (emphasis added)..
[22]Ibid., p. 300.

Chambers does not leave BAMers without hope or a cure to this lurking danger. On June 19 he promises, "If I am devoted to the cause of humanity only, I will soon be exhausted and come to the place where my love will falter; but if I love Jesus Christ personally and passionately, I can serve humanity though men treat me as a door-mat."[23]

BAM before family. Paul is quite clear when he says that family is the first temporal priority of a BAMer. He even goes so far as to declare that it is better for anyone who is thinking of going onto the mission field or into ministry to stay single, but that those who do marry are worse than unbelievers if they neglect their families for the sake of the mission (1 Cor 7:32-34; 1 Tim 5:8). This is far easier said than done, as any missionary and businessperson knows. Businesses (and missions) are consuming, demanding mistresses. Mutual covenants and accountability among BAM team members and their spouses are perhaps the best hedge against this danger. Failure to heed this warning results not only in seriously damaged marital and parental relationships, but in premature abandonment of the mission field. So, too, untended children of BAMers can often wander into harmful, even life-altering, relationships and practices.

Spiritual warfare: Lions and bears. Like any growth process, forward progress in building the kingdom of God is never a straight line. It is inevitably marred by our own unintentional misdirection, missteps and backsliding. But it is also the direct target of increasingly serious opposition, seemingly impenetrable walls and overwhelming discouragement. These come from many sources, but frequently from sources within one's own family, church or company.

Jesus warned Peter that Satan was going to "sift you as wheat" (Lk 22:31). Peter was indeed sifted and passed on the warning, "Be self-controlled and alert. Your enemy the devil prowls around like a roaring lion looking for someone to devour. Resist him, standing firm in the faith, because you know that your brothers throughout the world are undergoing the same kind of sufferings" (1 Pet 5:8-9). Just as he did with Peter (and Job), Satan can be expected to attack the CEO, the team and their families at their most vulnerable spots. Certainly if the BAM enterprise is being effective in its mission, Satan will sift and stalk them

---

[23]Ibid., p. 171.

like a lion after his prey. He may even come in the form of friends and family, advisors and confidants, or disciples and fellow Christians. Even Jesus experienced this as Satan tempted him through his most faithful disciple, Peter. Jesus spoke harshly to Peter but was actually rebuking Satan, when he said, "Get behind me, Satan!" (Mt 16:23). Regardless of the disguise, the CEO can be assured that the lion will come and that he is hungry and strong.

In short, such warfare and suffering will be manifest in the life of the Christian CEO who challenges Satan's territorial claims. The BAM CEO and his or her team can expect to be attacked in all aspects of their business, health and families. Satan will seek to exploit any and every vulnerability and weakness to derail the CEO's spiritual progress. As an old proverb says, "Don't kick a sleeping bear unless you want to do battle and to kill him." God's people who seek to use their businesses for God's purposes are indeed kicking a bear and will find themselves under attack and in serious need of God's protective armor. Certainly, in BAM as in other kingdom service, Paul's familiar warning about our spiritual vulnerability is ignored at our great peril:

> Finally, be strong in the Lord and in his mighty power. Put on the full armor of God so that you can take your stand against the devil's schemes. For our struggle is not against flesh and blood, but against the rulers, against the authorities, against the powers of this dark world and against the spiritual forces of evil in the heavenly realms. Therefore put on the full armor of God, so that when the day of evil comes, you may be able to stand your ground, and after you have done everything, to stand. (Eph 6:10-13)

A reality check. The four warnings given here are of such supreme importance to everything that follows in this book that I would be severely remiss in not giving them—for they pose significant barriers to successful BAM. Preparing to overcome them is, however, more than training, devotionals and personal commitment. It involves steeling the heart and mind into a total commitment to Jesus, hearing his call with clarity and believing—with all of your heart, mind and soul—that prayer works. The CEO and BAM team must start with prayer, continually bathe their activities, plans and people in prayer, and celebrate their victories and their setbacks with prayer, praise and thanksgiving. If so, their passion and prayers will be more than a match for Satan and will help them consume whatever dish he, his dark angels and a lost humanity see fit to serve.

In a very tangible way these barriers take the gloss off of BAM and remove the romanticism that often accompanies a first encounter with BAM concepts. But they also allow committed Christians to better discern the depth of their faith, calling and commitment, and in that process, maximize the chances of making the BAM adventure both successful and joyful.

DISCUSSION QUESTIONS

1. Why is it necessary for the proposed BAM Company to have "buy-in" to the BAM vision? Who needs to buy in? Why? What if they do not? Do non-Christian employees need to buy into the vision? Explain. If so, is this unfair or illegal discrimination? How should a manager resolve the apparent tension between religious core values and a BAM calling with respecting the religious freedom of employees?

2. Why are Christians within a company sometimes the largest barrier to becoming a BAM Company, as the author suggests? What could the CEO and BAM team members do to align these Christians with the company's values and BAM mission? Is the BAM proposal an infringement of their freedom of religion and an abuse of executive power? Explain.

3. Are relationships fundamentally important in the workplace, as the author suggests? Why? Are they important in a BAM Company to a greater or lesser degree? Why? How are workplace relationships best improved?

4. Define what is meant by *core values* (do not give examples). In what ways can a company (BAM or other) go about defining its core values? What process would you recommend? Who should be involved? What limits would you place on the process and the company's definition?

5. Of the four warnings the author gives, which are you particularly susceptible to? Why? What can you do now to avoid falling into that trap in the future?

6. BAM engagement: What level of faith integration intentionality is your employer aiming for, if at all? What level of faith integration are you intentionally and personally aiming for in your place of work? What ways

do you see that you could better live your Christian faith within your place of work? What systemic changes could you make at your workplace that would make it more of a Christ-honoring place? How? When will you do it?

7. BAM engagement: Given your definition of core values in question 4, think about your life. What are your core values, your nonnegotiables? Think about where you work. What are the core values of your company? Does the company measure *everything* in the company by them or are they just words on a plaque, in advertising or in annual reports? Are they compatible with your personal core values? Why? What compromises are you making or are willing to make to keep your job?

10

Stages of BAM Development

*"Like newborn babies, crave pure spiritual milk, so that
by it you may grow up in your salvation, now that
you have tasted that the Lord is good."*
1 PETER 2:2-3

*"In fact . . . by this time you ought to be teachers. . . .
Therefore let us leave the elementary teachings
about Christ and go on to maturity."*
HEBREWS 5:12; 6:1

*"To be a Kingdom Citizen, be an Aggressive
Responder to what God is doing."*
BRUCE BICKEL

WHERE DOES A CEO BEGIN THE faith integration process?[1] That will emphatically depend on his or her personal level of spiritual maturity and understanding of and commitment to the process. In the end, mature commitment is the true platform from which the process must be launched and sustained within the company. Accordingly, it is important to understand that there are certain stages in the faith integration process that a believer CEO in

---

[1]The chapters that follow pointedly focus on the CEO, because that is the person who sets the culture and agenda of a company and who is ultimately responsible for the company's performance. In a BAM setting, the CEO is also the person who selects and empowers the BAM team. The discussion can, however, enlighten and help the small business owner, the entrepreneur, the non-CEO Christian in business, the business student and other stakeholders in the BAM enterprise on both the process and their individual or organizational place in it and response to it.

business goes through. Similarly, the CEO who wants to go beyond basic faith integration and enter the BAM world must also pass through an additional series of predictable stages over a period of indefinite duration, perhaps days or months, but often years.

These stages are usually taken in succession, with each stage building on the previous one. In that sense the stages describe not only a company's progress, but the CEO's maturation process in his or her personal pilgrimage (walk with Christ) and company leadership. The ten successive stages are: conversion/salvation, discipleship, paradigm shift, faith integration, Kingdom Company, BAM Company, Great Commission Company, sustainability, replication and transformation. In a nutshell, the essence of each of the ten stages is:

1. *Conversion/salvation.* The CEO comes to a personal, saving knowledge of Jesus Christ and invites him to be Lord of his or her life.

2. *Discipleship.* The CEO is discipled, grows in Christian maturity, develops personal faith practices such as Bible study, church participation and personal witnessing.

3. *Paradigm shift.* The CEO comes to realize that God intends him or her to live faithfully 24/7 in every area of life, including business, and subsequently starts questioning what it means to be a Christian in business.

4. *Faith integration.* The CEO seeks ways to lead the company for Christ, to integrate biblical principles into the business and to use the business as a platform for ministry to those within his or her immediate sphere of influence: employees and their families, customers and clients, suppliers and vendors, creditors and investors, and competitors.

5. *Kingdom Company.* The CEO moves beyond ad hoc faith integration and seeks to institutionalize faith integration into the DNA of the company in such a way that it will survive his or her tenure. The company exists to glorify God in all that it does and, to that end, embraces multiple bottom lines. These points are understood and agreed upon by all of the company's significant stakeholders.

6. *BAM Company.* The CEO maintains efforts to be a Kingdom Company and adds crosscultural community development as a major emphasis of the company's agenda. Usually this phase occurs with companies that are

operating in an international environment, but in today's pluralistic world, mission can also be next door as well as overseas.

7. *Great Commission Company.* This is a type of BAM Company that usually has a larger number of employees, higher volume of sales and greater presence in a community. In that sense, a GCC also has greater potential of having a major kingdom impact on the communities in which it operates.

8. *Sustainability.* The BAM Company CEO recognizes the difficulties presented by the dual mandate of business and mission. He or she intentionally plans and manages the company's BAM efforts to maximize kingdom impact while maintaining business profitability, growth, financial independence and long-term survivability.

9. *Replication.* The BAM Company CEO implements a deliberate plan to bring other BAM companies into his or her business area or to grow such companies from among the indigenous local Christian-led businesses.

10. *Transformation.* The BAM Company has a major kingdom impact on the people and communities it engages, so that they experience real spiritual and temporal transformation.[2]

These ten stages are presented in sequence for analytical purposes to help explain the company's and the CEO's maturation process. Given the infinite ways that God works in people's lives, however, the sequencing may be misleading. It is probable that many of these stages may be experienced concurrently or in a different order by individual CEOs. The younger businessperson may go through each of these stages. The older, more mature believer will have already passed through the earlier stages and may have a different entry point on the faith integration spectrum or may be actively engaging several different stages simultaneously.

In any event, the stages will usually overlap as the CEO learns, experiments, grows and matures. Many will stumble along the way or tragically

---

[2]There are a wide range of definitions of the various companies described here. The ones given here and in the following chapters are how I see these companies and their relationship to each other. Although definitions may vary, the scheme presented here should help clarify and solidify the would-be BAMers' understanding of their personal and spiritual progression and that of their teams and companies.

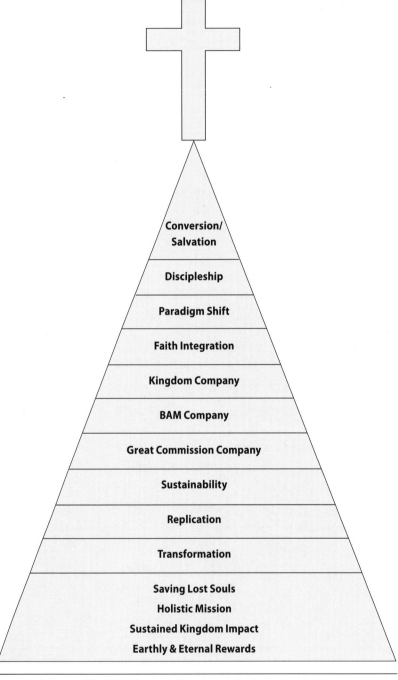

Figure 10.1. Stages of BAM development

become satisfied with their own (token?) progress and cease to grow or even drop out. Others will become discouraged by satanic attacks, outright betrayal, suffering, apparent failure or spiritual doubt. Still others will forget their first love, when their faith was fresh and new. A few, however, will persist in their quest and find victory and satisfaction, knowing that they, with Paul, "fought the good fight" and served their Lord well with the resources he placed in their hands.

The cumulative steps in this journey lead the CEO to an evolving, even compelling, understanding of the reality of his or her situation: God has placed in his or her hands company resources, networks and influence that intimately affect the lives of people, families and communities; God has given the CEO stewardship over an awesome power to further God's purposes (or not) through this leadership position in the company and the broader marketplace; and God will exact an accounting for how the CEO used that position and how (or whether) he or she positively influenced lives for God's kingdom on earth.

CONVERSION/SALVATION

The first stage, not surprisingly, is for the nonbelieving CEO to come to an intimate and personal relationship with Jesus Christ as Lord and Savior. This *conversion/salvation stage* is, as experienced believers all know, a rite of adoption into God's family that he has mandated through belief in Jesus Christ. It comes in many forms and denominational labels (e.g., being saved, coming to Jesus, being reborn), but it involves a voluntary submission to God the Father, a personal encounter with Christ the Son and an indwelling of the Holy Spirit. The CEO may be assisted in crossing the chasm from unbelief to belief by individual believers, the church, parachurch organizations, television or radio programs, or it may come through personal reading, reflection or crisis. Regardless, it is so foundational and critical that many marketplace ministries worldwide are focused almost exclusively on this and the second stage.

DISCIPLESHIP

The second stage, discipleship, is the learning stage that the newly believing CEO passes into and continues throughout life. Those who assist and teach the CEO have been called by Jesus to this task: "go and make disciples of all nations" (see Mt 28:19-20; see also Acts 1:8; Is 49:6). Initially, it involves taking a new, immature or lukewarm believer, frequently referred to as a babe in Christ, and helping him or her grow and mature in the faith. As such, it forms the basic building block for all mission, including BAM. The methods by which this is accomplished are legion, but in the end it often comes down to a more mature Christian caring enough about the new Christian's growth to teach him or her the tenets of the faith in all of its facets. Christ calls each of us to a lifetime journey. The *discipleship stage* is a maturing process for which the writers of the New Testament, particularly Paul, provide considerable instruction. Absent this growth, the new babe in Christ will likely wither and die spiritually. With this growth, the CEO discovers new meaning and excitement for life, both personally and professionally.

All too often, however, CEOs and businesspeople in general never seem to go much beyond this stage. They seem satisfied with being Sunday Christians, with moderate service to the church and minimal engagement with the living Christ. Others may not know how to grow beyond this, but may be too content, embarrassed or self-righteous to seek help. It has been said that the greatest threat to the church is complacent Christians. Certainly, businesspeople in the pews are as susceptible to this malady as others, but equally certain is the danger that their ultimate accountability may well be greater. Anyone who doubts this is invited to study Jesus' parables and to take seriously his admonition, "From everyone who has been given much, much will be demanded; and from the one who has been entrusted with much, much more will be asked" (Lk 12:48).

PARADIGM SHIFT

Third, during the process of discipleship, probably sometime after the early stages, the maturing CEO will inevitably be challenged in his relationship to God as a businessperson and, more particularly, the relationship of his business to God. This *paradigm-shift stage* often involves a major mindset change as he or she grapples with basic questions: Who owns the business, me or God? If God does, then what is my role in it? Is there a kingdom purpose for this business? If so, what is it? Are profits really evil? Should I leave business to be in "full-time ministry," as so many in the church have told me? Is it possible that God could call me to business just as a pastor is called to the pulpit? Can I be both a successful businessperson and an obedient follower of Jesus Christ, or are these mutually exclusive? If I can be both, can I reconcile my understanding of business rules with biblical principles? Do biblical concepts work in business? If so, which ones? How?

The questions are endless, but they represent a basic stage in which the growing CEO wrestles with how to live in faith in the business context. It is not an easy stage. For centuries the church has erroneously taught that there is a secular-sacred divide between the pulpit and the pew, between the church and the marketplace, between good Christians and businesspeople. The church has tacitly preached that those in the marketplace are playing in Satan's territory and that they are engaged in spiritually inferior, even sinful enterprises. That teaching is under attack today, and many churches are coming to see its error. It is, however, a teaching that has infected millions of businesspeople and will not easily be erased or reconciled. Nonetheless, the CEO who is serious about faith integration must overcome it. Once CEOs see themselves as God's children who have been placed by God in a position of considerable community influence—precisely because of their business—they are ready for the next stage.

Faith Integration

Fourth, the maturing CEO eventually asks, How can I lead my company for Christ? How can I manage this precious resource the Lord has placed in my hands to have kingdom impact? How do I honor Christ in the operation of my business? As a Christian, how do I integrate my faith into decision-making, marketing strategy, production process, product designs and employee and customer relationships? In short, how can I integrate my faith and biblical principles into the DNA of every aspect of the company's culture? And, perhaps most importantly, how can I begin living with integrity and wholeness, faithful to my Lord in every sphere of my life? This *integration stage* is still a questioning stage, but it moves the dialogue from one of relationship to one of active engagement in ministry, from questions about *what* and *whether* to *how*.

Kingdom Company

Fifth, the CEO who intentionally takes the journey beyond the questioning stage to proactive faith integration is seeking to become a Kingdom Company. While the literature is replete with various names and definitions for a KC, to me the best description of a KC is a for-profit company that has intentionally, largely integrated the Christian faith into every aspect of the business, its leadership, decision-making processes, operations, goals, objectives and bottom lines. It is a company that is mature in its faith integration efforts, has institutionalized those efforts and is committed to a process of continual improvement, of continually seeking to be more Christlike in every way.

Like personal maturity, this *Kingdom Company stage* is a never-ending journey of growth, evaluation, adjustment and learning on the go. There is never an actual point at which we can say, "We have arrived!" Rather it is a stage in which the CEO, leadership team and all of the employees are continually alert to new ministry opportunities and to the dangers of backsliding and spiritual drift.

In this fifth stage the focus is on the company and its sphere of influence: its shareholders and board, employees and their families, customers and clients, contractors, suppliers, vendors and agents, investors and creditors, trade associations and labor unions, and competitors. It is usually monocultural in its outreach, but with the ever-increasing, global pluralization of communities and workforces this will undoubtedly change. It is, however, a stage of inward focus on the company and of outward focus on its immediate sphere of influence.

BAM Company

Sixth, there comes a point in the CEO's and the company's maturation process that although the CEO and executive team are realizing the goal of becoming a Kingdom Company, they have an itch, a gnawing dissatisfaction that produces a deep-seated desire—a calling—to have greater kingdom impact. Often the company is drawn to those social-justice issues embedded within Scripture and our Christian morality:

> And what does the Lord require of you?
> To act justly and to love mercy
>   and to walk humbly with your God. (Mic 6:8; see also Zech 7:9-10)

In this stage the company mindset turns beyond ministry to mission. While the distinction between ministry and mission has been hotly debated by church scholars for decades, for our purposes the term *ministry* means serving others in the name and love of Christ monoculturally and locally (Winter's E-0 and E-1 outreach), while *mission* means performing ministry service across cultural boundaries (Winter's E-2 and E-3 outreach). Such crosscultural outreach traditionally has been thought of as overseas or international, but as already noted, it is readily apparent in today's world that mission is next door as well as overseas. Christian service to the Mississippi Delta, Appalachia, Watts or the New Mexico Apache or Navajo reservations, when led by outside Christians, is clearly as much mission as outreaches to India, Peru, China or Ukraine. It may not be as sexy to travel across town to the "other side of the tracks" as it is to do mission to Uganda, but often the need is the same and the cultural divide is just as great.

This *BAM Company stage* is characterized by a company exhibiting a high degree of intentionality about seeking to be a Kingdom Company and simultaneously engaging in crosscultural Christian mission and community development. For both a KC and a BAM Company, the company itself is a vital, integral part of its ministry or mission, but there are at least three critical distinctions between these companies. First, the KC usually has a monoculturally focused ministry; that is, its major sphere of influence is among people of its own culture. It is a Christian-led company reaching out to its immediate employees, customers, suppliers and community, most of whom are of the same cultural or ethnic origins. It is a German company ministering to Germans within Germany (or to the German community in the U.S.) or a South Korean company ministering to Koreans (at home or abroad) or an Hispanic American company ministering to Hispanic Americans. BAM, on the other hand, invariably ministers crossculturally and usually internationally.

Second, a KC affects people almost exclusively through its business efforts; that is, it ministers to people who are touched by its business activities. While this is also true of BAM companies, BAMers deliberately go beyond being a KC to becoming proactive in community development. In that sense, a BAM Company is a KC *plus* community development.

Third, an obvious, albeit important, aspect that is often overlooked is that a company can be a KC without being a BAM Company, but as noted earlier, it cannot be a true BAM Company without first being or seeking to be a KC. By analogy, a person can be a Christian without being a missionary, but a person cannot be a missionary without being a Christian.

It bears emphasizing that just as a traditional missionary cannot be effective on the mission field without a deep, abiding faith that is exhibited in his or her personal life, so too a company cannot effectively engage in God-honoring community-development mission if it is not striving to honor Christ in its internal management practices. Certainly, a company does not have to be perfect before engaging in mission; by no means is the church perfect internally before it sends missionaries into the field. The would-be BAM Company does, however, have to care deeply about being a KC and to make daily efforts toward that end if it is to be an effective, long-term community witness for Christ. Absent that Christian distinctive, the BAM Company may be doing good community-development projects, but it probably will do so in ways that are no different than secular companies that practice corporate social responsibility.

Notwithstanding these differences between KC and BAM companies, a final, overarching point must be emphasized. To say that all BAM companies are KCs, but not all KCs are BAM companies, is not to say that one is holier or better than the other; they may simply represent different stages of spiritual development and engagement, or they may represent different callings. It may be that (1) the Lord has called the KC CEO to exactly that ministry and only that ministry (which is wonderful in itself!), or (2) the KC CEO has been called to BAM, but for some reason has laid that broader calling aside temporarily or permanently, or (3) the CEO or the company may simply not have yet reached a level of maturity in which the Lord is expanding their vision of the company's kingdom usefulness to include BAM and the ability to implement it, or (4) the Lord has not yet called the KC CEO to BAM; that is, God is simply not ready, in his infinite sense of perfect timing, to use the CEO or the company that way.

GREAT COMMISSION COMPANY

Seventh, just as a BAM Company is a KC that has been called by God beyond its immediate spheres of influence to work crossculturally (or even internationally) and in community development, a Great Commission Company (GCC) is a special type of BAM Company that is called to work at a higher, more complex corporate level. It is a BAM Company that maximizes the economies of scale to achieve greater kingdom impact. In a word, the *GCC stage* applies to BAM companies that are simply larger, with more employees, greater production capacity, higher sales volume and often multiple locations. As such, they have more resources and a superior presence in the communities where they do business and, thereby, have greater community and regional influence and potentially greater kingdom impact.

As noted earlier, the term *Great Commission Company* was coined by Steve Rundle and Tom Steffen. Building on the work of Sharon Bentch Swarr, Dwight Nordstrom and others, Rundle and Steffen broke new ground in and beyond tentmaking. They noted that the traditional micro- and small-business model of tentmaking calls for businesspeople and entrepreneurs to go into the crosscultural mission field and support themselves through their work. That may happen by working for existing companies, by starting their own businesses or by being a teacher, health worker, government employee or consultant. Regardless, each involves a single individual or small team working with sole proprietors or within a small firm to achieve their evangelistic and church-planting goals. While they may work within the context of a larger sending agency or church, their efforts are at a relatively small level.

Rundle and Steffen suggest that it is far more effective and sustainable to do BAM through larger business enterprises that take a holistic ministry approach to the business and have wide ranges of stakeholders. For example, rather than simply planting a church made up of scattered workers, why not buy or manage a large company in a closed country, one that employs hundreds of workers and consider that your flock?

Calling such companies Great Commission Companies, Rundle and Steffen define each one as "a socially responsible, income-producing business managed by kingdom professionals and created for the specific purpose of glorifying God and promoting the growth and multiplication of local churches in the least-evangelized and least-developed parts of the world."[3] Although much of this definition also applies to all kinds of BAM companies, the GCC's distinguishing characteristics are its size and its community-development agenda and capacity.

There is no special rule as to what size a BAM Company should be before it is considered a GCC. The gauge I find most useful is one of organizational structure. If a BAM Company operates through an executive leadership team,

---

[3]Steve Rundle and Tom Steffen, *Great Commission Companies* (Downers Grove, Ill.: InterVarsity Press, 2003), p. 41.

it is in the GCC category. For example, if a company has so few employees that the CEO personally manages all of the company's operations, it would either be a KC or a BAM Company, but not a GCC. On the other hand, if the company is of sufficient size that it has several divisions in its operations, with different people leading each division, that company would be in the GCC category. In this situation, each of the division leaders would comprise the executive leadership team, which would report directly to the CEO or to an executive vice president, who would report to the CEO.

In practical terms this distinction is largely irrelevant for our discussion and may even be unproductive hairsplitting. There is, however, a practical difference that is worth noting: because of their greater size, resources and financial profits, GCC's can engage BAM more effectively and efficiently than smaller companies. First, they can hire a fulltime specialist on staff to do chosen in-house and external projects. If community development, hire a community-development specialist; if health, hire a doctor or set up an in-house clinic; if counseling, hire a professional, trained clinician; if education, literacy training or agricultural guidance, hire an appropriately experienced teacher; or if construction, hire qualified contractors, carpenters, masons or other tradespersons. Small firms have no capacity to provide these services on staff. Second, GCCs have the option of retaining someone in-house or simply contracting with specialists, NGOs, churches or universities and colleges worldwide in each of these disciplines to come alongside the company and the community on an as-needed basis as consultants, adjuncts and workers. Again, smaller BAM companies do not always have the luxury of accessing these people.

In either case, because GCCs are a type of BAM Company, when we speak of either one, the remarks are generally applicable to both. Most of the discussion in this book, however, addresses the GCC since it is more difficult to manage and has the greatest potential for kingdom impact. Nonetheless, smaller BAM companies can profit from the GCC discussion in at least two important ways: first, many aspects of GCCs are directly applicable to them, and, second, envisioning GCCs can inspire BAMers to pray about growing their BAM companies into a more influential presence in their mission field.

For both BAM companies and GCCs, the community-development aspect of their agenda is key to their BAM status. Similarly, both *what* they do within the community and *how* they do it are also key: both goals and methods must always be Christ-honoring and "worthy of the gospel" (Phil 1:27), and, where possible, they should overtly, publicly proclaim the presence and love of Jesus and all should be done in his name. In so doing, the company goes beyond the social-responsibility efforts of international companies and the community-development efforts of secular NGOs. It lets the people know that Jesus wants to visibly demonstrate his love for them by sending this company to help alleviate their pain, to meet their needs—and to meet him.

This differentiates it from its secular counterparts. This distinctive is more often demonstrated than proclaimed, more often shown through actions than words, through example than statements. It means being different because we are Christ-sent Jesus followers, not because it is simply good business.

In summary, a GCC is a larger BAM Company that seeks to incorporate the Great Commission, the cultural mandate and the great commandments into its core goals. It does so domestically by reaching crossculturally beyond its business interests and influencing the community in which it operates. It does so internationally by expanding its business operations to reach people in other nations or by starting/buying a new business overseas. Although this may take place domestically or internationally, GCCs have historically been focused on the world's poverty-stricken areas, especially those that deny access to traditional missionaries.

Sustainability

Eighth, as the CEO and executive team pursue KC and BAM goals, they will quickly realize that sustainability and its offspring, replication (stage 9), are key elements of being a viable company that seeks to thrive long-term. This *sustainability stage* is not an easy one to transit successfully and will be an ongoing challenge to every KC, but especially for every BAM Company.

Initially, it is critical to recognize that the KC or BAM business (and the BAM team) must find ways to be sustainable financially, culturally, structurally and spiritually. Financially, it is undeniable that there is a cost to being good. While we firmly believe that being a KC or BAM Company is good business in the long run, there are continual challenges and obstacles that will cost the company money, customers and sales. Culturally, a BAM Company and its expat BAM team must adapt (including language mastery) to survive within the alien context in which they operate. Cultural sustainability requires focused contextualization which, in real life, is no easy task. Without it, however, the company will have little chance of becoming a viable economic force in the community or of having any significant, long-term kingdom impact. So too, the team and their families will soon grow discouraged, weary and vulnerable to abandoning the BAM mission field.

Structurally, the BAM Company must organize itself to maximize its opportunity to handle the enormous pressure that a BAM Company faces from its dual business and mission mandates. Failure to do so will inevitably lead to spiritual drift, distorted priorities and inept or neglectful management of one or the other of these mandates. Resolving the structural dilemmas appropriately to the context is essential for long-term BAM Company sustainability.

Spiritually, the BAM Company must meet the personal and family needs of the team and their families. Without an active regimen of connectivity to Christ and to each other, without effective support systems and security, and without faith-based survival strategies and mutual encouragement, the team will lack the sustainability so necessary to remaining on the mission field. The team is there for Christ, but in the midst of serving others and spreading the good news, the team members often encounter a spiritual dryness that can become a bitter root within the BAM Company and community.

Similarly, a BAM Company's mission outreach and community-development efforts can and undoubtedly will drain corporate assets, energy, people, productivity and earnings. If there is not proper alignment between the community-development goals and the business-survival goals, the company's management can strain the corporation and its people beyond their capacity. For a BAM Company to sustain itself, boundaries must be established that keep the business alive and well. It is an obvious fact, but one frequently overlooked by nonbusiness, mission-minded enthusiasts, that in BAM, without the *B* there is no *M*, without the business there is no mission.

Sustainability of a BAM Company is always a critical issue and it comes in many guises. In that regard, succession and slippage deserve special mention because of their inevitability.

Succession. Sustainability is a particularly difficult, sensitive, even hurtful issue when a KC or BAM Company faces management or ownership succession. Succession is, after all, nothing short of a major transfer of power—the power to chart the future of the company in every aspect of its being. Such succession is an inevitable reality in every company, whether it arises from death, resignation, retirement, sale, merger or acquisition. It is particularly difficult in intergenerational succession where a parent is being succeeded by a son or daughter.

With virtually every such succession, a company goes through a reassessment of its culture and structure. It usually causes a major realignment of people, style, purpose, policies, process and, not infrequently, products and image. New CEOs and owners quite simply want their own people and their own stamp on the face of the company. Anyone whose favorite restaurant has changed hands understands the implications of having a new chef in the kitchen.

In short, when there is a change of management and ownership, every aspect of the company's existence is literally up for grabs. Successfully meeting those challenges and institutionalizing kingdom intentionality into the company's very essence is critical if the company is to survive these changes as a KC or BAM Company. How that can be done is as different as each company's culture, but for now, it is sufficient to note the latent dangers posed by succession for each KC or BAM Company and its ability to continue making a positive impact for the kingdom.

Slippage. Another danger to sustainability that is inherent in any business is the onerous pressures of day-to-day business and the constant demands business makes on time, energy, relationships, motivation and resources. Running a business is a full-time, difficult task. Maintaining a successful, profitable business, especially in today's technological, globalized business environment is neither easy nor certain. In the midst of such pressure, even for the best BAM companies, there is a constant tendency to drift back into business as usual and to allow an erosion of kingdom focus and kingdom goals. It happens subtly, creeping up on a company and its leadership incrementally, until the company is virtually devoid of intentional kingdom impact.

Scripture speaks of the constant war between the flesh and the Spirit, between the "natural man" and the "righteous man," between the ways of the world and the ways of God (see Rom 8:1-14; Gal 5, especially vv. 1, 13-25; and Eph 4:25–5:5). In our fallen world the natural human tendency is to follow the way of the sinful nature. It takes a continual spiritual alertness and

activism to reorient our lives to the ways of the Spirit and to sustain that
mode of living. Staying the course spiritually, remaining obedient to our
Lord and his gospel is a constant, lifelong struggle. That is true of us as
God's children. It is equally true of the business enterprises that we lead. No
matter how intentional and well-meaning we are, the danger of corrosive
slippage away from kingdom goals and impact is very real and pervasive. As
Peter warned, it lurks in the company halls, lunchrooms, offices, plant
floors, executive suites and boardrooms like a prowling lion ready to devour
its prey (1 Pet 5:8).

REPLICATION

The ninth stage is not altogether distinct from the BAM Company stage. In
many ways, it is a natural outgrowth of that stage and is another, albeit not
readily apparent, dimension of sustainability. I call it the *replication stage*. As
with any good family, if a business is to survive from one generation to another, progeny are required. Having offspring is basic to the survival of humanity and to the fulfillment of God's cultural mandate. Accordingly, he
commanded, "As for you [humankind], be fruitful and increase in number;
multiply on the earth and increase upon it" (Gen 9:7).

While replication is not basic to business survival, it is increasingly clear
that it is a key element in being an effective BAM Company. That is, part of a
BAM Company's outreach to the community is to help plant, pray for, nurture
and incubate other KCs and BAM companies. Although replication will be
discussed in greater detail later, it deserves special mention here as a key stage
in a CEO's progress toward maximizing the company's potential as a BAM
Company.

Another aspect of replication is peer-group participation. Through this
means, KC and BAM Company CEOs and executives come together on a periodic basis, often weekly, to discuss real business problems and collectively
look for Christ-centered, Bible-based alternatives for addressing them. As
noted above, becoming a member of one of these groups, or creating a local
group among business peers in a given city, is an important, even necessary,
step for any BAM Company that has a long-term commitment to its kingdom
goals. It is also a highly useful tool for helping a new, replicated BAM Company find its place in the community of local Christian businesses.

TRANSFORMATION

Tenth in the progression of CEOs and BAM companies is the realization that they have within their hands a God-given opportunity not only to transform their company culture, its people and its immediate environs, but quite literally to transform each community in which they do business. This transformation stage is a natural spinoff from the preceding stages and a natural goal for all BAM companies. There are major Christian-led, ecumenical, city-transformation movements going on throughout the United States and globally. All of them recognize the vital role of business and the power of the marketplace in effecting city transformation. In fact, the business component of the marketplace is now seen as a *sine qua non*, an essential element, of effective city transformation. Without the business community being completely involved and committed, long-term city transformation is generally not possible.

Ed Silvoso, although primarily focused on city and national transformation within Argentina, notes,

> Nowadays there are multitudes of believers in the marketplace who hold strategic positions in business, education and politics. They need to know that they are called to play a vital part in the establishment of God's kingdom on Earth. Without their active participation *and leadership*, our cities will not be transformed. . . .
>
> God has explicitly called them and *anointed* them for it. . . . [T]hey can bring transformation to their jobs and then to their cities—as happened in the first century.[4]

McCartney agrees, but asks an intriguing question: Is it possible that a third Great Awakening could take place in our times, also led by believers in business?[5]

Many of us are convinced that one company can change a city. It does so by example to other businesses, whether Christian-led or not, and by increasing Christ's presence, gospel and values in the business community. Through its own business activities and through replication of other KCs and BAM companies, the BAM Company provides proactive leadership and engagement in meeting community needs out of the love of Christ. By full

---

[4]Ed Silvoso, *Anointed for Business* (Ventura, Calif.: Regal, 2002), pp. 23-24, 18.
[5]Bill McCartney, foreword to Silvoso, *Anointed for Business*, p. 13.

partnership with the ecclesiastical church, nongovernmental organizations and others, the BAM Company can share the goal of reclaiming its city for the Lord and effecting sustainable community transformation. This can happen domestically and internationally, wherever the Spirit of God is nurtured by the business community.

Summary

As noted earlier, these ten stages of BAM development are not independent, isolated, sequential steps. Seeing them that way is useful for analytical purposes, but life, spiritual growth and business dynamics are messier than that. Rather, these growth stages frequently occur in overlapping, often cumulative ways in which multiple stages are being engaged simultaneously. For example, a mature Christian business leader may simultaneously be continuing his or her own personal discipleship, participating in a Christian business peer group to assist others and refining the company's policies, practices and personnel to gain greater kingdom impact and to ensure the sustainability of his firm as a Kingdom Company, while also undertaking major mission outreach efforts, incubating other BAM companies, and partnering in a community-transformation effort, not to mention devoting time to his or her family and community. And, believe it or not, the CEO also needs personal leisure time.

In any event, being the CEO of a BAM Company is an enormous undertaking and is clearly not for everyone. But, as we will see later, he or she does not have to do this alone—and should not. It is a team effort that must be planned and structured to be effectively managed. Regardless, that is why it is essential for the CEO to stay perpetually close to the Lord, beginning each day by asking the Boss what should be the day's focus. Prayer, continual prayer and listening prayer, are vital. Paying attention to those checks from the Holy Spirit will help avoid major missteps. Paying attention to clear direction from the Holy Spirit and seeking confirmation before acting will help show the way. Maintaining humility and avoiding spiritual arrogance (e.g., believing that he or she alone hears, or hears correctly, from the Lord) are necessary if the CEO's leadership is to be effective and if the BAM team and employees are to forge a persistent commitment to the BAM Company, its values and its goals.

Finally, it is important to understand these stages so that CEOs who are fully committed to finding ministry within the context of business can assess both their starting point and long- and short-term goals. Knowing the possibilities and having a clear vision of where they can take their companies is often the key impetus that motivates them to engage in BAM and to see it as a holy quest personally and for the people whom God has placed in their lives.

DISCUSSION QUESTIONS

1. The author offers a paradigm for progressive growth in faith integration by a company CEO. Which stages are personal to the CEO, and which are applicable to the company? How would you describe each stage? Are they sequential? Explain.

2. Which stage best describes your CEO and company? Why do you think so? What would have to change to move your CEO and company to another stage? Is that likely to happen? Why or why not?

3. What are the stages of a person's spiritual journey in Christ? What stages describe your faith? Are you continuing to grow, stuck on a plateau or declining? What makes you think so? What can you do to experience spiritual growth and maturity more rapidly?

4. The author speaks of three types of companies: Kingdom, BAM and Great Commission Companies. What are the differences? Diagram them and explain how they relate to each other. Are these distinctions important to mission or are they hairsplitting, as one commentator suggested? Why?

5. What does the author mean by *slippage*? Is this real? Give examples of where you have seen it in your life. How does a person avoid it?

6. What is meant by BAM Company replication? What are the various ways that this is done? What tangible benefits derive from a BAM Company replicating itself?

7. *Transformation* seems to be the buzzword in today's Christian mission circles. What does it mean? What are the different types of transformation? The author speaks of city transformation. What does that mean? What would a "transformed city" look like (building on your answers to question 5 at the end of chapter 3)? Discuss and diagram. Is this a realistic possibility? Explain.

8. BAM engagement: Many people speak of the desire/need to dedicate their

lives to a larger purpose. Do you agree? Why? What is meant by "larger purpose" (think beyond glib generalities and politically or religiously correct answers)? Does your life have a larger purpose to which it is dedicated? If so, what is it? Is it worth your life? Why? What are you doing to move ever closer to achieving that purpose?

11

LEVELS OF FAITH INTEGRATION
AND ACCOUNTABILITY

"Now to each one the manifestation of the
Spirit is given for the common good."
1 CORINTHIANS 12:7

"Whatever you do, work at it with all your heart, as
working for the Lord, not for men. . . . It is the Lord Christ
you are serving. Anyone who does wrong will be repaid
for his wrong, and there is no favoritism."
COLOSSIANS 3:23-25

"His master replied, 'You wicked, lazy servant! So you knew that I
harvest where I have not sown and gather where I have not scattered seed?
Well then, you should have put my money on deposit with the bankers, so
that when I returned I would have received it back with interest.'Take the
talent from him. . . . And throw that worthless servant outside, into
the darkness, where there will be weeping and gnashing of teeth.' "
MATTHEW 25:26-28, 30

AT FIRST BLUSH, FAITH INTEGRATION seems a simple matter, but when
the CEO attempts to incorporate biblical principles into the company, the
complex *how* question can be overwhelming and incredibly discouraging. The
CEO's understanding of the various levels of integration is vital to the efforts
to successfully meet this challenge and to further the quest to become a Kingdom Company or a BAM Company. As we will see, these levels roughly parallel the stages of development outlined in chapter ten, but they are substantively

different. Whereas the stages address the *what* and *when* of the CEO's (and the company's) maturation process, the levels of integration address both *how* and *for whom* integration is affected. Whereas the stages set out a roadmap showing where the CEO can take the company conceptually, the levels show where and how to actually integrate faith into the company's daily operations.

FAITH INTEGRATION

Clearly, faith integration is neither rote nor routine. Nonetheless, it can and must be approached systematically to help institutionalize the concept and its sustainable application, and to obtain maximum kingdom impact. To achieve this, three levels of faith integration must be considered: *inherent integration*, seeing the company's products and services as blessings in and of themselves; *internal integration*, seeking kingdom impact opportunities in every function of the company's operations and every area of the company's strategic business plan; and *external integration*, going beyond the business plan with a variety of company-sponsored initiatives in the community at large. Let us briefly look at each, then turn to the especially sensitive issue of accountability for the CEO and the BAM team.

Inherent integration. It may be that the company's processes, products or services have inherent kingdom impact in and of themselves; that is, the company produces a product or service that helps people live better. Examples of such products and services are those that provide improved safety, health, sanitation, nutrition, housing, clothing, aesthetic beauty, education, transportation, communications and recreation, as well as medical, legal, accounting, financial, technological and other professional services. Indeed, benefiting and adding value and quality to people's lives is what every company, Christian-led or not, should strive to achieve.

Unfortunately, a quick glance around the world shows that such beneficial services are often the exception rather than the rule. Millions of dollars are being made from business products and services that exploit, damage, degrade and often enslave people, with disproportionate tragic consequences to the poor, the marginalized, the elderly, women and children. Some obvious examples are illegal drugs, human trafficking, alcoholic beverages, tobacco products, gambling and casino operations, pornography, sex trade, abortion clinics and the like. Less obvious examples include usurious lending rates, price gouging, tainted foods or toys, substandard wages or working conditions, exploitation of undocumented workers, slum housing, shoddy or cost-cutting construction, careless medical treatment, placebo drugs, misleading advertising and de facto discrimination.

The list of products and services that are not inherently God-glorifying is virtually unlimited, but this in itself vividly demonstrates how important the nature of our businesses is to our Christian walk and witness. Our vocations are, in fact, a key element of our witness for Christ and visibly proclaim our obedience to his commandment to love our neighbors.

The greatest biblical commandment is to love God with all of our heart, soul and mind, and the second commandment is to love our neighbors as ourselves (Mt 22:36-39). Gene Edward Veith, citing Martin Luther, points out that one of the primary ways we love our neighbors—and have kingdom impact—is through our vocations:

> When we pray the Lord's Prayer, observed Luther, we ask God to give us this day our daily bread. And He does give us our daily bread. He does it by means of the farmer who planted and harvested the grain, the baker who made the flour into bread, the person who prepared our meal. We might today add the truck drivers who hauled the produce, the factory workers in the food processing plant, the warehouse men, the wholesale distributors, the stock boys, the lady at the checkout counter. Also playing their part are the bankers, futures investors, advertisers, lawyers, agricultural scientists, mechanical engineers, and every other player in the nation's economic system. All of these were instrumental to enable you to eat your morning bagel. . . .
>
> When God blesses us, He almost always does it though other people. The ability to read God's Word is an inexpressibly precious blessing, but reading is an ability that did not spring fully formed in our young minds. It required the vocation of teachers. God protects us through the cop on the beat and the whole panoply of the legal system. He gives us beauty and meaning through artists. He lets us travel through the ministry of auto workers, mechanics, road crews, and airline employees. He keeps us clean through the work of garbage collectors, plumbers, sanitation workers, and the sometimes undocumented aliens who clean our hotel

rooms. . . . The fast-food worker, the inventor, the clerical assistant, the scientist, the accountant, the musician—they all have high callings, used by God to bless and serve His people and His creation.[1]

Seen in this light, there is a noble aspect to business, one that is inherently good and God-glorifying. As such, it underscores the plain truth that business in and of itself is not evil. It is an activity ordained by God since before the Fall and fulfills both a need in those being served and in those serving. It brings us our daily bread and, when done in the Spirit, gives us great inner peace and personal satisfaction in a life well spent.

Internal integration. With inherent integration, the company has a positive kingdom impact from merely providing goods and services that benefit people's lives. However, BAM is more than that. It involves being very intentional about maximizing the company's kingdom impact, both internally and externally, that is, both within the company and in the community it serves. Internally, the process is not complex, but it does require focused commitment on the part of management. This will be explained in detail in later chapters, but as a preview, it is important to understand that at the outset the BAM CEO and his or her BAM team have a choice to make. They can either approach faith integration internally on an ad hoc, case-by-case basis, or they can deliberately plan for it. If they plan for it, which I highly recommend, there are different levels of planning from which to choose. These range from a simplistic, basic planning approach to a full-blown strategic master BAM plan. Regardless of the level chosen, the planning exercise should involve as many of the company's personnel and stake-holders as possible, and at its heart it should include a prayerful, thoughtful, thorough functional analysis approach. This approach, which will be explained in detail in chapters fifteen and sixteen, is a way to systematically examine every department and function within the company to see how each can be improved from both an efficiency and financial perspective *and* from a kingdom impact perspective. From this analysis the multiple bottom lines for the BAM Company can be identified and made a part of the company's annual plan and, eventually, become institutionalized within the company's DNA.

External integration. The process of integrating the kingdom bottom line into the company's DNA begins with a healthy appreciation of the inherent

---

[1]Gene Edward Veith Jr., *God at Work* (Wheaton, Ill.: Crossway, 2002), pp. 13-15.

kingdom impact of the business and its products or services in and of themselves. BAM calls for companies to go beyond that and to examine every internal aspect of the business to determine how to maximize the company's usefulness to God's mission. BAM also calls on each company to examine its place in the external community and ask, How can this business be leveraged to help this community and its people, especially those on the fringes who are in pain and marginalized by society?

While the term *external integration* seems to be an oxymoron, it is actually quite descriptive of the process. To begin with, ironically, external integration does not start outside of the company. It begins by bringing together a team of local employees to talk with the BAM team about their community, its needs, its power structures and its leaders. These employees are an invaluable resource. They live in the community and more often than not have done so for their entire lives. They know the local terrain and are the company's eyes, ears and hands to see needs, hear pleas, discern obstacles and barriers, and ultimately to implement the various community-development projects that the company decides to undertake.

The BAM team members will also make their own observations. Often an outsider can see the needs, the things that can and should be changed, in ways that insiders cannot. But outsiders (the etic) also have little or no right to make changes in a community on their own initiative. To have a long-term impact the changes must be made by those whose lives are most directly affected and who are insiders to that culture (the emic).

The two working together—the outsiders and the insiders—can, however, achieve wonders that neither of them could do alone.[2] Gird these with the power of the living God and the active involvement of the Holy Spirit, and it is a formula for genuine, Christ-honoring transformation within the life of the community.

From this beginning, the inquiry must also reach into the community to involve those formal, informal, civic, business, church and governmental leaders who have the power and influence to assist or to obstruct the compa-

---

[2]This is a concept long recognized by modern missiologists, which is unfortunately based on the tragic consequence of Christian missionaries' failure to adhere to it. It is referred to by them and by anthropologists as the *emic* (insiders' view of their world) and the *etic* (outsiders' view of that world). For a greater discussion of this concept and its applicability to BAM, see chap. 1. Also, see Paul G. Hiebert, *Cultural Anthropology* (Grand Rapids: Baker, 1983), pp. 50-54, and Charles H. Kraft, *Anthropology for Christian Witness* (Maryknoll, N.Y.: Orbis, 1996), pp. 76-79.

ny's efforts. Local cultural protocol must be followed to avoid giving unnecessary offense. Through dialogue with these leaders, the BAM team can both
assess the wisdom of the employee committee's recommendations and discern
what specific community projects will find community support. The object is
to help, not to hinder; to bless, not to anger or threaten; to build relationships,
not tear them down; to become a valued member of the local community, not
a disruptive presence; and to empower, not to dominate. This requires special
sensitivity, God-given discernment, patience and active listening.

The object is not to be an obnoxious outsider who comes into a community
saying, "We know your problems and needs. We know best and we will fix
things!" Rather, it is to come to them with listening ears, a slow tongue, humility and curiosity; to have them tell the company what their community needs
and priorities are; to hear their suggested solutions; to dialogue about possible
alternatives; to discern what help is within the company's capacity; and to seek
an invitation to join the community in meeting the identified need(s). The
object is not to do the project for them, but through company resources—especially money, people, talent and time—to come alongside of them as a paraclete (helper) to jointly accomplish the task.[3] One of the most effective, exciting ways for doing this is through a process known as "appreciative inquiry."

> Appreciative Inquiry is an exciting philosophy for change. The major as-
> sumption of Appreciative Inquiry is that in every organization [and com-
> munity] something works and change can be managed through the identi-
> fication of what works, and the analysis of how to do more of what works.
> . . . The tangible result of the inquiry process is a series of statements that
> describe where the organization [community] wants to be, based on the
> high moments of where they have been. Because the statements are grounded
> in real experience and history, people know how to repeat their success.[4]

Again, throughout the relational process, the community needs to know
that the CEO and BAM team are committed Christians and that they have
been sent by Jesus to help because Jesus loves them. This can be done in a va-

---

[3]There is considerable literature available on community-development methods and traps. The
BAM Company should avail itself of these resources as well as community-development experts in its own context as its leadership team seeks to serve the community.

[4]Sue Annis Hammond, *The Thin Book of Appreciative Inquiry,* 2nd ed. (Bend, Ore.: Thin Book,
1998), pp. 3, 7.

riety of ways, from simply spending time with each other, getting to know one another and becoming friends, to more purposeful activities such as conducting adult-learning programs or teaching community Bible studies.

Many of the needs that will surface during the community inventory will be social or environmental. If the company decides to participate (and invest its resources) in these projects, they will become part of the appropriate bottom line goals (see chap. 12). The only questions remaining then are how to maximize the kingdom impact with these efforts, and how to work the final corporate decisions into the company's master plans.

ACCOUNTABILITY FOR INTEGRATION

One aspect of being a KC or BAM Company that is often overlooked is the need for the CEO and the leadership team to be held accountable for their commitment to integrate biblical principles into the business and lead it for Christ. Generally, one person cannot hold another accountable unless there is a relationship between them that gives rise to that obligation.[5] Accordingly, let's briefly examine a few of these relationships, especially the CEO's special accountability, the role of his peer group and how we measure accountability.

Relationship accountability. The law recognizes and mandates accountability in certain formal, familial and social relationships. For example, the parent-child relationship, teacher-student, priest-penitent or in legal or employment relationships, such as attorney-client, doctor-patient, trust officer-beneficiary, lifeguard-swimmer, parents-babysitter, employer-employee. Similarly, it can arise from informal, voluntary requests or commitments, such as those covenant relationships found between God and the Jews, Jesus and Christians, or friend and friend.

Any company, whether large or small, is a network of relationships and hierarchies, formal and informal, legal and moral. As such, it embodies a mixed web of accountability, both up and down the chain of command and horizontally among those who are on peer levels. Often formal accountability is found in the employee's position description, but far beyond that is a general

---

[5]The issue of accountability is key to any successful mission and BAM enterprise. I highly recommend that a study of John Wesley's approach to accountability be undertaken by the BAM team as they prepare for the mission field. For example, see <http://home.snu.edu/~hculbert/selfexam.htm> and other Internet sources under "John Wesley Accountability."

accountability that every employee has to every other employee. Although seldom spoken, except in rhetorical, motivational ways (e.g., at management pep talks or all-employee gatherings), every company employee—from the CEO to the night watchman and janitor—is in the same lifeboat, one that provides them and their families with their provision for living. That mutual dependence on each other raises a general, mutual accountability for each person to do his or her best to promote the company's success and prosperity in whatever job is assigned, no matter how menial or tedious. While this general accountability is not often recognized, in a BAM Company it is preeminent and scriptural. Further, I submit that each person in a BAM Company is morally and ethically responsible—and accountable—for helping others in the company who are struggling, and for looking out for each other's well-being.

The CEO's accountability. In a business setting the CEO is directly accountable to the board of directors and the shareholders, and indirectly to all of the stakeholders in the business. If the CEO of a BAM Company is also sent by a church or a mission-sending agency, that raises an institutional accountability similar to the corporate board relationship. In either case, this institutional accountability emanates from the contractual, legal relationship and is usually governed by the standards it sets.

There are, however, other levels of accountability that affect every business, especially one that is seeking to have kingdom impact. First, in a KC or BAM Company the CEO comes to realize that God is the true Owner of the firm, that he or she is CEO by appointment from the Owner, and is accountable to that Owner on an hour-by-hour, decision-by-decision basis for the stewardship of the company. Jesus told several parables about the duty of the steward to the owner. Those Scriptures are powerfully and directly applicable to business. They illustrate not only to whom the CEO is accountable, but for what. Particularly instructive is Jesus' parable of the minas in Luke 19:12-27. In that story, the master expected a diligent investment of his money so that it would return a reasonable profit to him, and he held the unfaithful servant directly accountable for the results. Because of the servant's failure to be a good steward with the resources entrusted to him, the master chastised him, "You wicked servant!" Then the master punished the servant by taking away all he had and warning all like him, "Those enemies of mine who did not want me to be king over them—bring them here and kill them in front of me" (v. 27).

While this seems quite severe by today's standards, CEOs must recognize that they are being judged by God's standards, which are quite high, and that God takes our stewardship of his resources and gifts quite seriously. The Lord makes this imminently clear when he says, "I will judge you according to your conduct. . . . The king will mourn, the prince will be clothed with despair, and the hands of the people of the land will tremble. I will deal with them according to their conduct, and by their own standards I will judge them. Then they will know that I am the LORD" (Ezek 7:8, 27).

It is important to see that this accountability to God is at both a company *and* a personal level—and that these are inextricably entwined. Believers in every walk of life are accountable for how they are walking with Christ and what steps they are taking to grow spiritually. A Christian CEO is not immune from this scrutiny, not only because it is a personal growth obligation, but without that growth and maturity, efforts to lead a company for Christ will inevitably be stunted.

If the CEO is not continually walking with the Lord, investing time in Scripture, diligently praying to the company's true Owner and for all of those in the organization, he or she and the company are being set up for failure. Kingdom impact cannot be obtained without the company having been blessed by the Lord and prospered by his hand. When a CEO attempts to attain these goals solely through personal strength and business acumen, he or she perverts the kingdom impact by removing the goals from under the Lord's purview and placing them under human purview.

Second, the CEO nearly always has a family. Contrary to modern business practices, scripturally the responsibility to one's family comes before business. Paul is very clear in 1 Timothy 5:8 that one who does not take care of his own family is worse than an unbeliever. It is true that God gave us vocations as a way to be fruitful for him, but as Veith says, he also gave us the vocation of being a husband or wife and parent:

> Every Christian—indeed, every human being—has been called by God into a family. . . . The family is the most basic of all vocations, the one in which God's creative power and His providential care are most dramatically conveyed through human beings. . . . Marriage is a vocation from God. . . . Not only do parents—like God—bring the child into exis-

tence—they also—like God—sustain the life of the child. . . . God is operating in what they do. He is hidden in the vocation of the parents.[6]

Business is important, but too many businesspeople have sacrificed their families on the altar of business. This is not healthy from any perspective, but from the perspective of leading a KC or BAM Company, it is also a counterproductive witness, especially to the employees who also have families. It is also a double act of disobedience to God: not only is the CEO neglecting his or her own family (and perhaps damaging his or her own health), but is often abusing the company family if he or she models or requires similar business sacrifices from them. In short, balancing family and business is critical to leading a scripturally sound business.

Third, the Christian CEO is accountable to the wide variety of direct company stakeholders, specifically, the investors, board, creditors, employees, suppliers, vendors, customers and clients—and often their families. These people have, in one way or another, voluntarily contributed value to the company and its success or failure. Expectations are created by that contribution and by the relationship to the company that it creates. In their individual ways, each is depending on the company's CEO to be a faithful steward of that investment and trust, and to answer to them for sound stewardship.

Fourth, the CEO is also accountable to the community in which the business is located and to other communities that are possibly affected by the business. Being a *good corporate citizen* is a mantra of modern business ethics and development. For the KC or BAM Company it is not just a matter of looking good for the public and improving the image of the company by some high-profile community project. For the KC and more especially the BAM Company, it is a major component of its reason for being.

One of the BAM Company's major Christian distinctives is, after all, community development, especially development that empowers company employees to fully participate and even lead the effort to build the life of their hometown. How one goes about that in effective, empowering and contextually appropriate ways raises issues with which each BAM Company must wrestle. That discussion is broad enough to be an entire book in itself. The point here is that these community outreach efforts are points of accountability.

---

[6]Veith, *God at Work*, pp. 78-79, 85.

It is important to emphasize that accountability to the community arises in at least three ways. It arises first to the employees who are members of the community and whose lives will be affected by what the business does and, second, to the community at large that will have to live with the consequences of the company's actions. If they are well-conceived, well-coordinated and well-executed, these projects will add to the life of the community. Conversely, if they are not, they can actually do damage to the community, the company and the employees. Third, bad management practices *within* the BAM Company constitute a negative witness to employees and their families as to the desirability of following Christ. So, too, bad management *outside* the company through abortive or damaging community projects constitutes a negative Christian witness to the entire community.

Any company that holds itself out internally or externally as a BAM Company is especially vulnerable to criticism. Accordingly, it needs all aspects of its policies, projects and presence to "be worthy of the gospel" (Phil 1:27) and to be appealing to the non-Christians who are watching, especially in an international setting. If the CEO is to truly incorporate such projects into the company's DNA and to do so wisely, there is perhaps no better safety valve than a board of advisors who are part of the local Christian community but not an official part of the business.

Peer group accountability. Resolving the frequent tension between different levels of accountability, making timely, wise management decisions and threading the needle in complex relational issues are difficult tasks. In general, the CEO cannot be at his or her best in resolving the matters when isolated and alone. The Christian CEO, to sustain the dual efforts to personally mature in Christ and to bring the gospel into the company in a long-term, sustainable way, needs to ally with fellow believers who are in similar circumstances. Certainly the CEO can receive some spiritual help from his or her church and pastor, but often it does not carry the informed insight and wisdom that is most helpful. Pastors often know little about business and, accordingly, have no base of empirical expertise to understand its nuances and pressures. The Christian CEO needs advice from other mature Christian CEOs who have wrestled with the same issues. That is why Christian business peer groups have become so popular and are so useful to the CEOs of Kingdom and BAM companies.

As mentioned earlier, whether accountability comes from peer group participation in such organizations as Christ@Work, Convene or CBMC-Forums, or through independently structured affinity groups, the structure of the CEO's advisory group is critical. The group needs to consist of mature Christian peers who have business and leadership experience, who will covenant with the CEO to meet on a regular basis, who will hold the CEO accountable on all aspects of personal, spiritual and corporate life, and who will maintain the confidentiality he or she needs to be open and transparent. Scripture certainly affirms the advisability of this course of action (e.g., Prov 12:15; 15:22; 20:18; 24:6).

Measuring accountability. In each business, the CEO is ultimately accountable for reaching the goals he has contracted to attain (i.e., the company's agreed upon bottom lines). In every situation there is a financial bottom line, and the CEO is responsible for obtaining a good return on investment ($-ROI) for those who have invested money in the business. When there are other bottom lines, such as the social or environmental goals of secular companies, the CEO is also accountable for the company's measurable progress in meeting those. When working with a KC or BAM Company, however, the CEO is also responsible for the company's kingdom bottom line.

Measuring those spiritual bottom lines can often be difficult, for kingdom impact is not just measured in terms of good works, as for example, helping disabled people acquire marketable skills and a job. It is measured in terms of kingdom motive or intentionality. In Kingdom ROI (K-ROI) terms, *why* something is done is equally important as *what* is done. If there is no Christian, God-filled distinctive, then it is no different than a secular, good-works program. Christian NGOs doing poverty relief and development work wrestle with this continually, asking, How are our work and our impact different than similar efforts undertaken by the United Nations? Christian schools of higher education ask, How are our curricula qualitatively different and better than those offered at the secular school? and, more specifically, What is the Christian worldview Jesus and Scripture espouse, and how is it integrated into our curricula in an effective, paradigm-changing way? Kingdom Companies must also ask, How are we different than our secular competitors? What is it about our business that sets it apart as a better way, a higher road, a more attractive business model? BAM companies also assess their community development and outreach programs, and ask, What is the Christian distinctive we bring to this effort? These questions will be fully explored in chapter twelve as we wrestle with the various bottom lines of a BAM Company.

Summary

In summary, accountability is a key element of any KC or BAM Company. Accountability raises issues of to whom one is accountable, for what and why. How such accountability can be measured and institutionalized within the KC or BAM Company is a matter of BAM team preference, context and prayer. The need, desirability and necessity of doing so—including forming or joining a spiritual board of advisors—is, however, good for both business and mission.

Discussion Questions

1. What are the three levels of faith integration suggested by the author (pp. 252-57)? How would *you* define them? If you were the BAM Company CEO, how would you implement them into your company?

2. BAM engagement (individual or group exercise): Briefly design a hypothetical company in a major American city you are acquainted with (or select an actual company and specify that company's products, size of labor force, suppliers, markets, prices and other relevant factors. Next, suppose that you have just been made CEO of this company and have the active support of the board and the shareholders to repurpose it into a BAM Company.

    *   What is the best *process* you could use to determine your company's kingdom impact opportunities? Why? Who would you involve? Why?

    *   How would you achieve inherent integration? Why? Who would you involve? Why?

    *   How would you achieve internal integration? Why? Who would you involve? Why?

    *   How would you achieve external integration? Why? Who would you involve? Why?

    *   What level of accountability would you require? Who would you

hold accountable for what results? How would you measure the results? How would you hold them accountable?

12

BAM's Multiple Bottom Lines

Money makes the world go around . . .
A mark, a yen, a buck, or a pound . . .
Is all that makes the world go around . . .
Money money money money money money . . .
When you go to get a word of advice
From the fat little pastor
He will tell you to love evermore.
But when hunger comes a rap,
Rat-a-tat, rat-a-tat at the window . . .
Who's there?
Hunger!
Ooh, hunger!
See how love flies out the door . . .
For
Money makes
The world go around.[1]

"Greed is Good . . . good. Greed is right. Greed works."[2]

"The main thing about money, bud,
is that it makes you do things you don't want to do."[3]

"No one can serve two masters. Either he will hate the one and love the other,
or he will be devoted to the one and despise the other.
You cannot serve both God and Money."
MATTHEW 6:24

---

[1]"Money," Styrics.com <www.stlyrics.com/lyrics/cabaret/money.htm>.
[2]Michael Douglas as Gordon Gekko in the film *Wall Street*.
[3]Hal Holbrook as Lou Mannheim in the film *Wall Street*.

BEFORE GOING FURTHER, it is essential to discuss a key element of being a BAM company: the bottom line. Although used loosely, the term *bottom line* universally refers to the end result of a process or effort. It is the ultimate, actual goal that, for example, a BAM company wants to achieve as a result of its operations for a particular period of time. Usually, most bottom lines are measured by calendar or fiscal years and may be as simple as, "We made a profit of $352,874 this year, which is slightly below our bottom line goal of $360,000." Further, most actual bottom lines will be expressed in plural goals, not singular ones. These can be thought of as sub-bottom lines, measurable progress goals or benchmarks on the road toward the ultimate bottom line. In the previous example, the company may have had benchmarks of $12,000 per month. Similarly, bottom lines can be expressed in many ways (e.g., flat figures, percentages, ratios, event completed, person hired, patients served or students registered), depending on what is appropriate to the goal being measured. These must, however, all be capable of measurement, or they become only vague pipe dreams and one never knows whether they have been achieved.

I was president of a community bank when I came to Christ. The first thing I did after my conversion was turn to the church to ask a fundamental question: How can I best serve Jesus? I was told that Jesus said I could not serve both God and mammon (money), and further, that to truly serve Jesus I had to leave the business community and especially leave my trade as a money-lender (banker), and go into full-time ministry. After all, the church said, the marketplace is Satan's territory, Satan's playground, filled with temptation, greed, corruption, and evil.[4]

This attitude reflected a longstanding stereotype of business within the Christian community, which equates business and its drive for profits with oppression, exploitation and injustice.[5]

---

[4]The animus between the church and business has been experienced by countless Christians in business and is well documented in Laura Nash's two influential books, *Believers in Business: Resolving the Tensions Between Christian Faith, Business Ethics, Competition and Our Definitions of Success* (Nashville: Thomas Nelson, 1994) and with Scotty McLennan, *Church on Sunday, Work on Monday: The Challenge of Fusing Christian Values with Business Life* (San Francisco: Jossey-Bass, 2001). While an in-depth theological discussion of the role of money and profits is beyond the scope of this book, the serious student will want to explore those issues further. See, however, the brief discussions in chapters six and seventeen.

[5]There is considerable misunderstanding within the church, especially over the concept of *profits* and its spirituality. It is my prayer that this book will help dispel many of those stereotypes and replace them with (1) a vision of how influential the Christian business community can be

While such harsh impressions are reinforced daily in many business practices globally—practices which are to be roundly condemned by every right-thinking Christian—to lay such evils at the feet of business per se is patently and logically absurd and unsupportable both theologically and biblically. The problem is not with business but with people. Since the dawn of humanity and the Fall, people have abused organizational structures of every kind, including business, government, schools, families, entertainment and even churches for godless purposes. That does not mean that there is no redeeming value in these institutions or that we should categorically reject them because they are ill-used by evil people. That is throwing the proverbial baby out with the bath water. The world has massive problems, but they will not be solved without finding ways to use all of these institutions for good. Their potential to help people, to provide for human needs, to improve civilization and to serve God and his purposes is virtually limitless.

But what about business? Consider this: business is the lifeblood of the world's economies. Without business and its endless benefits, humanity would not, could not, survive. Business provides the essentials of our lives, both primitive and modern: our food, clothing, housing, energy, transportation, communications, health services, computers, iPods and cell phones. Business, in one form or another, is the innovative center, technological birthing place and distribution system for meeting virtually all consumer needs worldwide.

As such, isn't it reasonable, especially in today's globalized world, that God would choose to use business—and the profits so necessary to its existence—as a tool for his purposes?

The Financial Bottom Line

Traditionally, business has had only one bottom line: maximizing shareholder value. That means operating the business to maximize profits for the company and its owners (i.e., to produce a positive financial bottom line). This goal of business is fundamental to every business, including all BAM businesses. Quite simply, to be effective a BAM company must survive. To survive and be sustainable, it must have a positive financial bottom line—it must make a profit.

---

in bringing about the genuine transformation of our cities and nations through the love and gospel of Christ, and (2) an understanding of how vital profits are to keep the Christian business community healthy, productive and socially beneficial.

Further, to have credibility in its gospel witness, a BAM company must be a real business that delivers valuable goods or services to its customers the same as any other business. If it ignores the fundamental rules of business it will, quite simply, cease to exist, and any mission potential of the business will be moot. It is axiomatic that in BAM there is no long-term kingdom impact unless there is a real, viable, profitable business.

While the financial bottom line is an imperative to sustainability and credibility, it would be a mistake to conceive of a BAM company as simply a financing mechanism for doing mission. The very existence of the business in a community helps meet the community's needs. It creates jobs that pay wages, that gives people purchasing power, which in turn stimulates the economy by helping produce profits for other businesses. This multiplier concept is well known by economists and is a basic building block in economic development.

For example, give a woman employee of the BAM business $100 and she spends half buying food at the market and the other half buying clothes for her children. This gives the food merchant and the tailor each $50 they would not otherwise have had. They then spend their money in various ways, creating income and wealth for still other people. The usual multiplier can be as much as five to ten times the wage, that is, a wage of $100 will produce $500 to $1,000 of economic growth in the community.

While it should be obvious to all, it bears emphasizing that simply giving money to an individual as a gift, even with the best Christian charitable or altruistic intentions, is not the same. While admirable, a gift is usually a one-time gesture or, at best, short-term assistance. It will not produce the same steady, reliable revenue stream that is so necessary to help people overcome their economic poverty. The gift is also devoid of many of the other intangibles that come with having gainful employment and may even be demeaning and insulting.

The business also teaches people a marketable trade and management skills and helps them enhance their career potential. Those who have been without a job, as so many people in the developing world have, understand that there is so much more to a job than a paycheck. There is a sense of dignity, of belonging, of self-worth and pride that comes with being wanted and needed— and knowing that people are willing to pay good money for their labor. Hope replaces fear. Enthusiasm replaces depression. Smiles replace tears. Productive citizens replace outcast discontents. Jobs also give people a stake in the stability of a society and in helping communities become healthier, happier, more peaceful places to live. Stability is a priceless commodity in civilization and is a prerequisite for economic development and effective BAM outreach.

In summary, the BAM business, which exists because of its positive financial bottom line, is both a platform for mission outside of the business and a sanctuary—a refuge—within which mission and ministry is performed. In that sense, it is like the old Spanish missions in California: both an influential presence of God within the community at large, ministering outside of its walls, and also a safe haven internally, meeting people's needs within its wall. In truth, both the internal and external mission components of a BAM business depend upon a healthy financial bottom line.

CORPORATE SOCIAL RESPONSIBILITY

In recent years many secular businesses have recognized that good business requires more than mindless, even heartless service to the financial bottom line. It also involves leveraging their company and its resources to help the local community in which they do business. Companies that have moved toward this new frontier have created a business movement called "Corporate Social Responsibility" or CSR. Some CSR companies are motivated by pure altruism while others see it as a moral obligation. In so doing, each builds on earlier business traditions that say a business that makes its living from a community needs to be a "good corporate citizen" and to give something of value back to the community.

While altruism and morality drive certain segments of the CSR movement, other companies practice CSR more cynically. They see CSR programs as just another marketing tool that makes good business sense. To them the CSR programs might build the life of the community, but more importantly, in so doing they also build the company's business image and reputation, promote its long-term sustainability, and thereby ultimately build its business profits.

In the end, whether motivated by altruism, profits or just plain greed, all CSR managers have to weigh their community-minded activities by the impact on their financial bottom line. Good works are not free. They require the use of company resources that drain bank accounts and strain profit margins. They must also be justified to the company directors, investors and shareholders. This tension between CSR programs and the financial bottom line is inherent in every CSR setting. Unfortunately, all too often, if the CSR program doesn't add to the financial bottom line or doesn't feather an important stakeholder's nest, it doesn't fly. CSR is not, after all, the primary reason for a secular company's existence.

Triple Bottom Lines

To its credit the CSR movement has spawned innovative experiments that are helping communities and people worldwide. One good example is Cascade Engineering Company in Grand Rapids, Michigan, which recognizes that it must keep a financial bottom line, but has expanded its corporate agenda to include two other bottom lines: A *social* bottom line and an *environmental* bottom line. All aspects of Cascade's corporate life have been focused on identifying, defining, promoting and achieving the goals and objectives under each of three bottom lines. Of necessity, they must also harmonize the tensions that inevitably exist among these bottom lines as they compete for the same limited company resources.

Balancing these three bottom lines has not been easy or always possible. In fact, there have been many false steps and even outright failures along the way. Nonetheless, Cascade's leadership has boldly persisted and through considerable trial and error is now achieving a high level of success in all three. In fact, it has been so successful in its approach that it has formed a for-profit consulting subsidiary, Quest—Sustainable Solutions, that will work with other CSR-minded companies to institute their own triple bottom lines.

Cascade's annual Triple Bottom Line Report is available on their website, and it is truly impressive.[6] The company's host of public-service awards attests to the effectiveness of its efforts and to the good works that it is doing both within the firm and within the community.

Given our current BAM emphasis, it is important to note that although Cascade is led by a devout Christian team, the CEO admits that he is not intentionally giving his CSR program a Christian spin or brand. Although personally motivated by Scripture, he has chosen not to be overt about his or the

---

[6]"The Cascade Engineering 2005 Triple Bottom Line Report," Cascade Engineering, Grand Rapids, 2005 <www.cascading.com/sus/triple.htm>.

company's Christian witness or motivation.[7] This may prompt mission-minded Christians to ask, "Although the public sees his good works, no one knows the true source or motivation. Then, is it fair to say that they glorify the Father in heaven?" On the other hand, others query, "Is it fair to say that they don't? Or to even judge them?"

MULTIPLE BOTTOM LINES

For a company to intentionally move from a strictly secular business model, even one focused on CSR, to a kingdom model requires a deliberate, prayerful, planning approach. While secular companies, by delivering quality goods and services to meet the needs of a community, can have definite kingdom impact, such results are only a byproduct of the company's primary reason for being: increasing shareholder wealth. That is, the businesses are profit-driven, not kingdom-driven.

On the other hand, the BAM business, while motivated by the necessity of producing profits, nonetheless has other bottom lines which are equally important to the company. Mats Tunehag has suggested that a BAM Company also has a triple bottom line: financial, social and spiritual.[8] At the time of writing, this was insightful and arguably groundbreaking, but today it seems far too limited. It is more likely that the true BAM Company will have a variety of multiple bottom lines, depending on its location, contextual opportunities, products, business model and mission calling. Further, multiple bottom lines will evolve as God uses the innate gifts and creativity of believers in business to push the limits of current thinking.

Identifying BAM's bottom lines. At the heart of any BAM business is the concept of the multiple bottom lines. Defining the multiple bottom lines that are peculiar to each company is a primary responsibility of the company's executive team. From a generic perspective it is appropriate to speak of at least four bottom lines that are essential for a BAM Company, each of which needs a different measurable or metric. Briefly, those bottom lines are the financial, social, environmental and kingdom bottom lines.

First, the *financial* bottom line is the traditional bottom line driving most

---

[7]Fred P. Keller, chairman and CEO, Cascade Engineering, remarks made to visiting scholars, including the author, Grand Rapids, July 20, 2007.

[8]Mats Tunehag, "God Means Business! An Introduction to Business as Mission, BAM," unpublished monograph, 2008, p. 8.

businesses: making a profit for the shareholders. This is also an essential bottom line in any BAM Company, since the company must first be a viable, sustainable business if it is to remain in existence and have the capability of supporting or doing mission.

The financial bottom line is traditionally measured in money by the company's chief financial officer (CFO) and will include various ratios to indicate the health of a company as an investment. Of those ratios, return on investment or ROI, is probably paramount to the investor, who will ask how much profit was made on his or her money. That is, for every dollar invested, how many dollars of profit did he or she make, expressed as a percentage? For example, for $100 invested, a company makes $15 over a given period of time, giving it a 15 percent ROI. For simplicity, and because it is the currency of choice in business globally, we use the U.S. dollar and call the collective, generic metric for the financial bottom line its $-ROI.

Second, the *social* bottom line(s) comes from the peace and justice themes of the Bible and the basic Christian faith. A meager but poignant sampling of these dominant biblical themes is instructive:

> And what does the Lord require of you?
> To act justly and to love mercy
> and to walk humbly with your God. (Mic 6:8)

> Seek justice,
> encourage the oppressed.
> Defend the cause of the fatherless,
> plead the case of the widow. (Is 1:17)

> This is what the Lord Almighty says: "Administer true justice; show mercy and compassion to one another. Do not oppress the widow or the fatherless, the alien or the poor. In your hearts do not think evil of each other." (Zech 7:9-10)

> Defend the cause of the weak and fatherless;
> maintain the rights of the poor and oppressed.
> Rescue the weak and needy;
> deliver them from the hand of the wicked. (Ps 82:3-4)

> Do not withhold good from those who deserve it,

when it is in your power to act. (Prov 3:27)

This is the first and greatest commandment. And the second is like it: "Love your neighbor as yourself." All the Law and the Prophets hang on these two commandments. (Mt 22:38-40)

These verses are perhaps the signature Scripture for holistic business as mission. Jesus said,

For I was hungry and you gave me something to eat, I was thirsty and you gave me something to drink, I was a stranger and you invited me in, I needed clothes and you clothed me, I was sick and you looked after me, I was in prison and you came to visit me. . . .

I tell you the truth, whatever you did for one of the least of these brothers of mine, you did for me. . . .

[And] whatever you did not do for one of the least of these, you did not do for me. (Mt 25:35-36, 40, 45)

In *Christ Outside the Gates*, noted missiologist and theologian Orlando E. Costas addresses these themes when he describes the difficulties in mission theology today. In so doing, he supports the scriptural mandate for a social bottom line for BAM. Costas is seriously concerned about the Western, Eurocentric bias of today's theology of mission and pointedly says that he is speaking as an outsider (etic) to bring a new perspective. His view is from outside the gates of the "holy city" (where Jesus was crucified), "outside the gate of a comfortable and secure ecclesiastical compound." As such, it is an attempt "to articulate the reality of rejection and marginalization of the Latin American peoples, the Hispanic community in the United States, and all oppressed women, men, and children everywhere."[9]

---

[9] Orlando E. Costas, *Christ Outside the Gate: Mission Beyond Christendom* (Maryknoll, N.Y.: Orbis, 1982), pp. xiv, 194. Costas (1942-1987) is perhaps my favorite missiologist and theologian, next to Charles Van Engen. Costas's biography is remarkable, but especially for such a young man— he died of stomach cancer when he was only forty-five. He was a "pastor, missionary to Latin America, community organizer, internationally known missiologist, contextual theologian and theological educator. He was Thornley B. Wood Professor of Missiology and director of Hispanic Studies and Ministries at Eastern Baptist Theological Seminary, and later the Judson Professor of Missiology and dean of the Andover Newton School of Theology, and was an ordained minister in the American Baptist Churches, USA, and the United Church of Christ." See a more complete account of his inspiring story in the biography by Elizabeth Conde-Frazier, "Orlando E. Costas," Talbot School of Theology <www.talbot.edu/ce20/educators/view.cfm?n=orlando_costas>.

Costas articulates a theology that came to be known as Liberation Theology. While it led to excesses that in hindsight are regrettable, the basic point he makes underscores the reason for BAM companies going into the world. Costas argues that mission is not an academic matter but must speak into "concrete life situations."[10] Van Engen fully concurs, saying mission must be done in the streets where people live or it is not truly mission.[11] Writing in 1982, Costas prophetically saw the dangers of globalization and blatantly warned that there are major areas of human and demonic oppression in which spiritual warfare is raging and Christ's gospel is desperately needed. If mission does not reach into those areas, he says it has failed.

> [The world is] a complex web of institutions that need to be called to accountability by the new order of life. . . . It is a network of global relationships that determines the life of people and their institutions, that deforms God's creation and opposes the work of his kingdom. Such a demonic and oppressive network needs to be resisted by God's People and overcome by the liberating power of the gospel as it is incarnated in concrete life situations.[12]

BAM is a direct response to this call to liberate the oppressed. Its primary focus is in nations and with people groups that are hopelessly mired in poverty. Their primary pain is often economic, and by creating jobs with wages and hope BAM companies are directly engaged in their liberation. But there is so much more to holistic BAM mission. We call it community development, but in reality, it is an acknowledgment that we Christians are called to use the resources that the Lord has placed in our hands for good, not evil, and to build up people, institutions and cities, not to tear them down. We are called to action to help people holistically improve their lives and to see Jesus as the source of that transformation. One major tool for accomplishing that is BAM and its social bottom line.

A laundry list of social goals that has been adopted by BAM companies

---

[10]Ibid.
[11]Charles Van Engen, "Mission *of, in* and *on* the Way," in *Footprints of God: A Narrative Theology of Mission*, eds. Charles Van Engen, Nancy Thomas, and Robert Gallagher (Monrovia, Calif.: MARC, 1999), pp. xvii-xxviii; and Charles Van Engen, *Mission on the Way: Issues in Mission Theology* (Grand Rapids: Baker, 1996).
[12]Costas, *Christ Outside the Gate*, p. 172.

would be as varied and infinite as the social needs and cultural contexts the companies operate in. These business social practices are areas of needed future research and undoubtedly will include such goals as employee health and prenatal care, employee family health (perhaps, a family bottom line?), nutrition and literacy programs, child care centers, educational programs, help for the community's handicapped, employing the community's untouchables, training the community's unemployed or underemployed youth, drilling for clean potable water, business incubators, drug and rehabilitation centers, and building projects like schools, parks, athletic fields, and paved roads.

Note that these are examples of goals a company may *choose* to pursue, based on the needs of its environment, the context of the company and its financial, human, and managerial capacity to support such efforts. The point is, these things will not happen unless the company's management and ownership intentionally decide to set such goals for the company and then take steps to institutionalize the means by which those goals can be met. Ironically, many companies that initially resisted the social bottom line are now finding that it is good stewardship, good Christian witness *and* can also be good business.

How the company measures its social bottom line will depend entirely on the project or events that the company chooses to engage. It is not a difficult task: look at the specific project or event and determine what outcome or results you want to achieve. After that, determine what the significant benchmarks or stages are in the process of reaching those results. If it is a building project, the relevant measurements might be (1) what is accomplished, (2) by what date, and (3) at what cost. If it is employing the handicapped or training people in job skills, then the measure will undoubtedly be in terms of people engaged, impacted, trained and placed in permanent jobs. Again, these numbers should be broken into significant benchmarks or stages. For example, a training program might look at the number of people contacted for a particular class, the number responding, enrolling, starting the class, successfully completing the class, finding gainful employment, the cost of the entire program, the cost per student completing the class, and the key ratios (e.g., the number contacted to the number enrolling; the number starting to the number finishing; the number finishing to the number employed).

Third, the *environmental* (or "green") bottom line commits the company to assess the environmental impact, both negative and positive, of every aspect of the company's operations and to manage it in a manner that is environmentally friendly—even protective, proactive and enhancing. Such environmental stewardship goals are fully consistent with Christian values and are an implicit part of the cultural mandate to be good stewards of the earth.

Environmental bottom lines are measured similarly to the social bottom lines. The social goals are often community projects, but they do not exist for themselves. They may be measured by the project's *people impact*, asking perhaps, How many people were served? So too the green goals may be measured in *earth impact*, asking perhaps, How many tons of paper were recycled? or How many gallons of water were saved? In both instances, the benchmarking process discussed under social bottom lines is the best approach. Look at the end results, certainly, but the progress along the way is also significant—measure goal-achievement victories and define sub-bottom lines.

Fourth, the *kingdom (or mission)* bottom line, being both the primary *raison d'être* for the BAM Company and the most complex bottom line, deserves greater discussion. First and foremost, it is a set of specifically identified measurable goals that have an intentional impact for the kingdom of God (i.e., a kingdom impact). These goals are arrived at through a process of examining the company, its personnel, products, locations, markets, networks and resources, and through focused prayer, determining what God would have the company do to accomplish these. Because of the critical nature of these bottom lines to the BAM Company's mission, the next section and the next several chapters (especially chap. 13 on kingdom impact and chaps. 15-16 on functional analysis) will flesh out what a kingdom bottom line looks like, how it is implemented for obtaining results and how it is measured.

Reconciling BAM's bottom lines. All four bottom lines describe multiple goals that the company hopes to achieve during a specified period of time, usually one year. Whereas the social and environmental goals are very narrowly construed and apply to specialized areas of the company's activities, the financial and kingdom goals are general in nature and cut across the entire spectrum of company activities. The financial bottom line is limited in its own way, however, in that it solely addresses the monetary resources that the company has to accomplish all of its goals.

On the other hand, the kingdom bottom line encompasses and permeates all of the other bottom lines, including the financial, and seeks to address the holistic kingdom impact implicit in both (1) the actual accomplishment of each of the other bottom lines (the ends), and (2) the actions taken toward meeting those bottom lines (the means). Take, for example, a company's choice of how to package its product. The financial and environmental goals should require an examination of alternative product packaging options for their relative environmental impacts. The kingdom bottom line asks, Other than the kingdom benefit of efficient use of resources and good stewardship of the earth (which is good and worthy), what other kingdom impacts, if any, might be achieved in this decision? Could the package be used for other holistic mission purposes, for example, carrying educational, health or nutritional information; promoting local churches, NGOs or community events/projects; or proclaiming gospel truths?

This simplistic illustration highlights the special, all-encompassing nature of the kingdom bottom line. It requires an assessment of everything the company does and an inquiry into what greater kingdom impact the company could have through that function or activity. It may also include direct evangelism or discipleship (through company-initiated and driven programs) or indirect efforts (e.g., through partnership with local churches or ministries). Examples might include Bible studies, prayer walks, conversions, baptisms, discipleship programs, church planting, support for local churches and mission agencies, increased ethical standards and practices, daily prayer over company offices, counseling for employees and their families, instituting a corporate chaplaincy, revising corporate human relations or safety manuals, standards and practices to reflect sound biblical principles or sponsorship of Promise Keepers, Character First, or community transformation events. The list is as infinite as the Lord's leading and as finite as the company's resources— and faith.

In short, the company examines itself and makes deliberate choices to obtain specific kingdom results through its operations, products and presence, balanced by its capacity. This tension between the company's capacity—financial, human, time—and its desired goals, and between its capacity and its calling, is the "stuff" BAM Company managers must continually contend with. It calls for tough decisions, focused prayer and spiritual discernment.

This is made even more difficult by Henry Blackaby's challenge that God's people should not be limited by their physical resources and human capacities. Rather they should seek God's leading and call, then have a "faith goal" that is beyond human reach but wholly within God's capacity *if* the company's faith is strong enough.[13]

Measuring BAM's bottom lines. The kingdom bottom line must also be measurable if it is to be sustainable and to allow discrete, meaningful evaluation of the underlying programs. How it is measured will depend on the nature of the company activity or function that is being examined, but generically it can be referred to as the kingdom impact, or the kingdom return on investment—the K-ROI, if you will. The K-ROI will vary widely depending on the function or activity addressed. Stated differently, we are accustomed to speaking of the dollar return on investment, $-ROI, as a guiding principle to improve the efficiency of a company and to inform its major managerial decisions. We suggest that the BAM Company should do the same thing—to infuse K-ROI thinking into every aspect of the company so that it permeates its corporate DNA. To that end, the financial, social and environmental bottom lines must have identifiable and measurable K-ROI goals and objectives, as well as $-ROI.

Notice that having a K-ROI does not override or preclude the $-ROI. Quite the contrary. As explained earlier, in order to have a long-term, sustainable, viable business, a positive $-ROI must be maintained. It is not only a *sine qua non* for survivability, but a reality check on what can actually be accomplished in the K-ROI programs, absent extraordinary divine intervention.

The two ROIs will, however, always be in tension. Resolving that tension is the challenge of any Christian-led management team, since these two ROIs must co-exist in harmony and balance. The company is not a church and should not seek to be one. The company is, however, owned by God (all things are his) and should seek to maximize its potential for kingdom impact in every aspect of its being.

Summary. Christian-led companies that want to have a kingdom impact will need to go beyond the traditional single bottom line and define their additional bottom line categories and kingdom goals. Whether those bottom

---

[13]Personal discussions with Blackaby, as well as his classic, Henry T. Blackaby and Claude V. King, *Experiencing God* (Nashville: Southern Baptist Convention Sunday School Board, 1990).

lines are two, three or more, it is essential that they be specified, quantifiable and measurable. Vague goals that have no way to benchmark progress or to measure attainment are not goals, they are only wishes, hopes and dreams. While valuable, they do not form the basis for a deliberate, effective, long-term, sustainable program for kingdom impact.

Each company, large or small, should assess its bottom lines at least annually. This not only allows the company to see its progress toward established goals and to lay its plans for the coming year, but it allows an opportunity to publicly or semi-publicly proclaim the vision and values of the BAM Company. This is customarily done through the company's annual report, which specifies each bottom line and then recites the specific results toward attaining those goals. This report will usually be addressed to the major stakeholders, but with a BAM Company greater dissemination may be desirable.

The relationship among the various bottom lines in a BAM Company is graphically illustrated in figure 12.1.

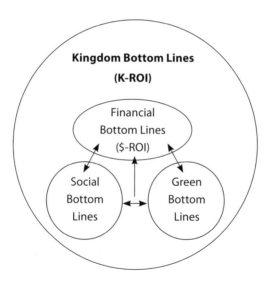

Figure 12.1. Multiple bottom lines

Is BAM Merely a Christian CSR?

Since BAM bears remarkable resemblance to some of the best practices of companies in the corporate social responsibility movement, we must ask whether, in reality, BAM is merely a Christian-led CSR movement. While this in itself is not a bad thing—far from it—we believe that BAM is something much more. There are at least four primary distinctions: First, the purpose of the BAM business and the intentionality of its CEO and BAM team are quite different. They are focused on Jesus and the promotion of his gospel *in deed as well as word* as the driving force and reason for the business. They are choosing to do business as a vehicle for holistic mission outreach, not to do good works as a sideline to doing business. Often the difference is subtle, but it is very real and can make the difference in the business's long-term success and survivability. Where a CSR company would choose to continue in business and to make money without the CSR component, the BAM business would not. BAM's purpose is the good-works component; the money-making component is merely the engine that moves the vehicle, not its reason for existence.

Second, the BAM team's overall commitment to be a Kingdom Company, and ultimately a Great Commission Company, requires an overt commitment to manage the business by biblical principles and for the glory of God. That is a daunting task in itself. On the other hand, a Christian-led CSR company (C-CSR) like Cascade may be scripturally managed and motivated, but they believe that giving overt credit to the Lord poses unacceptable business risks and is somehow counterproductive. That may be true given their context and industry, as there is always a price to publicly proclaiming our allegiance to Jesus the Christ. There are also drawbacks, however, to being a closet Christian, especially where the company has high community visibility. How the community and the employees view senior management and its motivations is a testimony in itself. If it is a testimony only to a humanistic program like CSR, that leaves little room for God and certainly diminishes his glory.

BAM companies recognize this and do not usually overtly proselytize. Instead, they make it known in their personal and professional daily speech, actions, lifestyles, management styles, decisions and testimonies that they are ardent followers of Jesus and are doing their best to conduct all aspects of the business in a manner worthy of his gospel. That includes the goals, objectives and actions to achieve each of the company's multiple bottom lines.

A third way that BAM companies are distinct from C-CSR companies is their kingdom impact. It seems axiomatic that a different focus produces a different kingdom impact. Christian CSR companies, by the very definition of their secular bottom lines, exclude any conscious goal of having an intentional kingdom impact. BAM companies' primary goal, on the other hand, is for each and every bottom line to serve a kingdom value and have a defined, God-pleasing kingdom impact.

Fourth, if a BAM Company were a C-CSR, "CSR" should probably stand for corporate *spiritual* responsibility, not corporate *social* responsibility. CSR, by its very nature—even where motivated by Scripture, as in the case of Cascade, is not focused on improving the community's life to directly promote God's glory and the furtherance of his kingdom. CSR is doing good works for the purpose of doing good works, which is certainly admirable, but glory to God, if any, is only an indirect byproduct.

BAM, on the other hand, is doing good works as a natural fruit of the Spirit, or as the book of James would say, as *evidence* of our faith and as a light that leads people to Christ (Jas 2:14-26, esp. v. 20). Jesus commanded, "Let your light so shine before men that they may see your good works, and glorify your Father which is in heaven" (Mt 5:16 KJV; see also Jn 14:11-12). Note that the good works are not for their own purposes—an end in themselves—but rather a means to promote God's glory and to lead people to a desire to know him.

A NEW SECULAR-SACRED DIVIDE?

While this division of bottom lines—especially separating out the kingdom bottom lines—may be suspect as perpetuating the secular-sacred divide, I hasten to emphatically deny this. In fact, the opposite is true. The kingdom bottom line is necessary as a separate component of the company's major goals. Otherwise, in the rush of ordinary daily business, it will inevitably be watered down, polluted or lost altogether. To ignore the reality of this human tendency toward slippage and degradation is to sow the seeds of unsustainability, drift, destruction or futility into the business's kingdom impact. Therefore, quite paradoxically, to avoid the secular-sacred trap and to assure kingdom impact, it is essential for the company to have a separate, distinct, defined kingdom bottom line that directly engages all other company bottom lines (and all efforts to obtain those bottom lines). In short, to be a BAM Company, there must be a sustained effort to eventually have a measurable K-ROI on every aspect of the company's operations and every bottom line, goal, objective and means.

DISCUSSION QUESTIONS

1. What does *profit* mean to you? Is profit inherently sinful? What caused the church's stereotype of profits? Is the view justified, even partially?

2. Should every business have a financial bottom line? Why or why not? Support your opinion with Scripture.

3. Which of the bottom lines discussed in the text challenges your thinking the most? Why? Which one bothers or even irritates you the most? Why? What other bottom lines might be legitimate primary goals for BAM companies?

4. Given the Scriptures on social justice, should a BAM Company have a political bottom line as Costas intimates? Why or why not? What would such a bottom line look like in actual company goals and actions? Would it make a difference where the company is located (e.g., a BAM Company in inner-city Los Angeles versus one in today's China, in South Africa during apartheid or Germany during Hitler's regime)? Why?

5. The author argues that BAM is not simply a form of Christian CSR. Do you agree? Why or why not? How would a non-believing businessperson view this author's arguments? Why is this important?

6. BAM engagement: How will you be intentional about incorporating multiple bottom lines into your company, workplace or job? Describe the possibilities.

13

KINGDOM IMPACT

"I am the true vine, and my Father is the gardener.
He cuts off every branch in me that bears no fruit,
while every branch that does bear fruit he prunes
so that it will be even more fruitful."
JOHN 15:1-2

"By their fruit you will recognize them. . . . [E]very good
tree bears good fruit, but a bad tree bears bad fruit."
MATTHEW 7:16-17

"The ax is already at the root of the trees,
and every tree that does not produce good fruit
will be cut down and thrown into the fire."
MATTHEW 3:10

"And we pray this in order that you may live a life worthy
of the Lord and may please him in every way: bearing fruit
in every good work, growing in the knowledge of God."
COLOSSIANS 1:10

IT SEEMS SIMPLE ENOUGH TO SAY whether something has a positive impact for the kingdom of God on earth, but on closer analysis, kingdom impact can be a very tricky, even elusive matter. It has as much to do with the intent of the actor as it does with the consequences for those acted upon. It may also have no immediately perceived benefit, and yet have profound long-range effect. On the other hand, it may have immediate consequences that

seem good and come from right intentions but that naively result in significant long-term or secondary harm.

Regardless of its nuances, kingdom impact is central to all that a BAM
Company does. Without kingdom impact there is no eternal fruit to show for
the missionary labor. Without an intentional kingdom impact there is no
Christian distinctive that differentiates the KC or BAM Company from its
secular counterparts. Stated positively, kingdom impact is the major goal that
a BAM Company seeks, and it is the measure of the fruit that a BAM Company produces.

Examining the concept of kingdom impact broadly, we will look at its role
in management, especially in the crucial areas of planning and decision making. Examining kingdom impact at the operational level, we will look at its
role in the functional analysis approach to planning outlined in chapters fifteen to sixteen.

PILLARS OF MANAGEMENT

A detailed discussion of basic business principles is hardly necessary since the
bookstores and libraries are filled with works on virtually every aspect of
management. Unfortunately, however, few of those books are written from an
overtly Christian perspective or even a biblical worldview. And yet, the Bible
is filled with advice on each one. As Steve Marr notes, "The Bible is still the
best business book!"[1]

Bob Briner heartily concurs, "I examined the principles of Jesus—the greatest manager ever . . . and the Bible—the greatest business manual ever."[2] So do
Ken Blanchard, Bill Hybels and Phil Hodges in *Leadership by the Book*, where
they speak of both Scripture and "the leadership genius of Jesus."[3] Many others have studied Scripture through "business eyes" and drawn the same conclusion. Larry Burkett, for example, pioneered the investigation of business
principles in modern times, published *Business by the Book* and launched two
ministries to teach those principles. He says,

I can tell you with certainty that the business school I attended taught

---

[1] Steve Marr, *Business Proverbs* (Grand Rapids: Revell, 2001), p. 3.
[2] Bob Briner, *Business Basics from the Bible* (Grand Rapids: Zondervan, 1996), p. 12.
[3] Ken Blanchard, Bill Hybels and Phil Hodges, *Leadership by the Book* (New York: Waterbrook,
1999), p. xii.

the bottom line: If it doesn't make money, forget it. But since graduating from business school I have been studying another text book: It's called the Bible. . . . I am not the first person to discover the principles of business taught in God's word. In America the use of the Bible as a business text goes back hundreds of years. . . . Prior to the twentieth century, business courses, and indeed law schools themselves, were based on biblical principles.[4]

It is generally recognized that there are five basic pillars of business management: decision making and planning, organizing, leading and directing, coordinating, and controlling. While a theological exegesis of each of these pillars is far beyond the scope of this book, two of the pillars—decision making and planning—are foundational to every other pillar and deserve special comment. Why? Because without good, consistent, God-honoring decision making and planning, there will be little if any long-term sustainable kingdom impact by the BAM Company.

Decision making. Decision making is never value neutral. Whether decision makers realize it or not, they examine a problem within a value context that makes up their own personal worldview. Those values may be Western, Asian, African or Latin; Christian, Muslim, Buddhist, Hindu, humanist or secular; and they may be driven by personal ambition, national fervor, racist hatred or humanitarian altruism. They may be good or evil, but they are never neutral.

Decisions are, perhaps, the key element in life. Our lives are the sum total of all of our decisions, large and small. Think of the thousands of decisions we make each day: from the functional decisions like what to wear, where to go, where to work, how to do my job, what to eat and which direction to turn the car, to the more important, life-altering decisions like where (and whether) to go to college, which profession (vocation) to pursue, who to marry, what job to take, and whether to become a follower of Jesus Christ.

The same can be said of a business. There is virtually no important aspect of its existence that was not the direct or indirect result of someone's decision. Even accidents and events that are beyond our control are usually the product of another person's decisions. The only real exceptions are natural disasters

---

[4]Larry Burkett, *Business by the Book* (Nashville: Thomas Nelson, 1998), p. 4.

like hurricanes, tornadoes, earthquakes, tsunamis and droughts, which are euphemistically called "acts of God."

That being so, the CEO who is intentional about leading a BAM Company will want his or her decisions to be the best, and, like Solomon, will want to seek God's wisdom. In that regard, Proverbs gives the CEO excellent advice on wisdom for business and life. A commentary on Proverbs 2:1-11 summarizes Solomon's definition of wisdom as "the ability to consistently make right choices—choices that are just, fair and moral."[5] Given this subject's paramount importance, it seems appropriate that we briefly survey some of the other standards that contemporary Christians have urged upon the business community. Certainly this offering is only a small limb from a gigantic oak. It does, however, give the CEO a taste of the judgments that must be made in setting the decision-making standards that will guide the company's future.

Core values. In the process of determining the guiding core values of a Christian-led company, the CEO and executive team will be setting boundaries on their future decisions and all company policies. It is invariably an ongoing, never-ending process of refinement, but once the basic overall boundaries are in place they (1) begin to define the company's true character and culture and (2) establish a standard against which decisions are to be made and judged. This is not a checklist, formula or litmus test, but rather a code to live and manage by.[6]

It must be noted that the infinite variety and complexity of decisions that must be made each business day make all generic core value statements necessarily incomplete. For the BAM Company, that means that in addition to weighing each new decision against the core values, the leadership may be required to take a fresh journey of exploration into Scripture. That will, of course, depend on the CEO's spiritual maturity and biblical literacy, but even the most mature will find that Christian business peer groups and spiritual boards of directors are extremely valuable. Wise counsel is invariably needed—and is scripturally encouraged—in every aspect of decision making and, hence, in every aspect of life.

Honoring Christ. Beyond the company's core values, it is a truism that each of

---

[5]Sid Buzzell, Kenneth Boa and Bill Perkins, eds., *The Leadership Bible: Contemporary Leadership Principles from God's Word* (Grand Rapids: Zondervan, 1998), p. 730.
[6]For a more complete discussion and listing of sample core values see chap. 9.

the key elements of business is, from conception to implementation, determined and fashioned by decisions. If an individual or a company sincerely desires to honor Christ in all aspects of life, then the place to begin is with the quality of the decisions they are called to make. With each decision, large and small, the decision maker needs to ask such questions as, Who/what is directly and indirectly impacted by the decision? How? How, if at all, does this decision (and the actions that emanate from it) honor Christ? How does Scripture inform me about making a wise, God-honoring choice in this situation? What do my godly counselors advise me to do, and what is the basis for their advice?

What would Jesus do? As discussed earlier, over one hundred years ago Charles Shelton advocated making every personal and business decision by asking and answering one simple question, "What would Jesus do?" The book and its challenge were so powerful that it is still in print today and has sold over thirty million copies.[7] Many Christians wear bracelets, T-shirts and lanyards imprinted with *WWJD*. Sheldon's premise, that the WWJD standard could be successfully applied to Christian-led businesses, led to the founding of the Fellowship of Companies for Christ (FCCI) by Atlanta businessman Bobbie Mitchell over twenty-five years ago. Today, FCCI (now known as Christ@Work) is perhaps the largest, most influential marketplace ministry in America and is seeking to expand to all parts of the globe. The WWJD standard has served FCCI businessmen and women well over the past three decades and should be taken seriously by any BAM Company CEO.

The Four-Way Test. Rotary International, the world's first service club of business leaders worldwide, has over 1.2 million members in 32,000 clubs in virtually every nation on earth. Among its primary purposes is the constant promotion of ethical business practices and decision making in every society and nation in every cultural and religious context. It has adopted a standard called "The Four-Way Test." The test says that in every business decision, "in all we say, think or do" we must ask four questions:

1. Is it the truth?

2. Is it fair to all concerned?

3. Will it build goodwill and better friendships?

---

[7]Charles M. Sheldon, *In His Steps: What Would Jesus Do?* (New Kensington, Penn.: Whitaker, 1979).

4. Will it be beneficial to all concerned?

The test specifies that if the decision maker cannot answer all four questions in the affirmative, it is not a wise decision, and the contemplated action should be rethought, revised or discarded. Decisions made in violation of any one of the four standards, Rotarians have found, are always bad decisions in the long run.

According to the test's author, Herbert J. Taylor, it was God-inspired and the result of purposeful prayer.

> We [Taylor's company] believed that "In right there is might" and we determined to do our best to always be right. Our industry, as was true of scores of other industries, had a code of ethics—but the code was too long, almost impossible to memorize, and therefore impractical. . . .
>
> One day in July 1932, I decided to pray about the matter. That morning I leaned over my desk and asked God to give us a simple guide to help us think, speak and do that which was right. I immediately picked up a white card and wrote out The 4-Way Test.[8]

Shortly thereafter, Taylor discussed The Four-Way Test with four businessmen: a Presbyterian, a Roman Catholic, a Christian Scientist and an Orthodox Jew. All four agreed that the test "not only coincided with their religious ideals, but that if constantly applied in business, they should result in greater success and progress" and that all of a business's "proposed plans, policies, statements and advertising" should always be checked first against the test to see that it is satisfied.[9]

In the years since its adoption, Rotary International has spread worldwide and has members from every religious group on earth. None have found any incongruence between The Four-Way Test and their religious tenets. For Christians, we find that The Four-Way Test is not only consistent with Scripture, but we are moved by the fact that Taylor, a committed Christian, penned it in answer to focused prayer. Certainly BAM Company CEOs and their executive leadership teams would be well advised to make this test a part of their decision-making filter.

---

[8]Herbert J. Taylor, "The 4-Way Test," Rotary International <www.rotary5440.org/4wayfldr .html>.
[9]Ibid.

Glad you asked. Another filtering matrix for sound business decisions has been graphically illustrated more in the violation than in the doing by such business scandals as Enron, WorldCom and Tyco. This contemporary filter is the "Glad you asked!" standard. It asks simply, If investigative reporters from *60 Minutes* arrive at the CEO's office and ask about a particular company practice, can the CEO honestly and enthusiastically say, "I'm really glad you asked about that! We are proud of what we have done and would like nothing better than to boast about it to you and America!" This standard is reputed to have been first employed in a governmental setting by the Secretary of the Air Force some years ago, but it certainly has great general applicability to business today, especially for Christian-led BAM companies.[10]

The maximizer principle. As a past district governor of Rotary International, I have been significantly influenced by the Four-Way Test and the "Glad you asked!" standard. I have, however, developed a decision-making criteria that goes beyond those standards. I call it my maximizer principle. It says that in making decisions I ask, Which of the alternatives before me will maximize (1) my personal growth, (2) my professional growth, (3) my spiritual growth, (4) the growth of those whom I love and (5) the positive impact on friends, work colleagues, society, humanity and the kingdom of God? We are born to continually grow and mature physically, mentally, emotionally and spiritually until we die. We are also expected by our Creator to make the most of the time, gifts, relationships and opportunities he has given us. "From everyone who has been given much, much will be demanded; and from the one who has been entrusted with much, much more will be asked" (Lk 12:48).

Applying the maximizer principle has led me to understand that when two roads diverge in the woods, as Frost says, we can take "the one less traveled by" or we can take the common, well-traveled path. So, too, by age fifty we can either have lived one year fifty times or lived fifty different years. We can maximize, minimize or moderate. We can, as Jesus said, be hot, cold or lukewarm—and he spits the lukewarm out of his mouth (Rev 3:16). I have chosen to maximize—to make decisions that hold the greatest promise of maximizing some key aspect of growth for me or those people or causes I care deeply about. I can state unequivocally that decisions made by this principle have

---

[10]C. Neal Johnson, "Glad You Asked," in *How to Succeed the Biblical Way*, ed. Ron Jenson (Wheaton, Ill.: Tyndale House, 1981), pp. 19-21.

invariably led me along the harder, more arduous path, but they have also led to a richer, more vital, vibrant, interesting life. So, think and pray on the choices you have, and find the decision-making standard that will maximize your opportunities to have the life you want. There are no guarantees in life, but whatever standard you select, do not short-change yourself by choosing one worthy of the gospel and person of Christ and the precious gift of life that the Lord has given you.

Holy worldliness. Richard Mouw, president of Fuller Theological Seminary, addressed a Christian consultation on ministry in daily life and spoke on what he calls "Holy Worldliness." He started by assuring the businesspeople in the audience that their business was as much a godly calling as being called to the pulpit, and that their businesses are full-time ministries as much as is his position or that of a pastor. He went on to share an approach to godly decision making that was somewhat unique but resonated with the audience. He noted that in each decision we make, if it is to be wise, we need to carefully define the reality of the context in which the decision is being made (i.e., contextualize the decision). But, he explained, in this "reality defining" exercise we need to be aware that both God and Satan are at work. They are engaged in a continual battle for the human spirit, and Satan as well as God seeks to influence our lives and hence our decisions.

Accordingly, Mouw borrowed a concept from his friend, David Tiede, president of Luther Seminary in St. Paul, Minnesota, and proposed that each business decision and its context be subjected to two additional questions. These questions are phrased in street language, he said, because they are meant for the street and not academic halls, for real life and not ivory-tower reflections on life. The first question is, What in *heaven's* name is going on here? This is, of course, to discern what God is up to in this circumstance. The second question is, What in the *hell* is happening? This is to remind us of Satan's presence, as well as his lies, tricks, deceits and desires to shape our decisions in destructive, self-wounding ways. That awareness will hopefully help the decision maker discern what Satan is up to in this circumstance.[11]

Dave Tiede said, "You know the language of the street that people use loosely and without thinking has theological significance. When someone

---

[11]Richard J. Mouw, "The Call to Holy Worldliness," Fourteenth Annual Consultation of Christian Ministry in Daily Life, keynote address, Pasadena, California: April 21, 2006.

says, 'What in the Hell is going on?' or, 'What in Heaven's name is going on?' they're pointing to two features of our theological reflection. That it is important for us to discern the hellishness of what's going on around us, including in our businesses and in our entertainment activities and the like, but also what in Heaven's name is going on?" And in every way, every day in our work, in our interactions, in public life, we need to be asking those two questions theologically, not out loud, of course.[12]

Other more sophisticated approaches have been taken, but none, I suspect, are as practical and useful as Sheldon's and Mouw's. They both emphasize that all of our decisions, regardless of circumstances, need to be Christ honoring, Bible based, Spirit filled and spiritually astute.

Planning. There is no formula for being an effective BAM Company. There are, however, choices that CEOs (and their leadership team) can make. If they want the company to have a kingdom impact, they must measure their own intentionality, commitment and resources, and then decide which of several courses they will take. The CEOs can approach the matter ad hoc on a daily basis or be more intentional and actually develop appropriate plans.

Corporate planning makes good business sense and is the starting place of every new business and an annual exercise by all successful, dynamic companies. This is absolutely true for CEOs who seek to make their companies into BAM companies. Kingdom impact does not happen on a regular, productive basis without prayerful, thoughtful planning. Without planning, any kingdom impact is, as Steve Rundle and Tom Steffen so artfully say, strictly serendipitous and purely by happenstance.[13]

CEOs have at their disposal several planning choices. On the one hand, the company's plans can be phased, the goals incrementally implemented and the action steps gradually incorporated into the company's operations. On the other hand, CEOs may choose to develop and implement a full-blown strategic master BAM plan. Each of these approaches will be examined at length later, but at this point, it is important to understand what Scripture says about planning, what levels of planning are available to the CEO, and that planning is crucial to kingdom impact.

---

[12]Ibid.
[13]Steve Rundle and Tom Steffen, *Great Commission Companies* (Downers Grove, Ill.: InterVarsity Press, 2003), p. 40.

Scriptural support for planning. Throughout the planning process, it is useful to turn to Scripture for guidance. Some businesspeople will be surprised to find that the Bible actually has a great deal to say in favor the planning. Here are some samples.

Solomon notes:

> The plans of the diligent lead to profit
> > as surely as haste leads to poverty. (Prov 21:5)

> Commit to the LORD whatever you do,
> > and your plans will succeed. (Prov 16:3)

> In his heart a man plans his course,
> > but the LORD determines his steps. (Prov 16:9)

Jesus speaks to the crowd:

> Suppose one of you wants to build a tower. Will he not first sit down and estimate the cost to see if he has enough money to complete it? For if he lays the foundation and is not able to finish it, everyone who sees it will ridicule him, saying, "This fellow began to build and was not able to finish." (Lk 14:28-30)

The Lord God himself is a planner:

> "For I know the plans I have for you," declares the LORD, "plans to prosper you and not to harm you, plans to give you hope and a future. Then you will call upon me and come and pray to me, and I will listen to you. You will seek me and find me when you seek me with all your heart." (Jer 29:11-13)

Paul commented on God's plan:

> In him [Jesus] we were also chosen, having been predestined according to the plan of him [the Lord] who works out everything in conformity with the purpose of his will. (Eph 1:11)

But the Lord warns:

> "Woe to the obstinate children,"
> > declares the LORD,

"to those who carry out plans that are not mine,
forming an alliance, but not by my Spirit,
heaping sin upon sin." (Is 30:1)

Clearly, our Lord recognizes the importance of planning and advises us to do so in all of our endeavors. On the secular side, there is considerable business literature advising businesses of the necessity of proper business planning. That is sound advice, backed by Scripture, for every BAM business on both the business and the mission aspects of its enterprise. But there is a caveat: a stern warning that all BAM planning, while necessary, is useless and void of true kingdom impact without God's direction, approval or will.

Continuum of BAM planning. The spectrum of approaches available to the CEO forms something akin to, but a step beyond, the Rundle-Steffen continuum of corporate intentionality previously described (see pp. 219-20). The difference is that this continuum of BAM planning speaks to how CEOs convert their intentionality into reality, how they move from good intentions to good actions. At one end of this continuum of BAM planning are those CEOs who elect to ease into BAM practices, to test the waters and move slowly and cautiously on an ad hoc basis. At the other end are those CEOs who have caught the full BAM vision and want to move ahead at flank speed, but with deliberate, thought-out, prayed-over, vetted plans. The ground between those polar extremes is populated by CEOs (and their companies) who, in one degree or another, are leading their companies toward kingdom goals gradually and incrementally, with an ever-increasing mixture of both ad-hoc methods and partial planning. The BAM planning continuum is represented in figure 13.1.

Figure 13.1. BAM planning continuum

It is important to reiterate that this continuum is *not* a hierarchy of holiness. Rather, it marks the stages of development in a company's pilgrimage. It is, however, a fact that some Christians in business seek to maximize the resources over which God has given them stewardship and others do not. For both groups, seeing the range of possibilities allows them to weigh their management alternatives and to assess which is appropriate for their companies. This is especially critical for those that want to realize their highest potential and maximize their company's kingdom impact.

The continuum focuses on planning because, as Rundle and Steffen correctly point out, that is perhaps the single most important factor that distinguishes a GCC or BAM Company from merely Christian-led companies. "Christian companies can and quite often do have a positive impact in their communities. But the process is usually more serendipitous than intentional. It is not *centrally coordinated* or the result of *planning,* equipping or accountability."[14] Effective planning, of course, includes proper attention to equipping one's people for mission and holding them accountable for the results.

Note that the BAM planning continuum is not for those CEOs who reject any method of deliberate, intentional faith integration. Rather, it assumes that each company on the continuum has made a decision to have a kingdom impact with its operations—to one degree or another. The remaining management decision, therefore, is determining where the company will initially (and ultimately) rest on the continuum. It is not an understatement to suggest that this decision is critical to the current and future success of the company. It represents a fundamental, often seismic, shift in company purpose, goals, focus, strategy, image and decision-making criteria.

Who makes the decision is, therefore, of major concern and will vary from company to company. It may be made individually by the CEO or in consultation with his or her leadership team or the board of directors. As noted above, their buy-in is a critical prerequisite to becoming a BAM Company. In making that decision, however, the CEO, executive team and board should be mindful of the observation made by Oswald Chambers:

> Every now and again, not often, but sometimes, God brings us to a point of climax. That is *the Great Divide in the life*; from that point we either go towards a more and more dilatory and useless type of Christian life, or we become more and more ablaze for the glory of God—My Utmost for His Highest.[15]

---

[14]Ibid. (emphasis added).
[15]Oswald Chambers, *My Utmost for His Highest* (Westwood, N.J.: Barbour, 1963), p. 362 (emphasis added).

I suggest that the decision about the company's level of commitment and place on the continuum may well be a similar point of climax—a great divide that separates (or not) this company from the pack.

Three approaches to kingdom impact. The process of planning how to identify and then integrate the kingdom bottom line into the other bottom lines is perhaps most easily done in the three complementary approaches. Each approach can be engaged individually from the outset, but for companies new to faith integration, engaging them sequentially, with each one building on the previous one, may be the preferred path. The choice is up to the BAM CEO and leadership team, but it is a choice that must be made if the company is to move deliberately into genuine faith integration.

The three optional choices are what I call the ad hoc approach, the incremental planning approach and the master planning approach. Each approach is a part of the BAM planning continuum. If the three are taken sequentially, the company will gradually move from left to right along the continuum. Virtually the only limiting factor is the company leadership's growth and maturity and its understanding and commitment to genuine faith integration.

1. The *ad hoc approach* means, as its name suggests, that something is done on an unplanned, case-by-case basis, each incidence is special, separate and distinct from every other incidence. Each is approached randomly, rather than as a preconceived, planned series of events or actions. It is limited to that situation and is usually temporary.

As an approach to BAM, the ad hoc method is primarily done on the job as each decision is made, each relationship is impacted and each opportunity is taken or lost. It is an unplanned mission or ministry outreach and is reactive rather than proactive.

Rather than focusing on projects, the ad hoc approach takes its cue from the second great commandment (love your neighbor) and looks at people and the ministry opportunities they present, almost moment by moment, encounter by encounter. It involves looking at all internal stakeholders (their people) from the board members to temporary employees, being sensitive to their needs and watching for opportunities to minister to them. In short, the ad hoc approach is a process of living out the faith in daily decisions, interactions and opportunities to engage people where they live and to make their lives better. Again, all of this must be balanced by the limited resources, capacity and constraints of maintaining and growing the business.

The kingdom impact of such practices is difficult to calculate because few attempts are made to quantify or measure them. Further, it is our experience that few CEOs who avoid a systematic, planned, purposeful approach to faith integration ever get beyond shallow, surface measures or have serious kingdom impact—and fewer still realize their dreams of becoming a Kingdom Company, much less a BAM Company, by the ad hoc approach.

Stated differently and without in any way diminishing the kingdom impact a CEO has on his company through these commendable ad hoc, case-by-case approaches, we want to suggest that there is another more effective way. This supplemental approach will not only augment the KC's efforts, but will help lead it far beyond the KC level toward becoming a BAM Company. Quite simply, that way is by *planning the company's kingdom impact*. This approach is not only foundational to all good management practices, but conforms both to common sense and to Scripture.

Lest I be misunderstood, I am advocating a planning approach *plus* an ad hoc approach, because any viable plan must incorporate the implicit concept of *planning for the unplanned*, spontaneous intervention of the Holy Spirit. That is, the plan must always create alertness to unplanned, spontaneous ad hoc opportunities for Christian service and kingdom impact.

2. The *incremental approach* to internal faith integration recognizes the old adage that *he who fails to plan, plans to fail*. Most business books strongly advise all businesses, from startups to international conglomerates, to develop detailed plans for their businesses. Unfortunately, many businesses pay lip-service to this and merely draft a token business plan, which they promptly put on a shelf to gather dust until the next year's planning exercise. For BAM companies, planning is certainly advisable for both the business and mission aspects of its enterprise. The more detailed the planning, the better.

How a gradualist, incremental planning approach works for a BAM Company depends greatly on the company's context, experience and resources. CEOs who want to be intentional about their BAM ambitions must examine the continuum of BAM planning and decide the initial, appropriate level of planning for their company. Then they must slowly, incrementally ratchet it up, closer and closer to the right end of the continuum, as experience, good sense and focused prayer dictate.

Initially, CEOs may be well-advised to take tentative baby steps into faith integration and to have the plan reflect limited faith goals that can be successfully met. Building on victories, CEOs should then gradually expand the nature and direction of the integration process. This is prudent and recommended. For existing companies, it gives the CEOs, their staff and other stakeholders an opportunity to buy into the integration concept and to see that it can be both good business and good ministry or mission. This gives the startup BAM Company an opportunity to solidify the business base and to ensure business survival before moving heavily into missions.

Since the process of faith integration, especially for the BAM Company and its community development agenda, is in tension with the company's limited financial and other resources, a step-by-step incremental approach minimizes that tension, moderates the risks and allows balance to be maintained. In flying, any mature pilot will tell you that small maneuvers make for small mistakes, large maneuvers for large mistakes. Accordingly, the most prudent way to fly is to stick with your filed flight plan, keep your risk exposure low, and make your banks and turns so gradual and smooth that your passengers hardly notice.

Even though the company's faith integration may initially be limited to specified operational areas or departments, the master planning approach (discussed next), especially utilizing the functional analysis methodology (described in chaps. 15-16), will be helpful to CEOs who are taking the incremental planning approach. It will inevitably help them assess the best paths (albeit limited) to take within the few company divisions and functions that they have chosen for initial faith integration. Hopefully, it will also inspire them to be aggressively intentional about becoming a full-blown BAM Company and a GCC as quickly as possible.

Before moving on, it may be useful to briefly examine two approaches that BAM consultants have used to help a company walk through the process of actually implementing the incremental model. First is Leadership Development International (LDi), an educational and consulting ministry. Although LDi is currently focused on China, it has long-term plans for expanding beyond China and "back to Jerusalem" via the ancient Silk Road.[16] LDi has both

---

[16]The discussion on LDi is based on personal visits with Chan Kei Thong, Roy Smith and Randy Ebeling, vice president of U.S. Operations, as well as C. K. Thong's "World Christians Through

an educational arm specializing in K-12 schools for the families of expatriates living and working in China and also has a BAM arm. The BAM side includes both revival-type activities to bring Chinese business leaders to Christ and consulting services to help those CEOs make their companies into KCs and eventually BAM companies and GCCs. Chan Kei Thong, an ethnic Chinese from Singapore, is the president of LDi, and Roy Smith, an American businessman from Austin, Texas, is vice president for LDi training, which includes BAM-type education and consulting.

Thong and Smith have developed a simple but effective analytical matrix for Christian-led businesses. The simplicity of the model helps communicate a basic message to the Chinese CEOs: to have a kingdom impact, the company's faith practices must result in both "good business and good mission." LDi examines a company and puts its practices into one of three quadrants. Figure 13.2 illustrates the process.

Figure 13.2. LDi business analysis diagram

The goal of LDi's consultation is to identify which business practices and functions fit into which category and to modify those practices to fit within the "Good Business and Good Mission" category. So, too, the company's efforts to expand its kingdom impact can be assessed within this matrix. For any new initiatives to be accepted by the company and incorporated into its DNA, it must be both good for the business and good for the kingdom.

A similar approach is propounded by Tetsunao (Ted) Yamamori. He uses the term *kingdom entrepreneurs*, defining them as "business owners, called by God, to do ministry through business." He says, "I have identified three basic types of kingdom entrepreneurship." Those are businesses that have a (1)

Business," presentation in West Lake Bible Church, Austin, Texas, June 18, 2005.

strong business and weak ministry, (2) strong ministry and weak business, and (3) strong business and strong ministry.[17] To this we might add a fourth type: Weak business and weak ministry. Not every business succeeds in either or both of its dual mandates.

The LDi and Yamamori models are quite useful exactly because of their simplicity. They especially have utility for CEOs who are encountering the KC and BAM concepts for the first time and are attempting to discern a direction and initial steps for their companies. These models are, however, just that: an initial program of faith integration. For the truly serious CEO, the analysis must eventually go far deeper and expand into the fuller strategic master BAM approach and its functional analysis methodology.

3. The third approach to planning the company's faith integration, the *master planning approach*, is for those who want to be quite intentional and increasingly comprehensive in their faith integration process. This approach will be discussed at length in chapter fourteen. Nonetheless, even those seeking to make their company a KC or BAM Company by the ad hoc or incremental approaches would be well-advised to carefully examine the formal process of how to conduct master planning. Since *it can be implemented piecemeal or in whole*, it can give valuable insight into future possibilities and growth areas for every company's faith integration process. So too for those companies that already have a master plan, it is my hope that the suggestions found in the master planning approach will have a beneficial, informative impact when the company updates and revises its plan.

It should be emphasized that this master planning approach can be costly in time, energy, diverted resources, immediate productivity and expenses, but that the long-range benefits to the company are, as the saying goes, priceless. The master plan gives focus to all that the company does, helps limit or streamline its operations to those activities that are goal enhancing, and gives a lighted path to ever-increasing kingdom impact.

Plan for the unplanned. The framework for faith integration is scripturally sound, as the Lord does call us to count the costs, prepare our plans and lift them up to him at each step of the way. It would be spiritually naive, theologi-

---

[17]Tetsunao Yamamori, preface to *On Kingdom Business: Transforming Missions Through Entrepreneurial Strategies*, eds. Tetsunao Yamamori and Ken A. Eldred (Wheaton, Ill.: Crossway, 2003), pp. 7-10.

cally unsound and missionally inept, however, not to end this discussion with a major caveat: all of this planning is well and good, but be assured that if God is in it, the Holy Spirit *will* intervene in some dynamic, totally unexpected and unanticipated ways that may (and probably will) significantly interrupt, disrupt or totally obliterate much of the careful planning. This admonition finds its roots both in Scripture and in the ancient, humorous but poignant proverb: "To make God laugh, tell him your plans!"[18] In other words, part of our flexibility in planning is to recognize that *when working for God, the unexpected is expected. And invariably, his way is always better.*

By the same token, if God is in it, you can also expect Satan, the liar, deceiver, trickster and charlatan, to show up trying to pawn his wares. Sometimes an interruption or wrench in the gears occurs. Determining whether it is of the Spirit or of the devil is not always easy and requires special discernment. In such situations it would be well to remember Mouw's sage advice and ask, "What in *heaven's* name is going on here?" *and* "What in the *hell* is happening?"

Closing Observations

The previous discussion focused on three positions on the continuum: first, on the left end is the ad hoc approach, which is a natural starting point for a company that is making its initial foray into the BAM world. Second, the space between the poles of the continuum, which is for companies doing their master plan by the incremental approach, one or two steps at a time. During this planning stage the company becomes more acquainted with the full implications of and options for faith integration. It allows its faith integration process to proceed on a more cautious basis, but with intentionality and commitment to expand its efforts. On the right end of the continuum is the full-blown strategic master BAM plan, which will be discussed at length in the next chapters.

These three approaches have been given as sequential steps or alternatives to help guide CEOs to the most appropriate, balanced mix for their companies and to define the boundaries of their planned kingdom impact. Before closing this discussion, however, five points must be emphasized: the need for continual flexibility, the critical importance of persistence, the value of patience, the necessity

---

[18]Robert Ludlum, *The Janson Directive* (New York: St. Martin's, 2002), p. 26.

of staying before the Lord in prayer and fasting, and the absolute need to make certain that God and his kingdom, not the plan, are always the primary foci.

Flexibility. Everything in life and ministry or mission—including our plans—must allow room for the Holy Spirit's movement and spontaneity. Further, no matter how thorough the company's BAM plan is, it will and should always continue to move in response to new opportunities, changed markets, profits, personnel, circumstances and contexts, and (as noted above) to new insights from the Lord and unexpected leadings of the Holy Spirit. Further, by definition a plan is for a defined period of time and must be revisited and reworked at regularly scheduled intervals in the light of experience, feedback and new insights. In planning, it is axiomatic that a workable, effective plan must be dynamic, ebbing and flowing with the daily movements of life. In a word, it must be flexible.

Persistence and patience. It is a given in business, ministry and life that not everything attempted will be successful or beneficial. In fact, there will be many disappointments, missteps, miscalculations and outright failures along the way that will educate the company and its leadership team. These are to be expected and will either motivate the BAM team to redesign and refine its plan, moving it ever closer to the desired results, or demoralize, de-energize and derail it and its BAM efforts.

Scripture recognizes the danger of the human tendency to find defeat in failure and setback, and calls God's people to be persistent in their quest to build the kingdom of earth.

> Consider it pure joy, my brothers, whenever you face trials of many kinds, because you know that the testing of your faith develops perseverance. Perseverance must finish its work so that you may be mature and complete, not lacking anything. . . .
>
> Blessed is the man who perseveres under trial, because when he has stood the test, he will receive the crown of life that God has promised to those who love him (Jas 1:2-4, 12; see also Jas 5:11; Rom 5:1)

A key aspect of persistence is patience. James, the half-brother of Jesus and leader of the Christian church in Jerusalem, admonishes us to be patient and to understand that kingdom fruit is only borne in due time and season, "Be patient, then, brothers, until the Lord's coming. See how the farmer waits for the land to yield its valuable crop and how patient he is for the autumn and spring rains" (Jas 5:7).

When building a business, the work is monumental and the progress slow. When the business is also a BAM mission outreach, the work will increase monumentally and the perceived kingdom impact will often be long in coming. Persisting in the face of negligible impact requires a patience that can only come from the Lord. That patient trust in God's divine leadership when little provides encouragement keeps the BAMer on the field. It is the twin virtues of persistence and patience that allow the CEO to fight off discouragement, hopelessness, apathy, depression and the often overwhelming temptations to throw in the towel, quit the field and return home.

The gold miner patiently persists day after day, seeking that valuable, tiny vein of gold hidden in the vast mountain range. So too the BAMer must patiently persist as he or she seeks to improve lives and rescue lost souls in the vast sea of impoverished humanity. Just as the miner willingly eats dust, knowing that he or she might be only inches or hours away from striking it rich, so the BAMer eats the bitter fruit of rejection and persecution, knowing that he or she may be only hours away from blessing others with eternal riches. Both understand that to reach their goals, monumental persistence and infinite patience are often required.

Prayer and fasting. Unlike the secular miner, the BAMer is not alone in the quest. The BAM CEO knows that his or her full partner in the BAM enterprise is none other than the One who placed the gold inside the miner's mountain and created the human souls inside the BAMer's employees, customers, governmental officials and beggars at the gate. The CEO also knows that the primary way to communicate with his or her Partner is through prayer. More importantly, the CEO understands that any BAM initiative that is not the result of focused, prolonged prayer, both within the company and from outside intercessors, will face long odds in having genuine, long-term kingdom impact.

Scripture is replete with calls to continually pray, to bathe all of our decisions in prayer and to seek the Lord in prayer on every aspect of life. Such prayer may also involve another scripturally sound spiritual discipline: fasting. (e.g., Mt 4:2; 6:16-18; Mk 2:18-20; Acts 13:2; 14:23).

God's people everywhere seem to grasp this concept, but a simple example may be helpful. An indigenously led church in Sierra Leone, Africa, recognized the importance of BAM as a key to their holistic mission outreach. But before moving forward with the plan they felt God was giving them, they entered into a full thirty-day time of prayer and fasting *as a congregation.* The reaffirming, positive impact on each member of the church, as well as the increased effectiveness of their mission effort cannot be overstated. The profound communion and intimacy they experienced with God during this period was, as their leader put it, "As essential as it was earth-shaking."[19]

This level of devotion and commitment is what God wants. It is also what he expects from those of us in BAM who are totally sold out to him, and it is what he deserves as our sovereign Lord and Creator—and as the true CEO of our BAM Company.

Discussion Questions

1. The text speaks of the "pillars of management" (pp. 284-300). What does this term mean? What are the pillars? Define and discuss them. Why are they central to successful management?

2. What standard(s) do you use in decision making? How did you arrive at it? How does it help you? Give some examples of major decisions that you have made using that standard(s)? Before this exercise, had you ever written it down? Why or why not?

3. Do you make periodic written plans personally or at work, or both? What process(es) do you use? Which of the three approaches to planning mentioned in the text most resembles your planning style? How important do you think formal planning is for a company? Why? For a ministry? Why? For your personal life? Why? How does planning align with the postmodern culture's values and worldview? Explain, giving examples.

4. What are the various types of prayer? Define them. What is fasting? How does it relate to prayer? Support your opinion with Scripture. What role does prayer and fasting have in a BAM Company? In your life? In your workplace?

5. BAM engagement: Of the four decision-making standards given in the text, which one resonates most with you? Why? How could you specifically use that tool in your life? Your workplace?

---

[19]Don Lewis, chairman of ARK Ministries, interview by the author, Newport Beach, California, December 22, 2007.

14

WRITING THE BAM PLAN

"Commit to the LORD whatever you do,
and your plans will succeed."
PROVERBS 16:3

"In his heart a man plans his course,
but the LORD determines his steps."
PROVERBS 16:9

"Our goals can only be reached through the vehicle
of a plan, in which we must fervently believe,
and upon which we must vigorously act.
There is no other route to success."
STEPHEN A. BRENNAN

"The first question any Christian businessperson should
ask about planning is not why plan, but how to plan."
LARRY BURKETT

AS WE HAVE SEEN, the decision *to plan or not to plan* is not the question. Planning is critical to success. The real question is how extensive the planning should be. The answer to this is not simple and must be reexamined prior to each fiscal year and each planning cycle. The continuum of BAM planning (see p. 293) illustrates the different choices companies have for planning kingdom impact. As we have seen, the far right end of the continuum is reserved for those companies that want to be highly intentional about the planning process and about maximizing their kingdom impact. It is to those companies that the following planning process is addressed. After reviewing this process in its entirety, some companies may *not* want to undertake such an extensive exercise and, instead, may want to opt for the more gradual, incremental planning approach, or they may see other effective ways of achieving the same or similar results.

By the same token, some companies will just be starting their KC/BAM pilgrimage, while others may be mature companies that want to re-envision their firms to have a more deliberate, intentional kingdom impact. That is as it should be—each plan and its process should be individualized to meet the status, needs, goals, character and culture of the company (including its products, services, markets and clientele), the mission context it is contemplating, and the leaders' discernment about God's call.

The value of my suggested planning process is not that it provides a wooden template that must or should be followed. Quite the opposite—it is one approach of many. Nonetheless, it is a fairly comprehensive approach which I hope will be a useful point of reference or departure, or a self-directing planning guide for those who are struggling with *how* they become a KC, BAM Company or a GCC.

Dual Mandate, Unified Plan

The company that wants to be Christ-honoring in all that it does, and to have bottom lines beyond the financial, is immediately faced with a dual mandate: (1) business and (2) mission/ministry. Although companies will approach these mandates differently, I strongly recommend that the company develop a written strategic master BAM plan (SMBP) which consists of the following nine steps:

1. The context—the strategic area/country analysis (SAA). The BAM team should develop a comprehensive understanding of the context in which business will be operated, often through a formal, written study of that context (the SAA). The SAA is essential to inform all aspects of the company's business plan and its mission on how to be culturally appropriate, sensitive and relevant to that country, especially to its business and religious environments. (See appendix two for a sample format; see also appendix three.)

2. The business—the strategic business plan (SBP). The BAM team should draft a traditional, written strategic business plan (SBP) that fulfills the business mandate and takes into account the contextual factors learned from the SAA. The SBP will, of course, address every aspect of the business's prospective goals, operations, products and markets, including its structure, strategies and multiple bottom lines. (See appendix four for a sample format.)

3. The mission—the strategic mission analysis (SMA). The BAM team should address the mission mandate by: (1) analyzing and refining every aspect of the SBP from a faith-integration, kingdom-impact perspective, utilizing the functional analysis approach described in chapters fifteen and sixteen; and (2) conducting an in-depth mission/ministry analysis of the company's workforce, the external labor pool and those people's circumstances and lives, and the community at large (as revealed both by the SAA and additional God-led investigation). These steps will assist the company to determine kingdom-impact opportunities both internally and externally. Once the opportunities have been identified, they should be used to augment the appropriate parts of the SBP and to propose additional kingdom-driven bottom lines to be added to it. (A sample format of a "plan" that might serve as an analytical guide to the SMA is found in appendix five).

4. The tensions. The BAM team must identify and resolve the inevitable tensions between the goals and resources of the business mandate and the almost universally more expansive and ambitious desires of the mission mandate. This may also include resolving tensions between the business and mission advocates within the company. These tensions come from such critical issues as limited capacity, goals incompatibility, financial and organizational costs and business feasibility, and the enthusiasm (or lack thereof) for undertaking the recommended faith-integration actions or the proposed social, environmental and kingdom projects and activities. Resolving these tensions will help refine the plan into a coherent whole that (1) harmonizes the goals and action steps necessary to achieve all of the company's agreed-upon, God-given multiple bottom lines, (2) maintains the measurability of each individual bottom line, and (3) keeps the company fiscally viable and missionally engaged.

5. The *initial* strategic master BAM plan (SMBP). Develop a comprehensive, but initial written SMBP that seamlessly weaves the SAA, SBP and SMA into a unified whole, with defined multiple bottom lines and action steps to achieve each of them.

6. The coordination effort. Fully coordinate the *initial* SMBP with the key stakeholders, including all of the employees and, when appropriate, selected members of the community.

7. The *final* SMBP. Based on the input received during the coordination phase, draft a final SMBP that can be taken to the board of directors for approval.

8. The feedback cycle. Once the final, approved SMBP is operationally active, the BAM team should continually (1) monitor and evaluate every aspect of the company's business and mission activities, both pro and con, and (2) adjust the plan as necessary and desirable to improve efficiency, productivity, morale, bottom-line results and kingdom impact.

9. Annual review. Repeat the process as often as needed to maintain freshness and vitality to the SMBP, but conduct a comprehensive review and update not less than annually.

Just as a symphony has different scores for each instrument and all blend harmoniously into the final production, so the SBMP has these different subcomponents (the SAA, SBP and SMA) that are intended to blend into the whole. Nonetheless, the central document to the BAM planning process, like the conductor's central score, is and always will be the strategic business plan. The SAA and SMA are essential albeit very different analyses that are *intended to inform the SBP* and help shape it into an effective business and mission strategy for the BAM Company.

Or, looked at another way, the entire process is similar to that of an architect preparing plans for an office building. In this case it is a business structure designed for God's purposes and glory. In developing his plans, the architect first does a rendering (an artistic picture or portrait) that shows the completed project. Next, with the help of engineers, geologists and other experts, he develops schematics for each aspect of the building's character. There will be site preparation plans, grading plans, floor plans, electrical, plumbing, and heating and air-conditioning plans. These are prepared separately, but they are not designed to be the finished building itself. They are only parts of the whole that come together to make the building what it is.

In the end, the architect overlays these components on each other and merges them into a functionally sound, harmonious whole. They are then augmented with landscaping plans to add aesthetics and make it pleasing to the eye. Throughout the process, the architect continually presents the preliminary plans (1) to his clients for their approval and (2) to the city for building permits, quality inspections, a seal of approval and a certificate of occupancy.

So it is with master planning a BAM company. The plan's components—the SAA, SBP and SMA—are overlaid on each other and melded into one strategic master BAM plan, which is designed for one purpose: to glorify the one, yet triune God. Throughout the process, the plans are continually referred to our Lord to seek his guidance, approval and blessing.

In that regard, if the consolidated SMBP is to be successful, if it is to be blessed by God, if it is to have true kingdom impact "in all its ways," it must be consistent with his will and calling, compliant with Scripture and undergirded in prayer. As the psalmist warns, "Unless the LORD builds the house, / its builders labor in vain" (Ps 127:1).

In summary, the SAA is integrated into (informs) (1) the SBP to assure that the business is in harmony with the local business culture and (2) the SMA to keep all mission activities both biblically based and contextually relevant and effective. Once the SMA is completed, its kingdom impact goals and their action plans are woven into the SBP and become one with it, as dye works into the whole fabric of a beautiful garment. In the end, the three parts, the SAA, SBP and SMA, will converge into one overall, socially responsible, values-driven, fiscally sound, contextually informed, impact-focused, culturally relevant, effective strategic master BAM plan (SMBP) for the company—a master plan for our Master's glory. The goal is to design a final SMBP that will ultimately be his plan for the company, not the company's plan for him.

Figure 14.1 may be helpful to give the BAM strategic planning process greater clarity before addressing each aspect more specifically on subsequent pages.

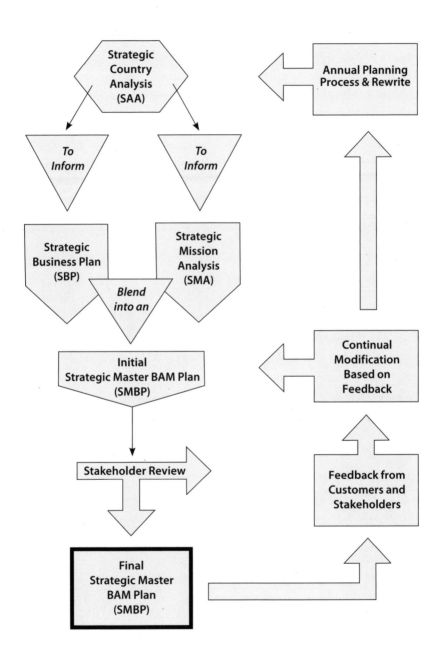

Figure 14.1. Annual BAM planning cycle

In the remainder of this chapter we will look at each of the four key components—the SAA, SBP, SMA and SMBP—in greater detail. Then chapters fifteen and sixteen will introduce the functional analysis approach to refining
the plan; chapter seventeen will speak to the difficult issues of money and
people; and chapters eighteen and nineteen will give a step-by-step guide to
help the CEO and his BAM team navigate this entire process in a fairly
straight-line, user-friendly way.

Strategic Area/Country Analysis (SAA)

An essential element of any mission is to know the area or country and culture
of the people to whom the mission team is taking the gospel. Innumerable
missteps, many quite tragic, have occurred because well-meaning missionaries did not fully understand or appreciate the environment they were entering.
Missiologists call this process *contextualization.*

Appropriate contextualization. Based on centuries of empirical data, missiologists have concluded that successful mission requires appropriate contextualization, that is, mission strategy and methods that are appropriate to the
context in which the mission is engaged and, as much as possible, that are in
harmony with it.[1] That is, to be effective and to give the target population true
ownership of Jesus as *their* Lord, mission must be culturally appropriate to
those people's worldly context.

Context is defined by many factors: cultural, anthropological, historical,
sociological, geographical, and environmental, as well as religious practices,
traditions and worldviews. In addition, overriding every person's context are
the prevailing economic and political power structures in that society. In
terms of basic necessities, every person must make a living or be supported,
and every person is subject to a prevailing economic and political regime.
These factors influence people's survival strategies, national and international
economic practices, and governmental policy and laws.

Unfortunately, mission-sending agencies often fail to analyze, consider
and prepare crosscultural missionaries (whether domestic or international) to
understand the basic economic and political power centers that they will confront when they set foot into their mission field. This failure can leave mis-

---

[1]Charles H. Kraft, ed., *Appropriate Christianity* (Pasadena, Calif.: William Carey, 2007).

sionaries dangerously ill-equipped for their service and set the stage for potentially disastrous consequences. The resulting costs can be exceptionally high, not only for the church, the mission and the individual missionaries, but also for the people and the hurting, needy communities of lost souls they fail to reach.[2]

International business has long known about contextualization. It is a guiding principle of most international and transnational companies doing business in today's globalized world. After all, a business is not simply a business, but a business in a particular city and country, with its own unique culture, markets and power structures. Just to survive, a business's plans and operations must be in harmony with its local context. It is almost as simple and as complex as knowing your market before you attempt to sell your wares there. As one leading international business expert said:

> International business is different from national business because countries and societies are different. . . . One of the biggest dangers confronting a company that goes abroad for the first time is the danger of being ill-informed. International businesses that are ill-informed about the practices of another culture are likely to fail. Doing business in different cultures requires adaptation to conform with the value systems and norms of that culture. Adaptation can embrace all aspects of an international firm's operations in a foreign country.[3]

---

[2]For greater insights into the critical role of contextualization for all mission efforts, including BAM, see Robert J. Schreiter, *Constructing Local Theologies* (Maryknoll, N.Y.: Orbis, 1985), pp. 16-18, 91-93, 115, 119. In this study, Schreiter examines each of the dominant models of contextualization, gives their advantages and disadvantages, and attempts to guide the reader through the various situations in which each might be applicable. Of particular usefulness to the practice of BAM is his outstanding discussion of the praxis model.

Dean S. Gilliland edited a major work in contextualization, *The Word Among Us: Contextualizing Theology for Mission Today* (Dallas: Word, 1989), and Stephen B. Bevans authored *Models of Contextual Theology* (Maryknoll, N.Y.: Orbis, 1992), in which he refines and explains each of Schreiter's models and provides an excellent explanation of the praxis model. More recently, Van Engen provided a summary of "five perspectives of contextualization that have developed over the past several centuries of missionary activity" as well as a methodology for deriving contextually appropriate mission theology. See Charles Van Engen, "Five Perspectives of Contextually Appropriate Mission Theology," and "Toward a Contextually Appropriate Methodology in Mission Theology," in Kraft, ed., *Appropriate Christianity*, pp. 183-202, 203-26. See also Frecia Johnson's new model of "Reciprocal Contextualization" unveiled in Kraft's *Appropriate Christianity*, pp. 475-89.

[3]Charles W. L. Hill, *International Business*, 3rd ed. (Boston: McGraw-Hill, 2002), p. 103.

Since BAM by definition includes both business and mission, understanding the cultural context in which the BAM enterprise will exist is obviously critical. In fact, it is perhaps the key to the BAM Company's survival. Ken Eldred notes:

> Above all else, the evidence suggests that it is culture that drives the economic success and blessings of a nation. The most fundamental need of developing nations is not an infusion of capital, a higher level of education, a democratic government or even a more robust form of capitalism. The most fundamental need is cultural change that involves a transformation of core values, attitudes and practices. Economic, political and social improvements will occur as byproducts of that transformation.[4]

Eldred defines these core values, attitudes and practices as a culture's "spiritual capital" and says,

> Think of Spiritual Capital as the faith, trust and commitment that others will do what is right—not only what is right in their own eyes or what benefits them the most, but what is right in the eyes of God. Showing integrity, being accountable and honest, offering hope, being loyal and trustworthy, loving and encouraging others, exhibiting good stewardship, being fair, creating order and serving others.[5]

Understanding something as complex as a country's culture is, however, quite difficult and necessarily involves a great deal of research and study. Simply learning the language can be an onerous, time-consuming but essential undertaking. Nonetheless, with the advances of the Internet and its flood of information at everyone's disposal, with modern communications technologies, the growth of globalization and its resources, and the pluralization of our cities (i.e., our ability to find and meet members of a target people group), the task of contextualizing is infinitely easier, albeit no less critical.

Preparatory phase. Conducting a Strategic Area/Country Analysis (SAA) of the BAM Company's targeted nation should be done in several stages. Usually, the initial phase is a preparatory one, involving basic research and tenta-

---

[4]Ken Eldred, *God Is at Work* (Ventura, Calif.: Regal, 2005), p. 117.
[5]Ibid., p. 98, but see all of his chap. 5 for a fuller explanation of this meaningful concept.

tive planning. It is for the purpose of screening the possible country alternatives and selecting the one(s) that fits the BAM team's profile.

This preparatory phase involves learning as much as possible about the country, its geography, language, people, history, culture, worldview, economy, politics, religions and business climate, as well as security and stability issues, existing infrastructures, entry and exit procedures, imports and exports requirements, tariff structures and the like. It also includes, if available, interviews with people who are indigenous to the country but may be living in the BAM team's vicinity. (Appendixes two and three each contain a detailed outline of what a written country assessment might include.)

This preparatory phase is also useful in identifying the city, village or region within the country that best suits the team's purposes. Sift through the business and mission opportunities in that locale, sketch an initial business plan, formulate ideas about possible mission activities, make preliminary decisions about divisions of labor in the new business, discuss sources and uses of capital for the business, and begin language lessons.

In the end, how the team conducts the SAA and which facts and circumstances it focuses on will be guided by the overriding purpose of the SAA: to successfully inform every aspect of the SBP and the SMA about the environment in which the business will be operated and the BAMers will live. Accordingly, the SAA, if done correctly, will greatly aid the success of the BAM enterprise. If done poorly, it can jeopardize not only the business and mission, but in some contexts the very lives of the BAMers and their families.

In-country visitations. The preparatory phase is not to be short-changed. It must, however, be followed by one or more vision trips to that country. Such trips are invaluable as a *reality check* on the preliminary observations and decisions made during the preparatory phase. It will assist the BAM team members to gain an understanding of what they and their families will face and to reassess whether this is where God is calling them, whether the business they contemplate doing there will succeed, the special challenges and obstacles to living and doing business in that context, the resources that will be needed, the range of possible indigenous partners, the possibilities of having meaningful kingdom impact, and in the end, the measure of their individual and team commitment. As plans progress for the business, additional trips will usually be necessary and are encouraged before making the final move to the country.

Some BAMers even enter the country for one to two years just to live there, do language study, and define and refine their plans while immersed in the actual context before starting their businesses.

These visits should be thoroughly prepared. Before departing, the team needs to know what they want or need to learn, where they want to go, who to talk with, questions to ask and information to obtain. On the business side the team members will also want to maximize their understanding of (and compatibility with) local customs, laws, permits and licenses, import-export regulations, markets, rents, labor costs, and the availability of office space, manufacturing and warehousing facilities, equipment, communications, Internet, transportation (truck, rail, shipping, air), interpreters, appropriately skilled labor force, sources of raw materials, and other infrastructure resources.

On the mission side, they will also need to explore the kingdom impact opportunities, social conditions, levels of development, local missions, NGOs, churches, other BAM companies, community development and mission history. Throughout the visit, it is vital that they watch where God is already working and discern whether he is inviting the BAM Company (and family members) to be a part of his work in progress. In that regard, they need to prayerfully observe the mission opportunities and callings that God might be showing them which are within the company's (and the team family members') capacity to perform.

On both sides, they will need to identify the area's existing formal *and* informal power structures: political, governmental, economic, social and religious. Knowing who to contact (and why and how), who to avoid, whose favor to curry, and who to co-opt is a reality that can spell success or failure for the BAM enterprise from the beginning.

On the living and lifestyle side, they must consider such things as visas, travel and currency restrictions, housing, transportation, schooling (if children are involved), churches, shopping, food, clothing, medical care and health facilities, spiritual and personal support systems, language training, personal assistants, security, and the like. The list is quite long, but it is important to the BAM team's family members and, therefore, to the longevity and sustainability of the BAM enterprise. In that regard, during at least one of the in-country visits, key spouses need to accompany the team to allow focused investigation from the family and living perspectives.

In addition to this extensive planning, the actual in-country visits need to be flexibly structured allowing plenty of time for overcoming jet lag, for rest and reflection, for planned events *and* for expected, but unknown, unplanned, divine appointments and leads. The team must not forget that God is already in the country and has people and resources in place for the team to discover. He will also accompany the team every step of its way. The team may have its own travel agent, but the Holy Spirit is its true guide. The team's visits may well include visitations in many forms.

Once in the country, the BAM team should visit a variety of people: government officials, foreign businesses (especially those from the BAM team's home country), local businesses, banks, chambers of commerce, trade associations, port authorities, import-export brokers, the commercial section of their home-country's consulate, schools, churches, resident missionaries, tentmakers or BAM businesses, and any others who can enlighten them on the entire scope of living, traveling and doing business and mission in that locale.

Above all, these visits provide an opportunity to begin the relationship-development process. Bar none, relationships are the single most important source of the deep, rich, personal, professional and spiritual satisfaction that can result from engaging in BAM. The relationships will, of course, be useful for business and mission purposes, but that is incidental to the blessings of friendship that the Lord has for them on the BAM field. Through relationships, God literally opens heaven's floodgates and bestows blessing after blessing that can make the entire BAM experience a treasured, joyful high-watermark in their lives.

The singular importance of relationships is vividly portrayed in a recent book about mission in Afghanistan, *Three Cups of Tea*. The Afghan saying behind the book's title is, "Here, we drink three cups of tea to do business; the first you are a stranger, the second you become a friend, and the third, you join our family, and for our family we are prepared to do anything—even die."[6]

When the in-country visits are completed, the BAM team should then amend their initial SAA and subject it to intense scrutiny both within the team and with those outside of the team, including their family members. This scrutiny

---

[6]Haji Ali, quoted in Greg Mortenson, *Three Cups of Tea* (New York: Penguin, 2007), back cover.

will test the objectivity of the SAA's assertions and conclusions, and serve as a reality check on the entire project. After all, the SAA will be performing a vital function in the BAM enterprise by informing the SBP and the SMA of the situational realities ahead. If the SAA is well done, thoughtful and bathed in prayer, it will provide a sturdy foundation. If the SAA is weak, the structure standing on that foundation will be drastically compromised. Jesus recognized this when he admonished his audience about wise and foolish builders:

> Therefore everyone who hears these words of mine and puts them into practice is like a wise man who built his house on the rock. The rain came down, the streams rose, and the winds blew and beat against that house; yet it did not fall, because it had its foundation on the rock. But everyone who hears these words of mine and does not put them into practice is like a foolish man who built his house on sand. The rain came down, the streams rose, and the winds blew and beat against that house, and it fell with a great crash. (Mt 7:24-27)

Drafting the SAA. An initial SAA should be prepared during the preparatory phase. Upon returning from the initial vision trip (and each subsequent trip), the BAM team should reduce their data and analysis to writing, preferably in a continually improving SAA. Although a written SAA is not always necessary, it is highly recommended—as are individual BAM team member and family journals—to record initial observations, first impressions, insights, conclusions, facts and assumptions (right and wrong ones). It *is* certain that if these are not recorded contemporaneously or soon after they are formed, they will fade and inevitably be lost with the passage of time. Writing and synthesizing them in one place—the SAA—is by far the best way to maximize the BAM team's collective wisdom about its opportunities, choices and mission context. Not only will this help clarify and document what they have learned, but the writing exercise invariably helps identify areas needing further research. Once established, a BAM business can serve as a most welcomed, useful bridge for other BAM businesses that want to establish a presence in the same area. The SAA can be a valuable asset and orientation material in that process.

STRATEGIC BUSINESS PLAN (SBP)

America's bookstores are overflowing with books on how to start a business and how to prepare a business plan. Most universities and business schools have courses on entrepreneurship that highlight the critical steps in this process. Even grade schools and secondary schools have business clubs such as Junior Achievement that teach young people the basics of business startups. The U.S. government's Small Business Administration (and its SCORE program of business counseling by retired executives) exists solely to help would-be entrepreneurs achieve their goals. Every U.S. state has its own economic development agency to assist business growth and startups within its borders. The U.S. Peace Corps has a worldwide program for using retired professionals to help entrepreneurs and businesspeople launch successful businesses in developing, emerging and transitioning economies. Some churches, mission-sending agencies and NGOs even have their own version of business training specifically designed for each cultural and economic context. And this only touches the surface.

Businesses that already exist and are contemplating revisioning (repurposing) themselves into a KC or BAM Company, or are already a KC and want to expand their operations internationally or crossculturally and become a BAM Company, will also need written business plans. While this discussion is pitched to the new BAM entrepreneur, it is equally applicable and useful to established, expanding businesses.

It is foolish to start or operate a business of any type without planning, and it is extremely important to do so in writing. That is especially true if we are starting or operating a business internationally or in a country or culture other than our own. It is even more critical if the challenges are compounded with an intentional BAM emphasis. Such plans often begin on a café napkin and morph into short, simple outlines and plans. Others may be highly complex and replete with graphs, charts and pro forma financials, or anywhere in-between. The extent of needed business planning depends on any number of factors, including the nature of the business and its product(s); the selected area or country and BAM context; the experience, biblical literacy and educational level of the BAM team; the number of employees to be hired; the volume of business expected; the projected earnings; the amount of available capital; and the sources, expectations and demands of those underwriting the business.

Every business plan, whether simple or complex, begins with a short but demanding exercise of defining the vision, mission, core values and goals (business bottom lines) of the company. Once these elements are clear, the company then addresses other aspects of the plan which, in one way or another, describe how to move the company from where it is to where it wants to be. The process is no different with a KC, BAM Company or GCC. Each is, first and foremost, a business.

In sum, regardless of the business's size or sophistication, the company needs to do a serious, thoughtful, written business plan. Because there are numerous books, materials and agencies available to help would-be BAMers accomplish this task, I will not address how to write a strategic business plan, except to reiterate five points:

1. Written plan. The SBP must be prepared correctly and put in writing. Do not take shortcuts. This will only hurt the BAM team and the business in the long run. The process of writing a plan will discipline the team's thinking, which is critical to the business's success. There is no substitute for having to think through and define every aspect of a business ahead of time.

2. Individually crafted. There are literally hundreds of formats that can be used. There are a considerable number of "fill in the blank" software packages available on the market, but using such software usually defeats the purpose of causing the entrepreneur to thoroughly think through every aspect of his new business.[7] The real value of a business plan is not only found in the ultimate product, the plan itself, but equally important in the *planning process* that produced the plan. Accordingly, I recommend an old-fashioned, handcrafted approach that is an individually tailored variation of the SBP format found at appendix four.

3. Contextually appropriate. The SBP must be contextually appropriate to the country and city in which the business is to be operated. To do that, it should thoroughly incorporate, even absorb, the SAA into every aspect of its DNA. This is especially true of the operational side of the plan—both strategic and tactical—which should be in great detail and as specific as possible. If the BAM team fails to do so, the business and its team are in for a bumpy, if not futile (even tragic), ride.

4. Totally inclusive. Again, to the extent possible, the process of writing this

---

[7]One possible exception is PaloAltoSoftware's *Business Plan Pro* <www.paloalto.com/business_plan_software> which has been highly recommended to me.

plan should include every member of the BAM team and its company's employees, if any. This takes maximum advantage of the expertise of the team and helps include all participants in both the planning process and the company's financial and operational success. It is critical that those charged with carrying out the plan be onboard and in alignment with the BAM team's vision and objectives as early as possible.

5. WWJD. Every aspect of the plan and the planning process should be approached from a prayerful kingdom impact, kingdom-building perspective.

STRATEGIC MISSION ANALYSIS (SMA)

The third component of the process to become a BAM Company is to conduct a strategic mission analysis (SMA). Such an analysis is an overarching attempt to look at every aspect of the SBP, the company, its resources, people and power, and to identify and define kingdom impact opportunities by asking how these aspects of the company or community life can be leveraged by the company for kingdom impact.

The SMA is best done through a systematic process of opportunity identification, impact analysis, viability assessment, resources allocation and prayer. As previously explained, it initially requires the BAM team to comb through the SBP and the company departments during the SBP's functional analysis process (see chaps. 15-16) and identify fresh opportunities for kingdom impact inherent in each aspect of the plan, at every level, in every department and through every business function. In the process the SMA will undoubtedly bring to the SBP new and separately identified corporate goals, measurable benchmarks, impact-assessment criteria and measures, and even individual or departmental goals, objectives, tasks and assignments. This exercise may even add to the business plan a variety of kingdom-driven bottom lines that were not seen in the initial business-planning process.

In addition, the SMA process examines the existing workforce, the people's working and living conditions, demands, expectations and needs, to identify kingdom opportunities in serving these people and their families with Christ-honoring love. It also examines the potential labor pool in the community to determine what kingdom opportunities might exist there, such as hiring the handicapped, preemployment training or addressing prevailing discriminatory practices based on gender, race, tribe, caste or ethnic background. Beyond that, the SMA analyzes the community to identify kingdom-driven, community-development opportunities for the company.

With that in mind, these questions still remain: If a mission analysis is called for, how do you conduct and write it, and how does it relate to the company's business plan?

On one hand, it would be foolish, even presumptuous, to think that I could give a definitive template for a strategic mission analysis, much less a mission plan. After all, mission, *missio Dei*, is God's venue, and as we know and as biblical history reveals, God really does work in infinite, often mysterious ways. On the other hand, Scripture admonishes us to develop our plans, and to do so under God's guiding hand. Admittedly, developing a mission analysis is a challenging process, especially since it depends on such factors as the gifts and the calling of the individuals involved in the business, the nature of the business, its product(s), target markets, manufacturing base, supply sources, competition, financial resources, prior and existing missionary efforts and local church resources. In addition, the SMA, being informed by the SAA, must account for the contextual realities of the company, its people and its clientele/customer base. While these are key factors in traditional business planning, they take on new and added significance in the BAM Company, and are equally key to the SMA's development.

Identify kingdom impact opportunities. Basically, how to develop an SMA is found in six steps:

1. Listen to God and to the culture.

2. Think expansively, prayerfully and boldly with the BAM team. And through appreciative inquiry (see p. 256) or some similar asset-inventory system, identify the larger mission opportunities—kingdom impact opportunities—that exist internally and externally in context and that are consistent with the gifts (and calls) found in the BAM Company and in the community.

3. Using the functional analysis approach (see chaps. 15-16), identify and define the internal kingdom impact opportunities as they relate to each specific function, product and activity of the business in context.

4. Explore the community that the company serves and identify its social, environmental, kingdom and other needs that would be good community-development projects for the company and that are in harmony with the SAA. Consultation with a CD specialist is advised in order to gain the best input from this community and to avoid missteps that could injure company-community relations.

5. After inserting these kingdom impact opportunities, goals, objectives and projects into an SMA, integrate all of these into the SBP.

6. With the entire BAM team, prayerfully select and prioritize those kingdom impact opportunities and kingdom bottom lines that fit within the company's resource base, capacity and calling, modifying the SBP as needed into the initial SMBP.

The sixth point may seem fairly routine, but it is perhaps the most difficult part of the process: prioritizing; selecting among the "goods" to find the "best." Given every company's limited resources and capacity (money, time, people, facilities), prayerful prioritization is called for. The company is, after all, a business first and not a church or charity. Nonetheless, with its leaders' God-given creativity and imagination, even the most resource-restricted company can undoubtedly find many previously undiscovered, affordable ministry and mission opportunities. Such opportunities abound within every company's policies, procedures, operations, organizational structure and community presence. They also exist within the workforce (and their families), client/customer base, and other spheres of influence. Each one of these areas can be an arena for kingdom impact with only minimal expense. It is even possible to find kingdom actions that may actually help stimulate or improve the company's financial bottom line and increase its capacity for greater service in the future. This is particularly so in the human resources field, which is discussed in chapter sixteen.

Each of these steps and each decision requires a listening, discerning, prayerful heart, an intimate knowledge of the SAA and an assessment of the ministry and mission opportunities that exist at each of the three different levels of integration: inherent, internal and external. But more than that, each step and each decision is deeply personal. Each has the opportunity to make someone's life better in some tangible way.

Three special areas require special comment. First, an environmental and BAM impact assessment. Second, the hands-on requirement. Third, pet projects.

BAM impact assessment. Clearly, when evaluating its environmental bottom lines the BAM Company needs to develop an environmental impact statement (EIS, AKA environmental impact report or EIR), whether or not it is required by local law. The purpose of the proposed actions and goals is to improve God's natural environment and to avoid causing harm. Unfortunately, harm can easily result from the company's well-intentioned (but ill-considered), good-faith actions. This danger should always be in the forefront of the BAM team's thinking.

Although we do not often associate an EIS with nongreen issues, we should. When missionaries (whether holistic, as with BAM, or more traditional) enter a foreign culture, they do so as outsiders (etic) who are deliberately attempting to be change agents. As outsiders, they are often inadequately informed about the impact certain actions can have on those within the culture (emic). Sometimes these actions can have far-reaching consequences that the missionary would never have conceived nor wanted. Three examples may suffice. The first illustrates the illusive power of tradition; the second, the daunting power of established local interests; and the third, the potentially destructive power of charity.

First, on the San Blas Islands off the east coast of Panama, the islanders lived for centuries in virtual isolation, with none of the amenities of modern life. Having no water supply of their own, the Indians were required to canoe daily to the mainland jungles to collect water and bring it back to the crowded village. Well-meaning missionaries tried to solve this situation by installing a pipeline from the mainland to the islands. The pipeline solved the water problem, but created a major, unforeseen social problem. Since the islands are flat and barren, there is no privacy except in their thatched huts, which are usually quite open and busy. As a result the young people have no place to date (i.e., to explore relations with the opposite sex and look for mates). To resolve this issue, for decades the Indians allowed the young people to fetch the water from the mainland, thereby giving them the privacy and time they needed in the mating rituals. Once the water pipeline was in place, these trysts were unavailable and the social equilibrium was significantly upset.

The second example comes from Southeast Asia. A businessman in Arizona designed a solar still that could produce fresh drinking water from salty or polluted water. It was basically a glass greenhouse that was sealed so that the water vapor could not escape but would condense on the glass and drain into a collection vessel. He successfully sold these in arid areas around the world and, at one point, obtained a contract from the national government to provide them for a remote fishing village. The village was located where there were plenty of fish but no pure water to process the fish for market. In addition, the women had to walk to an oasis each day with pots and buckets for their only drinking water.

The Arizona Christian businessman showed them how to make the stills and to produce enough water for both drinking and processing their fish. All was well—or so it seemed. When the man returned to the village a few months later, he found that the women were returning to the oasis as before and that the fishing business had failed. The reason was a local power struggle. The man who sold water at the oasis did not like losing his income, so he hired two thugs to raid the village at night and break all of the glass in the stills. As the reporter of the story said, "Since they had no more glass, they had no more water and history began all over."[8]

The third example is of a Christian businessman in El Salvador who manufactures low-priced prosthetics for the poor, which created jobs for himself and several others. Citing this business as "a truly inspiring example of BAM in action," Rundle makes an insightful comment, "The proprietor of this business believes that the emotional and spiritual hurts of his customers are often more significant than their physical limitations. An important part of his rehabilitative ministry, therefore, is helping people heal emotionally and spiritually."[9]

All went well for both the man and the poor until a group of well-meaning foreign Christians saw the need for prosthetic devices in El Salvador, returned home, raised money, purchased prosthetics from outside of the country, and gave them to the poor in El Salvador free of charge. While this was beneficial to the immediate recipients, it threatened to drive the entrepreneur out of business and dry up the long-term supply of prostheses. This action also endangered valuable jobs in a country desperately needing entrepreneurship

---

[8]Don Lewis, e-mail to the author, January 19, 2008.
[9]Rundle, e-mail to author, January 25, 2008.

and economic development, and since the charity's efforts were short-termed (just long enough to bankrupt the businessman), there may be no low-priced prosthetics available in that area for the foreseeable future. This is a "widespread problem," Rundle said. "Christian charities, in their eagerness to address needs in the short term, often stifle entrepreneurship and economic development. (It is hard to compete against products offered for free.)"[10]

The only way to avoid or minimize these types of adverse effects is to conduct a BAM impact analysis and create a BAM impact statement (the BAM equivalent of an EIS) as part of the SMA for each good-works project that a BAM Company contemplates. Such a statement is or should be part of all thoughtful projects, but unfortunately this approach is exceptionally rare. As a result, because of many BAMers' ethnocentric worldviews, inadequate cultural knowledge or negligent planning and due diligence, they fail to see the train wreck they are creating and the many people who may be hurt as a consequence.

Hands-on. The second area requiring special comment is the hands-on requirement. Quite simply, all BAM Company community projects (and as many internal projects as possible) should involve the full, hands-on participation of employees at all levels in the company. It is an encouraging aspect of such hands-on employee involvement that the employees often benefit as much, if not more, that the community. This is because the project gives them the joy and satisfaction of having helped improve the lives of their neightbors and the life of their community. It also teaches them the value of volunteer service and self-help, and is an object lesson to other local businesses (and the community), showing them a better way to treat people—the Jesus way.

Admittedly, the project creates a bond among the employees that rebounds to benefit the company, improves morale and satisfaction with their working environment, and may increase productivity and profits. That is, however, not the primary motivation of the BAM Company, which is to help the people of the community holistically in the name and love of Jesus and, through the goodwill generated, to increase their receptivity to the gospel.

Pet projects. Without belaboring the point, there is another danger that the BAM team must avoid. That is when employees, members of the community

---

[10]Ibid.

or even BAM team members mislead the company into supporting a pet project. That is, a project that promotes the interests of an individual or some small group, thereby increasing their personal power, status, prestige or standing in the community or company. The ability of an individual to deliver a needed project or to boast about being able to access the company's resources can be a source of power-brokering within the community. All of this will usually occur outside of the BAM team's knowledge, but they must be sensitive to it and take steps to avoid any semblance of it. Otherwise, the company projects become instruments to promote people and their agendas, and they cease to honor Jesus or truly serve the community or the kingdom.

A Working Outline

At this point, I would be remiss not to offer a suggested format for drafting a stand-alone strategic mission analysis. My proffered SMA format is found in appendix five.[11] Before proceeding, three points must be re-emphasized. First, the central document is the SBP. The SMA is only designed to inform it of kingdom opportunities available in its operations, among its employees, within the local labor pool and in the community. The SBP is like a naked Christmas tree, with the SMA being the accompanying ornaments, offerings and gifts. Second, each company and context is unique, making any suggested format presumptive, if not dismissively, inadequate. My format does, however, represent a considerable body of experience, as well as prayerful reflection, and is so central to the purpose of this book that it deserves thoughtful attention. If nothing more, perhaps it will provoke meaningful, even high-spirited discussion within a specific BAM Company and lead to the SMA and SMBP format most appropriate to the company's own circumstances. Third, although a written SMA is not required, it is strongly encouraged. The SMA process is, after all, one of analysis. If the findings of that analysis are not in writing, there is a great danger of their being lost in the process of examining other areas of the SBP. The written findings also form a tangible checklist (and prayer list) of kingdom impact opportunities that, if not incorporated into this year's SBP, may be feasible in the future.

---

[11]The topic headings of appendix five are fairly self-explanatory, but each section might better have been left with blank spaces so that the reader can begin to make modifications as moved by the Spirit, reflection and experience.

STRATEGIC MASTER BAM PLAN (SMBP)

The SMBP is a document that passes through three initial phases. First, it is the product of a blended SAA, SBP and SMA, and as such reflects the dual mandate of BAM—business *and* mission. Second, after the *initial* SMBP is completed, it is incubated in a refiner's fire, being subjected to intense scrutiny by the company's executive team, all managers, and ultimately, if possible and appropriate, all employees and affected members of the community. This final review is quite useful to obtain their last minute corrections and revisions, as well as their buy-in and ownership of the plan. These stakeholders are the very people who will be responsible for implementing the plan and seeing it work, fail or fall into mediocrity, tokenism or worse. It is therefore vital that they not only have a hand in crafting it but also eagerly choose to undertake the work required to give it life. Once the initial SMBP is fully coordinated and approved by the board of directors, it is ready for implementation.

Third, the resulting document is redrafted into a *final* SMBP that reflects the best thinking of community members, employees and company leaders. It is, of course, restricted in time (usually one year), at the end of which the process will be repeated. With each repetition, the SMBP will hopefully be further refined by the experience gained in its implementation.

This last point is also important because in the end (and annually) the company's leadership team will be judged by the stakeholders based on how well it has met the demands of its two competing mandates—business and mission—and whether it has done so in a unified, harmonious, virtually seamless way. Admittedly, the act of balancing these mandates is not simple, but it is necessary if the company is to achieve its multiple bottom lines. I hasten to add, however, that *if done correctly, the balancing process—and the creation of the final SMBP—can be an incredibly joyful, even fun, process for everyone involved.* Through it, they will have the rare opportunity of seeing their best, creative thinking and their dreams for a different kind of company being fleshed out into a viable pathway to the future.

That said, each BAMer must understand that the final SMBP is not just another plan. Yes, it is a master plan for the company's future efforts to realize its several bottom lines. But it is so much more. By actually developing an SMBP and committing the company to its attainment, the BAM Company raises the bar significantly, taking the company to an entirely new plain, far above ordinary business. It also increases the stakes in an already difficult, even dangerous, undertaking, for it is also a sacred covenant that entails a time of judgment and of testing.

A covenant. Drafting and implementing an SMBP is more than just a carefully crafted business faith plan; it is a *covenant*—on three important levels. First, it is a pledge among the BAM team members, one to another, to faithfully carry out the plan, to use their collective and individual best efforts to attain the kingdom bottom lines, and to be held accountable to each other for those pledges. Second, it is a commitment by the BAM team to all of the stakeholders, both within the company and the community, to meet the high expectations that have been created by the plan. This is particularly so in the social, environmental and other nonfinancial bottom lines.

But third and most important, by its very nature and the prayerful process used to craft it, the SMBP is a binding covenant between the CEO, BAM team and God. It is the team's sacred pledge to do all it possibly can to achieve the kingdom bottom lines. Further, it is a promise to do so through hard work, persistence, prayerfulness and methods that are always worthy of the gospel of Jesus Christ.

From another perspective, it is a vow that the team must take seriously because God takes it seriously. Jesus said, "Simply let your 'Yes' be 'Yes,' and your 'No,' 'No' " (Mt 5:37). By committing to the SMBP, the BAM team has laid itself bare before the Lord and submitted to being held accountable for its yes. Psalm 76 speaks clearly about God's righteous anger and "wrath against men" who do wrong in his sight. The psalmist admonishes those who voluntarily take vows or oaths before the Lord to be "survivors of [his] wrath" by the simple act of fulfilling those vows. "Make vows to the LORD your God and fulfill them" (Ps 76:10-11).

A time of judgment. The standard for the initial SMBP review (by the employees and the community on those items that affect them) should be as uncompromising as that employed by Jesus when he confronted the barren fig tree. Seeing that it bore no fruit and could satisfy no one's needs, Jesus immediately caused it to wither (Mt 21:18-19).

Further, the review standard should be as honest and forthright as Jesus' confrontation of the church at Laodicea, "I know your deeds, that you are neither cold nor hot. I wish you were either one or the other! So, because you are lukewarm—neither hot nor cold—I am about to spit you out of my mouth" (Rev 3:15-16). Jesus then severely admonished the Christian businessmen and women in this thriving commercial city and, implicitly, those of us in business today:

> You say, "I am rich; I have acquired wealth and do not need a thing." But you do not realize that you are wretched, pitiful, poor, blind and naked. I counsel you to buy from me gold refined in the fire, so you can become rich; and white clothes to wear, so you can cover your shameful nakedness; and salve to put on your eyes, so you can see. (Rev 3:17-18)

By applying these severe standards, the final SMBP will represent the best efforts of Christians in business to leverage the company, its products, services, people, assets, networks and community influence to have kingdom impact. He does not call us to perfection but to a committed, pure heart. In addition, paraphrasing Jesus, be hot or cold about your BAM efforts and your SMBP, but never be lukewarm. You are not required to do BAM, but if you do it, do it right, with passion and commitment, working as unto the Lord. Otherwise your efforts are futile and will fail, to your everlasting shame and suffering.

A time of testing. Make no mistake. The final SMBP, being the company's foundational plan for joining and affecting God's kingdom on earth, will be tested by God.[12] He will subject it and its authors to his refiner's fire to separate the precious metal from the dregs (Mal 3:2-3). Paul makes this abundantly clear when he tells the church at Corinth,

> But each one should be careful how he builds. For no one can lay any foundation other than the one already laid, which is Jesus Christ. If any man builds on this foundation using gold, silver, costly stones, wood, hay or straw, his work will be shown for what it is, because the Day will bring it to light. It will be revealed with fire, and the fire will test the quality of each man's work. If what he has built survives, he will receive his reward. If it is burned up, he will suffer loss; he himself will be saved, but only as one escaping through the flames. (1 Cor 3:10-15)

---

[12]The entire concept of God testing his faithful is a fascinating study. Scripture is replete with examples of God testing men, and men testing God. See for example, Deut 13:3; Ps 66:10; 81:7; Prov 17:3, Eccles 3:18; Jn 6:6; 1 Thess 2:4; Jas 1:3.

To the faint-hearted or half-hearted, the warning is clear: do not aspire to becoming a BAMer or to design an SMBP. This is not particularly encouraging news to many would-be BAMers, but it is the reality of stepping out for God. It is not for the ambivalent or timid soul, nor is it for those with shallow, feckless faith. Further, if the SMBP is for and of God, Satan will certainly mount strong opposition. But be wary: so will God.

That being said, why would God test the BAM endeavor? The answer seems fairly clear: he wants to know whether the SMBP is purely of and for him or if it serves the BAM team in ways that diminish his glory. Is the SMBP an innocent lamb of God to be nurtured, blessed and shepherded, or is it (intentionally or otherwise) a wolf in sheep's clothing? Is it an honest business effort, albeit quite imperfect, to honor our Lord, or is it a shrouded charlatan, "playing the religion card" to garner people's favor, increase market share and reap higher profits? This added dimension is not one we often talk about, but Scripture is clear.[13] So, before moving forward, take a few minutes to consider once again the cosmic reality of what BAM is about and ask whether this master plan truly is the Master's plan or our plan for the Master.

To those who truly love the Lord and want their lives and businesses to have eternal significance, his testing should not only be expected but welcomed. It is the path God has mandated for those who choose the narrow gate. As Scripture says, being with God, even if it means suffering, is better than any alternative. So to those hearty souls, I say, choose BAM. Prepare for it, then go for it. Risk it. Seek his face, his guidance, his blessings and, with the godly counsel of others, make a commitment that will become that "great divide" in your life that has made all the difference.[14]

DISCUSSION QUESTIONS

1. The author speaks of a "dual mandate" for a BAM Company (p. 305)? What does this mean? Do you agree? Are there other mandates that are equally important? Doesn't this negate the earlier argument against a secular-sacred divide? If so, how? If not, why not?

---

[13]To those who doubt the importance of this admonition, I commend a careful study of such stories as the death of Ananias and Sapphira in Acts 5:1-11, and Peter's chastisement of Simon the Sorcerer in Acts 8:9-25.

[14]Oswald Chambers, *My Utmost for His Highest* (Westwood, N.J.: Barbour, 1963), p. 362.

2. Do you believe it is important to begin the planning process with a thorough strategic area analysis (SAA) as the text suggests? Why? Discuss what information is most critical from the extensive suggestions in appendixes two and three.

3. Have you ever written a business plan? If so, share your experiences with the group. Was it for a business in a foreign country or a crosscultural setting? How did this influence your approach? Was the business successful? Why or why not? In light of that experience, how do you respond to the suggested process in this chapter and the format in appendix four? Explain.

4. BAM engagement: Later you will be asked to consider an actual BAM business that you and your friends might launch in a crosscultural setting. Part of that exercise will include preparing a business plan for that company. If you were to actually attempt to carry out this plan, do you believe that God may test you and your plan? Why? Is your opinion supported by Scripture? Do you believe that Satan will attempt to thwart your plans? Why? Is your opinion supported by Scripture? If your answer is "yes" to the previous questions, what can you do before the plan is written to prepare yourself and your team for testing by God and for attack by Satan?

15

The Functional Analysis Approach

SECTION 1

*"Focus on the journey, not the destination.
Joy is found not in finishing an activity but in doing it."*
GREG ANDERSON

*"To look backward for a while is to refresh the eye, to restore it,
and to render it the more fit for its function of looking forward."*
MARGARET FAIRLESS BARBER

*"Therefore let us leave the elementary teachings
about Christ and go on to maturity."*
HEBREWS 6:1

ALTHOUGH EACH COMPANY WILL HAVE its own approach to the planning process, I propose the functional analytical approach for the company that is truly dedicated to an intentional engagement between Scripture and work. It is recommended at two levels. The first is the generalist approach discussed in chapter thirteen, in which the pillars of management are examined from a scriptural point of view and a set of overall guidance for management decisions emerges. The second is a more detailed approach in which the company examines the various operational functions of the business, seeking ways to realize kingdom impact from each. We now will examine this second approach, because it is at the heart of how the dedicated CEO should approach the faith integration process in his or her company.

OPERATIONAL FUNCTIONS

All too often when we explore how to integrate faith into a business the discussion focuses on the larger questions, such as core values, vision, mission and overall fairness, tithing, and the like. That is good, and these must be addressed. However, if the company is to truly reflect Christ in *all* of its ways and to be transformed into a KC or BAM Company, it must go beyond the generalist, pillars of management approach. It must delve into *each* of the company's departments and *each* of the functions within those departments—from the board of directors to the night watchman and cleaning crew—to determine their God-honoring potential for having individual and collective kingdom impact. The analysis must be carried out department by department, function by function, by both the organizational leaders accountable for the various departments and by the workers intimately involved on the front lines performing the function, doing the work. Only then will the functional analysis approach be a useful exercise that has both long-lasting kingdom impact and becomes an integral part of the company's method of doing business.

This functional analysis approach emanates from two key precepts: first, the Bible has sound advice for us in every situation, for every decision and in every relationship; and second, the shape of our individual lives and those of our companies are determined by the sum total of *all* of our decisions. In the real world of business, those decisions—both large and small—are made at every level in every business act every day. The importance of this cannot be overstated, because the customer is directly affected by many, if not most, of the company's decisions. In today's information age, the consumer is well aware of broader decisions that previously have been internal secrets of the company. In addition, in today's global environment, competition for the company's products and services is stiff, and public scrutiny of internal decisions can turn the company's fortunes upside-down overnight.

In short, the decisions made by the company are seen by others and are the stuff that make and break a company, whether BAM or not. The company's identity, reputation, image and character are formed by the quality of its service or products, its prices vis-à-vis the perceived value, how it responds to its customers, how the employees treat the customers and how the company treats its employees, the wages it pays, the benefits it gives, the cleanliness of its premises, the friendliness of its personnel, and the like.

An outstanding example of a company whose services, products and prices are quite good, but whose image has suffered horribly because of real and perceived bad management practices vis-à-vis its employees is Wal-Mart. The company has been so severely castigated that some cities have passed resolutions and public referenda banning Wal-Mart from their communities. It has learned a very expensive lesson the hard way: there is virtually no aspect of a company's operations that does not either advance or diminish its goal attainment. For a KC or BAM Company, that is doubly so; not only is there a business to promote but there is a God to serve. The dual mandate of business and mission carries a formidable challenge—and opportunity—to advance both, but it cannot be successfully done if any aspect of the company's operational functions is ignored or neglected.

As CEOs examine this process and contemplate the God-sized task they have signed up for, they should become quite excited about the fascinating journey on which the functional analysis approach will take them and their people. It is always exciting, even exhilarating, to contemplate the enormous potential good that can come to so many people for generations from such a journey. It is, after all, an exercise that marries the power of Scripture and the Holy Spirit with the power of the corporation into a potent, unified force for good. That oneness parallels the oneness that Christ has with the church, which is awesome to contemplate.

IDENTIFYING KINGDOM IMPACT OPPORTUNITIES

It must be remembered that the functional analysis approach is simply a method to identify opportunities hidden within our work to have a positive impact on people who need God and his kingdom. Nothing more, nothing less. It is looking at each function and collectively asking, How can we gain more kingdom impact from what we are doing? And then doing it. In many senses, it involves what some might call *theologizing* about traditional business functions, that is, extracting from Scripture those values and principles that should inform and even fashion the performance of given business functions.

Such in-the-field, contextual theologizing is a key element of any mission enterprise. Charles Van Engen defines the biblical theologizing process for the church, but his words are equally applicable to business and the BAM CEO.

He notes that "biblical theology of mission is a multidisciplinary field that reads the Bible with missiological [marketplace] eyes and, based on that reading, continually reexamines, reevaluates, redirects the church's [BAM Company's] participation in God's mission in God's world."[1]

Applying this continual theologizing approach to business, Van Engen notes that there are three different aspects of the mission theology process, each of which is critical: Mission must be "of the way" (Christ-centered), "in the way" (it must happen within the world) and "on the way" (it is dynamic, moving forward over time as part of the faith pilgrimage of the BAM team "as they anticipate Christ's present and coming kingdom").[2]

Those who undertake this functional analysis, lay-theologizing process should realize up-front three foundational truths:

Hard work. All too often Christian business leaders buy into the concept of faith-work integration but shy away from rigorously pursuing its application to their companies. The reasons are many, but central is the reality that such application can be quite demanding financially, physically (especially time), intellectually, emotionally and spiritually. In a word, it is hard work. It would be naive and misleading to suggest otherwise. CEOs who enlist in Christ's armada to do BAM must expect no less. They must also take steps to prepare themselves, their family and their team for these realities. To sustain them all, they need to always keep in mind the enormous good that can come from these extra efforts, the very real growth that they will experience and the realization that when it is finished, they will have fought the good fight.

A process, not an event. It is important to understand that integrating faith into a business (whether it is a KC, a BAM Company or just a Christian-led enterprise) is a process, not an event. It is a never-ending cycle of continually questioning and refining all of the business's practices to maximize its kingdom impact. The daily stream of challenging business issues will keep the process moving. The key is to keep asking questions about how to make the best, most Christ-honoring, scripturally sound, viable business decisions.

This refining process is also one of incremental spiritual discernment, of growing in *how* to integrate faith over time, on a daily and even hourly basis.

---

[1]Charles Van Engen, *Footprints of God*, ed. Charles Van Engen, Nancy Thomas and Robert Gallagher (Monrovia: Calif.: MARC, 1999), p. xviii.
[2]Ibid.

It requires starting with the larger issues—like the company's core values as they apply to the pillars of management—and gradually working down to the finer points and applying biblical principles to specific functions. It does not have to be done overnight and indeed cannot be. The ancient proverb that life is in the journey, not the end, was never more true than in the faith integration process. It is the faith journey, in itself, that is as valuable to the CEO, the BAM team and the company as the end goal. Here they will encounter the living Christ and they will have their first kingdom impact.

The refining process of faith integration is like a farmer who sees his barren, rock-infested plot of land and decides to make it into a productive agricultural field. The first task is to prepare the land, which means clearing the rocks and stones. On his initial pass through the field the farmer loads the wagon with the large boulders and obvious rocks. At the end he or she is pleased with the progress and thinks the job complete. But when the field is surveyed again, the farmer sees thousands of smaller rocks missed the first time through. They too must be cleared to produce the best crop. At the end of the second pass, the farmer is again pleased, but later sees all of the missed rocks. Again and again, day after day the farmer goes into the field, each time removing the rocks that seem to be sprouting from the field. Each pass through the field is hot, tedious, back-breaking work involving long hours, sore hands and aching feet. But because of the farmer's persistence, unwavering commitment and faith in the eventual outcome, he or she knows that each pass through the field is enhancing the quality of the field and its capacity to produce abundant fruit far into the future.

There are several lessons to be learned from the farmer's experience. First, producing a rich harvest depends on thorough preparation of the field; second, successful farming (like rearing a child) is a daily and tedious task that requires patience, persistence and commitment; third, both our lives and our companies are like this, and the process of sanctifying them and steadily improving their fruit-bearing potential is worth the effort and in the end will be rewarded; and fourth, each function in the company, each stakeholder, each customer or client encounter can be viewed either as a stone in the company's shoe that keeps it off balance and produces pain, or as a glass slipper fit for turning a servant into a princess.

The company is one body. The functional analysis approach is one that can be approached piecemeal or in whole. At each stage of the process, however, it will become clear to the BAM Company CEO and BAM team that this is an exercise in striving for excellence in all that the company does, all that it is and all that it stands for. As they drill down into some of the functional specifics, they quickly discover that none of them is usually found in isolation. A business is much like a living organism in which each part is somehow related to every other part. Paul recognized this organic aspect of the church and the individual gifts of its congregants, saying that all are unique, but when working in harmony, their collective synergy is multiplied. Quite simply, the whole is greater than the sum of its parts. The same can be said for a business, especially a KC or BAM Company.

> Now the body is not made up of one part but of many. . . . If the whole body were an eye, where would the sense of hearing be? If the whole body were an ear, where would the sense of smell be? . . . As it is, there are many parts, but one body.
>
> The eye cannot say to the hand, "I don't need you!" And the head cannot say to the feet, "I don't need you!" On the contrary, those parts of the body that seem to be weaker are indispensable, and the parts that we think are less honorable we treat with special honor . . . so that there should be no division in the body, but that its parts should have equal concern for each other. If one part suffers, every part suffers with it; if one part is honored, every part rejoices with it.
>
> Now you are the body of Christ, and each one of you is a part of it. (1 Cor 12:14, 17, 20-23, 25-27)

The Functional Review Process

Early in the preparation of the SMBP via the functional analysis approach, the BAM team literally needs to leave the executive suites and go to the plant floor; the loading dock; the warehouse; the manufacturing, assembly and distribution points; the janitorial basement; and into each of the company's offices; and interrogate each manager, employee and contractor about each function, activity and program in the business. They need to ask at each station, "What can we do to create or improve this function for greater business profits and efficiency, for greater value for our customers, and for greater kingdom impact?" In short, the BAM team needs to critically examine and interrogate every aspect of the company's operations, functions, management and stakeholders, existing and planned, and ask, "How can God be honored in this?"

Once answers are found, they then ask such questions as:

- How can we institutionalize these business and kingdom goals and objectives?
- How do we measure the impact?
- How do we hold people accountable for fulfilling these goals, objectives and tasks?
- How do we institutionalize this accountability?
- How do we build in a feedback loop to systematize continual improvement and find new avenues for kingdom impact?

Drilling down. As with any continual-improvement process, the devil is in the details—which is a very apt pun for faith integration. How to do this is vividly illustrated in modern computer software. We start with the general menu; when we click on an item, we discover that underneath it is an entirely new, previously invisible subsidiary menu. We click on one of those options and a third, wholly new, comprehensive menu appears; similarly, fourth, fifth and sixth menus are only a click away. In sophisticated software, the process—called *drilling down*—seems almost infinite.

In performing the functional analysis to improve the business and the kingdom impact of a BAM business, the same concept can be profitably applied. The first pass at examining the functions will probably yield measurably positive results, but as the company becomes comfortable with the process, the real meat is to be found in drilling down below the surface and discovering the underlying realities and opportunities. For example, if the function or issue is, Why is Maria, the second-floor maid, not having her assigned hotel rooms ready in time for the next guest? the usual knee-jerk solution is that Maria is at fault, and she should be disciplined along with her supervisor. On the other hand, by drilling down, we may find that the problem and its solution lay elsewhere. It may be because her training was inadequate; her supervisor is too strict; her language capabilities are not strong enough to understand her instructions; her room cart with sheets, towels, cleaning and mini-bar supplies and toiletries is not adequate or has bad wheels; her electric floor sweeper is out of date or the cords are too short; the sheets are not finished by the laundry in time; the check-out and check-in times are unrealistic; she has too many rooms to cover in the time allowed; the way she was taught to make the bed is inefficient; the other maids are critical of her for working too hard or quota-busting; the night supervisor is hitting on her; the rooms are old—the list goes on.

The point is that drilling down gets into the nitty-gritty details of every aspect of a business and seeks solutions to problems, as well as the opportunities for improved efficiency, higher customer value and greater kingdom impact, from the people who are on the front lines, actually doing the job, not from remote executives.

In most companies this functional analysis should be a continual exercise, but all too often it will take place only every year or so, if at all. I encourage the company to consistently drill deeper as each problem or issue occurs, or as each opportunity for better service or greater kingdom-impact opportunity arises. Certainly, each year's planning should go deeper than the year before, steadily moving the company toward greater Christlikeness and kingdom impact.

Assessing stakeholder needs. Another part of the functional analysis approach is to address the needs of each class of company stakeholders. One of the major internal stakeholder classes is the work force. The BAM team and its SMBP will be woefully inadequate if it does not assess the employees' and their families' needs and consider how the company might be able to assist. This is especially critical in a BAM, crosscultural, international setting. Some examples of employees needs might be: counseling; day care; elder care; prenatal care; nutrition, health, hygiene, literacy and computer training; grief and life event ministries; after-school and summer-school activities and education; housing; food; and transportation. Meeting some of those needs may directly benefit the company, others will not; but all of these services are part of a BAM Company's holistic mission and are delivered explicitly in the name and love of Jesus, showing that he loves them and, as his disciples, so do we.

Prioritizing. Since the BAM Company cannot be all things to all people, the following questions must be answered:

- How should the needs of these employees and their community be prioritized?

- Which of these needs is within the company's capacity and calling?

- Of those, what is the best way to address them, by whom and with what expected results?

- What is the kingdom impact of these projects, and how do we maximize that impact?

Such prioritization is not easy, but with the inevitable tension between the infinite human needs facing each community and the finite resources of the company, it is an essential task. It must, of course, be based on the most complete information possible about each option so that a cost-benefit analysis can be prepared with integrity and sensitivity. Seeking the counsel of those most directly affected by the various proposed projects will be as invaluable as it is essential in making the final assessment. Above all, seeking divine guidance and discernment is absolutely essential if the selected priorities are to reflect Solomon-like, godly wisdom.

Institutionalizing. The answers to all of the questions raised (and the initial priorities that flowed from those answers) should be recorded and institutionalized within the SMBP. They must also become key factors in the tactical action plans emanating from that plan. Ultimately, the overriding goal is to infuse these answers and the values they represent into all of the company's formal and informal policies, procedures, practices, processes and products, and into the worldview of everyone associated with the company, inside and out. If done correctly, persistently and continually, kingdom bottom lines will eventually find their way into every nook and cranny of the company's operations, culture and ethos—and beyond.

Product by Product

Clearly, the product or service a company renders to its customers or clients is the single most important aspect of its business health. Accordingly, it may be proper for the BAM CEO to start the functional analysis approach with the company's products. A few of the critical issues that might be considered in such a review are the type of product; its usefulness (or harm) to both the public and the environment; the presence of any harmful ingredients or design flaws; the functionality, safety and user-friendly aspects of its design; the excellence and quality of its performance and manufacturing; its obsolescence, price, packaging (including waste disposal), instructions, warranties (what and how honored), branding, advertising, distribution; and how returns, repairs and complaints are processed.

This is a fertile field for meaningful analysis from not only a business perspective but also a kingdom-impact perspective. It is helpful to view the product through the eyes of the customer—that infinite variety of people who may be affected by it—and to weigh the message the product sends about the company and its kingdom standards.

DEPARTMENT BY DEPARTMENT

After completing (or as part of) the product review, the company's organizational chart is not a bad place to start when thinking about the next steps in the functional analysis approach. The object will be to have each department conduct a similar review of its personnel, structure and workflow to seek new operational efficiencies *and* kingdom impact opportunities. Since each department and its area of responsibility is defined by senior management, and since they are responsible for setting the culture of the company, as well as its core values and modeled behavior, I strongly suggest starting the review at the top of the organizational chart. That usually means the CEO and BAM team, but it should also include the board of directors, boards of advisors, retained professionals (e.g., attorneys, accountants and marketing specialists) and influential shareholders. Regardless of how the review is handled, the review of the top echelons needs to be done with visible rigor, complete integrity and a high degree of transparency. If not, the word will quickly spread throughout the company, endangering the reliability of similar surveys outside of the executive suites.

As the audit of the company continues from one department to another, the initial efforts can even take a *zero base* approach. That is, they should ask: Can the department's existence be justified? Is the personnel strength well aligned with the demands of the jobs? How is the department's morale? What are the strengths and weakness of the department as a whole and its supervisors and workers individually? Does it have the right people assigned to jobs well suited to their gifts, skills and joys? How are its training, turnover, overtime and error rates, promotion rates and opportunities, and skill sets? How is the workflow, lighting, heating, cooling, access to restrooms and break rooms, overall comfort and aesthetics? How is it equipped, furnished and cleaned? This exercise can be difficult, time-consuming, stressful and even threatening to the status quo, but if done correctly, it can also breathe new life and purpose into the company.

In short, the examination should address every aspect of the department as a department. At first blush this seems like a standard secular business approach. It is, but with a twist—through Jesus' eyes and the scriptural Golden Rule. The way a company answers these questions will be reflected in how it takes care of both its people and its customers. While the answers are critical for the business of the company, embedded within them is a larger issue: the company's kingdom impact on and Christian witness to its own employees, their lives and their families' lives—and to the people who are being served by the company's products.

FUNCTION BY FUNCTION

The actual work of the company is accomplished within each department. Each employee in the department is assigned a variety of tasks or functions that must be performed. These are usually found in typical position descriptions (PD), but as any employee knows, actual performance requires a plethora of other tasks and functions that are far too detailed for formal PDs. Each of those additional tasks is, however, often highly useful, if not essential, to the proper performance of the job. It is in each of these—formal and informal tasks and functions—that we find a rich treasure of opportunities for having a positive kingdom impact. That is especially so when multiplied across the company in every position.

As figure 15.1, a chart of traditional business functions, vividly demonstrates, these functions are like the good soil of the farmer's field: it is ripe with potential for reaping a large kingdom harvest. It is not difficult to see the kingdom potential in some of these business functions and relationships; others require greater discernment, sensitivity and prayer. The reader is invited to study figure 15.1 with an eye to what kingdom-impact opportunities might be had in each function and relationship. (Chapter sixteen will attempt just such an analysis for four of the more important aspects of company life.)

Traditional Business
Relationships and Functions

Stakeholder Relationships

Shareholders/Owners
Boards of Directors and Advisors
Chief Executive Officer (CEO)
Executive Management Team
Managers
Employees
Families of each of the above
Customers/Clients/Alumni
Suppliers/Vendors/Contractors
Creditors
Community/Government
Industry/Trade Unions
Competitors

Functions

Management
Administration/Planning
Human Relations
Finance/Accounting
Operations (internal)
   Design
   Manufacturing
   Distribution
   Retail
   Warehousing & Inventory Control
Marketing
Sales
Maintenance
Customer Service
   Orders
   Returns
   Repairs
   Complaints
Quality Control
Legal
Security
Information Technology
Audit

Businesses/Industries

Professionals
   Doctors/Dentists
   Attorneys
   Accountants
   Bankers/Trust
   Brokers
   Computer/IT
Service Industries
   Construction Trades
   Auto & Truck Dealers
      Insurance
   Appliances
   Real Estate
   Transportation

Manufacturing
Wholesaling
Retailing
Government
Education
Science and Research
Consumer Goods/Services
Agriculture and Fishing
Lumber and Paper
Information
Media
Petroleum, Mining
Steel
Pharmaceuticals
Entertainment

Figure 15.1. Traditional business relationships and functions

When addressing a particular function or aspect of the company, whether in the SBP, SMA or initial SMBP, it is important to involve everyone who will be working on that business function. Where possible, let the business and mission agendas and the functional questions come from those who will be responsible for carrying out the business function(s) being examined. On the business side, ask questions such as, How can we do this particular function better, improving its quality, efficiency and cost? On the mission side, ask such questions as, How can we honor God through this particular function or aspect of our business? or, where non-Christians are involved in the planning process, How can we honor our company's *vision* and *values* through this particular function or aspect of our business? or, How can we better serve our customers or employees in this situation? These questions, of course, need to be bathed in continual prayer.

The Community: Need by Need

The same approach can be undertaken for each encounter with the company's external stakeholder groups: investors and creditors, customer and clients, suppliers and vendors, independent contractors, and the community at large. It must be remembered that there are many different ways in which the BAM Company's community presence is felt. For example, a new company creates jobs, pays wages and taxes, builds buildings (which employs others for labor, construction materials, inspections and permits), buys furniture, fixtures, equipment, machinery, raw materials, and transport, and purchases professional services from attorneys, accountants, translators, interpreters and tradespeople.

BAM companies have a similar economic impact, but with their special community-development and spiritual agendas they can also have very positive social, environmental and spiritual effects. In that regard, they bring substantially more good to the community than ordinary businesses.

Since community-development is one of the BAM Company's prime directives, a few observations are in order. It is axiomatic that any project that the BAM Company selects for community-development should meet real needs of the people within the community. There are many ways of identifying those needs, but I want to emphasize five foundational points.

First, community-development (CD) is not an easy or simple task, but regrettably it is a term that is loosely bandied about BAM circles with little or no appreciation for its complexity or dangers. CD is actually a highly developed, professional specialty and is no place for amateurs. In spite of best intentions, CD projects that are ill-conceived, poorly executed or fail to take into account the full range of people or cultural traditions that will be impacted can do a great deal of harm to the community, its people and the local church, not to mention the company. I cannot emphasize this too strongly. Failed CD projects are wasteful, counterproductive, harmful, hurtful and can actually reverse or set back any positive community relationships and witnessing opportunities that they were intended to produce—for years.

The BAM Company should realize that CD is an active mission field in its own right and that it has generated considerable, valuable resources. CD consultants and professionals spend years in education, training and mentoring contexts to gain an understanding of the complexities of their trade. Hundreds of volumes have been written about CD, citing both good and bad methods and case studies. These materials are all available to the company to learn from past mistakes and successes, and all underscore the invasive nature of CD and the need to be well-versed in how to do it, especially in crosscultural contexts.

Accordingly, when a BAM Company is engaging in CD, it needs to proceed with caution, conduct a formal or informal BAM impact analysis (see pp. 322-24), and when possible, consult or hire a Christian CD specialist to advise the company or possibly lead the company's CD effort. These specialists are available from a wide range of Christian NGOs. In addition, each GCC should seriously consider hiring such a specialist as a permanent member of its BAM team. Either way, proper training in Christian CD is invaluable for selected members of the BAM team, especially the CMO.

Second, the company and its BAM team are outsiders (etic) and have no legitimate right to simply declare what the community's needs are and impose their priorities on its citizens. Stated positively, when proposing to do good works within the community, the BAM Company should begin with an assessment of the community's legitimate needs—as seen by the community. This is best done by proactively listening to the employees, the community citizens and the community leaders. By going to the employees, the company enlists them as active agents in the development process. By going to a variety of people at all ends of the local political spectrum, the company seeks several results:

- Discerning the legitimate community needs as the people themselves perceive them and as they prioritize them. Avoiding being sold a "bill of goods" that represents the local power brokers' agendas for lining their own pockets or for increasing their power, but that does little to help the people of the community.

- Co-opting the power brokers into not raising opposition or creating barriers to the project's chances of success.

- Engaging the local citizens in leading the effort to improve their community. In that sense, the company is merely coming alongside the locals to partner with them in the project, rather than doing it for them turnkey.

In summary, this is an effort (1) to obtain the best thinking of the people who will implement or be affected by the project, (2) to visibly demonstrate the company's commitment to serve and listen, rather than rule or impose, (3) to reach consensus and hopefully wholehearted acceptance of the project by all concerned, as well as receive unconditional commitment to seeing it accomplished, and (4) to identify and mutually resolve any resistance, opposition or questions about the project ahead of time.

In the process, there are at least four sets of people who should to be consulted: (1) the employees who will carry out the various elements of the project, (2) the community participants who will be affected by it, (3) those formal and informal community leaders who can be allies or opponents of the projects, (4) any specialists, professionals or consultants (e.g., engineers, environmental experts, social workers, accountants, attorneys, contractors, technicians) who may be needed for their expertise in an area that either affects the project or is being affected by the project, and (5) the CEO's and company's Christian advisors and intercessors.

Third, there are other people and companies that have worked in this city or country, perhaps with the same goals, who should be consulted, and there is probably a history of economic community-development in this community that should be studied with great care to avoid the pitfalls of the past.

Fourth, the project should be one in which the employees themselves have a major role (if not *the* major role) in identifying the community's needs, selecting the specific need that the company will address and organizing or participating in its implementation. The project should not be about spending company money for the community as much as it is about the employees' hands-on involvement in meeting the identified need. Through this participative model, the company can establish its own bona fides with the community and simultaneously instill in the employees a new or renewed sense of citizenship, personal responsibility and voluntarism in helping to build the life of their community.

This level of employee involvement not only empowers and energizes the workforce, but it gives them an ownership stake in the business's success and educates them on the faith integration process. It also tends to make each one of them a valuable, *self-appointed* quality control (QC) monitor in the heart of the business production chain. That is no small matter both in business QC terms and in Christian witness. From a business QC perspective it demonstrates to the workers that they, their work (and its quality) and their opinions are valued by the BAM team. From a witnessing perspective, it shows the higher standards that characterize a Christ-centered, gospel-following company and points them favorably to the author of those standards, our Lord. Further, and perhaps most informative, the workers are able to actually see the CEO's faith in action. This, more than anything, sends them a powerful message about the company, its values and purpose, and the Christ it serves. In the end, it may well be *the* critical piece of the CEO's testimony that helps them actually come to know Jesus.

Finally, whether the BAM Company's projects include building local schools, parks or playgrounds, paving roads, digging wells, helping children at risk, tutoring students or adults, training in literacy, nutrition, hygiene, sanitation or computers, operating medical clinics, or working with local NGOs and churches, the company's opportunities for doing good in the name and love of Jesus are almost infinite.

These projects are part of the company's efforts toward external integration—witnessing through word and deed outside of the company. If these projects are to be meaningful in terms of holistic kingdom impact, they should be carefully planned. Not only will this maximize the possible kingdom impact, but it will hopefully hedge against the negative witness that can result if the project does not go as contemplated or has unintended negative consequences.

In that regard, it is imperative that the planning process for the CD project include the functional analysis approach: looking at every part of every stage of the project, including the identification, selection, organization, implementation or evaluation stages. If performed correctly, this approach will cause the participants to be methodical, thoughtful and prayerful, and to ask questions they might never have asked before, including, Why are we doing this project? What will be the environmental, cultural, economic and kingdom impacts of this project? What might be the unintended, negative impacts of this project? How do we measure the project's various impacts?

Certainly, the BAM Company will not transform the local business culture or civic-mindedness quotient overnight. Long-term, however, it can have a very significant effect merely by being a positive presence in the community year after year. Its continual, consistent witness over the long haul can serve as a valuable example of community service that will be attractive to and perhaps emulated by other indigenous and international companies in the area. Simultaneously, it can help build the image of Jesus in the community and hopefully move many people toward seeing him as their Lord and Savior. Holistic mission is neither easy nor short-term. That is why BAM, because of its long-term incarnational nature, is well-suited to the task, and if approached correctly it can be highly useful to the people in meeting their legitimate community needs and in facilitating their introduction to Jesus and the Holy Spirit.

DISCUSSION QUESTIONS

1. In your own words, define and describe what the functional analysis approach is and how it is done. What is your reaction to it? Explain. Is such an analysis reasonable or useful for a BAM business with the pressure of its dual mandates? Explain.

2. In what way would you equate the process of applying functional analysis in a business to contextualizing the gospel?

3. The process of applying functional analysis to a business may be a long, hard, tedious task. How can a BAM Company build methods and procedures into the process that will encourage the company to continue it on a long-term basis? Are there ways to make the process fun for the employees? What might those be?

4. Is it important to do a functional analysis on products before releasing them onto the market? Why? Select a common product (e.g., a loaf of bread, cereal, a bank account, breakfast at the local café or an item of clothing) and describe what factors might come out of a functional analysis of that product.

5. BAM engagement: How can you use the functional analysis method to improve the efficiency, customer value and kingdom impact of your job? Be specific and descriptive.

16

The Functional Analysis Approach

SECTION 2

"But after observation and analysis,
when you find that anything agrees with reason
and is conducive to the good and benefit of one and all,
then accept it and live up to it."
SIDDHARTHA GAUTAMA

"Finally, brothers, whatever is true, whatever is noble,
whatever is right, whatever is pure, whatever is lovely,
whatever is admirable—if anything is excellent or praiseworthy—
think about such things. . . . [P]ut it into practice."
PHILIPPIANS 4:8-9

IN CHAPTER FIFTEEN, I INTRODUCED the concept of the functional analysis approach as a baseline for identifying, achieving and institutionalizing kingdom impact within the Christian-led company. This is basic to all KC and BAM companies. This chapter will build on that concept with practical examples of how it is performed, and identify five dangers that can undermine it both operationally and spiritually.

FUNCTIONAL ANALYSIS EXAMPLES

Let's briefly consider four primary departments or functions (see fig. 15.1) with an eye to producing kingdom impact: human relations, marketing and sales, quality control and finance. As we discuss these departments and their functions, think of the numerous ministry and witnessing-by-deed opportunities found within each that are *not* mentioned.

Human relations functions. The human relations department (HR) or function is perhaps *the* critical element in the company organizational mix. With the right people, properly selected, trained, motivated and incentivized, any company can accomplish great things. Without the right people or with the wrong people, it is virtually impossible for a company to successfully achieve its mission, regardless of the value of the product or service. With the right people the company can thrive; with the wrong people the company will be fortunate just to survive. Selecting the right people for the right job can be a source of personal and corporate growth, productivity, satisfaction, fulfillment and joy. Selecting the wrong people for a job can create nightmarish situations involving hundreds of wasted hours, diminished productivity, wounded people, damaged reputations, low morale, added expenses, protracted legal wrangling and bitter roots.

Quite simply, no matter how good the deal, how great the product, how attractive the dream, it will not work if the wrong people are involved.

Aside from hiring the right people for the right position, HR, at its essence, is simply how we take care of people, especially people in our own corporate family. The apostle Paul said that those who do not take care of their own, especially those of the family of God, are worse than unbelievers (1 Tim 5:8). Certainly, a BAM company, like a family in the marketplace, should take care of its own.

One illustration of this viewpoint is worth noting: Dennis Bakke, founder and former CEO of AES, one of the world's largest producers of electrical energy with over forty thousand employees in some thirty-five countries, saw the HR department as an obstacle rather than as a valued aid to human relations within the company. He says,

> I was becoming skeptical about [employee] handbooks and most of the other programs administered by human resources departments. . . . [A]nd I began asking questions about the handbook. What if we eliminated it altogether? What if we did away with procedure manuals? They are always out of date, and no one follows them anyway. What if we did away with detailed job descriptions? What if we didn't have an organization chart with boxes representing people and their jobs? What if we

didn't have shift supervisors? What if there were no written limits on what individuals could authorize the company to spend? What if all the specialist titles given to employees were eliminated? What if we created teams of people around areas of the plant to operate and maintain the facility, instead of letting bosses assign tasks and run the plant? What if each group could set its own hours of work? What if each member hired and fired their own colleagues? What if you could make important decisions rather than leave them to your supervisor or the plant manager? I gave no answers, just asked questions.[1]

From this questioning evolved a revolutionary management concept that he called "Honeycomb," based on the individual freedom of bees in the hive to work toward the production of honey. "The basic thrust of my idea was to try to create an environment based on the same principles of trust, freedom, and individuals acting for the good of the larger group."[2] In practical terms, it meant a *radical redesign* of AES plant management and eliminating the HR department, but spreading the HR functions across the company in innovative ways appropriate to each function. This generated the fascinating book *Joy at Work: A CEO's Revolutionary Approach to Fun on the Job*, and an equally evocative Harvard Case Study on the "Missing Department," which challenges corporate leaders everywhere.[3]

Looking at the HR functions and how they intimately affect people's immediate lives and livelihood reveals why HR is so important both from a business and a spiritual point of view. HR functions include recruitment, interviewing, hiring and rejecting, orientation, training, salary and benefit administration, medical care, sick leave, vacations, retirement plans, promotions, evaluations, counseling, layoffs, discipline, firing, safety, communications, legal compliance, records keeping, manuals and documentation, employee relations, and company events, just to name a few.

Each function affects people's lives in ways that can be life-changing, positively or negatively. Seldom are such effects neutral. Each of these also requires

---

[1]Dennis W. Bakke, *Joy at Work* (Seattle: Pearson Venture Group, 2005), p. 84, but see the entire chap. 4 for a detailed understanding of the concept of honeycombing.
[2]Ibid., p. 85.
[3]Jeffrey Pfeffer, "Human Resources at the AES Corp.: The Case of the Missing Department," Harvard Case Study, Harvard Business School, 1997.

endless decisions as to proper policies, procedures, practices and people. More to the point for present purposes, each function offers an opportunity to see the gospel lived out in ways that can lead (or not) to sharing with others the abundant life that we seek and are scripturally promised.

In all of these functions, the methods of performing them and the motivation behind the actions speaks volumes about the company and its leaders as individuals, about what they actually value most, and about their integrity as witnesses for Christ in every situation and aspect of life. Max DePree says that "the first responsibility of a leader is to define reality." It is not inappropriate to suggest that how each HR function is performed (through our policies and procedures) is a de facto testing ground that *defines reality*, the true reality of the company and its leadership, warts and all.[4]

That being so, HR functions also create remarkable opportunities for the CEO who wants to be intentional about having kingdom impact, about making his or her company into a Kingdom Company and a BAM Company. Jesus says that the first two commandments for each Christian are to love God with all of our heart, mind, soul and strength, and to love our neighbors as ourselves (Mt 22:37-39).

In the business setting, it is no stretch to see that our "neighbor" includes all of those we hire and their families, all of those we interview but don't hire and their families, all of those we terminate, all of those in the community labor pool from which we draw, and ultimately all who interact with our company. This last group includes actual or prospective customers, vendors, suppliers, creditors and even competitors. Loving these neighbors through our HR function is not only good business, it is good witness. Steadily improving our HR function, and aligning it with the great commandment and biblical Golden Rule is taking a major step toward being a KC or BAM Company. It is what Mouw calls "holy worldliness."[5]

Before moving ahead, it is important to emphasize a point made earlier. While a Christian-led company seeks to do all it can to engage its functions scripturally, this must be done within the *defined reality* of the business itself. As I have repeatedly emphasized, without business there is no mission. Ac-

---

[4]Max DePree, *Leadership Is an Art* (New York: Dell, 1989), p. 11.
[5]Richard J. Mouw, "A Call to Holy Worldliness," Fourteenth Annual Consultation of Christian Ministry in Daily Life, Pasadena, California, April 21, 2006.

cordingly, there are boundaries to which the BAM business must adhere if it is to keep its business license, comply with the copious volumes of laws (especially in HR), make a profit, survive and have the opportunity of continuing to serve its people and the community. Defining those boundaries and maximizing all of the company's multiple bottom lines is a balancing feat that will bring out the best in management.

In short, the dual mandate challenges and stretches the Christian business person in ways that are stressful but exciting, healthy and extraordinarily rewarding, both professionally and spiritually. And perhaps nowhere is this more prominently seen than in the HR function.

Marketing and sales functions. The marketing and sales functions are the *sine qua non* of business. There can be no company without actual sales of a product or service. This sounds so basic and so obvious that it is almost insulting to discuss it. But many would-be BAM companies have floundered for failure to understand this fact of business life: BAM requires sales of the right product or service to the right target audience (to meet their real or perceived needs in a timely manner) at the right price (right for the customer, the company, the competition and the market) in a manner that helps bond a customer to the company, its brand or image, which usually encourages repetitive purchases by the same customer.

Given the enormous, worldwide competitive pressures within the established capitalist markets for any given product or service, there is great pressure on every business to design and maintain a sustainable marketing and sales model. Successful marketing requires defining and packaging the business, product, service and brand in such a way as to promote sales within the defined contextual market. It can include all or any number of the following functions: company image-making; brand, product and packaging definition and design; extensive market analysis, including market trends, demographic distribution assessment and target market profiling; packaging and price point differentiation; media selections; message creation, production and distribution; public relationship development; and damage control.

Successful sales work in tandem with marketing. While technically different, I include sales here under the marketing umbrella because they are two sides of the same function. In simplistic terms, marketing creates the demand; sales satisfy the demand. Although very different, sales and marketing both include determining how to cause a buyer to exchange his cash assets for the product or service being sold. They require the buyer to perceive real value in acquiring the product and deciding to purchase this product at this price at this time, as opposed to all of the alternatives he or she has available for exchanging hard-earned cash for other products now or in the future. As we will see, BAM sales and marketing go further by providing products and services in a godly manner that serves as a witness to Christ and his teachings.

Media manipulation. Marketing and sales today have the power to manipulate people, especially through the vast media resources that dominate modern society. This manipulation occurs through the overt message content, the subliminal or subtext messages, the media method used, the messengers chosen for delivery, and the implicit associated values, status and stigmas. No one in Western society today can avoid the avalanche of advertisements, images and marketing ploys. To many people it is a daily blitzkrieg that attacks their lives, their children, relationships, values and culture, and that distorts their national, social, economic and public-policy priorities. It can be reasonably, albeit cynically, argued that media advertising is a sophisticated effort to convince people to buy something they don't need and can't afford. More specifically, that it creates perceived needs where none existed before; it instills desires and hunger for something that may not even be good for the customer; it shapes public perceptions and opinion about a company, brand, product, service or person that may bear no relationship to reality; it creates a famous or infamous persona out of the most ordinary or eccentric objects (even a duck or gecko); and it pressures customers to buy beyond their needs, their capacity to pay or their best interests.

While marketing and sales do meet the legitimate needs of literally billions of people daily, they can also be something more sinister. Through time, the art of marketing and sales has developed techniques and technology to manipulate and motivate people to act in ways that they otherwise would not. As such, it is a power that invariably raises special ethical and moral issues. When that power is in the hands of Christians or is used by Christian-led companies, the issues are even more sharply defined. Scripture admonishes us to follow the Golden Rule, to think more highly of others than of ourselves, not to do something that will cause our brother or sister to stumble, to always deal fairly with others, to be truthful, to never bear false witness, to give full value for the price charged and to work for the Lord, not humans, with excellence, honesty, and integrity.

A witness to the integrity of Jesus Christ and his gospel occurs when a Christian-led company puts its product before the public, has its name and reputation at stake in the quality of that product and in the excellence of its service, and then markets, sells and services its products to people who are God's children, or could be. Witnessing for Christ is what we do, not just what we say; being a follower of Jesus is how we live his gospel in the real world with real people in real time.

Accordingly, any company that wants to have a kingdom impact cannot afford to have its methods of marketing and sales reflect anything less than complete honesty, morality, decency, transparency and fairness in every respect: from first contact to the closing of the sale to servicing customers and meeting their needs and complaints afterward.

Achieving this is no easy task. Doing so within the constraints of non-Christian competitors and international markets, within the financial realities of profit-and-loss statements, and within the international or crosscultural business context is especially challenging. Marketing and sales are difficult tasks under the best of circumstances. Doing them from a Christian worldview to achieve kingdom impact—while remaining a healthy, competitive, financially viable company—is a God-sized task. It is a task, however, placed on us for God-sized purposes. It is also an excellent place to prove that the gospel message works in every setting, including successful marketing and sales. After all, if it does not work there, it cannot be relied on to work anywhere.[6]

Sales representatives. The sales function includes a salesperson who will often have face-to-face contact with a buyer to show the product and close the sale. In the days of Willy Loman this included traveling salesmen and catalogues, hawkers and barkers.[7] Today, direct sales occur through a variety of infinitely more sophisticated methods: networks of sale representatives; international call centers; QVC and similar marketing and direct sales channels;

---

[6]For an excellent discussion of how to integrate faith into teaching a broad range of subjects, including business, see David Claerbaut, *Faith and Learning on the Edge* (Grand Rapids: Zondervan, 2004).

[7]On Willy Loman, see Arthur Miller, *Death of a Salesman* (New York: Chelsea, 2003).

infomercials; e-commerce, websites and the Internet; personalized direct mail; and in-store sampling and promotionals. In each case, directly or indirectly, at some point people engage and influence other people.

How those sales representatives deal with the public, how they represent the product and the company, and how they *are* the company to their customers should be a matter of great concern to every company, whether Christian-led or not. Equally important, but often overlooked, is how those people are treated by the company. All too often sales reps are forgotten as people or members of the company's family. Often they are merely objects to be used, abused or discarded at the company's whim. They are usually independent contractors or part-time laborers dealing in the very dog-eat-dog competitive environment of sales. They are faced with enormous pressures, not only from the companies they represent but from the faceless blitz of modern technology and e-commerce that threaten their markets and their livelihoods. Moreover, questions arise as to how they are chosen, supported, supplied, compensated, honored, communicated with and made to feel a part of the company's team.

These issues are particularly important in a Christian-led company, especially if the reps are ethnically or culturally different, or the BAM Company is operating in a foreign or multinational business context. Not only is the actual sales volume affected positively or negatively, but so is the company's witness and ministry to these people who are, after all, also created by God and in need of Christ. The Christian CEO is encouraged to effectively evaluate and define all of the sales functions and not to neglect the company's sales reps.

Quality control functions. Perhaps the number one commandment of BAM and any effort to integrate faith at work is *Thy product and service shall continually be a thing of value, excellent in all of its ways.* Scripture repeatedly calls us "work . . . with all your heart, as working for the Lord, not for men" (Col 3:23; see also Eccl 9:10; 1 Cor 10:31; 1 Pet 4:11) and "in the same way, let your light shine before men, that they may see your good deeds and praise your Father in heaven" (Mt 5:16). The very act of meeting a real need that people have through our vocations and companies is an act of ministry in the name of the Lord.

In God's design, each person is to love his or her neighbors and to serve them with the gifts appropriate to each vocation. This means that I serve you with my talents, and you serve me with your talents. The result is a divine division of labor in which everyone is constantly giving and receiving in a vast interchange, a unity of diverse people in a social order whose substance and energy is love.[8]

The Lord meets people's needs through other people's vocations. He meets their needs through businesses, as well as the love that accompanies the delivery of their products or services. If it is a product or service that is rendered "as for the Lord," by definition it should be "without blemish" and the best of the best, perfect in every way possible.

How the quality control (QC) function of a company is institutionalized or organizationally addressed is vital to the BAM Company's witness for the Lord. One sterling example is the Ritz Carlton Hotels. Its founder, Horst Schulze, is a faithful follower of Jesus Christ. When he established the high standards of service that have made his five-star brand name synonymous with the "most excellent" and "best of the best" hotels in the world, he started with a basic Christian concept of service. He taught his people that "you are ladies and gentlemen, servicing ladies and gentlemen." The staff, rather than being inferior or subservient to the patrons, is elevated to their status but further graced with the privilege of helping make others' lives more comfortable and better. QC at the Ritz Carlton Hotels is maintained by empowering every employee to provide whatever assistance is needed by the guest, then and there. Problems in service delivery are not resolved by management but by those at the lowest functional level possible (i.e., at the level at which the service is actually delivered and where the solution must be implemented). And if a problem occurs twice, it is deemed to be a service flaw that must be addressed systemically at the service level rather than the management level—that is, the solution to the problem must address its root cause in order to avoid repetition, and the people best suited for that investigation are those on the front lines of service.[9]

China is learning by painful example that QC must be given top priority. The recall of products manufactured in China has become endemic, with the repetitive rejection of a major range of its products by the United States, Eu-

---

[8]Gene Edward Veith Jr., *God at Work* (Wheaton, Ill.: Crossway, 2002), p. 40.
[9]Horst Schultz, "Creating a Passion for Excellence in Your Company: The Ritz-Carlton Hotel Story," FCCI Execute with Excellence Conference, Cancun, Mexico, October 2, 2002.

rope, Australia and New Zealand. Those include toys, pet food, toothpaste, lipstick, certain sea foods, automobiles, contaminated milk powder, and medicines.[10] One BAM Company in China has addressed this issue, placing high standards on its people and making each person on the production line a voluntary, self-motivated QC expert for company. The system it has instituted penalizes bad production, rewards good production, gives the workers pride in their craft and in maintaining the company's high reputation.

In summary, the QC functions of a company are not only good business but are at the heart of providing service in a Christlike manner. Christian-led companies that seek to have a kingdom impact (and to truly become BAM companies) must, first and always, seek to consistently deliver the most excellent, well-designed, well-made, well-serviced, fairly priced, value-laden products and services they are capable of. Nothing less is truly loving your neighbor (your customer) or living out the biblical Golden Rule through the company's efforts.

Financial functions. Nowhere is faith more challenging than in the area of money. Money has a power of its own that Satan uses to drive a wedge between Christians and their Lord, between Christians in the marketplace and the church, and even among marketplace Christians themselves as they participate in the pervasive worldly practices of business. Thomas Merton poignantly said, "Money has demonically usurped the role in modern society which the Holy Spirit is to have in the Church."[11] Martin Luther, speaking more pragmatically, said, "There are three conversions necessary: the conversion of the heart, mind, and the purse."[12] Richard Foster amplifies this:

> Jesus makes it unmistakably clear that money is not some impersonal medium of exchange. *Money is not something that is morally neutral, a resource to be used in good or bad ways depending solely upon our attitude toward it. . . .* According to Jesus and all the writers of the New

---

[10]Jyoti Thottam, "The Growing Dangers of China Trade," *Time,* June 28, 2007 <www.time .com/time/magazine/article/0,9171,1638436,00.html>; Austin Ramzy "A Chinese Toymaker's Mea Culpa," *Time,* August 14, 2007 <www.time.com/time/world/article/0,8599,1652707,00. html?iid=fb_share>; Austin Ramzy, "China's Melamine Woes Likely to Get Worse," *Time,* November 4, 2008 <www.time.com/time/world/article/0,8599,1856168,00.html>.
[11]Thomas Merton, quoted in Richard J. Foster, *Money, Sex and Power* (San Francisco: Harper & Row, 1985), p. 19.
[12]Martin Luther, quoted in Foster, *Money, Sex and Power,* p. 19.

Testament, behind money are very real spiritual forces that energize it and give it a life of its own. Hence, money is an active agent; it is a law unto itself; and it is capable of inspiring devotion. . . . What we must recognize is the seductive power of mammon. Money has power, spiritual power, to win our hearts. Behind our coins and dollar bills or whatever material form we choose to give to our money are spiritual forces. . . . [These ask] for our allegiance in a way that sucks the milk of human kindness out of our very being.[13]

Money can be used for good or for bad. The challenge facing the BAM Company is to learn how to use it for good and to minimize the potential for its destructive forces being unleashed. That said, let's look at the company's financial functions, which include banking and credit relationships, bookkeeping, accounting, payroll, accounts payable, accounts receivable, collection policies and often product returns, discounting and refund policies, foreign exchange, and money management. Each of these functions has far-reaching consequences both within the company and beyond, especially for the Christian-led company.

Alan Ross, former president of FCCI, tells the story of how he attempted to lead one of his company's creditors to the Lord and was told bluntly, "I don't want to hear about how honorable your Lord is until you, as his follower, start paying my bills on time."[14] How we deal with others directly reflects our witness for Christ. If we do not pay our company or personal bills in a timely manner, if we stretch our suppliers out ninety days or more because we have the power to do so, if we use imprudent or harmful collection policies against those who owe us, if we lie to our banker or cheat on our taxes, if we keep two sets of books, if we do not make our payroll, if we overcompensate our executives at the expense of our employees, shareholders, customers and community, if we do not act as good stewards of the funds within our possession—these and countless other ifs tell the story of ways we can dishonor Christ and his gospel. Conversely, they spell out major opportunities we have to positively

---

[13]Foster, *Money, Sex and Power*, pp. 25-26.
[14]This statement was made by Alan Ross in discussion with the author, September 2001, and to audiences for FCCI. Ross also authored two books on faith in the workplace: Alan M. Ross, *Beyond World Class* (Chicago: Dearborn, 2002), and Alan M. Ross and Cecil Murphey, *Unconditional Excellence* (Avon, Mass.: Adams Media, 2002).

witness to the world about who our Master is—and to persuasively demonstrate that it is not money.

If we do not understand the importance of this, we have only to hear Jesus' own admonition. In words reminiscent of his parable about the servant who did not properly invest the master's money (Lk 19:13-27), Jesus told a second parable of the ungrateful servant who sought mercy and debt relief from his master but did not extend it to his own debtors. Upon learning of this duplicity, the master seized the man and said, " 'You wicked servant. . . . Shouldn't you have had mercy on your fellow servant just as I had on you?' In anger his master turned him over to the jailers to be tortured, until he should pay back all he owed." Jesus then said, "This is how my heavenly Father will treat each of you unless you forgive your brother from your heart" (Mt 18:23-35).

While the parable is about mercy and forgiveness, it is also about accountability and justice, meeting one's financial obligations and extending fairness and equity to those we deal with. Jesus was fond of using marketplace and money parables to teach us that in all of our financial dealings we are to observe the Golden Rule, God's commandments and Jesus' gospel teachings. He taught us to make each of our encounters with others over money special *teaching moments* in which we actively demonstrate the true qualities honesty, fairness, justice, mercy, compassion and accountability taught by our Master.

In short, how each function on the financial side of business is managed speaks volumes to all of our stakeholders about our true values, treasure and Lord. Quite simply, no Christian-led company (much less, a KC or BAM Company) can have a sustainable kingdom impact without managing its money in kingdom-honoring ways.

All of its ways. We have briefly examined four business functions and even with these have only scratched the surface, only begun the drilling-down exercise that is needed. Similar discussions can be had at every level and about every function within the company. If a company is to truly incorporate biblical principles into its DNA, it can and should subject *all* of its ways to in-depth scriptural scrutiny to determine their potential of kingdom impact. Doing so is the hallmark of a BAM Company. Like clearing a field of boulders, it is a never-ending process, but one that reaps great rewards, both here and in eternity, for those who persist.

WARNINGS

The road to functional analysis is fraught with peril for the uninitiated. Accordingly, some warning flags need to be raised before proceeding further.

Employee buy-in. While it may be difficult to conceive of involving every employee in this function-crafting exercise, especially those who are not Christian, it is nonetheless highly recommended. Without the buy-in of those who are performing the functions, the quality of the results may suffer. The way to approach this, however, is not as a Bible-beating, evangelical exercise, but rather as a performance-enhancing effort by the company to make it the best in its industry, not only in quality of product and service, but in being one of the best possible places to work and to realize one's own potential. This degree of excellence can only be accomplished by senior management extracting from Scripture those universal principles that Christ taught, and then implementing them within the context of the various business functions.

Again, it is critical to understand that this functional analysis approach is *not* to be performed as a *Christianizing* exercise, but as a *kingdom impact* exercise. That may seem a subtle distinction, but it is important. The BAM team is taking gospel principles and seeking to use them in an ostensibly secular environment to maximize the company's service and love toward both customers and employees. The process of doing this does not have to be put in religious or theological language, but in language that emphasizes the universal scriptural values recognized by people of good will everywhere. The fact that the CEO is Christian and uses Scripture to extract these values should be no secret in the company, but its imposition on the functions (and people) of the company—without proselytizing—should be a positive, noninvasive, nonthreatening witness to all who deal with the company, both inside and out. It should result in insiders and outsiders alike asking why this company is so different, and Christian entrepreneurs asking how they can create this type of company.

Abuse of power. Faith integration is far from a simple process, and if done incorrectly or insensitively, it is latent with dangers of being misunderstood or even evoking charges of religious harassment and discrimination. It must never be forgotten that the CEO is a major power figure within the company's environment and holds sway over people's lives in very decisive ways. The employees will always be conscious of this, even if the CEO is not. It is a fact of business life that simply cannot be avoided or forgotten, especially in the midst of a faith integration effort.

A Christian CEO who acts out of well-intentioned zeal and enthusiasm can, and often will, overtly or subtly communicate directives to his employees that constitute religious harassment or religious persecution or that create a religiously hostile environment for nonbelievers, weak believers or people of faiths or denominations other than that of the CEO. Such actions, no matter how well-intentioned, can be an abuse of the power relationship within the business hierarchy that is first and foremost wrong and biblically condemned. Further, as a practical matter, it can result in charges of discrimination, lawsuits, union complaints, employee dissatisfaction, counterproductive witness and a collapse of the faith integration efforts and effectiveness.

Christ called us to live the gospel in every aspect of our lives, 24/7. In doing so, however, we must remember that Christ is a gentle man. He has the power to knock down our doors and force his way upon us, but he does not do that. Instead, he gently, albeit urgently, knocks on our doors and waits for us to invite him in. "Here I am! I stand at the door and knock" (Rev 3:20). So too we need to be Christians in the marketplace, to act as salt and light in an otherwise tasteless and dark place, but we are to do so as gentlemen and gentlewomen, letting the benefits of following our Savior be seen from our actions, lives, work, management and integrity.

In that regard, a major part of managing a BAM Company is to make certain that there are no real or perceived abuses of power by the Christian CEO or the BAM team. In integrating faith into the company and its functions, Jesus is not to be forced on anyone, nor is anyone to be discriminated against in the company by reason of their belief or nonbelief. Rather, the BAM Company is to be a sanctuary for all people of all faiths or no faith, exhibiting God's love, compassion and grace as well as his excellence, fairness and justice. In so doing, we are to make our God and his Son so attractive in action that they want to know him in person.

Doctrinal dogma. A corollary to the danger of abusing the CEO's power is avoiding all ecclesiastical, denominational and theological doctrines and dogma. To the greatest extent possible the biblical principles that are integrated into the BAM Company should be basic to the Bible—the core and only the core gospel. Throughout the centuries Jesus' core gospel message has been distorted and burdened by ecclesiastical traditions, practices and prejudices. Just as the cross has often become a gilded, jewel-encrusted ornament, so the gospel has been heavily ladened with nonscriptural concepts of what is holy, what is "proper church," what is acceptable music, dress, worship, doctrine and lifestyles and what is apostasy. Many of these change from church to church, age to age, culture to culture—and that very fact tells us much about what is and what is not the core gospel.

I do not reject this history, but adamantly note that these matters are often far from the gospel of love that Jesus proclaimed, the unity that the apostle Paul preached, and the profound simplicity of Jesus' message as seen by John or the active faith to which James calls us.

One of the wonderful aspects of the modern Marketplace Mission Movement has been its ability to avoid the pitfalls of denominational, doctrinal, theological and religious wrangling that has split the church for centuries. While the movement tends to be heavily evangelical and Protestant, it is neither; it welcomes within its ranks the people of "the whole church" from every Protestant denomination, as well as charismatics, Pentecostals, Roman Catholics, Orthodox, Coptics and other followers of Jesus the Christ. To date, the movement has been about businesspeople ministering to businesspeople to, within and through the marketplace; and they have done so in ways that focus on applying Jesus' core gospel to the details and realities of daily life and work. They proceed from the view that if the Bible is not relevant and applicable to business, it is not relevant or applicable to anything. If it doesn't work here, it doesn't work anywhere.

Unfortunately, there are some organizations within the Marketplace Mission Movement that are starting to press various theological agendas. That will greatly weaken the movement as a whole. For the KC and BAM Company the important message is: Stick to the basics and strenuously avoid letting the time-honored biblical principles be watered down and blunted by secondary matters, dogma or denominational practices.

Resistance. Satan will not be pleased with the BAM process, and the discerning CEO must know that there will be resistance to these efforts. Ironically, the greatest resistance often comes from well-intentioned, mature Christians within the company who do not understand the BAM concept and are steeped in their own ecclesiastical traditions of what constitutes proper faith integration. They believe, as the church has taught for decades, that business and profits are an inherently, albeit necessary, evil, or that business and faith should never be mixed. There may also be resistance from suspicious nonbelievers and, in today's pluralistic workforce, from people of other faiths and traditions.

How to overcome that resistance is a difficult, touchy subject. Douglas A. Hicks has even suggested that Christian faith integration in today's world is wholly inappropriate and abusive per se. Noting the prevalent "religious diversity in the workplace, especially in the United States," he advocates a faith-neutral environment which he calls "respectful pluralism," which is tolerant of all religious practice and an advocate of none.

> Respectful pluralism means resisting company-sponsored religion and spirituality while allowing employees to bring their own religions to work. . . . Company leaders, rather than promote any religious worldview, should create a culture of mutual respect that allows diverse employees to work together constructively.[15]

He unequivocally condemns the Marketplace Mission Movement, the marketplace ministry and BAM camps, and apparently all efforts by Christian CEOs to live out their faith in and through the workplace.

> Religion and spirituality in the workplace often refer to a religion or spirituality of the workplace. I have suggested that a critical distinction can be made between the beliefs and practices of individual employees, on the one hand, and the rituals and ethos of the organization, on the other. The wider question of organizational culture has received significant attention in the leadership and management literature. Some scholars have noted, in descriptive-analytical terms, the ways in which an organization's culture can be religious, quasi-religious, or spiritual. Other scholars have actually played a direct role in contributing to, or even promoting, the religion or spirituality of corporations, accepting the view that business leaders should serve as "spiritual guides" and that firms should develop their own "organizational spirituality." . . .

---

[15]Douglas A. Hicks, *Religion and the Workplace* (Cambridge: Cambridge University Press, 2003), pp. 2-3.

My concurrence [with proponents of the Christian workplace] in rejecting the fully secularist position, however, does not mean that I endorse either the Christian workplace or the generically spiritual workplace. To the contrary, I believe that each of these positions pays inadequate attention to the religious, spiritual, and moral diversity of employees and, in this omission each of these institutional approaches fails to respect equally the beliefs and practices of employees.[16]

Hicks, a Christian, misses the obvious point that faith integration actually fosters and creates a culture of mutual respect that allows diverse employees to work together constructively. It is not about proselytizing or denying employees their right to believe and practice their faith (or penalizing or persecuting them for it), or about imposing a religious view on the employees. Rather, faith integration is being obedient to Jesus to live the gospel 24/7, to love people through our lives and work, to show that love through actions that help people and communities holistically, to show respect for those who disagree with us, and even to love and help our enemies. Although the church historically has not had a particularly enviable record of tolerance, even within its own ranks, that seems to have changed measurably in the past two decades. Regardless, Jesus' gospel, which is the basis for BAM, is undoubtedly the most tolerant, loving, culturally respectful faith among today's global religious pantheon. Clearly, BAM's concepts are fundamentally the opposite of the global persecution and intolerance being exhibited toward Christians by many other faiths (and secularists). That persecution, intolerance and opposition—even from believing Christians like Hicks—reminds me of Jesus' warning that the world, ironically, would misunderstand us, hate us, persecute us and even seek to destroy us for preaching universal peace, love, respect and tolerance, and for attempting to live out our faith (e.g., Mt 5:11; 10:22; Lk 21:12; Jn 15:20-21).

To address the issue of resistance, it will be necessary for the CEO and his executive team to address it head-on with great wisdom and sensitivity. The process will require scriptural guidance; focused, direct and intercessory prayer; and wise counsel. As Scripture says, wisdom comes from many counselors (e.g., Ps 111:1; Prov 15:22). In the exercise of lay theologizing, it is especially true. How the resistance will be overcome or neutralized will vary from

---

[16]Ibid., p. 113-14.

case to case. If handled correctly, the process can actually strengthen the BAM movement within the company, actively demonstrate our concern for universal tolerance and be used by the Lord to help mature the BAM team.

Avoidance. A related warning is in order at this point: the necessity of avoiding culturally offensive faith integration. First, the faith integration process is to discern useful, universal concepts and values that God would have us apply in our daily work in every culture. Any efforts to the contrary will only diminish our witness and the effectiveness of the integration process and the attractiveness of our Lord to nonbelievers.

Second, because of the international, crosscultural locale of most BAM companies, the process must also be highly contextual. Where indigenous, nonbelieving employees are involved, it is important that the faith integration process and community-development projects be implemented in ways that offer no offense to the local culture, but even harmonize with it. The only qualification is that such contextualization be done without compromising the core gospel. As Paul said, he could be all things to all people for the sake of the gospel, as long as the core gospel of Jesus was not compromised (1 Cor 9:22).

Discerning what might be culturally offensive is a matter of due diligence, of doing your homework. That means consulting with people who have your best interests at heart, who intimately know the local culture and its power centers, and who will give honest, transparent, evaluative commentary and advice. It is usually best to check with more than one adviser to avoid his or her personal agendas or viewpoints that may be in error. Crippling mistakes can usually be avoided by such consultations. If the consultations reveal potential problems, those need to be dealt with in a straightforward manner that wholly avoids or mitigates any damage.

DISCUSSION QUESTIONS

1. How could God be glorified through the HR department of a BAM Company?

2. Define *marketing.* How does it differ from *sales?* In what ways can God be glorified through the sales and marketing department of a BAM Company?

3. What kingdom issues are raised by the marketing function? List, describe

and explain at least six such issues, with scriptural support for each. Study your local newspapers, magazines and television and find six product/services advertisements. Describe the theological/biblical viewpoint expressed in each and discuss.

4. What does Scripture say about financial matters? How should a Christian glorify and honor God with regard to money and finances?

5. What precautions, policies and practices should a BAM Company CEO mandate to assure that he or she and the executive team are not using their power over employees to force them into a Christian belief system? Does this eviscerate the BAM intentionality and emphasis that the author encourages? Why or why not? Would it be wrong for the CEO to invite employees to participate in company prayer, Bible study and devotionals? Explain the pros and cons of this viewpoint.

6. How do you or could you integrate the gospel into your life and work in such a way as to draw people to Christ without coercing (even unintentionally) through your power as a leader? How can this be applied in a BAM Company?

7. What are the extra challenges that may come with "drilling down" in a crosscultural context? Cite and discuss possible examples, both within the United States and in a foreign country.

8. BAM engagement: Assuming you are a BAM Company CEO, how will you and your team identify and deal with resistance to your BAM efforts, either among Christians or non-Christians? Is there a danger that such actions might adversely affect the company? Explain.

9. BAM engagement: Through a "drilling down" process in your proposed (or real) business, apply the functional analysis approach in two areas other than those addressed in the text (i.e., other than human relations, marketing and sales, quality control, and finances).

17

People and Money

*"Then I heard the voice of the Lord saying,
'Whom shall I send? And who will go for us?'
And I said, 'Here am I. Send me!'"*
ISAIAH 6:8

"The Spirit came into me and raised me to my feet, and I heard him speaking to me.

He said: "Son of man, I am sending you . . . to a rebellious nation that has rebelled against me. . . . [D]o not be afraid of them or their words. Do not be afraid, though briers and thorns are all around you and you live among scorpions. Do not be afraid of what they say or terrified by them, though they are a rebellious house. You must speak my words to them, whether they listen or fail to listen . . . . But you, son of man, listen to what I say to you. Do not rebel like that rebellious house; open your mouth and eat what I give you."
EZEKIEL 2:2-3, 6-8

*"Lord, where you lead me I will follow,
what you feed me I will swallow."*
MISSIONARY PRAYER

AT THIS POINT I DELVE MORE DEEPLY into what is perhaps the two thorniest issues of all: people and money (or capital). It is a simple but basic fact that businesses require both. They are necessary as early as possible in the BAM Company formation process and will be necessary every day of the company's existence. It is therefore appropriate that we plunge into these deep waters before we address the step-by-step process that is designed to bring convergence to all that has gone before.

People and Organization

Before the BAM Company can move far into the planning and implementation process, its leaders must think organizationally, asking three fundamental questions: How do we form the BAM team ? What organizational structure most effectively manages the demands of the dual mandate? How much difference does the organizational nomenclature we use affect our enterprise?

The BAM team. There are numerous Scripture verses that highlight the importance of formal planning for the BAM Company, especially planning that is committed to the Lord and seeks the advice of many godly counselors (e.g., Prov 12:15; 15:22; 16:3, 9; 20:18). I highly recommend this formal planning approach but believe that before effective, long-range planning can occur, the BAM CEO should form a collaborative executive BAM team to assist in that process and to manage the company once it is formed. One of the major tenets of secular business management today is the concept of working within the team context. That is even more important in a company faced with the additional challenges of BAM, its dual mandate and its multiple bottom lines. Many BAMers try to be "Lone Rangers," working alone, under no external authority and with no structured accountability. That is decidedly neither scriptural nor wise. Neither is it the way to secure the greatest blessings from the Lord or to maximize the company's opportunities for maximizing its kingdom impact.

Accordingly, after the CEO has made his initial selection of a country or city, product and business, I recommend that he or she is now in a position to develop a profile of the people needed on the BAM team. The elements of that profile will include, among other attributes: international exposure, country experience, language capabilities, Christian credentials, mission background, business expertise, skill sets, community-development experience, financial needs, personal characteristics, the right chemistry, family status, desire and availability.

A senior management team of seasoned individuals who have the gifts, professional skills and a solid commitment to the Lord, to missions and to the company, will be required for long-term sustainable success. Ideally, this BAM team will be crosscultural, and each member will have extensive crosscultural experience. Each member also needs an intimate understanding of the distinctly divergent demands and rigors of both international business and mission, especially in developing or emerging nations of the world.

Conversely, if the company is already formed and its Christian leaders want to re-envision it into a BAM Company, the team's makeup and commitment are equally important. In that regard, team members may need to be reevaluated in light of BAM's unique challenges. Let us consider some of those.

Integrity. First, in BAM businesses we seek Christ-honoring excellence in all things (see, e.g., Eccles 9:10; 1 Cor 9:23; 10:31; Col 3:23; 1 Pet 4:11). We are scripturally called to no lesser standard, which applies to the selection of the BAM team members. The men and women forming the company's executive leadership team must, in addition to their professional skills, have the highest character, integrity and faith calling. The criteria for selection should, in my judgment, mirror those Paul recommends for leadership of the church (see 1 Tim 3:1-10; 1 Pet 5:2). There is considerably more pressure on the selection process because of the additional multiple bottom lines envisioned for BAM and the expertise that is required to achieve them. That is all the more reason for careful, prayerful, discerning selection of the team that God has preordained to take the BAM Company into hostile fire. It should be reiterated that while it may be permissible and perhaps desirable to have non-Christians in the company, it can be divisive and even destructive if they are on the leadership team.

Hiring nonbelievers. Should a BAM Company be staffed by believers only? The answer is, "Absolutely not!" but with four qualifications. First, it is essential that the CEO and the board of directors, if any, be committed, mature believers. The CEO will set the culture of the company and lead it in God-honoring ways (or not). The board is that body to which the CEO of a BAM Company is accountable, both professionally and spiritually. Improper spiritual alignment between the board members and the CEO would be discordant at best and potentially disruptive of the entire BAM effort. It would be the modern corporate equivalent of the "unequal yoking" Scripture clearly calls us to avoid (2 Cor 6:14-18; see also Is 30:1-5; Jer 2:17-20; 5:5-7).

Second, it is highly preferable that the BAM team of senior managers also be mature, committed believers. These leaders of the company will shape its policies, practices and priorities. If they are not in alignment with the CEO they will invariably clash and may even work at cross-purposes. On the other hand, having all of the BAM team as believers may not be possible or prudent in view of the foreign business context, the complexities of the company products and markets, the availability of a competent local labor pool, and the Lord's guidance. Nonetheless, the CEO, board and intercessory prayer team should pray earnestly that the Lord identify and call qualified Christian men and women to work with the CEO and become part of the team that will implement and nurture the BAM vision and goals.

If no such believers are found, it is imperative that the BAM team be competent professionals who are, at the very least, not resistant to the CEO's faith leadership and the BAM concept. If these team members are also indigenous prospects for conversion, so much the better. Such conversions are certainly one of the company's kingdom goals.

Third, the other employees of the company need not be believers, but it would be helpful if some were. A major goal of the BAM Company's community outreach programs is to provide employment for those in need, regardless of their spiritual condition. In fact, much of the eventual story of a BAM Company will center on the faith journeys of these souls. They are, after all, the primary reason the company came to this particular place at this particular time.

Keep in mind, however, that although some local employees may be (or identify themselves as) Christians, the company should not assume they are spiritually mature, have much biblical exposure or are active in church. Almost certainly, their religious views and faith journeys have been shaped by very different social, political and religious contexts than those of the BAM team. Exploring their different pilgrimages can be, however, one of the special delights awaiting the BAM team members and their families.

Fourth, the company must recognize that its BAM emphasis may cause some nonbelievers within the workforce to feel left out, uncomfortable or even disadvantaged in their employment prospects. Others, including those employees who were initially receptive, may come to resent the company's spiritual basis. If left unchecked and not addressed immediately as problems arise, these individuals can cause serious disruption and contentiousness, thereby polluting or poisoning the company's morale, productivity and witness.

To minimize this danger and to respect each employee's God-given right to believe as he or she sees fit, during the hiring process all candidates for employment should be clearly advised of the company's faith focus, *and* the employee's religious freedom when exercised in harmony with the company's values and vision. At this point the issue is not one of promoting the Christian faith but of having all employees in alignment with the underlying business values and vision, which are derived from the Christian faith (e.g., honesty, integrity, character development, standards of excellence and caring for each other). Further, steps must continually be taken throughout the company's life to reinforce these values and vision with the workforce, both in words and deeds, in management policies and practices.

Accountability. Being an unaccountable Lone Ranger is not a healthy BAM business model. Each of God's ambassadors on the mission field, whether traditional or nontraditional (such as BAM), should be "under authority" and held accountable for their actions. As the U.S. Navy says, "That which is inspected is respected." While accountability and inspection are different sides of the same coin, the point is clear. People who are accountable perform better. With BAM, two questions must be asked: (1) Accountable to whom? and (2) Accountable for what?

First, the BAM team's primary line of accountability must be to the company's board of directors (or sending agency), to the CEO and, among the BAM team members themselves, to each other collectively. Accountability to an ecclesiastical church or parachurch body, locally or back home, should also be considered. This can, however, be awkward and counterproductive if the church or parachurch organization has a firmly established, traditional mission mindset that does not grasp the uniqueness of BAM mission.

Often, because of a BAM Company's nontraditional mission calling, it will be advantageous for the CEO and perhaps others among the executive BAM team to join or form a local peer group, such as Christ@Work, CBMC-Forums, Convene or C12. I highly recommend this. In addition, the CEO and BAM team may want a special advisory board of directors/counselors to serve that purpose.

Second, the BAM team is accountable for every aspect of their lives both on and off the mission field. BAM is not a 9-to-5 proposition. It is a 24/7 commitment. The reasons for this high level of accountability are many, but primarily it is to assure that the BAM Company stays on its kingdom track, that the leadership is making all of its decisions based on biblical principles, that they are practicing such principles in every aspect of the company's operations, that the team members and their families are making a positive witness for Christ within the community and the company, that they are having a positive kingdom impact in all they do, that they are living healthy, God-fearing lifestyles, that they are treating each other and their individual family members in God-honoring, healthy, uplifting ways, and that they are looking out for each other and those under their care.

Competent professionals. It is essential to the success of the business enterprise that the CEO and his BAM team members be competent business professionals who can perform their part of the company's work skillfully and efficiently. If a prospective BAM team member would not be hired by a secular company for a particular business role, then that person should not be added to the team in that capacity just because he or she is a willing, available Christian. The BAM business is, first and foremost, a business that has to succeed in business. It is an obvious but frequently ignored fact of business life that it cannot do so without the right people in the right places on the team.

Patrick Lai makes an interesting observation, however: "Though competence is important, if we must choose between two workers, one with good character and another with good competence, choose character. It is easier to teach competence than character." He then lists research findings for the "top ten qualities for effective tentmakers":

1. spiritually mature

2. socially adept

3. emotionally stable

4. persevering

5. evangelistic zeal

6. recruit others

7. language fluency

8. team player

9. clear objectives

10. accountable[1]

---

[1] Patrick Lai, *Tentmaking* (Waynesboro, Ga.: Authentic, 2005), p. 64.

Hiring ministers and missionaries. In the BAM team selection process the question is often raised about having traditional missionaries or pastors occupy prominent positions on the team. While there is considerable missiological tradition for doing so, there is often little BAM value. It has become an accepted consensus among most BAM practitioners that pastors and missionaries generally do not make good BAM team members. Although some may find this conclusion objectionable, even offensive, the prevailing wisdom among BAM advocates is that it is far easier to make a missionary out of a businessperson than to make a businessperson out of a missionary. It has been shown in the field that pastoral and missionary temperaments, nonprofit orientation and mindset, calling, gifts and skill sets are quite different than those required for a successful BAM business.

Accordingly, hiring pastors and missionaries as part of the BAM team must be (1) for specific purposes that are in harmony with the SMBP, (2) because they have special gifts that will be useful to the company and its SMBP, and (3) the result of their special BAM calling by the Lord. As harsh as it may sound, no other standard of hiring seems conducive to the long-term effectiveness of the team or the long-term satisfaction and joy of the individual hired. Setting people up for failure by placing them in an untenable environment that they are ill-suited for is neither good mission, good business nor good Christian practice.

Although this point is a generality that has its exceptions, it serves as a caveat to those who are forming a BAM team: They must carefully and prayerfully profile the skills required by the enterprise and, if at all possible, accept no compromises. It further underscores the need for careful, professional planning and cross-training in missions for the *businesspersons* selected to join the BAM team. Businesspeople may have the inherent *potential* of making better BAM missionaries, but that potential must be developed. That requires appropriate training in Scripture, mission, pastoral care and Christian community-development. Anything less diminishes the odds for success in the BAM enterprise.

Lifestyle evangelism. We often hear how important "lifestyle evangelism" is for missionaries. How the missionary and his or her family conduct their personal lives has perhaps the greatest impact, either positively or negatively, on how their messages of Christ's love, presence and salvation are received. Make no mistake, especially in foreign settings, those with whom the CEO, BAM team and their families interact definitely watch these Christians' lives more than they hear their words. They take their cue as to the nature of our God through the personal integrity, lifestyle and management style of the BAM CEO and his or her team.

Knowing the primary people group and their focus will dictate how the BAMer lives. It is a delicate but necessary task. If the company is an NGO focused on the poorest of the poor, the choices become easier. If, however, the person works for a BAM Company (a businessman or woman and a business owner/executive, even of a small enterprise), the choices are infinitely more difficult. Presumably, as part of the business community, the BAMer wants to be accepted by his or her business peers. It is necessary, therefore, to dress and act according to the standards appropriate for that class of person in that society. If the BAMer dresses higher or lower than the target group, he or she may not be accepted by the business community; if higher than his target customer base, he or she will not be accepted by the people. Lai, an Asian BAMer, feels quite strongly about this and requires all of his employees to dress in standard business attire daily—to dress appropriately for their station in this culture for his particular business. "How and where we live impacts who will befriend us. Our lifestyle needs to reflect our place in society. It does not make sense to the national [local people] for a business executive to be living in a slum."[2]

BAM is not easy in any aspect, but neglecting the lifestyle issues will clearly impede the mission. Here again, the lifestyle choices are not just for the BAMer, but also for his or her whole family. Obtaining family buy-in to these choices is important to both the mission success and to family harmony.

Management-style evangelism. Another aspect of forming a BAM team deserves special comment. Since one of their initial tasks is to integrate faith into their business, two points are clearly relevant. First, the CEO and each member of the BAM team need to know, understand and be in alignment on the biblical values that will govern every aspect of the company's existence, including its culture, policies, procedures, practices, products and services, decisions, and relations. That requires biblical knowledge and focused prayerful thought.

---

[2]Lai, *Tentmaking*, p. 250. See his broader discussion on lifestyles, pp. 249-57.

Second, the CEO and executive team must exhibit those same biblical principles in every facet of their lives and work to the maximum extent possible. When managers say they are leading their companies for Christ and then act in ways contrary to the gospel, this leads to a counterproductive witness. Whether on the plant floor, in the company lunchroom or boardroom, or in the community, people are watching and are very quick to find fault. When fault is found, innuendo, rumors, gossip, company grapevine talk, and even charges of personal misconduct or hypocrisy—whether valid or merely perceived—usually follow. If these are leveled at the CEO, BAM team or their family members, it can do irreparable damage to them personally and to the company and its SMBP, no matter how false or ill-conceived the rumors. When this happens, Satan wins and our Lord and his kingdom are compromised, if not shamed.

This calls for not only lifestyle evangelism, but what I call management-style evangelism. That is, what BAM Company managers say, think and do in every aspect and activity of the company will communicate more about the truth of the gospel than anything else. Accordingly, the CEO and BAM team's management style, policies and practices should always and only be performed in "a manner worthy of the gospel of Christ" (Phil 1:27) and be a winsome testimony to the attractiveness of following the Jesus way.

In his ministry, Jesus exhibited management styles and practices that all managers today can and should emulate. This is especially so when we realize that management is the exercise of power over others to achieve a desired result. In a creative, entrepreneurial vein, Laurie Beth Jones's book *Jesus CEO* introduces what she calls the "Omega management style" of Jesus, which incorporates both the "masculine, authoritative use" and the "feminine, cooperative use of power."[3] She then lists some eighty-five markers of Jesus' management style under three headings, focused on strengths of self-mastery, action and relationships.

In her later book, *Jesus, Inc.*, Jones posits a new, even more creative term for an emerging "new breed of business people," which she calls, "spiritreneurs," combining *spirit* and *entrepreneur*.[4] Defining spiritreneurs as "those who fully integrate their soul in a workplace enterprise," she says that they "are spring-

---

[3]Laura Beth Jones, *Jesus CEO* (New York: Hyperion, 1995), p. xiii.
[4]Laura Beth Jones, *Jesus, Inc.* (New York: Crown Business, 2001), p. xiii.

ing up all over" and are imitating Jesus of Nazareth, "the original spiritreneur . . . perhaps the ultimate spiritreneur—because he created a new category of work for himself and was able to make a living doing what he most loved."[5]

While I have difficulty with some of the terminology being proposed by Jones and others, these books give a sampling of the relationship people have seen between business and Jesus, his person, his message, his methods and his model. In so doing, they give needed guidance to the CEO and executive team as to how they should manage the BAM Company to simultaneously be effective (1) in moving the business forward, and (2) in making Jesus appealing and real to people who need him so badly.

Support systems. The BAM team as a whole, and each of its members and their families, need support systems to assist them in dealing with the personal challenges and crises that inevitably accompany mission work. That support must include an organized, intercessory prayer-partner ministry or prayer partners back home, online or within the group itself. The power of prayer is often the only thing that keeps those on the mission field from the clutches of the evil one. The prayer cover should not only address the safety of those on the mission field but their families back home. Satan is not shy about trying to pull dedicated Christians off of the mission field by creating family crises, sicknesses and even deaths. Scripture is replete with warnings about this danger and with admonitions to bathe every aspect of our work and lives in prayer. That is especially true when people are directly invading Satan's territory and seeking to gain a beachhead in order to move inland in righteous conquest. Quite simply, spiritual warfare is war. It is real and it inflicts casualties. Although war terminology is not politically correct in many church and mission circles, the apostle Paul's vivid reminder bears repeating here: "Put on the full armor of God so that you can take your stand against the devil's schemes. For our struggle is not against flesh and blood, but . . . against the powers of this dark world and against the spiritual forces of evil in the heavenly realms" (Eph 6:11-12).

On another front, the attrition rate of traditional missionaries serving in foreign lands is unacceptably high and a real concern. The reasons for prematurely abandoning the mission field are numerous, but they usually include

---

[5]Ibid., pp. xiv-xv.

some form of personal, family or faith crisis. Many of these crises could have been avoided or dealt with more effectively had there been support systems in place both on the field and at home. These systems should be as wide and varied as the living conditions demand and as the individuals need. They are especially important to expat members of the BAM team and their families who have never experienced crosscultural living, particularly within developing nations and in the midst of extreme poverty.

In addition to intercessory prayer, the following are a few support systems that might be considered: sanctuaries and retreats where the team can be spiritually fed in the midst of their efforts to feed others; activities for social integration, healthy entertainment and fun; opportunities to develop close, nurturing friendships; availability of counselors on marital conflict, parenting issues and emotional needs such as depression, loneliness, fear, stress, and coping skills; access to competent advisors on personal, legal and financial business; communications systems both within the country and with church, family and friends back home; availability of proper food, nutrition and medical care; adequate safety and security; tolerable housing; basic utilities (e.g., heat, water, electricity, telephones, cooking fuel, refrigeration), transportation and clothing; educational facilities for children; language and cultural training; personal indigenous assistants; and home leave.

In sum, while I am not aware of any studies that assess the attrition rate of tentmakers or BAM team members and their companies, these same pressures are to be expected in this nontraditional mission endeavor. Accordingly, support systems must become part of the planning that goes into forming the BAM Company and drafting its SMA and SMBP.

A dual organization structure. Once the BAM team is assembled, how does it organize for the dual mandate that it is operating under? How should the BAM company be structured to maximize its potential for achieving its multiple bottom lines? I firmly believe that for most BAM businesses, certainly all GCCs, the answers to those questions are found in having a dual organizational, management structure that reflects the company's dual business-and-mission mandate. The reasons for this are basic to successful management of the BAM Company and are rooted in humanity's fallen nature.

Humans, especially Christians in business leadership positions, have a natural, tradition-based, cultural tendency to allow the business to migrate toward the financial bottom line, to relegate the social and environmental bottom lines to second place, and to set the kingdom goals hopelessly adrift, destined to deteriorate and die. This slippage is often insidiously invisible and goes wholly unnoticed until kingdom impact ceases to be a part of the company thinking. If left unchecked, this process, which parallels the church's perennial experience with Christian backsliding, is almost as predictable as the sun rising in the east. The only practical way for the company to avoid this slippery slope is to include within the SMBP institutional mechanisms that continually keep the kingdom goals at the forefront.

Many organizational schemes could be adopted to achieve this, but in the end there should be a single person or department leader who is responsible for overseeing the mission or ministry mandate just as there is for the business mandate. Further, this person should have as much institutional status and clout as those who are answerable for the financial and business results. In my estimation, both should be of equal rank, both should report to the president or executive vice president, and both should be included within the company's executive team. If the company cannot afford such a person, but desires to be effective in its kingdom impact, the responsibilities should be placed with a top company officer.

In summary, just as there is a chief operations officer (COO) to oversee the business mandate and the SBP, so there should be a chief mission officer (CMO) to oversee the mission mandate and the SMA. In addition to being an efficient, effective way to divide the working and planning responsibilities, having two different squads working on both plans simultaneously will likely create a healthy competition of ideas and insights that can greatly add substance and joy to the planning process and help maintain all of the multiple bottom lines as priorities.

The CMO or other responsible officer would be charged with identifying kingdom opportunities for the company internally (functional analysis), externally (community-development) and serendipitously as the Holy Spirit reveals unforeseen, unplanned kingdom impact openings. He or she would also design, coordinate and implement the SMA's mission or ministry projects and activities, and be accountable for the kingdom bottom lines in the SMBP. As part of the SMBP, the CMO should also be assigned duties as corporate chaplain to minister to the company employees and their families, to lead the BAM team's devotionals, Bible studies and prayer sessions, and to create and monitor the company's intercessory prayer teams and support systems.

What about the secular-sacred divide? At first blush the dual mandate and the recommended dual organizational structure might seem to be in direct contradiction to the Marketplace Mission Movement's insistence that there be no secular-sacred divide—that we seek the full integration of faith and work. Accordingly, we could reasonably ask whether this dual approach is institutionalizing the secular-sacred divide within the company.

While that is a distinct danger, the greater danger is in not having a separate, specific faith-planning exercise, as well as a specified institutional guardian to oversee the faith goals and objectives. Scripture is replete with examples of the warring nature of humanity: the constant tension between the sinful nature and the spirit, the natural person and the Spirit-filled person, the ways of the world and the ways of God. This plays out in business as a natural tendency not to include the mission mandate in the business model. "Business as usual" and "That's business" are expressions used to illustrate the fact that the prevailing, worldly culture of business is often, if not usually, in direct opposition to biblical principles.

The duality of the initial plan and the recommended organizational structures are designed to overcome and compensate for this natural imbalance. This is akin to the checks and balances seen in the U.S. government and institutionalized in its Constitution.

Paradoxically, this system of three opposing branches is essential to allow competing interests to produce one unified, sustainable government. Our free-market economic system is premised on Adam Smith's *invisible hand*, which says that the collective greater good for all society is achieved by each person pursuing his own individual selfish interests in competition with every other individual. When resolving thorny public-policy issues, similar paradoxical forces must often be utilized to produce a healthier society. For example, consider our nation's efforts to correct the prevailing cultural imbalance caused by decades of institutional racism. We have done so, ironically, by mandating deliberate discrimination called "affirmative action plans." On a more personal level, our families find oneness through the merger of the distinctly different male and female attributes.

Similarly, we Christians go to the Bible and church for spiritual nourishment and guidance, and we go to business school and professional seminars for vocational nourishment and instruction. But we go to work, hopefully, as persons of integrity, that is, integrating both facets of our lives into a unified whole. So, too, when we build a KC or BAM Company, effective unified action can only come from a dual approach that separately identifies, then reconciles, the demands of both business and mission. It is a paradox, but one with which we followers of Christ—who was simultaneously fully human and fully God—are not unfamiliar.

What's in a name? Language is critical to mission. Words, phrases, idioms, euphemisms, even inflections convey defined meanings that have embedded connotations and cultural implications that go far beyond dictionary definitions. BAM planning introduces a number of key words that deserve special comment. Given BAM's illusive nature, a strategic BAM plan could go by many names. It might be called a kingdom plan or we might substitute the terms ministry plan, mission plan, outreach plan or even the more secular-sounding Christian corporate responsibility plan. Regardless of name, the purpose is to develop a plan in which a Christian-led company (usually in a crosscultural or international context) is intentional about having a positive kingdom impact, i.e., an impact for the kingdom of God on earth and eternally, both within the firm itself and to the community at large. Among other ways, it does this through its management practices, its products and services, and its community-development outreach.

In selecting the term *mission*, I have rejected *kingdom* because in certain international political contexts the word *kingdom* has quite different, even pejorative connotations. On the other hand, I have consistently used the term *kingdom impact* for two reasons. First, it is more descriptive of the end-game BAM seeks than any other term I have found. Second, it is used internally within the company and unlikely to have public visibility. I am, however, not wedded to the terms *BAM plan*, *mission plan* or *kingdom impact*, and each company will have to adjust its labels as needed, given the company's specific context.

Similarly, I reject the use of the term *ministry plan* because of the distinction drawn between ministry and mission. While their exact definitions have been the subject of considerable academic, theological and ecclesiastical debate through the ages, in this book I use the terms quite simply: *ministry* is reaching out to people in need in the name and love of Jesus Christ; *mission* is a subset of ministry in which we cross barriers—political, cultural, ethnic, geographic or faith—to minister holistically to people in need.

International business, by definition, involves crossing many types of barriers. Using international business as a purposeful tool to achieve kingdom impact would then properly fall under the rubric of mission and be a part of Business as Mission. Accordingly, I prefer to use the term strategic master BAM plan or SMBP when discussing how to do Christ-honoring business internationally or crossculturally.

Having said all of this, here is a major caveat: There are many places in the world where BAM is needed (e.g., the Middle East and Islamic nations) that will react with complete aversion, if not hostility and violence, to words like *mission, missionary, Christian, church* and the like. *Business as Mission* may be offensive to them and can lead to major missteps within those contexts. That is why the SAA is so important—it is far better to know about these hidden land mines before stepping on them. The appropriate risk-avoidance response is, of course, not to use any of these controversial or offensive words. If substitutions are necessary, be creative and contextual. The important thing is the substance of the enterprise, not its brand name or labeling.

MONEY

The money issue is one that haunts us at every stage of the BAM Company's genesis, development and operation. Money is needed for the exploratory inquiry and conceptual planning that roughly defines the company's mission field, product and business model. Money is needed to conduct the strategic area or country analysis and other preliminary due diligence studies, long before the formal business plan and faith analyses are begun. Money is needed to recruit, attract, train and pay members of the BAM team as they join the enterprise. Money is needed to write, vet and legally qualify the formal offering documents that may be necessary to approach venture capitalists or angel donors. Money is needed to develop the formal business plan and mission analysis. And all of this is *before* the company is operational. At that point, money is needed for startup expenses, equipment, facilities, initial inventory, wages, marketing, working capital and the like. In short, money is needed at every step in the process, except for the first one: the need to appeal to God for his provision and guidance.

The number one reason why most startup businesses fail and existing businesses struggle to survive and grow is undercapitalization. All new businesses or older businesses in new locations or with new products experience a lag time, sometimes quite significant, between the initial expenditure of seed money and the realization of any income on that investment. There is a saying in business that *cash is king*. In BAM we serve a different King, but the underlying truth in the saying is that a business must have capital *and* cash flow. Those are two quite different concepts, but both are critical to the business's ability to survive. There are no exceptions.

When I was in law practice, my secretary told me, "Neal, no dough, no go." When I was in Kazakhstan, with its infant market economy, I had to constantly remind my students of the need for capital. Before that time, under the communist command economic system, if they needed something, they simply requisitioned it from the government. There was no "cost of goods sold" and no real "operating expenses" as Western business understands them. In fact, for seventy years the words *capital* and *capitalists* were an anathema equated with oppression of the people, criminal activity and the hated Satan, America.

Hudson Taylor, the famous missionary to China from 1853 until his death in Switzerland in 1905, is reputed to have said, "God's work done God's way never lacks for God's provision." That has been quoted to virtually every missionary globally ever since, and is a sentiment that we all want to believe. The facts are, however, that while God does promise to provide for his people, he does it in ways that are different than we often expect or feel we need. As much as it pains me to say this, in my many years overseas, at seminary and associated with missions, I do not find Taylor's words supported by experience. I have seen literally dozens of well-intentioned, hard-working Christians with a powerful belief in our Lord who are willing to give their lives in his service. They have no doubt about their calling to the mission field and are highly motivated, but their mission efforts fail for lack of money, leaving them hurting, disheartened and disillusioned.

What is the source of funds for a BAM Company, and how much is needed? These are two questions that *must* be answered before the enterprise can hope to be more than a fanciful dream. To answer them fully would require a book in itself. Nonetheless, let me give a few "Capital/Money 101" type comments that may be helpful. First, everything belongs to God, so it is to him, the Boss, we must first appeal. As Scripture and mission experience show, however, God may be in it, but he often demands that we go to the limits of our abilities and capacities before he steps in with his blessing.

A case in point is William Wilberforce, who has been called "the greatest social reformer in all history."[6] Wilberforce had no doubt that God had specially called him to end the slave trade in England. Wilberforce was, however, often not sure that God had uniquely gifted him with the ability to accomplish what was truly a "mission impossible" assignment. Wilberforce did succeed, but at an enormous personal cost that wrecked his health and wealth, took decades to accomplish, and saw thousands of men, women and children sold into slavery before his mission was accomplished. Moses' experience was strikingly similar, as was Jesus'.

The point is that God calls us, God motivates us, God positions us and God allows us to struggle and suffer greatly to accomplish his will. Why that is so is one of the greatest mysteries of the Christian life. It is often the elephant in the room that everyone is afraid to acknowledge, because it might cast doubt on our faith. Quite the contrary! God is not afraid of our questions and doubts. He somehow sees these as the spiritual yeast in our lives that allow us to grow and mature in our relationship with him.

Second, there are three classic sources of money: debt, equity and retained earnings. In BAM there are six: debt, equity, retained earnings, donations, support and seconding. That is, the BAMer who is starting a BAM business from scratch can either borrow the money (with interest, no doubt); sell part of the company in exchange for common or preferred stock (equity); seek donations from others; raise support; have a church, NGO, mission-sending agency or business hire the BAMer and loan him or her full time to the BAM company, usually free of charge (seconding); or some combination of these. The BAMer who is already operating a profitable business has all of these options but also looks to the business's cash flow, retained earnings and profit projections as a promising source of new capital or as cash to service debt. The other most common places to acquire cash are from financial institutions

---

[6]Os Guinness, *A Case for Civility* (New York: HarperCollins, 2008), p. 97.

(e.g., banks and credit unions), private equity funds, venture capitalists, investor angels, private placement offerings of stock, and supporters who believe in the mission or company and who want to donate or invest. Typically these last sources of funds are family members, friends, churches, sending agencies and the BAM team itself.

Third, raising money for a business is a subject of considerable legal complexities within the United States and most developed nations. In the United States, each state has what are known as Blue Sky Laws to help prevent fraudulent stock offerings. Similarly, the U.S. Securities and Exchange Commission (SEC) has regulations that govern stock offerings. In the case of small businesses, their 500 series rules under Regulation D offer substantial relief, but still require certain informational filings and "full and fair" disclosure to all investors. There are also different rules for different classes of investors, some being considered sophisticated accredited investors and others not. Navigating these laws in a proper manner is not for the amateur, but requires competent legal counsel. Attempts at shortcuts can lead to fines, penalties, lawsuits and seemingly endless bureaucratic and investor harassment. Satan loves to play on this field!

Fourth, the BAMer must ponder how much money the company needs. This is not a simple matter and is one of the principle reasons for the BAM Company to develop a strategic master BAM plan. A key part of this plan is the pro forma financial projections. These usually cover the first three to five years of operations and represent the BAM team's best thinking about all capital requirements, capital and operational expenses, income, break-even points, and cash flow during that period. The amounts are important, but so is the timing. As every businessperson (and most individuals) knows, cash flow and liquidity are two elements to watch closely.

How much money? Do the homework, and if done well the answer will emerge. Be sure to plan for at least 10 to 20 percent overage because there are always hidden costs. Some cynics even advise taking the figure you have so carefully calculated in your financial projections and doubling it. That way, if your figures are right, you have a nice stash of extra capital for hard times or for expansion; if your figures are wrong, you have a nice stash of needed capital to see you through the startup phase.

Finally, the BAMer needs to understand that the process of developing sources of capital is an onerous process that continues throughout the business's life. So be prepared!

DISCUSSION QUESTIONS

1. Assume you are the CEO of a proposed BAM Company that will manufacture watches in China for import into the United States to sell to major, big-box retailers. Give the profile of your ideal four-member BAM team (e.g., what skills would you want, what criteria would you use for hiring, what contractual commitment would you require, etc.). Justify each. If you had two additional team members, what profiles would you have for them? Explain.

2. For the same company, as CEO what are your alternatives for raising the money needed to fund the venture, and how would you pursue those options utilizing your BAM team?

3. In an earlier chapter, the author suggests that money has a life and power of its own. How do you react to this? Is it a true statement? Why or why not? Cite and describe examples from your own experience. Why and how does the love of money corrupt people (even Christians), as Scripture says?

4. The author cites Hudson Taylor's aphorism that "God's work done God's way never lacks for God's provision." Do you agree? Why or why not? Cite and describe examples from your own experience.

5. The author is fairly specific about not having ministers and missionaries as part of the BAM team unless they have a specific job assignment for which they are competent professionals. Since a BAM Company has a dual mandate addressing both business and mission, is this wise advice—or a manifestation of a business bias? Discuss.

6. The author recommends a dual organizational structure to address the dual mandates of the BAM Company. What do you think about this approach? Why? What are the reasonable alternatives, especially in small BAM companies with limited staff and limited resources? As CEO with only four members on your BAM team, how would you structure the company to give proper attention to the mission mandate?

7. BAM engagement: What is "management-style evangelism," and how does

it manifest itself within the workplace? Is this a style that you could adopt in your workplace? Why? Assuming you could, what could or would you do to display it in your workplace?

18

How to Do BAM

STEPS 1-8

"A prudent man gives thought to his steps."
PROVERBS 14:15

"Blessed is the man who perseveres."
JAMES 1:12

"The journey of a thousand miles starts with one step."
LAO-TZU

JOHN BECKETT, AUTHOR OF *Loving Monday* and *Mastering Monday*, is arguably one the prime examples of a CEO who has successfully integrated his Christian faith into his business. Both of his books are must-reads for the serious BAM student. Beckett says, "As I've met with Christians in the workplace over the past several years, I've found a recurring heart cry. They want to know how to practically bring together the two worlds of faith and work."[1]

This echoes my own experience over the past several years of speaking and attending innumerable conferences, workshops, meetings and coffee-shop discussions. People inevitably ask, "How do I do BAM?" and "How do I find time to do it in the press of business?"

Hopefully, the previous chapters have helped address those questions. I conclude part two with two chapters that are designed to bring convergence for the

---

[1]John D. Beckett, *Mastering Monday* (Downers Grove, Ill.: InterVarsity Press, 2006), p. 39; see also *Loving Monday* (Downers Grove, Ill.: InterVarsity Press, 1998).

would-be BAMer: a broad-brushed, step-by-step approach to starting and managing a BAM business. The first four steps are initial steps in forming a BAM Company; the next seven steps take the would-be BAMer through the process of developing a strategic master BAM plan; and the final four steps address working the plan. Before proceeding, four explanations are called for.

First, while these two chapters address the startup scenario, they are equally applicable to those CEOs who want to repurpose their existing companies to have increased kingdom impact.[2]

Second, these chapters focus on developing a BAM Company internationally, but hopefully by this time it is understood that the same issues apply domestically, across town and next door. I address the international context because it is most difficult to engage and the most complex to understand.

Third, although these steps are given sequentially for analytical purposes, life is not that neat and tidy. Except for the first step, all of the others give only a rough approximation of the order in which decisions need to be made. In actual practice some steps discussed will be inadequate and may lead to many other steps only touched on here. Undoubtedly, too, several of the steps will be conducted simultaneously, and as information is received during one step, prior steps may be radically altered and must be revisited. It is much like the classic chicken and egg dilemma: which came first? Hopefully the would-be BAMer will recognize this issue and adjust these and other steps to fit the company's needs, resources and calling.

Fourth, the would-be BAM CEO will need to be extremely flexible because the Lord has a way of leading us down strange, even mysterious paths. This includes giving us completely unexpected divine appointments with total strangers that send us in directions never imagined. In such situations, which are *not* rare, the BAMer will need to jettison preconceptions and follow the leadings of the Holy Spirit. In doing so, however, he or she must be very careful not to be tempted to go in wrong directions by any false prophets, lying seductresses or insincere would-be partners. Here, Jesus' admonition that we be "as shrewd as snakes and as innocent as

---

[2]An apology to the seasoned, mature businessperson: Many of the following steps will be painfully obvious and simplistic to you, but please indulge me as many, less experienced business learners may find them useful and enlightening. This book and BAM are for both the "old business hands" who seek to re-envision their companies, *and* for the struggling entrepreneur and the young business student.

doves" is apropos (Mt 10:16), as is Jeremiah's warning of the tragic consequences to a nation, its leaders, and its people who follow false prophets
(Jer 23; 28).

STEP 1: TAKE IT TO THE BOSS

In BAM we teach the biblical, foundational concept that God is the Creator
and owner of all things on earth, including our businesses. Accordingly, he is
the *Boss* to whom all owners, managers and directors are accountable. As
Scripture reminds us, not too subtly, it would be wise to discuss the business's
future with the business's owner and Boss.

- God: "I am God, your God. . . . / [F]or every animal of the forest is mine, /
  and the cattle on a thousand hills." (Ps 50:7, 10)

- David: "The earth is the LORD's, and everything in it, / the world, and all
  who live in it." (Ps 24:1) (See also Paul in 1 Cor 10:26.)

- Moses: "[Y]ou . . . know that the earth is the LORD's. But I know that you
  and your officials [businessmen and women?] still do not fear the LORD
  God." (Ex 9:29-30)

- Solomon: "Unless the LORD builds the house, / its builders labor in vain."
  (Ps 127:1)

- Jesus: "Seek first his kingdom and his righteousness, and all these things
  will be given to you as well." (Mt 6:33)

How do we seek the kingdom first? In several ways. Start by asking God,
"How can we better honor you, Lord, in and through this business? Please
show us!" Then gather the BAM team together and bathe this request in prayer
and fasting. In addition, commit the issue to personal and group Bible studies
to hear from the Lord as to what he would have you do.

Throughout this process, which may take some time, seek wise counsel
from God-committed men and women, and reap the rewards. As Proverbs
says, "Make plans by seeking advice" (Prov 20:18). And "Plans fail for lack of
counsel, / but with many advisers they succeed" (Prov 15:22). And again, more
poetically, "Perfume and incense bring joy to the heart, / and the pleasantness
of one's friend springs from his earnest counsel" (Prov 27:9).

STEP 2: FIND THE MONEY

As discussed in chapter seventeen, where the money to fund the BAM Company comes from and how much is needed are two questions that *must* be answered before the BAM enterprise can hope to be more than a fanciful dream. A third pressing, but less obvious, question is, what legal requirements must be satisfied when raising money for the BAM Company?

The new BAM business will require money, legally raised, to investigate, form, operate, sustain, grow and expand the business until such time as it is capable of sustaining itself on internally generated cash. That money must come from sources outside of the business, and it is incumbent on the CEO and BAM team to raise it—before they make the company operational. As previously explained, to do so, they must investigate all of their options: debt, equity, donations, support, seconded employees or some combination of these. The amount will be determined by their business plan's pro forma financial statements, but those figures will only be as accurate as the team was diligent in its calculations. Launching the company with inadequate capital or reserves—at least one year's operating funds—is a sure formula for serious trouble, if not outright failure. The amount of money and the size of the reserve fund will vary with each company, its business needs and its context, but critical decisions identifying those amounts cannot be avoided.

STEP 3: INITIAL SELECTION OF COUNTRY AND BUSINESS

Once the CEO is in place and has consulted with the board (if any), advisors and the Lord, he or she will need to make an *initial* selection of (1) the most promising country, area and city (generically referred to here as "country") for doing BAM, and (2) the most promising business to engage in. The business selection may be the result of years of professional experience, consummate skill in a particular trade or vocation, knowledge of particular needs or opportunities, or the product of a long search during a vision trip or language-training sabbatical in a particular country. The people group or country selected may be the end game of a long association with a particular people group, one's family history or ancestry, a book, movie or TV program, random choice, or simply an insatiable fascination that is fueled by the Holy Spirit—a godly itch that has to be scratched.

There are two alternative, primary drivers of this initial selection process:

(1) the CEO begins with a product or business, then looks for a country with a promising market for that product or a site that favors its manufacture or distribution (e.g., labor pool, ports, transportation, legal and tax structure, infrastructure, etc.); or (2) the CEO begins with a country or people group that he or she wants to reach for Christ, then determines what product or business might thrive there. In my experience, most BAMers begin with the country they want to reach. *Either way, to succeed, a business must have a product with a ready, reliable market.*

The choice of business and country will be as mixed in motives as the people who make them, but they should be compatible. That is, the business needs to fit with the cultural, economic, political and business context of the particular country selected. Certain businesses require certain infrastructures (e.g., roads, ports, railroads, airfields, facilities, reliable electricity and other utilities, raw materials, workforce, banks, political stability, and the like), and absent those it is unrealistic to attempt such a business. No infrastructure, no business. Further, a product requires a market (whether in that locale or international), but not just any market. It must be a market that has sufficient people with sufficient purchasing power to buy sufficient volume at a profit-generating price, or the business will not survive. No market, no business; no business, no mission.

Assessing which product is right for which country is no easy matter under the best of circumstances. When the business is a BAM company, it is even more difficult because the BAM faith component may be incompatible with the local culture's religious power structure or tradition. If the incompatibility is extreme, the business, its product, its BAM team and even its presence may simply not be tolerated. Exploring these questions—having a reality check—is absolutely essential for the BAM Company's long-term survival. That is why this initial exploration (step 3) and the ultimate strategic area/country analysis (SAA) (step 5) are not merely suggested; they are obligatory (as is the Lord's counsel) in every decision every step of the way.

At some point during this process the BAM CEO will actually begin selecting a team, brief them on the progress to date and involve them in the selection process. Ideally these people will be in place to participate in all aspects of the SAA development in step 5.

STEP 4: FORM THE BAM TEAM

Chapter seventeen examined various factors that are essential in order to form and operate a BAM Company. Foremost among these, after the Lord's call and blessing, is the need to assemble a team of similarly committed believers who are willing to answer God's call to BAM. BAM is not an enterprise to be engaged in alone. This is not only good business and mission sense, but scriptural as well. God made us part of a family he calls to do his work. If he does not lead the CEO to individuals who are well-suited for the BAM team, the CEO needs to pause and consider why. Is it because the CEO has a faulty sense of calling? Did he or she hear correctly? Does the CEO have enough information? Is the country, business or time not right? Or are circumstances not ripe? Whatever the answers, the CEO needs to form this team early and prayerfully, keeping in mind the profiles of the people needed to do the right job the right way within the company.

STEP 5: CONDUCT AND DRAFT A
STRATEGIC AREA/COUNTRY ANALYSIS (SAA)

Once the BAM CEO has the team in place and has made an initial selection of the country and business, it is time for a full-court press on researching, conducting and drafting a strategic area/country analysis (SAA; see chap. 14 for a detailed discussion). Developing the SAA involves coming to an intimate understanding of the context in which the business will be operated, the mission will be performed and the BAM team will be living. In business terms it is called conducting *due diligence*. In more basic terms it is simply *doing your homework*. The bottom line is that BAM will not work if the company approaches its business or mission in an inappropriate manner to the country's culture, traditions and power structures. That is why I stress the concept of *appropriate contextualization*.

The first step in the SAA is the preparation phase, in which the BAM team extensively researches and discusses the issues in an appropriate format (see appendixes 2-3). The next step includes a series of country visits to provide a reality check to the information gleaned in the preparatory research and to expand and complete the SAA (see chap. 14).

Step 6: Finalize Country and Business Selection

Sometimes it is difficult to stop a runaway train or a bride who is walking down the aisle to marry the wrong man. Often, to prevent irreparable damage to countless lives, prudence and courage require that harsh judgments be made and brave actions taken. Such is the case in BAM when, in spite of the enormous investment already made in a particular country or business choice, there is a collective or even individual check in the team's spirit about those choices. The indwelling Holy Spirit often nudges us, perhaps gently at first or with a swift kick later, to say, "Don't go there!" Paul received such a message in Troas when he was contemplating his mission to Asia, Mysia and Bithynia, but the Holy Spirit said *no*. Instead, he received a Macedonian vision that led him in a totally different direction than he had contemplated—and that made all of the difference (Acts 16:6-10). By going to Macedonia, he launched a European mission that has had far-reaching global implications for two millennia.

So it may be with BAM. At some point during its original research, the BAM team may realize that something is not right. Perhaps the country is right, but the business, product or mission model aren't. Or perhaps everything is right except the makeup of the BAM team, its proposed partners or its strategies. Or maybe the team simply has a collective intuition about not moving forward. Whatever *it* is, once an issue has surfaced, the team should prayerfully closet themselves, listen to their inner urgings and engage in full, candid, vulnerable discussions, prayer, and fasting to determine where the Lord would have them go and what he would have them do. In any event, any reservations need to be openly discussed with love and sensitivity to each other. Disagreement does not have to lead to dissention—and should not if the Lord is first in the minds and hearts of the BAM team.

When consensus is reached, the BAM team needs to act. If necessary, it may even have to start over, as led by the Holy Spirit. Bad wine is best thrown out and not ingested. On the other hand, if the original selections are confirmed by the group or modified to reach unanimity, then they should be formally finalized in the written business plan (see chap 14 and step 8).

Now knowing the BAM Company's specific business and location, the BAM team should reexamine its own composition. This examination may reveal that some people no longer fit on the team and should consider dropping off or being reassigned. Analysis may also reveal certain holes in the team that need to be filled. Handling these situations with Christlike sensitivity is an absolute must. In any event, the CEO must move to make the team as complete as possible as early as possible. To that end, he or she should invite and initiate specific prayer that God would divinely guide the company to have the right people in the right positions in a timely manner.

STEP 7: DIVIDE YOUR FORCES—A DUAL ORGANIZATIONAL STRUCTURE

One critical element of organizing the BAM Company remains: purposefully dividing the workforce into a dual organizational structure, with one component (or individual) primarily responsible for overseeing the business mandate and another primarily responsible for overseeing the mission mandate (see chap. 17).

STEP 8: CHOOSE, PLAN AND PRAY

The process is now moving forward rapidly and tangibly. Up to this point it has been a fun but intensive exploration of ideas, places, businesses and prospects. At some point, however, difficult decisions and actions must be made, and resources committed. This is such a time. The BAM team, being called *to* business as mission, equipped *for* it and feeling led *by* the Lord to a specific country, area or city and business, must now become intentional.

Choose your BAM approach. There are basically three approaches the BAM team can take along the intentionality and planning continuums (see p. 293).

The first is the *ad hoc approach*, in which the business is planned and launched, but the faith integration decisions are made on a step-by-step, case-by-case basis, simply meeting challenges or mission opportunities as they arise or come to mind. The second is an *incremental planning approach*, in which some faith planning is undertaken, but it is limited in scope and will be expanded incrementally over time. The third is the *master planning approach*, in which the company undertakes a comprehensive survey of its entire operations, including a full-blown functional analysis (chaps. 15-16) from a kingdom impact perspective. The second incremental approach is recommended for most companies that are new to faith integration. The third approach, although more complex, is ultimately, if not initially, highly recommended for all companies and is the focus of the next several steps. Accordingly, companies wanting to take the less comprehensive approaches—ad hoc or incremental—will find that the discussion of the master planning approach sheds valuable light on their own selected approach and helps them envision a path for the future.

The primary point is that the CEO and BAM team must choose an approach. One is not more sacred or holier than the other, they are simply different stages in the development of the BAM Company. Once a decision is made, the team should then formalize its approach.

Plan your work. Planning is a time-consuming, energy-draining but thought-provoking and decision-informing futuristic exercise. It asks where the company currently is; where it wants to be in one, three or five years; what products or services it wants to provide; what results it wants to achieve; what it wants to be known for; what reputation it wants to have; what resources are needed; how these results can and should be achieved; what place God and Scripture have in every aspect of the business; and what faith-based action steps must be taken to realize the company's goals. Planning defines the ends, means and projected results or outcomes, and is designed to be a roadmap to guide the company from point A to point B by the most Christian, efficient, productive, profitable way possible. In the process it defines the faith, character, values, substance and identity of the company and its leaders. As such, it is a basic tool of any business, large or small, in every economic and cultural context, and is foundational to good Christian-led businesses. Its absence is an Achilles' heel to any company foolish enough to neglect it, no matter how good, noble or profitable the company's ideas, services and products. To my mind, its absence is also a serious disappointment to our Lord and saddens the Holy Spirit. (See chap. 14 and appendixes 2-5 for planning details.)

Work your plan. For the strategic master BAM plan to be a successful blueprint for the company's activities during the year, it must include specific action steps to be taken by specified individuals or departments to meet the plan's goals and objectives. That requires a system to continually monitor progress toward goals, to obtain feedback on needed systemic improvements, and to hold people accountable (as Christ holds us accountable) for performing their part of the overall plan. These will be discussed in steps 12 and 13 in greater detail, but at this point it is most important that the plan include actions that institutionalize the company's annual, formal business planning process; that systematically and continually update, revise, refine and improve its effectiveness and its responsiveness to changing circumstances and the realities of the company's business experience; and that bring fresh thinking, innovative ideas, new insights and renewed excitement to the BAM initiative, all in the light of Scripture.

Pray: God's plan, God's way. At this point it is imperative that the BAM team understand a basic fact of BAM planning: The call to BAM is a call to God's mission, *missio Dei.* It is not a call to the CEO's mission, the BAM team's mission or the church's mission. It is God's mission. If the team has any hope of success in BAM—in spite of their enormous sacrifices, hard work and investments of time, money, dreams and energy—it will not happen unless God blesses it. And he cannot be expected to bless it if they are simply asking him to bless *their plan,* rather than *his plan.*

Quite simply, if the team's efforts are to bear good, abundant fruit, *the master BAM plan must be the Master's BAM plan.*

Moreover, the plan must be thoroughly bathed in prayer at every stage of the BAM initiative, from first conception to final implementation to eventual termination. At every stage the cycle must be: Praying, planning the work, praying, working the plan, praying, revising/adjusting the plan, praying and so on. At no stage should seeking the will of the Lord be less than top priority. And this prayer is not only praising, asking and petitioning, but it involves proactive listening. Further, the company needs to have regular prayer sessions and Bible studies among its leadership, and it needs to garner outside intercessory prayer from loved ones, church members, supporters, the community, willing employees and other stakeholders.

DISCUSSION QUESTIONS

1. The author suggests eight broad, initial steps before the BAM Company begins operations. Discuss your understanding of each step. What additional steps (or substeps) might be useful at this stage? Discuss.

2. BAM engagement (for individuals or groups): Assume that you or your group are intent on setting up a real BAM business in a foreign country. Meet, discuss and do the following:

   a. Make a list of the selection criteria for the country that you would like to work in. Prioritize that list, and briefly explain your reasons for each criteria and its priority.

b. Based on your criteria, select a country that may be ripe for BAM and conduct an SAA for that country utilizing the relevant parts of appendixes two and three.

c. Based on your research and your team makeup, select a BAM business and product or service that you think you could realistically undertake in the next two years in that country. Give solid reasons for your choices. List the alternative businesses or products you considered and the rationale you used for eliminating them.

d. Based on your research and product or business selection, which city within the country would be the best host for your BAM Company? Give your reasons, both pro and con. List the alternative cities you considred, if any, and the rationale you used for eliminating them.

e. Prepare and flesh out an outline of a reasonable business plan for this business in that country in a format similar to that found in appendix four. Bullets are fine, but each must be accompanied by a short paragraph or two of adequate analysis and reasoning.

f. Based on your plan, research, travel and living costs for your team, how much money do you estimate will be required through the first year of operations? Give a detailed budget and, preferably, a detailed profit-and-loss statement for the first two years.

g. Write a specific plan of where and how you will raise the money for developing your business. Decide how much will realistically be from loans, investors and other sources.

19

How to Do BAM

STEPS 9-15

"A visionary who doesn't plan is only a dreamer."
DICK WYNN

"The plans of the diligent lead to profit
as surely as haste leads to poverty."
PROVERBS 21:5

"Many are the plans in a man's heart, but
it is the Lord's purpose that prevails."
PROVERBS 19:21

"The Lord Almighty has sworn,
'Surely, as I have planned, so it will be,
and as I have purposed, so it will stand.'"
ISAIAH 14:24

"'Woe to the obstinate children,'" declares the Lord,
'to those who carry out plans that are not mine.'"
ISAIAH 30:1

DOING BAM IS A COMMITMENT TO THE LORD that is neither easy nor short-term. It is a life commitment that God honors. He simply asks that in our planning, we consult him, seek his ways, his purposes and his glory, and be obedient to our call.

Planning is always difficult and at times arbitrary. We forecast, read trends and analyze our culture, but we can only make a "best guess." But leaders must do these things, or they cannot lead. . . . Trust and honor God both in the planning process and in working out the action plan.[1]

So it is with the faith-planning process. If we are called to BAM, we are called to use our gifts, minds, hearts, time and resources to do whatever is needed to make our BAM enterprise successful in kingdom terms. That includes planning our work and working our plan as led by the Lord.

Steps 5 through 8 in the previous chapter addressed the preparatory process before planning actually begins in earnest. Steps 9 through 11 speak to the actual planning process itself. Steps 12 through 15 address the process of working that plan and launching a sustainable, replicating BAM Company for the glory of God and for the transformation of hurting people in distant lands. All of these points already have been addressed at length, but they are summarized and prioritized here to give the would-be BAMer a feel for how all of this information flows together in a manageable, step-by-step process.

STEP 9: DRAFT YOUR STRATEGIC BUSINESS PLAN (SBP)

Chapter fourteen and appendix four discuss a basic business plan that can be a point of departure for the CEO, COO or other corporate officer charged with the company's business planning responsibilities. How the strategic business plan (SBP) is prepared will vary from company to company. For startup companies, the relatively small group of founders—or the CEO— undoubtedly will be drafting the business plan. For existing companies, however, it is highly recommended that a much broader advice process be initiated and that every employee and director in the company be intimately involved in the process. Advanced preparation for the planning exercise is required if it is to be successful in both planning results and morale building. For those who have not been through a corporate planning process, the following is a simple example that can work in most companies.

The process might begin with a company meeting that closely resembles a pep rally. It will be on paid company time and could include refreshments,

---

[1]Sid Buzzell, Kenneth Boa and Bill Perkins, *The Leadership Bible* (Grand Rapids: Zondervan, 1998), p. 822, commenting on Is 29:13-16.

decorations, music, posters, possible skits, "cheerleaders" and pep talks—all to inform and energize the company insiders and directors. It will highlight the company's faith-based intentions, the proposed planning schedule and broadly define why the company plans, what the planning process looks like, how it is used, and its critical importance to the company, the community, and themselves, and to their job security, advancement, and compensation. The opening session is to create genuine enthusiasm for the company, its BAM purposes and its future, as well as to initiate true bonding among the employees as to the higher purpose and adventure of their jobs.

Next is a planning retreat, often on a weekend or during the week, but away from the office. The dress and setting will be quite informal, which will set a relaxed, casual atmosphere that hopefully will lead to more creativity, insights and candor. Prior to the retreat, however, there is some homework that should be done by everyone involved. This homework will frequently include such exercises as obtaining employee attitude and 360 degree performance surveys (everyone rates everyone and everything), answering functional delineation and description questions, performing the functional analysis approach within each department, developing a departmental and company SWOT analysis (strengths, weaknesses, opportunities, threats), and holding futurist brainstorming sessions.

In addition, the CEO, COO, CMO and CFO should prepare and review initial financial projections for the coming year(s). These projections are not only a vital part of the ultimate SBP and SMBP, but they bring the reality of the company's financial bottom line to the discussion. It is fine to have splendid ideas about what the company can, should or might do, but they must be tempered by the company's worldly resources (capacity) and the company's godly calling. It is fair to warn that this latter call for the BAM Company may drive it to act in one of two opposing ways: stay within safe financial guidelines and projections, and only timidly venture beyond them, if at all; or have aggressive faith goals that lay an expectation of God's calling upon the company that is higher than human business sense would believe probable or even possible.

At the retreat it is usually best to begin casually with food, for example a continental breakfast, perhaps followed by fun, icebreakers, a few door prizes, but certainly *brief* inspirational and informational talk(s) from the chairman of the board, CEO, COO or a board member. It is vital for the employees to

know that this process is receiving the highest priority at the highest corporate levels and that the results will be used to fashion the company's future.
The retreat's opening is followed by an explanation of the day's or weekend's
agenda and procedure, then breaking into departmental groups to discuss all
aspects of the work and work product from both a business and a kingdom
impact perspective.

Following the retreat, the company's designated planning team, which is
usually led by the CEO or COO, will evalutate and compile the data, suggestions and survey results. Based on this analysis, the team will draft the company's initial written SBP (see appendix 4 for a suggested format). *As explained
in chapter fourteen and step five, it is critical at this stage and in each of the
preceding planning events that the findings of the SAA be fully discussed and
incorporated into this initial SBP.*

Step 10: Draft Your Strategic Mission Analysis (SMA)

Chapter fourteen and appendix five suggest an approach and format for a strategic mission analysis. It is through this analysis that the BAM Company seeks
to rise above its secular counterparts, both the strictly business-oriented ones
and those seeking multiple bottom lines under a corporate social responsibility
banner. The BAM Company seeks to have a sustainable, long-term, holistic
kingdom impact. This requires unique, Christ-focused planning—both at the
business mandate level (the SBP) and at the mission mandate level (the SMA).

Although drafting an SMA is not required, it is highly preferable for a variety of reasons. The purpose of the SMA is to inform the SBP of kingdom
impact opportunities both within and outside the company. How best to do
that will, in the end, depend upon the nature and needs of the company. If an
SMA is drafted, the process is quite similar to that previously described for the
SBP. In fact, for a BAM Company, it is altogether appropriate for the SMA to
be a major part of the company's planning rally and retreat on a par with the
SBP. In these meetings the concept of multiple bottom lines can be introduced
as well as the kingdom principles that support them. The gauge of how explicit
this BAM exposure will be, however, must be left to the prayerful judgment of
the BAM team, since the company employee base is decidedly not 100 percent
Christian, nor is the context often one that is compatible with Christianity. In
fact, the very act of proselytizing for Jesus may be a crime within the BAM

Company's context. So too the use of the term *mission* in BAM and SMA may require the company to rename the process the strategic community analysis or some variation of this.

Such dangers should not, however, keep the BAM Company from seeking or promoting holistic kingdom impact projects. The BAM team will do well to remember the three levels of faith integration—inherent, internal and external—and to realize that each level can honor Christ and help people (see chap. 11). The multiple bottom lines of a BAM company (see chap. 12) will each be addressed under the SMA. That is obviously true of the social, environmental and kingdom bottom lines, but it is also true of the financial bottom line since every other bottom line will have an associated measurable financial cost.

When addressing *inherent* and *internal* faith integration, the functional analysis approach should be applied, seeking ever greater kingdom impact from each function, process, product and service (see chaps. 15 and 16). When addressing *external* faith integration, the social and environmental bottom lines are prime areas for fruit-bearing. As the BAM Company surveys the community for holistic kingdom impact opportunities, it will undoubtedly be overwhelmed with the possibilities. That is the easy part. The difficult part is discerning which needs will be addressed, prioritizing them and then reducing them to writing within the SMP.

Step 11: Draft Your Strategic Master BAM Plan (SMBP)

It is up to the BAM team or the COO and CMO and their squads to synthesize and reconcile the results of the planning process and to produce an initial SMBP that takes full cognizance of the SAA, the initial SBP and the SMA. They must also assess the financial-bottom-line impact of the planned activities and resolve the inevitable tensions between the SBP and the SMA. Prioritizing, negotiating and compromising should result amid spirited debate, but if the process is of the Lord, it will be good, healthy and beneficial to all concerned.

In short, the SMBP is nothing more than a blended SAA, SBP and SMA. The three are overlaid on each other, then reconciled, coordinated and harmonized into a seamless whole. Doing this is a special adventure as the CEO, COO, CMO, CFO and other BAM team members, each with their own special expertise, interests and priorities, come together to advocate their positions and seek a solid, well-planned, thoughtful, prayer-based strategic master plan that defines the company's future and its identity.

This plan will harmonize two major mandates within the BAM company's context (SAA): A business mandate (SBP) and a kingdom mandate (SMA). These are respectively measured in terms of $-ROI and K-ROI for each aspect of the business. To achieve and align these mandates the company will set multiple bottom lines (chap. 12). At a minimum the financial, social, environmental and kingdom bottom lines should be included. All must be aligned in such a way as to resolve and balance their inherent tensions. Identifying them is a complex but necessary process that, in essence, defines the company's raison d'être.

The kingdom bottom line is not separate and distinct, but is deliberately invasive, injecting itself into each of the other bottom lines, infusing them with kingdom values and exacting a kingdom impact. It asks, How can this bottom line be achieved, this function performed or this service rendered in a better, Christ-honoring way that has a kingdom impact (see chap. 13)?

Once the initial SMBP plan is drafted (chap. 14), it will be taken to the experts—the employees who do the job and the community participants who are affected by the projects—for final input and a blessing. Then the SMBP can be finalized, taken to the board of directors for approval, and launched.

The steps already considered are merely preparation for the actual task of *doing* BAM. Without those steps there would be no end product for either BAM's business or its mission. Conversely, without the end product being actually delivered to the customer and being useful to him or her, all of the preceding expenses, energy and effort are wasted. Just as desire precedes decision, so decision precedes delivery. In the following steps, we explore how BAM is delivered to the end user and thereby has actual Kingdom Impact on people and communities.

Step 12: Work Your Plan

So many companies go through the laborious, expensive process of preparing a business plan only to put it in a nice binder, place it on a bookshelf and forget it until the next scheduled planning retreat. Others simply whip out a computer template and fill in the blanks, giving little attention to the individual, deep-seated issues that are involved in a true planning process. Both miss the point that a well-conceived plan (and its neglect!) literally defines the character of the company and the people who lead it. It must, however, be put into action if it is to be something more than nice-sounding words, ideas and dreams. So, too, it must be regularly and consistently reviewed to confirm that it is biblical and Christ-honoring.

Implementation. Planning is necessary to effective action, but it is only the means to an end. In the BAM context the ends are to achieve the multiple bottom lines that the planning process has identified and defined. That requires working your plan, that is, implementing the plan both strategically and tactically, putting feet on the words so that lives are changed. The SMBP itself should either spell out the details of each strategy or give rise to an action plan that describes what is being done, why, where, when, by whom, how and for how much, with what expected results.

"Plan your work; work your plan." A similar adage says, "Work smarter, not harder." These convey excellent advice for every company, from the transnational giants to the mom-and-pop stores on the neighborhood corner. Not only do they extol the virtue—and necessity—of working hard, but they recognize that company success depends on *how* we work, as well as *what* work we do.

These adages emphasize first that the people in the company must work to be successful. Implementation is, quite simply, hard work. Exciting, but nonetheless work. That means long hours, commitment and inevitable suffering, even in the most successful businesses, while also giving proper attention to professional and spiritual development, family and one's own quiet time. Second, it says that the work itself needs to conform to the plan. While flexibility is a necessity for a viable plan, ignoring the plan is not a smart option, especially if the plan was conscientiously developed by a process that includes the company's best and brightest, and its managers and workers at every level, in every department and locale.

Feedback, assess, revise. The SMBP needs to be evaluated, adjusted and modified based on experience gained from implementation. Such evaluation and adjustment cannot occur on a regular, sustainable basis unless both feedback loops and continuous planning mechanisms are built into the SMBP itself. Without such structural programs, there is little hope that the plan, no matter how well-conceived, will maintain its relevance, hold people accountable for its implementation or help the company realize its highest potential.

These feedback loops lead into a cycle that continues to adjust, refine and improve the SMBP over time and hopefully brings the company into greater and greater kingdom awareness and impact. The entire process must, of course, continually be bathed in direct, focused, specific prayer by the BAM team, the believers within the workforce and the company's intercessors.

Missiologists call this process "praxis" and recognize its critical importance to the mission endeavor; business scholars speak in terms of a "feedback loop" that informs company leadership what works, what doesn't and what can be done to improve results. Either way, in BAM enterprises, we suspect God simply calls it "obedience."

Accountability. While implementation feedback will lead to adjustments and revisions, another aspect is often overlooked: accountability. That is, the person or department that has functional flaws or inefficiencies that need correction also needs to be held accountable for shoddy performance. This is a delicate matter because the BAM team wants enthusiastic cooperation from all managers and employees in identifying opportunities for improvement in efficiency, profits, adhering to biblical standards and kingdom impact. Accordingly, where the recommended change leads to a better or more effective way to do a particular job or perform a unique function, the responsible employee and his or her manager should be rewarded. Conversely, where the change is needed because someone is not doing the job correctly or well, then appropriate, respectful discipline and retraining should occur.

Discipline in a Christian-led company is always a strained matter, but Scripture is full of admonitions to those in authority to rebuke, correct and discipline those who do wrong. Above all, discipline must always be administered in love, rebuking the action, not the person. Grace, forgiveness and encouragement can also help turn a negative into a positive and a careless or ill-equipped employee into a careful, productive member of the team who then becomes a quality-control advocate. Learning how to do this well is a matter of specific prayer, scriptural guidance, BAM team consultation and good management.

Step 13: Conduct Annual Planning Reviews

Each year at a specified time the BAM Company needs to conduct a formal planning process for the next year. It is a time to look back critically and honestly, but also to look forward eagerly. It means celebrating the prior year's blessings, auditing and evaluating the company's performance, and prescribing corrective action as well as new directions and dimensions of both business and mission service.

Celebrate the prior year's blessings. If the prior year's SMBP has been prayerfully designed and diligently executed, it will have produced unexpected blessings. Even if the year was unbearably hard, disappointing or fruitless, it should be celebrated. As Scripture counsels:

Rejoice in the Lord always. I will say it again: Rejoice! (Phil 4:4)

I have learned to be content whatever the circumstances. . . . I can do everything through him who gives me strength. (Phil 4:11, 13)

I press on to take hold of that for which Christ Jesus took hold of me. . . . Forgetting what is behind and straining toward what is ahead, I press on toward the goal to win the prize for which God has called me heavenward in Christ Jesus. (Phil 3:12-14)

You did not choose me, but I chose you and appointed you to go and bear fruit—fruit that will last. (Jn 15:16)

Rejoice, praise, celebrate, press on, win the prize and bear fruit that will last. These are words of encouragement for every BAM team and missionary. God has sent you; take joy in whatever ways he uses you.

Audit and evaluation. The BAM Company is well-advised to undergo an annual, Christian-led, company-wide audit that looks backward at last year's SMBP and evaluates the progress made toward each of its bottom lines. It tries to discern what worked, what didn't, why and what changes and improvements are needed if the bottom line goals and objectives are to be reached in the future. It is an audit that describes both where the company is (descriptive) and where its leadership wants to take it from both a business and a kingdom impact perspective (prescriptive). In both aspects the audit recognizes that progress is incremental and only realized over time. The audit can be performed formally or informally and by the company executives themselves, the COO and CMO, or by outside Christian consultants. Perhaps it is best done as part of the functional analysis approach (see chaps. 15 and 16).

The search criteria which drive the *descriptive* business part of the audit

are not dissimilar to those used by corporate investors and venture capitalists who perform due diligence on a business. They examine each major aspect of the company looking for indications of the company's health (or lack
thereof) and describing the conditions found in each department, product,
service, project and the financial bottom line.

The descriptive spiritual/kingdom audit goes much deeper, drilling into
the smallest recesses of the company. It identifies and assesses the company's business functions and activities from faith, ministry and mission perspectives, and weighs the cost effectiveness and metric measures of those
efforts. It not only examines each of the nonfinancial bottom lines but also
the means, ends and kingdom impact of each. At a minimum it should involve a detailed survey of the company's operations, existing organizational
structure, plans, goals and objectives, and interviews with company personnel and community leaders.

The *prescriptive* part of the audit should expand the discussion from the
"is" and "what happened" to the "what if" and "why not." This will require a
detailed examination of the company functions, seeking ways they can be refined and improved for business efficiency and effectiveness, and for opportunities to use those functions for greater kingdom impact. If properly performed, the audit will invariably underscore many unforeseen ways in which
the company can better serve and love its employees, customers, community
and other stakeholders.

The prescriptive audit will also include expanding the discussions with
company leaders, employees and perhaps community leaders to determine
what the company might do better within the boundaries of sound, viable
business practices. At this stage last year's multiple bottom lines are evaluated
and new ones identified, prayer is constant, and faith is tested. Out of this
stage of the audit the next year's SMBP is initiated. The final new SMBP will,
of course, be the end product of the step-by-step process that assesses the feasibility, appropriateness and organizational capacity and costs of the company's bottom lines, its faith-based initiatives and its kingdom impact.

Step 14: Replicate Your Company

Managing a BAM Company is a difficult and often lonely enterprise, especially in a foreign setting. To help alleviate this, I recommended that, if pos-

sible, the CEO form a professionally competent Christian BAM team in the beginning to give mutual support, encouragement, accountability, counsel and sharing of work (see step 4). So too the BAM team will want to give such support and counsel to others outside of the company. Four ways deserve special comment: replication, incubation, unification and indigenization.

Replication. I strongly recommend that a BAM Company attempt to replicate itself as soon as possible after successful launch by assisting and even sponsoring or hosting other noncompeting, expat or indigenous BAM companies in the immediate locality. This is the BAM equivalent of the well-known, well-recognized traditional mission method of spreading the gospel through church planting.

This assistance can take many forms, but it should be one of the major components of a BAM Company's kingdom goals. It may be as simple as helping another BAM team become familiar with the country by sharing the company's SAA. Or it may involve actually sponsoring another company and helping facilitate its vision trips, resolve the immigration issues, find suitable business locations and expat family housing, schools, transportation, shopping, language training, and the like. On the other hand, the assistance may go deeper and involve actual incubation of the new BAM Company.

Incubation. *Incubation* means helping to start or mentor a new company, possibly even having it co-located within the host BAM Company until it can operate independently. It may also involve having the host assume the new company's initial (possibly long-term) administrative tasks (perhaps for an agreed fee, barter or other compensation), such as visas, permits, leases, vehicles, personal assistants, hiring, payroll, accounting, legal and similar tasks common to all businesses. If the company's raw-material sourcing or product manufacturing, warehousing, marketing or transportation requirements are compatible with the host, the two may arrange for some or all of those functions to be permanently shared or outsourced to the host company for a fee.

This type of incubation is a win-win situation for both companies. It allows the new BAM Company to focus on its products, marketing and distribution, and thereby become operational, profitable and missional much more quickly. It also allows the host BAM Company to realize economies of scale in its existing operations or physical plant through the additional earned revenue. Both also share the advantage of their mutual Christian fellowship, encouragement, excitement and worship—and knowing that they are spreading the gospel in tandem with fellow believers.

We also recommend that each BAM Company, in addition to continuing to nurture any existing BAM progeny, try to assist or incubate at least one new BAM Company each year. The geometric, multigenerational growth and sustainability of such a business-replication model is exciting to contemplate. The multiplication not only adds jobs and wages to the local economy, but increases Jesus' presence and influence in the community-at-large.

Unification. As each BAM Company, host and hosted, examines its potential for positive kingdom impact, they may be able to do far greater things for the community together than either one could independently. Just as there is a synergistic advantage in ecumenicalism and interdenominational unity, there is great advantage in leveraging the resources and power of two or more BAM companies in joint ventures for the kingdom.

Accordingly, when these companies consider their kingdom goals each year, it is highly recommended that they share their ideas and information, seek common ground and literally become their "brother's keeper," always looking for ways to help each other. In so doing, they visibly assist the Christian community, both within and outside of the BAM companies, to move toward the unity that Jesus prayed for at the Last Supper:

> Holy Father, protect them [the disciples] by the power of your name—the name you gave me—so that they may be one as we are one. . . .
>
> My prayer is not for them alone. I pray also for those who will believe in me though their message, that all of them may be one, Father. . . . I have given them the glory that you gave me, that they may be one as we are one: I in them and you in me. May they be brought to complete unity to let the world know that you sent me and have loved them even as you have loved me. (Jn 17:11, 20-23; see also Jn 10:30)

The apostle Paul calls us to this same unity in Christ. In fact, part of his letter to the Ephesians could easily be a life verse for dedicated BAMers as they reach out both to other BAM companies (expat and indigenous) and to the community-at-large: "I urge you to live a life worthy of the calling you have received. Be completely humble and gentle; be patient, bearing with one another in love. Make every effort to keep the unity of the Spirit though the bond of peace" (Eph 4:1-3).

Indigenization. Early traditional mission efforts led to many aberrant, ethnocentric practices that were, at best, ineffective and, at worst, counterproductive, often leading to disillusionment, disaster or even death. These tragic experiences led to some innovative, even revolutionary (for the times) practices that focused on bringing Christ into the culture as it was. They attempted to harmonize mission practice with those cultural aspects that do not oppose the gospel and to minimize the friction between the two cultures. It recognized that Western missionaries are guests in the land and that Jesus is not a Western God, but is God of all people, in every land and every culture. It recognized that if church-planting efforts were to have long-term sustainability, the churches had to be turned over to and operated by the indigenous people.

Three-Self Churches. One of the concepts that grew out of an early period of mission experimentation in China is called the "Three-Self Principle."[2] It dictated that all local, indigenous churches should strive to become self-governing, self-supporting and self-propagating. It also recommended that when planting a church, the missionaries should have an exit strategy that includes turning over the church to the local leaders and moving on to other mission fields. It reasoned that the church, like a baby, needs to be weaned of its dependence on the mother church and its missionaries, and to become completely self-sufficient as soon as possible. Not only was this approach good for the indigenous churches, but they became sustainable even in the face of adverse changes in the political environment or the ejection or absence of foreign missionaries.[3] The Three-Self concept was, however, not entirely successful because Western missionaries often failed to give up control of the local churches,

---

[2]Ironically, the "Three-Self" label was so tied to the Christian movement in China that when the Communist Party determined to control the Chinese church movement, they adopted, as part of their campaign, the name Three-Self Church for their own state-run church and church governance system. This was a cynical move, distorting a concept that was originated to promote freedom of religious expression into a vehicle for religious oppression and persecution.

[3]This conceptual approach to mission originated in the late 1800s with Rufus Anderson from America and Henry Venn from England. It was quickly applied to the China Inland Mission, under the leadership of Hudson Taylor. Taylor himself shocked his supporters by insisting on an incarnational approach to mission: wearing Chinese clothing, speaking the Chinese language and living as the local people lived. For further information see Wilbert R. Shenk, "Rufus Anderson and Henry Venn: A Special Relationship?" *International Bulletin of Missionary Research* 5, no. 5 (1981):168-72; and Marlee Alex, *Hudson Taylor* (Peabody, Mass.: Victor, 1995).

never quite believing that the local people were able to successfully manage on their own.

The dilemma over how to make such a valuable mission concept effective was largely solved by John Livingston Nevius, an itinerate late-nineteenth-century American missionary in the Shantung Province of China.[4] Nevius adopted the Three-Self approach, but added one important caveat: The Three-Self principles must be implemented with each new indigenous congregation at the very start of the church.[5] If delayed, he explained, the local church becomes hopelessly dependent on the foreigners and the three selves are never fully realized. This approach became known as the "Nevius Method" and was successfully adopted by Western missionaries in the Korean church.[6] In fact, it is credited with being a critical factor in the subsequent explosion of evangelism throughout South Korea that has made it the home of the world's largest Christian church and the leading missionary-sending nation in today's Christian world.

Four-self business and BAM. There are important parallels and lessons to be learned from Taylor and Nevius in the management of a BAM Company. One goal of many BAM companies is to become independently and indigenously owned, managed, operated and financed as soon as possible. There are many different models for complete or partial indigenization of BAM businesses, but most advocate an eventual exit strategy for the expats. It is my belief that the more quickly a BAM Company (and its offspring BAM companies) can indigenize, the better it will be for the company itself and for the kingdom in that country. That is, the sooner these companies can become indigenous, Christian-led, self-supporting BAM companies—without expat and foreign involvement—the better. This is best achieved, I believe, by BAM

---

[4]"Revival in Korea: The Nevius Method and Self-Support," *A Mission-Driven Life*, September 26, 2007 <http://missionsforum.wordpress.com/2007/09/26/revival-in-korea-the-nevius-method-and-self-support>. Nevius first published his new ideas for mission in the *Chinese Recorder* journal in 1885, which was later published as a book *The Planting and Development of Missionary Churches* (1886) according to Hans-Ruedi Weber, *The Layman in Christian History* (London: SCM, 2000), p. 350.

[5]Everett N. Hunt Jr., "John Livingston Nevius 1829-1893: Pioneer of Three-Self Principles in Asia," in *Mission Legacies: Biographical Studies of Leaders of the Modern Missionary Movement*, eds. Gerald H. Anderson et al. (Maryknoll, N.Y.: Orbis, 1994), pp. 190-96.

[6]"Is It Too Late for Nevius? Taking a Look at the Korean Revival—Part 1," *A Mission-Driven Life*, October 12, 2007 <http://missionsforum.wordpress.com/2007/10/12/is-it-too-late-for-nevius-taking-a-look-at-the-korean-revival-part-1>.

companies adopting an expanded Three-Self posture—*four selves*—by become self-governing, self-supporting, self-propagating and self-replicating.

If, however, the BAM Company's CEO feels called to remain permanently with the company and minister to the people of that area incarnationally and long-term, he or she will almost certainly insist on retaining control of the company, its ownership and quite possibly its governance. That is entirely reasonable, and I have no quarrel with this model if that is the CEO's calling. I recognize that such a decision does not negate the high probability that the CEO will want the company to achieve the "four-self" status anyway, especially if he or she or the company is being subsidized by the church, denomination, individuals or other BAM companies. Achieving complete financial independence remains a primary goal of every business, including every BAM Company.

The CEO may also want to retain control over the company's ownership, but gradually turn over daily operational management to qualified local leaders within the company. Such a local manager can, as with any company, be incentivized by stock, stock options, bonuses and, of course, salary, benefits and other perks such as international travel, education, housing, vehicles and expense accounts. If stock is involved, the CEO will probably require buy-back options in the event the local manager does not work out satisfactorily or leaves the company. That way the CEO maintains oversight to ensure that the company remains true to its calling and the BAM vision and values. If the CEO sees any major deviation, he or she can return to the company and make necessary corrections before it is hopelessly sidetracked.

If retaining control is the model a CEO is committed to, then I recommend that the four-self principle be applied to the new indigenous companies that the original BAM company replicates, assists, hosts, sponsors or incubates. This allows the CEO to keep the mission base secure, while not quenching the Holy Spirit's movement within the local business community. This also allows the original business to remain a constant presence in the community, modeling for all new BAM companies the biblical way to manage a company and to help develop a community. The CEO's continued presence also strengthens his or her witness and allows the CEO to serve as a mentor, disciple and encourager to all Christians in business.

Regardless of the model adopted, the goal of four-self businesses is to see

Christ firmly established within the indigenous business community and to see each existing and new company well run by both business and biblical standards, with both kingdom impact and kingdom bottom lines of its own.

Four-self peer groups. As BAM companies are planted and new ones are incubated, the resulting clusters of BAM companies can become a potent force for holistic mission outreach within the community and beyond. This is especially true if, as I recommend, these BAM companies form and sustain peer groups of indigenous Christian CEOs and executives. Such indigenous groups directly reach the local business community (as distinguished from expat planted businesses) and indirectly affect all of their stakeholders within that city, region and country. By acting as mentors, coaches, encouragers and enablers to these indigenous business leaders, the peer groups further embolden and empower local Christian business owners and CEOs, teaching them to climb onto the ladder of BAM development and become KCs, BAM companies and even GCCs.

The four-self concept is directly applicable to the peer groups. This is especially critical in those CANs and RANs where Christianity is not welcome and may be against the law. Regardless, the peer groups can become a major source of spiritual as well as business sustenance, edification, encouragement and growth. The groups that have existed for some length of time become like a family and generate statements like "this is my real church" and "this is where I am fed." The sooner they can become independent from the founding BAM Company or outside group, the better. That does not mean that they should not associate with international peer-group ministries such as Christ@Work, CBMC-Forums, Convene, Full Gospel or the like. Quite the contrary. It simply means that the survival of these peer groups in the foreign context will, like an indigenous church, depend on indigenous businesspeople taking complete ownership of every aspect of their existence and growth.

Step 15: Transform Lives and Communities

Paul called Jesus' followers to be transformed in every way to Jesus' likeness:

> Do not conform any longer to the pattern of this world, but be transformed by the renewing of your mind. Then you will be able to test and approve what God's will is—his good, pleasing and perfect will. (Rom 12:2)

And we, who with unveiled faces all reflect the Lord's glory, are being transformed into his likeness with ever-increasing glory, which comes from the Lord, who is the Spirit. (2 Cor 3:18)

In 2008, St. Andrew's Presbyterian Church in Newport Beach, California, adopted new vision and mission statements that reflect this call to transformation. Their vision statement states they are "a vital life-transforming church"; their mission statement says, "Our Mission: Transformed by Jesus Christ and led by God's Word, we are connecting the generations and serving the world, so that lives can be changed through Christ."[7]

The words *so that* are critical to understanding the purpose of the church and of BAM companies. It is connecting with and serving the people of the world holistically, *so that* lives may be changed through Christ—*so that* people may come to know him, emulate him, grow in him and be transformed into his likeness.

In a word, BAM is in the "so that" business. When all of the planning is completed and the plans are implemented, it still comes back to the ultimate kingdom impact: *So that* people and communities are transformed through Christ into his likeness. BAM is merely a tool, a mission method and a means to help people holistically by reaching every aspect of their lives, thoughts, words, actions, pain and joy in the name and love of Jesus.

Far more important, it is a means to help people eternally by introducing them to the only one who can meet their need and heal their pain forever. *When all is said and done, the end game of BAM is Jesus.* He is our only real hope.

DISCUSSION QUESTIONS

1. What factors should a BAM company consider in deciding which additional companies they might incubate? How can a BAM company encourage and support other Christian entrepreneurs?

2. What are the indicators that a business's indigenous employees might be ready to manage it on their own? Explain. How can a BAM company plan for that eventuality?

---

[7]St. Andrew's Presbyterian Church bulletin, Newport Beach, California, February 17, 2008 (emphasis added).

3. BAM engagement: Based on the work that was completed for chapter eighteen's discussion questions, continue the exercise and refine your business plan, making sure it conforms to the SAA. Produce a final draft of your business plan.

a. Take each section in your business plan and brainstorm what you could do within each area to have a positive *environmental impact.* Add those to your business plan within the area being considered, put a parenthetical "(Green)" after each green line item to indicate its status as part of the environmental bottom line of the company.

b. Repeat the process with realistic ideas for your company to have a positive *social impact* on the community in which the company would operate. Add those ideas to your expanded business plan in the appropriate place(s). Place a parenthetical "(Social)" after each social line item to indicate that it is part of the social bottom line of the company.

c. Repeat the process with realistic ideas for your company to have a positive *kingdom impact* at each of the three levels of faith integration (see chap. 11). Add those to your ever-expanding business plan. Place a parenthetical "(Kingdom)" after each kingdom line item to indicate that it is part of the kingdom bottom line of the company. Note: Some line items in your business plan will have more than one bottom-line notation as they serve more than one purpose.]

d. Given the realities of your company's resources, your team's capacity and your callings, prioritize the items you would like to accomplish the first year, the second year and the third year, and those that should be put on long-term hold, unless the Lord moves unexpectedly.

e. Last, rearrange the business plan with all line items grouped by their bottom-line designation and their year of priority within each section.

f. Revise the draft into a form that can be presented to the class in both written and PowerPoint format and to the instructor as a class paper.

PART THREE

BUSINESS AS MISSION

Counting the Cost

"Always count the cost."
AMERICAN PROVERB

*"A well-worn adage advises those who
set out upon a great enterprise to count the cost,
yet some of the greatest enterprises have succeeded because the
people who undertook them did not count the cost."*
THOMAS HENRY HUXLEY

*"Surely there comes a time when counting the cost and
paying the price aren't things to think about any more.
All that matters is value—the ultimate value of what one does."*
JAMES HILTON

THROUGHOUT THIS BOOK I HAVE SPOKEN positively about the BAM experience and urged those who are feeling called to BAM to seriously engage it. I have discussed what BAM is, why people do it and how to do it. Hopefully, this has stimulated a diverse group—including existing international or cross-cultural businesses, domestic businesses that are considering expanding internationally, entrepreneurs who are feeling called to mission and business school students—to seriously consider engaging BAM as a life calling.

While we have provided warnings along the way, it seems prudent, even necessary, to spend the final part of this book discussing a subject that we generally do not talk about or only pay lip-service to: the enormous personal cost paid by most people who go into missionary service, whether traditional or nontraditional, such as BAM.

Jesus warned us in very clear terms:

If anyone would come after me, he must deny himself and take up his cross daily and follow me. (Lk 9:23)

If anyone comes to me and does not hate his father and mother, his wife and children, his brother and sisters—yes, even his own life—he cannot be my disciple. And anyone who does not carry his cross and follow me cannot be my disciple.

Suppose one of you wants to build a tower. Will he not first sit down and estimate the cost to see if he has enough money to complete it? . . .

In the same way, any of you who does not give up everything he has cannot be my disciple. (Lk 14:26-28, 33)

No one who puts his hand to the plow and looks back is fit for service in the kingdom of God. (Lk 9:62)

Truly, this is tough love, but Jesus says if we are his disciples and choose to follow him, we must put him first, above family, home, possessions and life itself. To those considering the mission field, he says, "first sit down and estimate the cost." Why? To see if our commitment is strong enough to withstand the enormous pressures that come with the mission territory and BAM. This exercise is an exceptionally difficult task, both from a planning and a personal perspective. It is, however, an essential task that cannot and should not be avoided or given short shrift.

Missiologists and church sending agencies are concerned that the attrition rate on the mission field (people leaving the field and their mission calling) is very high. The reasons for such defections are many, but they invariably have to do with spiritual warfare, unrealistic and disappointed expectations, inadequate planning or faith, and/or naive glamorization of the mission field. This is true even among well-intentioned, mature Christians.

RISK MANAGEMENT

Counting the cost of engaging in BAM means approaching the risks realistically, seeing how to manage them. Risk management is not new for the seasoned businessperson. It is part and parcel of going into the market to buy and sell goods or services. Let me briefly suggest how would-be BAMers can count the cost and then deal with it.

First, the BAM team must undertake detailed planning before entering the field. As part of these plans, the BAM team needs to accomplish four goals: (1) conduct a *threat assessment* and identify the specific risks in each aspect of the business and mission; (2) where possible, find ways to eliminate the risks altogether; (3) where risk elimination is not possible, develop strategies to minimize the risks or to hedge against them, thereby minimizing the effect of adverse events; and (4) assess the *risk tolerance* of the business and of the individuals going onto the field.

The threat assessment addresses the assaults—business, physical, emotional, health, safety, family, relational, political, economic, religious and spiritual—that will inevitably come with BAM. It identifies the sources and nature of the threats, the risk level each threat poses, and the potential damage that could result if the threats become reality. The assessment also examines all of the people associated with the business and the mission: expat and indigenous; BAM team and their families, locally and back home; and employees and community. In short, it determines who and what is being threatened, how, by whom, and to what end. The strategies for eliminating or minimizing those threats or risks are then included in the company's SMBP. The result is, in essence, the development of a *survival* or *coping strategy* for the people, the business and the mission.

Risk tolerance is a concept critical to the success of the BAM enterprise. It is the level of risk that the people or the business can tolerate and still function effectively. If the risk exceeds the tolerance level, the team should probably walk away from this particular enterprise or country because, apart from direct divine intervention, it is virtually destined to fail. On the other hand, if the level of risk is acceptable and accepted (two very different concepts), then the team can move forward with its plans. Assessing our own risk tolerance is not easy and should never be done alone. The people around us often know better than we what our real tolerance is for coping with stressful situations.

Similarly, assessing risk tolerance must be bathed in prayer, asking if God wants the BAM mission to proceed in spite of any indicated weaknesses. As mature Christians know, God often chooses weaker vessels to carry his message and ministry to the people groups of the world. Whether this is such a situation, however, is a matter of great spiritual discernment, not wishful thinking. If we are to be effective for Christ, we must face the realities of the situation and adjust to them. Jesus was clear about this, noting that a king who is thinking of going into battle without sufficient forces should reconsider his plans, make radical adjustments and sue for peace (Lk 14:31-32).

BAM RISKS

One of today's dominant realities is that the world is a very dangerous place. As would-be BAMers survey the actual context of their business and mission, that reality needs to stay in the forefront of their thinking. On an almost daily basis the media report that Christians, especially Americans, are under attack from radical Islam and other religious and political enemies. Kidnappings, beheadings, torture, mutilation, murder and mayhem are common. The stories that follow are not pretty or even politically correct, and they are not presented to scare well-intentioned Christian businesspeople away from the BAM mission field. Instead, they are presented to illustrate the significant challenges that BAM practitioners face apart from business as usual. After all, BAM is taking the gospel into enemy territory.

Jesus warned of this several times in Scripture, saying that Satan was like a prowling lion ready to devour and persecute Jesus' followers (1 Pet 5:8). "You will be handed over to be persecuted and put to death, and you will be hated by all nations because of me" (Mt 24:9).

In the following chapters, I have divided the major threats and risks into seven categories: macroeconomic, political, spiritual, business specific, mission specific, expatriate and lifestyle. Even this approach barely touches the surface of what is very real and relevant for all would-be BAMers. Hopefully, however, *to be forewarned is to be forearmed.*

Because this subject is so personal to me, the following discussion is approached anecdotally, based on my experiences on the mission field in Kazakhstan from 1991 to 1995, right after the Soviet Union collapsed and the fifteen republics were suddenly opened for evangelization. While these stories may no longer reflect the current circumstances in Kazakhstan, they are still highly instructive because of their universality. They are concrete examples that have been replicated in infinite variations in every mission since missions began—and will be as long as there is a need to spread the gospel.

I hasten to add that in spite of the stories that follow and the price that many have had to pay, I testify from personal experience and from long association with practicing BAMers that business as mission can truly be a source of great joy, incredible satisfaction and infinite eternal and temporal rewards. Using our business skills for Christ—especially in an underdeveloped country—adds vitality to life and to our relationship with God. The people we touch, the appreciation in their hearts and faces, the wonder in their eyes—knowing that we dared to leave America, the place of their dreams and hopes, to share their lives, work and pain—is priceless.

DISCUSSION QUESTIONS

1. Define *risk management*. What does it mean? How do you practice risk management in your everyday life? How does your company or employer practice risk management?

2. What is meant by *risk tolerance?* Give some examples from your own life. What is your risk tolerance (i.e., risk aversion)? Does it vary depending on the setting? Explain. Is your risk tolerance the same as other members of your immediate family? If not, what are the differences? How are these differences manifest?

3. How does a business do a *threat assessment?* What factors should be considered? How important is it? Does the context matter? Explain.

4. If the author had prepared a proper risk-management assessment, do you think he would have chosen Kazakhstan? Why? If not, why do you think he went there and took his wife? What factors influence someone to do BAM in a Third World country?

5. BAM engagement: In today's world, what country wouldn't you visit as a tourist? As a missionary? As a BAMer? Why? What does this say about your risk tolerance? Your faith?

20

Macroeconomic Issues

"History has shown that where ethics and economics
come in conflict, victory is always with economics."
B. R. AMBEDKAR

"We have always known that heedless self-interest was
bad morals; we now know that it is bad economics."
FRANKLIN D. ROOSEVELT

"The seven years of famine . . . will come upon Egypt. . . .
"So Pharaoh said to Joseph, 'I hereby put you in charge of the
whole land of Egypt.' . . .
"So Joseph bought all the land in Egypt for Pharaoh. The Egyp-
tians, one and all, sold their fields, because the famine was too se-
vere for them. The land became Pharaoh's, and Joseph reduced the
people to servitude, from one end of Egypt to the other."
GENESIS 41:36, 41; 47:20-21

MACROECONOMICS MAY WELL BE ONE of those courses that many
would-be BAMers have never taken. That is a shame, since the practice of
BAM, although a microeconomic issue, is significantly affected by a country's
macroeconomic policies. At the risk of oversimplifying, let me briefly explain
a few concepts. Microeconomics, as the name *micro* suggests, has to do with
individual economic units, like individual businesses and firms. Macroeconomics, on the other hand, deals with the collective or aggregate economic
issues at the national level and has two basic divisions: fiscal policy, which
deals with a nation's tax structure, and monetary policy, which deals with its

currency, money supply and banking system. Global economics, a newly bur-geoning discipline, addresses international, multinational, transnational and global economic issues.

In this context there are several macro issues that serve as a reality check for the would-be BAMer. As he or she counts the costs of doing BAM and prepares for how to manage the risk, the BAMer is subject to macro-economic forces over which he or she has little or no control. For example, the economic collapse of Thailand in the mid-1990s had what economists call a "contagion effect" that had a devastating worldwide impact, and the 2008 U.S. financial meltdown (that began with the domestic housing mar-ket) precipitated the worst global economic collapse (euphemistically called the "global economic tsunami") since the 1929 Great Depression. These are only two (of many) examples of macroeconomic forces beyond any individual's control that can sink all boats and with them, BAM busi-nesses.

Among other issues that deserve attention, I want to specifically, albeit briefly, address the following: money, the banking system, the tax structure, the accounting system, inflation, profit repatriation and natural disasters. Our discussion is not to educate BAMers on the technicalities of these issues, but rather to anecdotally share real-life experiences that I have faced on the mission field, primarily in the Republic of Kazakhstan, Central Asia and other parts of the former Soviet Union (FSU). While these examples are all interna-tional, variations on the same themes can be readily found in virtually every domestic crosscultural setting.

MONEY

Managing money is one of the key elements in any BAMer's survival strategy. Not only are the BAM team and its families dependent on this skill for day-to-day living, but the BAM Company must pay its expenses, meet its payroll, cover its taxes and, if it is to have any long-term viability, make a profit. While most BAM businesses start with an initial amount of cash capital, it often runs out quickly and leaves the original investment in jeopardy. As with any busi-ness, it takes thoughtful, knowledgeable planning to determine how much money will be needed and to develop pro forma profit-and-loss statements. The original capital investment and seed money must be sufficient to take care of the BAM team, to launch the BAM Company and to see it through the initial startup period.

First, startup businesses are notoriously difficult, especially with poor planning. The traditional failure rate in the United States is about 80 percent, most of which occur in the first two years. Accordingly, the BAM team needs to plan for two to three years of initial deficit operations before the business is independently profitable. The goal for any business, of course, is for the company to generate sufficient money/cash flow internally to cover all existing costs (including the BAM team's salaries), projected growth, capital reserves and investor dividends.

Second, there is also the issue of currency, both the local currency and the foreign currency of the BAM team's home country. In our case, the currency of Kazakhstan in 1991 was the Russian ruble. All of the countries of the FSU were within the Ruble Zone when the USSR broke into fifteen different republics. We brought U.S. dollars into the country and then exchanged them for rubles. This was necessary because the entire FSU was a cash-only (or barter) economy, which did not use checks or credit cards.

Since the ruble's value was fluctuating wildly, we had three issues to face. First was the high exchange-rate risk. This risk refers to the danger of having a fluctuating gap between the value of one currency and another. For example, the U.S. dollar is considered a hard currency, because it historically maintains relatively stable international value. Other hard currencies are the Japanese yen, the English pound, and today, the European euro. Currencies that fluctuate rather significantly are thought of as soft currencies. The Soviet ruble is such a currency. Therefore, when someone holds U.S. dollars and can buy 1,000 rubles for each U.S. dollar, there is no problem if both are stable. If, however, the ruble inflates to 2,000:1, the 1,000 rubles purchased earlier now has half the purchasing power. Therefore, to hedge against this risk, we exchanged the minimum amount of dollars we needed to cover our short-term cash requirements and tried to hold as much of our cash as possible in hard currencies. Similarly, as we received rubles in return, we either transferred those into hard currency as soon as possible or held them to meet our near-term cash needs, to avoid exchanging our dollars and paying the often hefty exchange fees.

Third, in the process of exchanging currency we had to decide whether to deal with the corrupt local government and their unrealistically low exchange rate and high exchange fees, or with the equally corrupt black market with its better rates and lower fees. Inherent in this last decision is, of course, a moral and ethical issue that affects our witness to the local people. If we go with the government to do everything legally, we are viewed as stupid, irrational, wasteful Americans whose business practices (and by implication gospel message) are suspect. If we go with the black market, we are engaging in criminal activity that undermines the ability of the local government to exercise effective monetary policy and to stabilize the nation's money supply. Further, dealing with the black market says that our Christian values are not relevant in Kazakhstan, or that they are flexible and relative to the situation (situational ethics), or that they are firm, but we do not practice them. Either way it puts the BAMer on the horns of a dilemma and can be a lose-lose situation.

Fourth, in Kazakhstan, as elsewhere around the world, the $100 bill was the favored currency on the street. Interestingly, however, both within the open and the black markets, people were suspicious of money that was dirty (literally), frayed, torn or did not have the newest embedded bar codes. So you might have adequate dollars to pay your expenses, but no one would accept them. The irony was that counterfeit currency is usually much newer and cleaner than legitimate, used currency. As a result, when we were on home leave, my wife and I would take dirty money back to the United States, go to our local bank and literally spend hours in the cash vault going through stacks of bills to select those that were acceptable for commerce. We would then redeem the old money (which would be destroyed by the Federal Reserve) with crisp, clean new bills to take back to Kazakhstan.

This raises the fifth issue. How could we safely transfer significant sums of money in and out of Kazakhstan? In the early days of its independent, national existence, there were no effective, safe methods of wiring money into the country. In order to move money to and from the United Sates and Kazakhstan, whether for personal, business or church use, we simply had to strap it to our bodies under our clothes and be very discreet. This was not particularly satisfactory, since the journey to Kazakhstan required twenty-seven hours through twelve time zones—literally halfway around the world. In those days the trip required us to land at Moscow's Sheremetyevo II International Airport. The airport is on the north end of this metropolis of over fourteen million people. After disembarking the aircraft and clearing customs, we had to walk through the mafia-controlled airport with all of our luggage. We then hired a taxi (also controlled by the mafia) and drove with this stranger and all of our possessions, including the money on our waist (to be declared to the custom's officer—another issue), for over three hours as we traveled to the domestic airport, Domodedovo, to catch an Aeroflot plane to Almaty, Kazakhstan.

At that time, Domodedovo was perhaps one of the filthiest, darkest, most dangerous and sinister airports in the aviation world. Its public lighting was in shambles; its signage virtually nonexistent in Russian (certainly none in English or other international languages); unruly crowds of people would literally push, shove, elbow and fight to get to the front of the line (orderly queuing was usually ignored in places like airports); large numbers of unemployed, disheveled and possibly homeless people blocked the passages; hoodlums hung out in the parking lots, entrances, and halls; and the public toilets were gross and stench-filled.

You get the picture—and it is a critical picture for our discussion. For as we progressed from stage to stage, all we could think of was the $10,000 I had belted around my waist. Muggings and deaths had been known to occur for much less, and as Americans we stood out in the dismal surroundings as if a spotlight were announcing our presence. We overcame these circumstances by having a trusted Russian friend meet us at Sheremetyevo, escort us past the mafia, drive us through Moscow to Domodedovo, take us safely through the airport's maze of people and rules, and see us onto our flight to Kazakhstan.

BANKING SYSTEM

This discussion of money raises another major concern. Once a person gets the money into their BAM country, how do they keep the money safe from vandals? Safekeeping money in a modern structured society usually occurs with a bank deposit. One of my ventures in Kazakhstan was to join with two local businessmen and a fellow banker from Dallas to found the first Western-style bank in that country. Under the fledgling banking laws and central bank policies, we found that it was easy enough to deposit our currency, either in dollars or rubles. But, since there were no checks, ATMs or credit cards, how could we get our money out?

When we first established the bank, this was a tricky issue, because the

Kazakhstan Central Bank required all banks to sweep the vault each evening and deposit all extra currency into their bank. They, of course, gave us a credit balance on our account statement, but the government was largely broke. In fact, they used our deposits (along with those from other banks) to finance governmental operations. Certainly, there was little understanding of the importance of bank liquidity to promoting a viable banking system.

Accordingly, in order to make a withdrawal, we had to physically go to the bank, fill out a request and be interviewed by a banking officer to see if our proposed use of the money was acceptable. Once an acceptable purpose and amount were negotiated and approved, it was entered on a clipboard in the order of arrival. The bank then waited for someone to make a deposit in order to have the liquidity (cash) to cover our withdrawal.

The procedure was much the same as waiting at an American restaurant for a table. If we are present when our name is called, we get our money; if not, it is given to the next name on the list and our name is stricken. That means, two things: (1) if we used a bank, we spent hours or days in the lobby waiting to transact business, and (2) most people avoided banks and stashed the money in the safest place they could conceive. It sounds almost humorous, but the waste of time is not only infuriating but emotionally stressful and depressing. There is a family to care for, a life to be lived, a business to be run and a mission to be performed. For the nation it was a disastrous procedure that encouraged people to avoid banking their currency, thereby limiting the Central Bank's ability to exercise effective monetary policy. It also stifled the government of Kazakhstan's (GOK) ability to rapidly move from a cash society to one compatible with the global economy and its financial instruments.

If that were not sufficiently bad, consider that if people did use the bank, the government had full access to all of their records. That means the GOK had information that could be used to convict these people of tax avoidance.

TAX STRUCTURE

How a country organizes its tax policies is of paramount importance to a BAM Company. Kazakhstan was totally unfamiliar with the complexities of taxation in its new market economy. It was also in dire need of tax revenues to support its governmental operations. Unfortunately, it structured its tax system in wholly counterproductive ways. For example, when all of the taxes that a business was lawfully required to pay were added up—the income, property, value added, import-export, and sales taxes at each level of government—the tax bills often came to over 110 percent of the *gross* income of a business. This meant that for every U.S. dollar of incoming cash, the company would have to pay $1.10 (U.S.) in taxes! Clearly, this did not allow any business to survive as a law-abiding entity.

The survival strategy that most foreign and domestic companies settled for was simple tax avoidance. The GOK bureaucracy was also so disorganized, understaffed and corrupt that the chances of being caught were minimal in the medium term. Predictably, the effect of these practices on the cash-starved GOK was disastrous. Not only did they have minimal tax revenues to fund government services, but they did not have sufficient cash to remedy the situation. Further, they did not have a database of businesses to determine who was cheating.

To say the least, the moral and ethical implications of that situation, especially for a BAM Company, were challenging. How does a BAMer develop a satisfactory, viable survival strategy for the company that will also reconcile with the Christian faith? How does a person render unto Caesar, when Caesar demands more than he or she has?

Accounting System

An important aspect of business is its accounting system. Without it, there is no way of knowing whether a business is profitable, where the profit is coming from, what the major expenses are, whether those expenses are in line with industry standards, which of the company's products give the best margins, what the margins are, what the capacity is for internally generated growth, and, of course, what taxes are owed. Western business models depend on Western accounting systems like GAAP (the U.S.'s Generally Accepted Accounting Practices). Such systems are, however, not present in many nations.

When we arrived in Kazakhstan, their accounting system was based on the communistic command economic system, not the market system. Accordingly, its chart of accounts was completely different. This created severe, adverse consequences for commercial businesses, especially when calculating profits and taxes. For example, under a Western system, employee wages are a deductible business expense for taxes; under the Kazakh view, the payroll was taxable income. In their view, if you paid wages, clearly you had cash coming into the business, which they considered to be hidden, unreported income. While this seems inconceivably naive from a Western perspective, it created direct conflicts between the business and the GOK taxing authorities, quite apart from the 110 percent tax burden. This raised issues of whether to engage in illegal tax avoidance or yield to the prevailing corruption of government officials. Again, for a BAM Company, the moral, ethical and Christian witness implications are enormous and may determine the long-term viability of the business itself and even the freedom of the BAM team.

INFLATION

Inflation is a danger for every society. It occurs when there is too much money in the system and the value of the currency falls, causing prices of goods and services to rise in order to adjust. One of the tragedies of the collapse of the Soviet Union was the collapse of the ruble through hyperinflation, that is, inflation that is greatly accelerated and causes the value of currency to plummet overnight.

We experienced hyperinflation in Kazakhstan. It began when other FSU republics like Belarus went off the Ruble Zone and adopted their own currency. Since they limited the amount that any one person could convert, those with excess rubles fled with their money to neighboring republics. That, of course, inflated the money supply in those nations and drove their prices sky-high and the value of the ruble down. One after another, each republic responded to this crisis by adopting its own currency. When this economic tsunami hit Kazakhstan, the GOK was unprepared to issue its own currency and ill-equipped to stem the flow of rubles pouring across its borders. Like the proverbial Dutch boy putting his finger in the crumbling dam, the GOK was rumored to have even declared a cholera epidemic alert in order to lawfully seal its borders to people with rubles.

One Friday morning we found that the ruble's value was approximately 2,000 rubles to $1.00.[1] By noon it had risen to over 5,000 rubles and by night to over 8,000 rubles. By Monday morning, it was in excess of 50,000 rubles to $1.00. The GOK immediately issued a proclamation removing Kazakhstan

---

[1]These figures are taken from memory and are only illustrative, but their magnitude and impact are not exaggerated.

from the Ruble Zone and outlawing the use of any hard currency. They announced that they were issuing a new currency, the Tenge. Unfortunately for the nation, bureaucratic problems prevailed, and it was over a week before the new currency hit the street. Even then, the GOK was very restrictive in what it allowed anyone to convert. Accordingly, those who held their life savings in rubles lost virtually everything.

During the week-long delay in issuing the Tenge there was no lawful money and the entire economy shut down. All shops closed because no one wanted to sell their tangible goods for worthless paper, and the police were out in force to strictly enforce the new currency laws. People scrambled to find ways to hedge against the hyperinflation and the revaluation of their currency. Everyone began dumping rubles, trying desperately to convert them to hard currency or to buy tangible goods that would maintain value.

I personally saw a Volkswagen bug stuffed to overflowing with rubles, while its owner stood on the street trying to buy hard currency. Overnight these bills became so worthless that they were even used for toilet paper.

Needless to say, a BAMer in the midst of this monetary crisis stood to lose everything he or she had built for years. It severely and adversely affected every aspect of the business: the financial bottom line, the flow of commerce, the ability to conduct business (and the wisdom of) until stability was restored, the capacity to keep employees on the job (how does one lawfully pay them when there is no lawful currency?), customers' ability to purchase goods with viable currency, and suppliers who are no longer getting product orders.

Ironically, it had a major positive impact on the BAMer's mission as ministry opportunities in this setting overflowed. People were scared and vulnerable. They needed reassurance and the Lord to help them through it. What better opportunity to give people the real currency of life here and eternally?

PROFIT REPATRIATION

Another issue that Western businesspeople are not usually familiar with is the fact that many nations around the world will not allow businesses to repatriate their profits, that is, take their profits out of the country. That means that the investors' cash in the BAM Company may be required to remain overseas. This creates problems for raising business capital, properly compensating investors and developing outside reserves that can be used to start BAM businesses elsewhere. On the other hand, it keeps the BAM Company profits within the country to grow the business. Although this is often the BAM Company strategy, repatriation is still an issue that must be taken into account when planning the BAM business. There are, of course, various accounting and billing techniques that are universally used to subvert the laws that restrict repatriation and to covertly export profits in the guise of expenses. These are, however, frauds on the local government and raise Christian accountability issues.

NATURAL DISASTERS

Geography is an important element in any strategic area/country analysis (SAA). It often determines the type of infrastructure that is available for the business, the type of business that is likely to succeed in this forum, and the local markets, labor pools, educational levels, and transportation and communications challenges that will be faced. We often forget, however, that every region of the world also has its own particular geographical challenges from nature that have far-reaching macroeconomic consequences. Some areas are prone to monsoon rains, mudslides, typhoons, floods, droughts, fires, earthquakes and diseases. These events can seriously, adversely affect the local and national economies, as well as all local (and international) businesses that are dependent on that nation's industries, crops, markets or infrastructure.

How a BAM business hedges against these disasters depends on a host of individual circumstances. Consideration of these issues in its risk-management planning is, however, not optional. Failure to do so can be fatal to the BAM enterprise. On the other hand, being in such areas provides opportunities for holistic ministry and truly credible witnessing through hands-on actions to relieve the people's suffering.

SUMMARY

The point of the foregoing discussion is to illustrate a few of the considerable macroeconomic issues that face a business operating in an international environment, whether it is a BAM or a secular company. BAM businesses, however, carry heavier burdens because of the higher standards they espouse. Although daunting, such macroeconomic issues should not dissuade a would-be

BAMer. Rather, they should be part of the BAM team's *forewarned is forearmed* planning approach. Risk management, risk allocation and risk tolerance all play a role in how the BAM enterprise eventually enters and performs on the mission field. These are critical elements of every SMBP and offer excellent opportunities for seriously evaluating the kingdom impact that the company can realistically expect to have.

DISCUSSION QUESTIONS

1. What is meant by *macroeconomics* and *microeconomics*, and what is the difference between them? How do they differ from global economics? Which macroeconomic issues have most affected your life? In the country you chose for the class exercise, which issues most affect your proposed country? How?

2. In light of this chapter and what you know about macro- and global economics, analyze the economic trauma of 2008. What were the major factors in that economic collapse? If you had been doing the business you proposed in the class exercise in the country you selected, what would have been the effect on your business and your mission? What is the effect on missionaries on the field today?

3. BAM engagement: List the various ways that the economic collapse of 2008 affected you and your family, if at all. Please share with the class your personal experiences from this major macroeconomic collapse.

21

POLITICAL ISSUES

"Men say that I am a saint losing himself in politics.
The fact is that I am a politician trying my hardest to become a saint."
MOHANDAS GANDHI

"No one will ever be held responsible, not legally, not criminally,
not politically, as long as this Liberal government is in power. . . .
A culture of waste, mismanagement and corruption is not going to fix itself."
STEPHEN HARPER

"Every culture has its distinctive and normal system of government.
Yours is democracy, moderated by corruption.
Ours is totalitarianism, moderated by assassination."
AUTHOR UNKNOWN

"Everyone must submit himself to the governing authorities,
for there is no authority except that which God has established. . . .
[F]or the authorities are God's servants, who give their full time to governing."
ROMANS 13:1, 6

WITHOUT BELABORING THE POINT of how different and often dangerous doing BAM on the mission field can be, there are a few critical real-politic
power issues (among many) that can confront a would-be BAMer. The major
power centers are often found in the formal and informal political structure,
the multilayered governmental systems, and the local, traditional chieftains,
fiefdoms and baronages. Such terms may seem antiquated to the modern businessperson, but regardless of labels, all societies have their well-entrenched

establishments. These are realities that the international business community and BAM companies must face when operating within other people's territories, particularly in nondemocratic societies. When playing in their sandbox, we either play by their rules or operate at our peril. For the BAMer this can be particularly challenging, since their rules are seldom in harmony with biblical rules or the Jesus way.

POLICE STATES

I have lived in a number of police states where individual privacy is routinely violated by governmental surveillance. In fact, it is a practice of many prevailing power systems to track the private lives of their citizens and all foreign visitors. The secret police and their brutal methods have been a part of despotic governments since time immemorial. These medieval practices have, however, been seriously refined in the last century through the advances of technology, particularly clandestine surveillance systems. The war on terrorism, 9/11, Al-Qaeda, and the U.S. invasion of Iraq have expanded such practices even by democratic governments, with the United States now publicly debating such issues as torture, CIA interrogation techniques, and detention practices at strange sounding places like Abu Ghraib (Iraq prison), Guantanamo, and clandestine CIA overseas centers. Whether it is right or not, like the Nazi SS and the Soviet KGB of yesterday, today's FSB (the KGB successor), the Indian RAW (Research and Analysis Wing), the Chinese MSS (Ministry of State Security), and their ilk are imposing realities of the political world in which we do BAM.

When in Kazakhstan, we experienced the KGB on several occasions. One instance particularly stands out. A Kazakhstani acquaintance of mine was imprisoned and intensely interrogated for three days because he had offered to help me obtain a topographical map of the nearby mountains for hiking. I frequently obtain these maps in the United States from the local REI sports store but was at a loss where to find them in the FSU. My request was innocent—and naive—because the KGB overheard our conversations on the eavesdropping bug they had planted on my telephone and, in a knee-jerk response that resembled the old Soviet mindset, equated that with potential espionage. They did not come after me, because I was working for President Nazarbaev's business school and was too high-profile. They could, however, go after their own citizens with impunity and with no accountability. After three days, my friend was finally released and, to his credit and my amazement, was embarrassed that he could not fulfill his promise to help me.

The lesson is clear. Police states exist around the world, they play by their own rules, and they are quite adept at what they do. They can directly affect the would-be BAMer and his or her business, ministry and family, or they can do so indirectly, often outside of the BAMer's line of sight. Further, with our Western mindset we can frequently create major problems for others through our inadvertent, innocent (perhaps naive) actions. Developing sensitivity to the prevailing context and staying alert to the possible consequences of our actions is a must. We must remember that when in such a state, we must always assume that they are watching, listening and monitoring all we say and do. This is true everywhere we are (whether in our home, car, office, a local café or the park) and everyone with whom we have contact. Quite simply, we must always act in the firm belief that there are no secrets under these regimes. All of this information goes into a detailed dossier they keep on every individual, his or her family, associates, and activities. I do not say this to create paranoia, but to illustrate that doing BAM is not child's play.

GOVERNMENT EXPROPRIATION AND NATIONALIZATION

In America, businesspeople have little concern about the government taking over their businesses if they become successful, but in international business this is a real concern. The record is replete with instances when national governments have nationalized businesses that are foreign owned and operated. Although there are hedges against such events (even U.S. government insurance programs), expropriation of a BAM business not only ends the business but effectively destroys the mission. Fortunately, because of their inherently small size and low visibility, BAM businesses are not likely prospects of lawful nationalization. There are, however, other threats that have the same effect. One is what I call informal expropriation.

INFORMAL EXPROPRIATION

An example of informal expropriation occurred in Kazakhstan to a close friend of mine. In the early days of Kazakhstan's independence there were no Western-style restaurants for the growing expatriate community to enjoy. My friend, an enterprising Lebanese with an American wife, saw this as a legitimate business opportunity and opened a restaurant with excellent Western cuisine. It was an immediate hit, particularly within the wealthier expat community, and became quite profitable overnight.

This success and the money it generated drew the attention of a local KGB official who wanted the business for himself. To accomplish this he conducted a military raid on the restaurant during business hours. Helmeted, gun-toting soldiers lined the patrons up against the wall, let the Americans leave (apparently to avoid the ire of the U.S. embassy), bludgeoned the owner and dragged him to their waiting vehicles. He was not heard from for ten days. During that time all appeals to the GOK foreign ministry were stonewalled and the owner's wife could not get any information on her husband's location or condition. Since Lebanon had no embassy in Kazakhstan, the family appealed to the U.S. embassy, but it was unable to obtain any better results.

During intense interrogation, the owner refused to sign papers deeding the business to the KGB official. After ten days, his family was notified that if they posted a ransom equivalent to the airfare from Almaty to Moscow, he would be released. They did so and KGB whisked the owner away to the airport and put him on a plane for Moscow. Although my friend subsequently returned to his Almaty business, the episode sent a chill through the expat business community.

This also serves as a warning to would-be BAMers that when operating a business, especially one that has an overt Christian agenda, the local rules are not the same as those they may be familiar with. Further, although a Western passport is a valuable asset, it does not offer immunity or even effective protection in all situations. Ultimately, it must be remembered that the BAM business is in a foreign nation and subject to foreign power structures that frequently have their own, often highly subjective rules of the road. That poses a real danger that must be addressed when planning and doing BAM.

LOCAL LAWS AND LAW ENFORCEMENT

The world has many different legal systems. Although Western democracies have recently set standards that many other nations seek to emulate, our rules, practices and procedures are alien to most cultures and often become severely distorted in the process of adaptation.

Local counsel. When practicing BAM in a foreign country (corruption aside for the moment), the local court systems simply do not work as well for foreigners as for locals. It is essential that the BAM Company retain the services of a local attorney who knows the system, is well enough placed to exert influence on the company's behalf and knows how to work the system to his or her client's advantage. If the lawyer is a believer, so much the better, but that is not always possible (and sometimes may even be a disadvantage).

Bribery. The Bible is clear that we are not to accept bribes, but Proverbs also says to give gifts to the decision makers (e.g., Prov 18:16, 18; 19:6; 21:14; see also Ex 23:8; Deut 16:19; Prov 17:23; Is 1:23).[1] When I was practicing law in Asia, a young American was jailed for getting drunk and fighting with the police. The judge let us know that a case of Chivas Regal scotch would be an appropriate gift for freeing the young man and keeping him from languishing in a rat-infested dungeon for years.

There are many different views on the subject of gifts for judges and other officials. This is an excellent example of the BAMer's need for local cultural and legal guidance. Though the Western system sees this as a blatant bribe, many foreign cultures see it as a way to thank the official for doing his duty. They point to the Western practice of tipping a waiter in a restaurant or baggage handler at an airport. It is a price paid over and above the standard fee to express thanks for ordinary, extra or exceptional service.

In another situation we were asked to pay a fee to a high governmental official to obtain a governmental permit that should routinely be issued. We refused and were delayed a full year before obtaining the permit and starting the project.

The U.S. federal Corrupt Practices Act forbids bribes to foreign officials, but the cultural practices of the vast majority of nations require special payments for usual services. How to deal with these issues is a critical point for any BAMer, especially given the Christian witness he or she is bringing to the people of that country.

Contracts. Another area of concern for a business is what we in the West call *the sanctity of contracts.* Business everywhere is based on commercial transactions that always require a contract, either written or oral, explicit or

---

[1]On a Christian view of bribery, see "Biblical Bribery," in Gary North, *God's Success Manual* (n.p.: GaryNorth.com, 2007) <www.garynorth.com/proverbs.pdf>.

implied. There are supply contracts, employment contracts, sales contracts, office leases, partnerships, technology transfer, nondisclosure and noncompete agreements, intellectual property licenses, and the like. The problem arises when the cultural context has a different view of these contracts, their interpretation and their enforcement than we do. Often Western businesspeople assume contracts can and will be routinely enforced, but that is not always the case. They are subject to many forces, particularly within a judicial process where personal power, arbitrary rulings or biases often reign. Learning these perils is part of contextualized planning, but it also requires local professional help. Unfortunately, that help often creates ethical and scriptural tensions for the BAM Company.

Torts. The word *tort* may not be familiar to many people. It refers to that area of the law in which a person is damaged (the plaintiff) by another person (the defendant) or by his or her property or possessions, through negligence, willful acts, or dealing in areas of strict liability. An example is an automobile accident in which one driver sues the other for damage to his or her person, car, earning capacity or emotional well-being. Other examples might be where a neighbor's loose dog attacks and injures an innocent child on a playground, a newspaper publishes a libelous article about a person, a company's truck accidentally backs over a child while delivering goods to a house, a company's products cause injury or make someone sick, or a company's customer is injured on the company's premises. The situations that give rise to tort claim disputes are endless and fill the courts.

It is critical for a BAMer to understand that the business not only has contractual liability and challenges in the foreign courts, but it also has exposure on the tort side of the law. The very act of operating within a foreign jurisdiction in a way that could cause injury to a person or damage property and interests raises a risk that must be addressed just as it would in the United States. Accidents are an expected part of business activity. In the United States we maintain insurance to cover these contingencies, but in many foreign countries such insurance is not available or is different than U.S. citizens and businesses are used to. In that event the BAM Company must have a strategy for dealing with these possibilities to avoid the economic exposure such accidents can cause, and in some situations the cultural, relational and mission damage that can result.

One excellent example is when a U.S. company's truck operating in Asia struck and killed a local man on a bicycle. There was a dispute over the amount of the wrongful-death claim, so the family simply brought the body into the company's office and laid it on the CEO's desk. Needless to say, the claim was quickly settled.

FREEDOM OF RELIGION

Although most modern governments pay lip service to freedom of religion and include it in their constitutions or other foundational documents, frequently there is a significant gap between rhetoric and practice. Religious persecution is at epidemic levels in various areas of the world and BAMers who openly practice their faith can expect to be subjected to harassment and persecution at each step. Not only is the BAM message likely to threaten the local governments and other social and economic power structures, but Satan is also threatened—and he often has major strongholds in the society that the BAM team is entering.

During one discussion among practicing BAMers, the subject of spiritual warfare precipitated highly impassioned and animated discussion. All of these BAM practitioners were rational, mature, evangelical Christian businessmen and women. They gave examples of actual encounters with evil that left them knowing beyond any doubt that Satan is alive and well, and that there are active witches and warlocks, demons and devils at work to destroy BAMers and their companies. Satan manifests himself everywhere, they say, but especially through the local police, the military, political leaders, crime bosses and neighborhood tyrants that rule over their fiefdoms with an iron hand.

Spiritual strongholds are spoken of openly in the Bible (e.g., Dan 10:13) and the would-be BAMer who is not willing to accept this reality and to be prepared to deal with it should stay home.

Any BAMer who is thinking of entering an Islamic, communist or totalitarian country must be forewarned. Most of these regimes deny true freedom of religion and frequently forbid any proselytizing of religious views (other than their own) within their borders. The penalties are often severe, including deportation, lengthy imprisonment, torture and continual official and informal harassment. In some extremist regimes it can also mean death by beheading or firing squad.

It is wise to remember that when entering a foreign culture, the BAMer does not enter a religious or power vacuum. There have been well-established prevailing power structures already in place, probably entrenched for decades if not centuries. These power structures are religious, economic, political and social. Ignoring this fact or not researching and preparing to engage these realities will set the BAM mission up for failure, frustration, mediocrity or counterproductive witness.

FREEDOM OF SPEECH AND ASSEMBLY

Similarly, the BAMer cannot innocently assume that he or she has complete freedom of speech in another country. In some countries, just meeting to worship may be a crime or a suspect activity. One of the quickest ways to run afoul of the dominant power structures is to speak out against them or to become actively involved in local peace and justice issues or public demonstrations.[2] This is not to say that BAMers should not be involved in such activities. That is between the BAM team and the Lord, and how the Lord would use the BAM initiative. But make no mistake; there is a price to be paid for such activities, and the BAM team should be in prayerful, complete agreement with each other in that regard before engaging those temporal powers.

Certainly, the United States is not immune from these abuses. The U.S. Civil Rights marches of the 1960s in the South drew Christians from every corner of America and were led by Christians such as the Rev. Martin Luther King Jr. Their combined efforts resulted in massive social upheaval and ultimate justice, but it was not before our society was racked by waves of murders, lynchings, beatings, church and house burnings, and other violence. Similarly, independent media, newspapers, radio and TV stations in the former Soviet Union that are critical of the government or its leaders have been and are being muzzled, closed down and driven out of existence by violence, intimidation, murder and persecution. And such atrocities are not limited to indigenous newspeople. A foreign journalist whose worldwide editorials had

---

[2]The movie classic *Missing* (1973) with Jack Lemmon, addressed the problem of official kidnapping and terror in Chile during the 1973 Allende revolution. In the years following the release of this movie, other films have vividly highlighted these issues and will give BAMer a visceral feel for some of the political realities that still exist today.

been quite critical of the prevailing power structure was even found bound and gagged in his apartment with his throat slit.

SECURITY ISSUES

In today's world we see jihadist Muslims vowing to destroy the West; angry young men, women and children strapping explosives to their bodies to savagely murder innocent civilians at public markets, festivals and weddings; drug cartels operating worldwide; the rise of Russian, Asian and other mafias; war and genocide being raged against innocents of every faith; tribalism reasserting itself in Africa, with thousands of mutilated bodies and burned villages in its wake; bellicose nations in the Middle East playing with nuclear weapons; masked mobs in Gaza firing their AK-47s in the air; small children in Sierra Leone using their AK-47s to terrorize the countryside; suicide bombers in Iraq, Israel, Spain and England; nationwide Islamic riots in France; American businesspersons being kidnapped by South American revolutionaries to fund their operations; American missionaries in the Philippines being captured by guerillas to publicize their protest against the government, and others in India being burned alive by angry Hindu militants; and young girls worldwide being kidnapped, sexually exploited and commoditized in human trafficking and modern slave rings.

The list of horrors never stops. Human cruelty and barbaric inhumanity is exhibited everywhere, every day. It is approaching global insanity and makes this an extremely dangerous world in which to do BAM.[3]

A BAM security strategy. The reality of these security issues abound and must be faced by any would-be BAMer. They must also be addressed in the BAM Company's SMBP as part of its risk management program. Conversely, in the midst of this violence and chaos—indeed, because of it—there has never been a more important time for the world to hear about Jesus and his message of peace. There has never been a more important time for BAM companies, individually and collectively, to focus on having a kingdom impact to help

---

[3]Movies that give a good sense of the danger are *Proof of Life* (2000) with Russell Crowe and Meg Ryan, about a South American business kidnapping; *Man on Fire* (2004) with Denzel Washington about a Mexican mafia kidnapping; *Body of Lies* (2008) with Russell Crowe and Leonardo DiCaprio about Islamic extremists and their terrorists activities; and a 1972 classic, *State of Siege*, with Yves Montand, based on the true story of the kidnapping of a U.S. governmental official in Uruguay.

transform this needy world. As Paul so succinctly says, How will they know about Jesus unless someone goes and tells them (Rom 10:14-15)?

Unfortunately, in the name of Jesus, Christians have filled history's pages with horrors of our own. The shame perpetrated by the church is legion. The Crusades, the Inquisition, the church's silence during the German-led Holocaust, the Ku Klux Klan—all are atrocities committed by professing Christians. But they bear no resemblance to the gospel of Christ and his teachings of love, peace and tolerance; and it is on that foundation—Jesus and his gospel—that BAM rests.

Think in practical (albeit, idealistic) terms: What would it mean to the world if everyone acted on the basis of the love and goodness that Jesus preached? If they ran their businesses, their governments and their lives on the values found in the Bible (whether they accepted the deity of Christ or not)? Certainly, it would be a brave new world that is far different than the one we have made without God. It would also be a world far different than the utopias we conceive.[4] Instead it would be a forerunner of the new heaven, new earth and new Jerusalem of Revelation 21. That is a cause worthy of our lives. We firmly believe that with God's help, the kingdom impact of BAM can make a significant difference—and an important step toward that new world.

Mafia, corruption and crime. Perhaps the major problem facing the governments of the developing and transitioning world today is corruption. It is at epidemic levels in virtually every one of these nations and has become so entrenched that it is virtually impossible to eradicate. It is a cancer that eats at the body politic and destroys trust, relationships, efficiency and progress at every level of society. Unfortunately, the business community is frequently as complicit in this corruption as it is trapped by it. After all, businesses must interact with these government officials in order to ply their trades, and at virtually every point in the commercial system, in virtually every nation on earth (especially in the developing world), the local and national officials have their squeeze points.

In many countries, the police are often powerless to help stem the tide of

---

[4]Think in terms of classic, toxic, utopian scenarios such as Aldous Huxley's *Brave New World* (1932), George Orwell's *1984* (1949), Ray Bradbury's *Fahrenheit 451* (1953), Ridley Scott's film *Blade Runner* (1982) or even Andy Wachowski and Larry Wachowski's film *The Matrix* (1999).

corruption and criminal activity, especially that of organized crime. They lack manpower, firepower, equipment, technology and funds to compete with these well-financed, high-tech criminals. On the other hand, the police in these countries (including our own) can also be the problem. In the nations of the former Soviet Union, the police are frequently in league with the mafia or *are* the mafia. Either way, corruption poses a very real threat to the BAM Company's ability to effectively carry on business in accordance with gospel standards.

In addition to the great threat to the BAMer from organized crime (the mafia), which is often operated from top levels of society, there is also the malevolence of simple street crime and/or neighborhood gangs at the lowest levels. These pose security issues for the business as well as the BAM team members, the employees and all of their families. When we were in the FSU, the various mafias had moved into major sectors of Russian commerce and were at war with each other and with the police for control of vital economic arteries. They especially targeted airports, seaports, trucking, railroads, oil and gas, banking, and the media. Each of these is a pressure point that can control the flow of commerce and affect all businesses, including BAM companies.

Private security forces. It is not uncommon for international businesses to use private security forces to protect their interests: vehicles and facilities, computers, shipments, people, homes and families. These forces range from security guards on trucks and trains (like the Old West *shotgun* rider on stagecoaches), to onsite guards, barbed fences, dogs, and special communications and surveillance systems, to bodyguards for key executives and their families. The larger company security forces are almost always well-armed, with weapons and special armor aboard every vehicle and at every facility.

Obviously few BAM companies are well-enough financed to take such measures, but the risks are no less real. On the other hand, the BAM Company is not just any business. It is a company with a godly mission beyond product or service delivery. It enters a community with the goal of becoming a permanent part of its fabric and to effect good works, create jobs and wealth, and minister holistically to the people there in the name and love of Jesus. Hiding behind security fences may be antithetical to the BAM agenda, but deciding how much risk to take and how to manage it are subjects that need to be clearly understood and discussed among the BAM team—and with the Lord.

POLITICAL INSTABILITY

Most of the issues we have discussed are capable of effective risk management that will offer comfort and reassurance to the BAMers, their families and employees. A risk that is less susceptible to management is that of political instability. This can vary from mild to extreme, from peaceful protests against the government to coup d'états and revolutions, from street riots and violent police/military intervention with gunfire, bombings, fires, wanton looting and destruction and murder to wars and terrorist attacks that purposefully attempt to destabilize the government and society.[5]

Such instability poses a risk at several levels. In its worst form it could mean that the legal, physical and economic infrastructure of the country collapses; that there are no open stores, banks, viable currency, safe roads or ports; and there are no operating police, fire departments, courts, laws or governmental functions. In such a situation, the BAM Company's survival is seriously jeopardized. In all probability, its inventories, facilities, equipment and vehicles will be damaged or destroyed; its employees and their families may be badly hurt or killed, kidnapped, or arrested, or they may have their homes uprooted and their possessions looted or destroyed. Expats and their families may also need to be evacuated, or they may be trapped, cut off from each other, from their embassy and from their established escape routes. In such an event the Christian mission and ministry opportunities may be so limited or dangerous that they must be completely, if not permanently, abandoned.

How the BAM team addresses these possibilities is a matter of risk assessment, risk tolerance and risk management, and will vary from country to country. In some countries the risk of political instability is historically low, while in others it is almost traditionally and culturally inevitable. Countries at both ends of this spectrum need Jesus and his gospel, and therefore BAM. But BAM is not a form of relief work. Its arena is development, which is quite different. Nonetheless, to be commercially viable (above the microenterprise

---

[5]The 2006 academy-winning movie *Blood Diamonds* had several scenes of intertribal violence, vigilante death squads, child soldiers, corruption and an unforgettable scene of rebels attacking the capital of Sierra Leone. Similar simulated realities are portrayed in *Hotel Rwanda* (2006), about the intertribal genocide of 1994, and the *Last King of Scotland* (2006), about the horrors of Idi Amin's terrorist regime in Uganda. While grim, these films offer a vivid picture of some of the realities that the BAMer might face when the local and national governments are not strong enough to maintain law and order or are so strong as to be the author of mass murder.

level), the BAM Company requires a modicum of social and commercial infrastructure—and that requires a fairly stable society.

This means that BAM cannot be practiced successfully in every country. Assessing the level of stability and infrastructure required for the particular BAM Company and its proposed product or service line is a matter of factual analysis and realistic discernment and prayer. If BAM is not a viable option, however, other forms of marketplace mission, especially microfinance and microenterprise development, may be more appropriate in that context.

SUMMARY

Going into a foreign country to do BAM is, by definition, subjecting ourselves to foreign political and governmental power structures. That involves dealing with the existing governing bodies at the local, state, regional and national levels, as well as the baggage that those bodies carry with them. Such baggage may include rampant corruption, crime, ineffective courts and police, mafia, anti-Christian bias or outright persecution, and restricted freedoms such as religion, speech and assembly. These are the realities that the BAM business may face. There is also the danger that these systems, as bad as they may be, will themselves be destroyed. Natural disasters, riots, war and revolution can, in a single day, wipe out a city or a nation. In such events, chaos and anarchy often replace the former despotism and corruption, leading to another cycle of social upheaval.

Whatever the BAM Company faces in its chosen context, the political issues must be carefully examined and the risk management decisions made a part of the SMBP. Any less response can place the BAM enterprise and the people associated with it in extreme danger.

DISCUSSION QUESTIONS

1. How would you cope with being watched, listened to and monitored all day, every day, by a police state? How would this change who you are in that setting and how you relate to others? How would it affect your family?

2. What could you do to safeguard your business from being taken over by the government once it becomes successful? By the mafia? Discuss.

3. How would you personally distinguish between a bribe and a "thank you"

for work well done? Can you support your decision biblically? Does the Bible view accepting a bribe differently than giving a bribe?

4. Corruption is a major problem facing developing nations. If bribes are necessary to obtain a business license, visas and other documents to do BAM business in a country, this is a signal that the citizens of this country need the gospel and biblical values in their civic life. How would you and your team operate in such an environment? What if it meant waiting a year to obtain the necessary documents to enter and/or do business in that country? How would you and your team utilize the time? Discuss alternatives and strains this would put on your plans.

5. BAM engagement: Of all the political risks in this chapter, which do you think are most likely to confront your proposed business in your chosen country in the class exercise? Explain.

6. BAM engagement: A righteous American, when going into Mexico to do business, once said, "I won't leave my integrity at the border." What is integrity? Is it ethnocentrically and contextually determined? The author spoke of an Asian judge requesting (through a third party) a case of whisky in exchange for not sentencing a nineteen-year-old American to ten years hard labor in a despicable prison. If the decision were up to you, would you give the whisky? Why or why not? What of the proverbial slippery slope? Where do you draw the line? What boundaries do you set for yourself and your family when in a foreign setting that the Lord called you to?

22

Spiritual and Mission Issues

"We're facing a new kind of enemy. We're involved in a new kind of warfare and we need the help of the Spirit of God. The Bible's words are our hope."
BILLY GRAHAM

"Finally, be strong in the Lord and in his mighty power. Put on the full armor of God so that you can take your stand against the devil's schemes. For our struggle is not against flesh and blood, but against the rulers, against the authorities, against the powers of this dark world and against the spiritual forces of evil in the heavenly realms."
EPHESIANS 6:10-12

WHILE TEMPORAL ECONOMIC AND political power issues are realities on the BAM mission field, they take backstage to the real power issues at play. The apostle Paul was quite clear about the spiritual realm being our dominant concern. In the final analysis, the BAMer is a business missionary carrying the gospel of Christ to a foreign people group and engaging in holistic ministry to those people. As discussed above and worth repeating over-and-over, the BAMer does not enter a spiritual vacuum.

Spiritual Issues

On the business-mission field the BAM team will be confronted and challenged by many, varied religious and spiritual issues. Four issues deserve special comment: entering enemy territory, the power of prayer, spiritual dryness and the threat of modern radical Islam.

Enemy territory. The world's great religions are only a fraction of those that exist on the mission field. Certainly, we know of such major faiths as Judaism, Islam, Buddhism, Hinduism, Confucianism, Baha'i and Taoism, not to mention the seemingly infinite variations of faith expressions such as Protestantism, Catholicism, Christian Science, Orthodoxy, Mormonism, Unitarianism, Universalism, Scientology and New Age, as well as organized secularists, atheists, Satan worshipers, Wicca and Voodooists. In fact, there are hundreds if not thousands of other spiritual groups, religions, sects and cults around the world. They have existed in one form or another in every country, among every people, in every era—and they exist today.

Each of these religious or spiritual groups has a territorial claim, whether it be over a given home, neighborhood, city or nation, or over a specific group of people. Christianity has received a mandate from Jesus Christ to disciple the world. In so doing, those who carry his message (whether traditional or non-traditional missionaries like BAMers) are entering these groups' territory and may be opposed. That, of course, depends on the context. In those places where several groups are already established, their responses to each other will run the gamut from living in relative harmony to chronic conflict to open warfare.

Where chronic conflict historically exists, the BAM team can expect strident opposition. In short, the BAM team is entering occupied territory where hostile spiritual power centers preside. These groups have a decided stake in the society and people they claim, and they are usually not happy with those who would disrupt that status quo. These groups may be used by Satan as soldiers in his army to mobilize against the BAM intruders. If so, the BAM team will quickly realize that the resistance is not so much economic, political or cultural opposition (although that may be the context) as it is spiritual warfare. As John Eldredge said in *Waking the Dead*, in these situations, "We are at war."

> There is something set against us. . . . We are at war. . . . How I've missed this for so long is a mystery to me. Maybe I've overlooked it; maybe I've chosen not to see. *We are at war.* I don't like that fact any more than you do, but the sooner we come to terms with it, the better hope we have of making it through to the life we do want. This is not Eden. You probably figured that out. This is not Mayberry; this is not *Seinfeld*'s world; this is not *Survivor.* The world in which we live is a combat zone, a violent clash

of kingdoms, a bitter struggle unto the death. I'm sorry if I'm the one to break this news to you; you were born into a world at war, and you will live all your days in the midst of a great battle, involving all the forces of heaven and hell and played out here on earth. Where did you think all this opposition was coming from?[1]

As in any warfare, we have to know our enemy.[2] In this case, as Paul warned, the enemy is Satan and his evil forces. In summary, if the BAMer does not understand this, he or she will simply be cannon fodder in this war and could be scarred for life. Spiritual warfare is hardball, and wherever the BAMer is vulnerable—family, business, home, health, finances, employees and their families, and even family back home—that is where Satan will attack.

Prayer power. The most effective weapon in this war is prayer—intercessory prayer and direct prayer by individuals, the BAM team, and believing employees. Great things happen through focused prayer. Scripture says that the "prayer of a righteous man can accomplish much" (Jas 5:16 NASB), but as I have repeatedly admonished, all BAMers must literally put on the armor of God to protect themselves during this battle (Eph 6:10, 13).

Constant, specific, focused prayer is a must for BAMers. It both demands and creates a close, personal, intimate walk with our Lord. It helps us understand him and his ways, and it helps us resist Satan. But equally important, it also brings encouragement, hope and a strong sense of expectation and excitement.

Listening prayer is also a must. If we genuinely want to know how God, the BAM business's Boss, wants his business conducted and how the BAM team is to deal with both strategic and daily decisions, that knowledge can only come by sitting at the Boss's feet and listening. BAMers must be like Mary *and* Martha (Lk 10:38-42). Daily they must be in the kitchen keeping things running, but they must also take time away from the kitchen to listen to Jesus.

There is also a form of prayer called inner healing prayer (IHP). It is an approach to prayer in which an individual can identify and resolve deep-seated emotional issues that have plagued his or her attempts at healthy living. This is

---

[1]John Eldredge, *Waking the Dead* (Nashville: Thomas Nelson, 2003), pp. 12-13.
[2]There are many excellent books on spiritual warfare to educate the BAMer and family. BAMers should not purposefully enter enemy territory unless they are called by God, equipped to do so and have adequate prayer cover.

especially important on the mission field, where such issues can be greatly amplified and thereby impede the mission's effectiveness. Dr. Frecia Johnson has established a unique and successful IHP ministry called "Experiencing Jesus."[3] Her prayer sessions lead believers to enter into a dialogue with Jesus about various emotional problems they are experiencing. Johnson says, "We invite Jesus and the Holy Spirit to lead the prayer time. They do the healing, I just facilitate the discussion." Both research data and anecdotal testimonies evidence significant long-term, deep, inner healing as a result of her ministry.

Training in how to conduct IHP is highly recommended in order to be effective and to avoid unscriptural activities. IHP can be exceptionally useful on the mission field. It not only helps the BAMers maintain stronger emotional and spiritual health for themselves and their families, but can transform their employees and those in the indigenous churches the BAMers serve.

Building spiritual cover for the BAM team, the business, the stakeholders and their families is also one of the elements of spiritual armor. This is accomplished by the team praying for each other, but it also means constructing a base of intercessory prayer support back home, which will pray for the team, their families and the mission enterprise. We do not understand how it works, but God has structured his support of our mission efforts in such a way that the heavenly forces are strengthened and more effective when they are energized by focused prayer. Given the nature of the forces arrayed against the BAM Company—cultural, market, political and spiritual—they need as much heavenly support as possible.

Spiritual dryness. One of the grave dangers of being on the mission field, both as traditional and nontraditional missionaries, is a case of spiritual dryness. Not only can it strike individual BAM team members directly, but it can have a corrosive, contagious effect on the entire mission force and their families. Traditional missionaries are so busy spiritually feeding others and ministering to their needs, that they often neglect their own spiritual nourishment. Similarly, in answering their call, they often neglect their families, who are exceptionally vulnerable. Frequently the family members are serving because of a call to ministry other than their own. They are the support team and may

---

[3]Dr. Frecia Johnson, whose Ph.D. is from Fuller Theological Seminary, is my wife, but this evaluation and recommendation on behalf of her prayer ministry is based on observing its effectiveness over a twelve-year period.

have cheered when the called family member raised the prospects of doing mission in a foreign country. But when the realities set in, the strains on the family begin to show. If the family is not 100 percent committed to the BAM calling, rifts are virtually inevitable. Family life is difficult enough in ordinary circumstances, but in the mission context it can even become greater.

The problem is multiplied with BAMers who are seeking to meet both the business and the mission mandate. The time constraints and demands are enormous, as are the emotional burdens. Discouragement, a sense of futility and hopelessness—all symptoms of spiritual dryness—can easily set in. If not dealt with immediately, they can destroy the cohesiveness of the BAM team as well as their marriages. Ideally, the spouses, if not the whole family, somehow need to be or become full partners in realizing the BAM venture.

To maintain balance, perspective and sustainability, everyone on the mission field must be fed spiritually and must be involved in meeting each other's inner emotional needs. How that is done depends on the dynamics of each family and each BAM team, but it must be addressed in the SMBP, in the daily interactions of the team and their families, and in simply looking out for each other. If this does not happen, the time on the mission field will likely be curtailed, seriously damaging the family and jeopardizing the mission.

The radical Islamic threat. Islam is on the move, and its more radical branches want to wipe both the country of Israel (and Judaism) and Christianity from the face of the earth. Radical jihadists, primarily under Al-Qaeda and the Muslim Brotherhood, are attempting to terrorize and destabilize both the Western world and Sunni Muslim nations like Saudi Arabia and Egypt.[4] Radical Muslims have also moved into Europe, creating major social and political problems, particularly for France, Germany and England. Many observers are concerned that Turkey's proposed entrance into the European Union (EU) as the first Islamic EU nation may be part of a Muslim strategy to Islamicize Europe.

The growth and movement of Islam is also testimony to the apparently unacceptable living conditions and restricted freedoms under Islam, since so many of its faithful are seeking to leave their homelands and emigrate to the West. Os Guinness argues that the future of Islam is one of the "grand ques-

---

[4]Cleo Shook, "Middle East Update," Sierra Madre, California, February 13, March 27, May 1 and May 8, 2007.

tions" confronting the world in the twenty-first century:

> [W]ill Islam modernize peacefully, forswearing its tendency toward militancy, pacifying its violent extremists, reversing its low view of women, acknowledging the right of religious liberty for all, including those Muslims who convert to other faiths, and accommodating to the fact of social diversity? Or will its continued violence, its insistence on coercing faith, and its adamant refusal to allow faith to be privatized be the catalysts that force the modern world to reconfigure its structures and policies, either or better or for worse?[5]

The reason this is relevant to BAM is radical Islam's direct, violent assault on Christianity (and other world religions) and Christians, especially missionaries. It is occurring worldwide and will undoubtedly be a major force to be contended with by BAMers—who will be on the front lines, in harm's way—perhaps for the next twenty or thirty years. Those who seek to organize a BAM Company in a predominantly Muslim nation or area will need to become thoroughly familiar with Islam, its basic tenets and its methods. This warning *is definitely not meant to be a wholesale indictment of all Muslims,* millions of whom also decry what is being done in the name of Allah and earnestly seek to live at peace with the rest of the world. But it is an unpleasant reality that must be honestly faced when preparing to do BAM.

MISSION ISSUES

The "mission" in BAM is perhaps *the* major area in which most BAMers, being businesspeople, are weak. Adequately exploring the mission issues that BAMers will face would take an entire course in missiology and more. Such training is well-advised for all BAMers in preparation for their field activities. However, the discussion here will be limited to a few items that deserve special comment.

Not a church. The church universal is rightly thought of as the people of God. And the local church is a particular congregation of believers. Some speak of this dichotomy as the *dispersed church* at large and the *gathered church* ecclesiastically and locally.[6] The primary activities of the gathered

---

[5]Os Guinness, *A Case for Civility* (New York: HarperCollins, 2008), pp. 29-30.

[6]For a discussion on the gathered and dispersed church see Charles Van Engen, *God's Missionary People* (Grand Rapids, MI: Baker, 1991), pp 35-46; see also Avery Dulles, *Models of Church,* expanded ed. (New York: Doubleday, 2000) for a Roman Catholic view, and Hendrikus Berkhof,

church are to worship the Lord, equip the saints and witness for Christ by word and deed.

Although BAM companies are nontraditional mission vehicles for taking the gospel to the world, they are also full-time businesses engaging the marketplace on a commercial level. In that sense, BAMers are part of the people of God (the dispersed church), but their BAM Company is not a church and should not aspire to be. It is a business that is using its economic position in the community to sponsor and effect holistic mission activities within the company and the community. It is first, last and always a business. Without the business there is no mission.

Bridges to the local church. The BAM Company should have a special relationship to local churches. Its team members and their families need a place to worship and be fed spiritually. Its employees, as they come to Christ, need a church home to join and participate in. Its community projects should always be done in such a way that honors Christ and, where possible, partners with the local churches and points people to them as a source of goodness, light and help. As part of their kingdom bottom line, the BAM Company can also assist local business entrepreneurs who are members of the local congregations (and others who are not) with business training, technical support and mentoring. This training will, of course, come from a biblical worldview and ethic.

With the help of the BAM Company, the local church can even establish an incubator for micro and small businesses started or owned by indigenous congregants. For those in the congregation it offers access to an improved standard of living and, through tithing, assists the church in realizing financial independence and growth. For those outside of any congregation, it offers an opportunity to see the church as an instrument of God to help them meet the economic needs of their lives.

Church planting. While a BAM Company is generally not called to plant churches in its area, it may see the need. How it responds to that need will depend on the company's available resources and its own special calling. Anyone who has planted a church (I speak from experience) realizes that church planting is a very specialized, skill-specific, time-demanding activity. There are numerous Christian agencies that specialize in church planting and bring

---

Christian Faith (Grand Rapids: Eerdmans, 1991) for a Dutch Reformed Tradition view.

a great deal of experience to the table. Rather than acting as a church-planting agent, I suggest that the BAM Company partner with one of those agencies. The BAM Company can bring people and resources to the task and, if the agency is not established in the BAM Company's locale, can offer the agency invaluable information about the local culture and local Christian resources and opportunities.[7]

DISCUSSION QUESTIONS

1. What is spiritual warfare? Is it real or merely an outdated metaphor to explain the human condition? Discuss. If you believe it is real, what is your specific plan to keep yourself, your family, your team and your business safe from spiritual attack?

2. BAM engagement: If you were to enter a country under heavy Islamic influence to launch a BAM business, how would you prepare yourself and your team for working in that country? Why does the author see Islam as a particularly dangerous threat to BAM? Do you agree? Why or why not? What are your views of Islamic activites in today's world? Discuss.

3. BAM engagement: Assume that you are on the mission field in the business and country selected for your class exercise (or your real situation, if applicable).

   a. What is your specific plan to keep yourself, your family and your team spiritually alive and well while doing BAM in that country? How do you plan to recruit and retain prayer partners?

   b. What is the country's main religion(s)? How will that religion affect your business? Before you enter the country, how can you prepare to interact intelligently, emotionally and spiritually with that religion?

   c. How do you plan to relate to the country's local churches? What is your plan to create relationship and to work with and through them? What are the pros and cons of such relationships vis-à-vis your primary mandates?

---

[7]Tom Steffen's books *Passing the Baton: Church Planting that Empowers*, rev. ed. (La Habra, Calif.: Center for Organizational and Ministry Development, 2000), and *Planned Phase-Out: A Checklist for Cross-Cultural Church Planters* (Bethesda, Md.: Austin & Winfield, 1993), are two of several valuable sources of information.

23

BUSINESS-SPECIFIC ISSUES

"Capitalism is what people do if you leave them alone."
KENNETH MINOQUE

"All business proceeds on beliefs, or judgments
of probabilities, and not on certainties."
CHARLES W. ELIOT

"Now listen, you who say, 'Today or tomorrow we will go to this or
that city, spend a year there, carry on business and make money.'
Why, you do not even know what will happen tomorrow. . . .
Instead, you ought to say, 'If it is the Lord's will,
we will live and do this or that.'"
JAMES 4:13-15

AT THIS POINT, I AM TEMPTED TO DISCUSS the many issues surrounding BAM overseas, such as obtaining licenses and permits, finding suitable locations, hiring local employees, mastering the local import-export system, solving electrical compatibility issues with Western computer hardware, navigating local banking and credit peculiarities, and the like. These are the usual issues that the BAM team faces during the due diligence phase. The answers, of course, should be incorporated into their strategic country/area analysis (SAA) and the strategic business plan (SBP). I will, however, resist the temptation to explore these topics—on which considerable literature has already been written and which will be the subject of the BAM team's in-country inquiries—and instead focus on some of the less obvious challenges.

PERSONAL ASSISTANTS

Personal assistants are often necessary for the expat BAM team and their families, especially in the early stages of residence within the country. These assistants help orient the expat BAMer to the local culture and the city, assist with shopping, transportation, translation, interpreting and even recreation, housekeeping, driving and security. They are often young people who want to practice their English and who see their association with you as a possible personal or professional advantage. By the very nature of their services, they frequently develop close personal relationships and become like members of the family.

Selecting the right assistants is important to avoid the dangers of bringing a dishonest, immoral, deceitful or unreliable person into the home and business. Obtaining recommendations from local missionaries, as well as known business and church sources, is usually a good way to find reliable help. Similarly, if the BAM business is being sponsored by another BAM business, reliance on their advice is advantageous.

If the BAM Company is in a country where such help is needed, it is wise to think ahead about the profile of the person who will be most useful to the team and their families. Different members will need different types of assistants. The factors determining which assistant is appropriate include sex, age, language skills, character, personality, image, maturity, networks, business experience, faith (and level of maturity) and, of course, compensation.

LOCAL PARTNERS

It is virtually impossible to negotiate a new culture and establish a BAM Company without the assistance of a local partner. In *emic* and *etic* terms, the BAM team is the outsider (etic) and the local partner is the insider (emic). Together they can do a great deal more, faster and more efficiently than either one could individually. Selecting the right partner is, however, a touchy subject, because the right person with the right contacts can be invaluable. Conversely, the wrong person can be disastrous and bring about the failure or ineffectuality of the enterprise.

As with personal assistants, the right local partner can often be found through local churches, NGOs, businesses and other BAM companies. This also should be bathed in prayer, asking the Lord to create divine appointments with the right people. Six points must be considered.

First, as with any employee that the company hires, the BAM team needs to draft a profile of the qualities they want in the local partner. Among other points on such a profile, the team wants someone who has a good reputation among local businesses, the NGO, BAM and church communities, and the home country embassy and consulate. The partner should be a person of excellent character, have a track record of successful business dealings and possess good people skills, direct industry experience, and a useful network of contacts that are relevant to the particular BAM business. The person needs to be fluent in the BAM team's mother language, as well as the local language.

Excellent contacts in key governmental offices and prominent social circles can also be useful both to the business and in reaching the movers and shakers of the city and nation for Christ. In Kazakhstan, two local partners, one U.S. partner and I started the country's first Western-style bank. Not only did the local partners prove to be bright and capable, but they mysteriously came up with one million dollars to capitalize the bank. They never shared how that could happen in an economy where the top wage was about $30 per month. It was soon apparent to me that the police and local mafia were keeping their distance from our business. This was quite unusual and raised questions in my mind. Those were settled when, on returning from the United States on a business trip, one of the local partners asked me to attend a private meeting with a high government official to discuss the bank and receive his blessing. I did, he did, and we continued to operate with little or no outside interference. Fortunately, there were never any requests or pressures to do anything unethical.

Second, the BAM team must address what being a *partner* means. Is the person to be an upgraded personal assistant, an employee or a true partner? Is the prospective partner to have a salaried position, equity ownership or both? If a salaried position, what are the terms of employment (i.e., salary, benefits, bonus, expense accounts, job description, etc.)? Is the partner a part of the executive management team? What authority does he or she have, and to whom does the partner report? If an equity position, what type, how much, when is it vested and under what conditions? Is it sweat equity or capital equity or both? Is the person a silent partner or an active participant in the business? What is the probationary period and exit strategy if the partner does not work out as planned? In other words, the person should be given the same consideration as a U.S. partner, but in alignment with the local context, which may be very different.

Third, should the partner be a Christian? If not, how does this interfere with realizing the BAM objectives, if at all? The earlier comments about the members of the BAM team seem appropriate at this point. Although it is not essential that the partner is a believer, it would certainly ease a source of possible conflict. In addition, depending on his or her status with the company, there is the very real issue of *unequal yoking*. Using an agricultural metaphor for his day, Paul warns Christians, "Do not be yoked together with unbelievers. For what do righteousness and wickedness have in common? Or what fellowship can light have with darkness? . . . What does a believer have in common with an unbeliever?" (2 Cor 6:14-15; see also Ps 94:20; Is 30:1-5; Jer 2:17-22; 5:5-6; 16; Eph 5:6). Commentators on this passage reiterate, "Paul urges believers not to form binding relationships with unbelievers, because this might weaken their Christian commitment, integrity or standards. It would be a mismatch. . . . [Believers] should not lock themselves into personal or business relationships that could cause them to compromise their faith." Believers should do everything in their power to avoid situations that could force them to divide their loyalties.[1]

If the partner is to be a Christian, other issues surface. How do you know this is so? How long has he or she been a believer? What references and evidences are there to verify the partner's bona fides? How does the partner grow in faith (e.g., quiet times, Bible study, prayer, church involvement, etc.)? What church does the partner attend? What has been the partner's role in the church and how is he or she viewed by the faithful? Are there any doctrinal issues that could conflict with the BAM team's faith? What is the partner's personal and family history?

The point is that there are different levels of faith and spiritual maturity, and tragically, mission history is replete with what are known as *rice Christians*. Those are local people who attach to the church and proclaim the gospel in their lives in order to get a job with the mission and thereby feed themselves

---

[1]Bruce B. Barton, ed., *Life Application Bible*, New International Version edition (Wheaton, Ill.: Tyndale; and Grand Rapids: Zondervan, 1991), pp. 2100-101. For a deeper discussion of unequal yoking see the commentary on 2 Cor 6 at <www.biblegateway.com/resources/commentaries/>.

and their families (hence, *rice*). They are probably good sincere people, but their commitment to Christ is a matter of convenience, even expedience, as a temporal survival strategy rather than an eternal one. Even if these people are true believers, political, cultural or family pressures may force them to take actions that are not biblical or in the BAM Company's best interests. Vigilance is called for to continually monitor this.

It was not uncommon in Kazakhstan for local partners with foreign companies to use that position to increase their status among their friends and peers. In fact, it was even chic for Kazakhstan business partners to brag about their U.S. partners, calling them their *pet Americans*.

Fourth, no matter how carefully we choose or how much confidence we have in our choice, we live in a fallen world and human nature is what it is. People in foreign countries look at expats (especially Americans), see that they are rich by local standards and recognize that at some point they will be going home. Further, the BAM team has passports and airline tickets in their pockets and can leave when the going gets tough. The local partner does not have that luxury. That, in a nutshell, is perhaps *the* critical divide that will always exist between BAMers and their partners. It is not always a matter of believers versus nonbelievers or of breach of faith; it is simply a fact of life. Partners are insiders (emics) who will probably live all their lives there. BAMers are outsiders (etics) who can—and probably will—leave.

That being the case, there will always be a distance that is hard to bridge with any local partner. Further, most local partners—no matter how good or Christian they are—will silently ask themselves, *How can I work with these foreigners to my advantage?* and *What's in it for me?* Whether they ask overtly or only subconsciously, they will usually look out for their own self-interest ahead of the BAM team's. I hasten to add that I have personally experienced *many* wonderful, inspiring exceptions—people who loved and took care of my wife and me at great personal risk and sacrifice to themselves and their families. They are perhaps the people I think of first when I look for real examples of Christlike, selfless, self-sacrificial friendship, service and loyalty.

Nonetheless, the world being what it is, the BAM team should not expect the exceptions to be normative when they hire, retain and evaluate a local partner, local attorney or other local professionals. It is easy to be lulled into a false sense of their loyalty because of the close personal relationships that often develop. This is not being cynical or negative; it is simply recognizing the reality of human nature. If God works an exception, that will be a true blessing. If not, the caution will have been well worth this hedge against the considerable risk.

Fifth, as potential or actual partners of foreigners, these people can find themselves in awkward, even dangerous, situations. It is not uncommon for them to play a dual role: your partner *and* an informant for the government. They may be on both payrolls, or they may be coerced into this duplicity. The secret police in most developing nations keep a close watch on foreigners, and they are not above bringing life-and-death pressure on BAM partners to obtain the information they desire about the BAMers, their personal routines, habits, weaknesses, lives and relationships, as well as about the company, their investors, finances, trade secrets, technologies, processes, designs, intellectual property and customers.

Similarly, BAM companies can be the object of industrial and business espionage. The internal secrets of the company may be coveted by local competitors within the industry. While BAM companies believe that direct competition with local businesses is antithetical to their mission goals and try to avoid it (primarily by focusing on exportable products), this is not always possible. It is not uncommon for employees to enter a company, learn a trade, receive the benefits of the foreign expertise and then quit to start a competing company. They may even steal company proprietary information and company employees. This is also true of local partners who have access to higher levels of valuable information.

BAMers often do not like to face these realities, but Jesus warned, "I am sending you out like sheep among wolves. Therefore be as shrewd as snakes and as innocent as doves" in this fallen world (Mt 10:16). This is excellent advice for BAM practitioners.

Finally, during the early stages of the BAM business, the team and company are often very dependent on the local partner. In fact, a codependent relationship can easily evolve to the peril of the BAMers. Codependent BAMers frequently find themselves at the mercy of local partners who have their own, often different, agendas. Avoiding this and achieving self-sufficiency within the local culture is critical to maintaining control over the business, its direction and its reception in the local community.

The danger of codependency is especially true of the local interpreter that the BAM team uses before they are language proficient. Just as the Lord tests his faithful, it is altogether appropriate and wise for BAMers to test all such local relationships. For example, there are many ways for interpreters to ply their craft: they may merely summarize what we want to say; they may only tell us what they think we want to hear (this is a common cultural characteristic); or they may go sentence by sentence but inadvertently not give the same meaning that we intend. Covertly testing the translation is absolutely necessary if the business is to communicate in a manner worthy of both good business and the gospel.

COMMUNICATIONS

Effective communications is one of the essential elements of a sound business. Much of BAM communication must be through interpreters who come in varying degrees of competence and maturity. That is why the lifelong Asian BAMer Patrick Lai says that learning the local language is *job one* for the BAMer. He believes in this so strongly that he requires all new expat hires to spend their first full year with his company immersed in language study.[2] Other communications issues that may escape the would-be BAMer are communications security, negotiating styles and the need to set boundaries.

Communications security. An issue BAMers may not be sensitive to is communications security. In most developing nations it can be assumed that the local and secret police will be monitoring all of the BAMer's communications. To avoid any provocative or mission-endangering communications the BAMer should assume, unless there is evidence to the contrary, that eavesdropping devices will be planted in cars, homes, telephones and offices; human surveillance and photographic histories of the people and their activities will be maintained; mail will be opened and inspected; e-mail will be intercepted and saved; banking records will be scrutinized; company files will be pilfered or copied; and private talks will be a thing of the past. If these things do not occur in a given context, then so much the better. No harm, no foul. But it is far wiser to start with a cautionary approach and ease off as circumstances dictate, than to naively assume that privacy in communications or in person is normative.

---

[2]Patrick Lai, *Tentmaking* (Waynesboro, Ga.: Authentic, 2005), pp. 35, 124-33.

This is not to suggest that the BAM Company has anything to hide or that it is acting in any disreputable way. It is to recognize that the "mission" in BAM makes the company a prime target for those forces that would oppose the Lord's work.[3]

Negotiating styles. A great deal has been written in the popular media about the widely differing negotiation styles used around the world. The Japanese approach business discussions very differently than do the Indians, the French, the Nigerians or the Americans. Without belaboring the point, learning the unique cultural style of the host country is an aspect of the BAMer's preparation that must not be neglected. Not only will the BAM Company be engaged in business negotiations, but it will be negotiating with the local culture missionally—to help them know Jesus.

Setting boundaries. Just as our lives are the sum total of our decisions, so our personal witness is often the sum total of our lifestyle and our management-style. Effective crosscultural BAM demands that the business and its activities be contextually appropriate. There are, however, lines that must be drawn to keep from tainting our witness. When interacting with the local people, we can be certain they will be watching all we do and drawing their conclusions about us as people and about our Christian message.

When in Kazakhstan, we found that the local businesspeople and governmental officials continually tested us with alcoholic beverages. Every social occasion (and many business ones) had a large stock of cognac, champagne and vodka. Our hosts did not drink socially, but imbibed liberally by proposing toasts to every conceivable thing. With each toast they drained a healthy shot of liquor. Often they would make individual toasts in which several people would toast the American guest, meaning that the guest would drink one shot for each of them while they only had one each. The object was to get the American drunk to ply him or her for information or test his or her character. We experienced the same hospitality in Taiwan, but the drink of choice there was rice wine and sake.

In each situation the problem we faced was that for personal reasons we do

---

[3]An excellent movie that illustrates the degree to which privacy in the United States has been eroded by new, sophisticated technology and growing governmental intrusion is *Enemy of the State* (1998) with Will Smith and Gene Hackman. Similar technologies are available to regimes that are less friendly to the Christian message and church.

not drink alcoholic beverages. And even if we did, the level of alcoholism (and resulting child and spousal abuse) in the country is so unacceptably high that we, as witnessing Christians, would be causing our brothers to stumble if we did anything that encouraged them to drink (see Rom 14:20-21; 1 Cor 10:32). Notwithstanding their knowledge that we were nondrinkers, they consistently plied us with alcoholic drinks during all of their social functions. We repeatedly, graciously refused, even joking about it, but insisted on having a soft drink or tea instead. This did not set well with our hosts, who continued to press us, even while reluctantly complying. Their motives may have been the purest, wanting to be the ultimate host to these strangers, but that made refusing them a constant source of tension between us and interfered with the level of intimate friendship we were seeking.

In those encounters, we drew a line in the sand and said we were not crossing it. From a character and witnessing standpoint, refusing to join them in drinking may have been admirable, but from a relationship-building standpoint it raised unfortunate barriers that were difficult, if not impossible, to overcome. It accentuated the fact that we were outsiders (etic) and presented insurmountable hurdles to being fully accepted or trusted. Since the message we brought depended so much on their acceptance of the messenger, there is no doubt that our actions cut some of them off from hearing the gospel—at least from us. These are regrettable realities and limitations that BAMers face every day in the field. We must pray that the Lord leads us to only create boundaries that are of and from him, and that exhibit great wisdom. We never want to draw lines that we create out of our own ethnocentric view of church or holiness. The former is acceptable mission; the latter quenches the Holy Spirit.

Discussion Questions

1. BAM engagement: Continue the class experience and answer the following questions about the BAM business and country you have proposed.

   a. Do you think that a business partner will be required in your proposed (your class exercise) BAM enterprise? Why or why not? What resources will you use to identify a reliable business partner? What is the profile of your "perfect partner"? How can you determine and confirm his or her character? What criteria will you use? What level of partnership do you need and want?

b. Do you think that you or your family will require one or more personal assistants in your proposed BAM enterprise? Why? If you do require assistance, what is the preferred profile of this person? What duties will you need performed by a personal assistant? What will you pay him or her? What days and hours? What resources will you use to identify a reliable personal assistant? What about a driver, cook and housekeeper? How can you confirm his or her character? By what criteria?

c. Would you plan to learn the local language? Why or why not? If so, by what method(s)? Is it necessary for you to become fully fluent in the language? What are the pros and cons? How long will it take to become fluent? How much time have you scheduled for language learning?

d. The author believed that he could not drink alcohol in this mission context, which had both positive and negative effects on his relationships. Are there similar issues you expect to encounter in your proposed business and country? What personal, relational boundaries will you set? Are they scriptural or personal? What about the many cultural issues that are gray areas? What are some of these issues? Should you adopt the cultural norm of the host country or adhere to your own more comfortable cultural norms? Give examples.

e. In your new context, how will you determine where to live and at what living standard? Is there a minimum living standard that is acceptable for you and your family? What standard is appropriate to your proposed business? your proposed mission? Discuss.

2. BAM engagement: Set the class exercise aside and think about your current circumstances, gifts, education, experience, burdens and dependencies. Assume that tomorrow you were selected by a prospective CEO to join a BAM team for a real company, but they had not yet selected the business or the country. Do an appreciative inquiry on yourself (see p. 256) and describe what you have to offer, for what types of businesses and in what countries, that would make you a valuable asset to the BAM team.

24

EXPATRIATE ISSUES

"We do not need to minimize the poverty of the ghetto or the suffering
inflicted by whites on blacks in order to see that the increasingly
dangerous and unpredictable conditions of middle-class life
have given rise to similar strategies for survival."
CHRISTOPHER LASCH

"We moved into an all-white neighborhood and that was a
culture shock. . . . I'd been used to being around all black kids."
HALLE BERRY

"Where you go I will go, and where you stay I will stay.
Your people will be my people and your God my God.
Where you die I will die, and there I will be buried."
RUTH 1:16-17

AS ALREADY NOTED IN VARIOUS OTHER CONTEXTS, the list of expatriate issues that BAMers and their families need to consider is virtually endless. Some of the more obvious issues are passports, entry and exit visas, work and travel permits, banking, currency and money transfer, housing, utilities, electric current, telephones, Internet access, health insurance, medical, immunizations, prescriptions, emergency evacuation, basic shopping, schools, transportation, security, entertainment, finances, home leave, language training, and food. All of these points need to be researched and addressed, but there are some less-obvious topics that deserve comment. The first is time management, the second (and closely related) is personal survival strategies, and the last four speak to lifestyle and family issues.

TIME MANAGEMENT

There are some excellent books on time management,[1] but the special time management issue that arises in the BAM context is as obvious as it is difficult to solve: both business and mission are full-time tasks. Both aspects of the dual mandate consume much energy, time and resources. The "business" of BAM is daunting, the "mission" of BAM is God-sized, and the combination is downright frightening to contemplate. How do we manage to do both and still have time for other priorities, such as family, Bible study, prayer and simply living?

First, each BAMer, especially the CEO, must recognize that one person cannot do it all—nor should he or she even try. That is one of the main reasons why a BAM team is recommended rather than a Lone Ranger approach. The team approach gives accountability, encouragement and companionship. It is also the key to the necessary division of labor between the business and the mission sides of the company. Second, I recommend that the dual mandate be managed through a dual organizational structure (see step 7 on p. 395) which spreads the burdens and the commitments among different people.

Third, the time-management issue is one that involves the entire BAM team and their families (including the children). Decisions need to be faced openly and discussed among everyone involved so that a win-win consensus is developed. The consensus should not only address what to do, but how to continually monitor and evaluate the time problem in the context of daily experience. Failure to do this can often have tragic consequences for the individuals, the business and the BAM families. Trying to *do it all* probably means not getting any of it done well, or doing one aspect of BAM well while neglecting other priorities. Either way it can quickly deteriorate into a lose-lose situation.

Fourth, and most importantly, I recommend that the dilemma presented by this overwhelming challenge be laid before the Lord with specific prayer for answers and guidance, consensus and harmony, productivity and family welfare.

PERSONAL SURVIVAL STRATEGIES

Each person on the mission field will react differently to the challenges of an alien culture. Culture shock is common and, while expected, must be success-

---

[1] I highly recommend Alec Mackenzie and Pat Nickerson's classic *The Time Trap*, 4th ed. (New York: AMACOM, 2009).

fully dealt with or the duration and quality of the BAM experience overseas will be greatly diminished. The object is to thrive in the foreign environment, not just survive. But, like adolescence, survival is a phase everyone must go through to reach adulthood. How that is done is called a person's personal survival strategy. Perhaps the would-be BAMer will gain some useful insights from the following three approaches.

Martha's Rule. Outside of his home country, the BAMer will quickly discover that time management and achieving efficiency are especially challenging. Not only do things not flow as smoothly as you are probably used to, but there are seemingly endless hassles in getting even the most ordinary tasks accomplished. In a word, efficiency tanks! Reality itself takes on a strange new pace and rhythm. Part of the reason is cultural and, perhaps, a bit of culture shock; another part is spiritual warfare. A third part is the simple fact that business is done and life is lived differently around the world. We are fish out of water, vulnerable new learners—unlearning lifetime habits and expectations we acquired as children.

While in Kazakhstan our fellow missionaries were Ross and Martha King, a wonderfully gracious, fun, loving, Christ-centered couple from San Marcos, Texas. As we all struggled with learning the new cultural and business realities facing us, Martha finally announced, "I have figured out how to survive and thrive in this environment. I usually have a long list of things to do and accomplish each day in San Marcos, but here my goal will be to do one thing a day. If I can accomplish that, it will have been a good day! More than that and it is a superb day!" This sounded like a joke, *Do only one thing a day!* and we laughed with her. But in the ensuing days, we discovered the wisdom of her suggestion. The reality was that our time was literally eaten up with so many hassles of living and coping that Martha's Rule actually became a major operating principle for our entire mission team.

Coming to the mission field from a Day-Timer (there were no Blackberries at that time), efficiency-based culture like the United States, another major difficulty was our high expectations. Through the application of Martha's Rule, we lowered our expectations and—almost magically—our lives flowed more easily; when we did achieve two or even three things, those became blue-ribbon days. Rather than see the things we did not accomplish, we celebrated those that we did—and that made all of the difference.

It is probably only a mindset or paradigm change, but Martha's Rule worked. Perhaps most important, it helped us maintain our joy in the midst of gross inefficiencies by Western standards. I saw the same thing while on the mission field in the Dominican Republic. My host missionary family went there to take the gospel and plant a church. They did this and much more, but at least half of their time each day was spent in basic living issues like getting water, fixing their truck, replacing the home propane tank, buying groceries and the like. Because of the context, they were not able to spend even half of their time in ministry. And unfortunately that half was often after their personal energy was depleted and exhaustion was setting in.

Noncoping days. We are all products of the culture we were reared in. Living in the alien culture of Kazakhstan, our American sensibilities and programmed acculturation were continually assaulted, especially in the early days. In spite of my extensive experience overseas (I have traveled in over seventy countries and lived in a dozen), Kazakhstan got under my skin. Periodically (but not frequently), I would come to the end of my ability to cope and was in danger of dropping into mild anxiety and depression. My personal survival strategy to resolve this problem was actually quite simple and fun. When those feelings swept over me, I would allow myself a *noncoping day*, in which I stayed home, didn't shave, slept, read a novel, ate peanut butter and jelly sandwiches, and worked jigsaw puzzles. In short, I gave myself permission to convalesce and allow my senses and perspective to regenerate.

These noncoping days were not superspiritual days; I did not retreat to read my Bible and pray. That was already part of my daily routine. Instead, the Lord allowed me to take these days off with a clear conscience, just as he did with Elijah when he ran away from Jezebel (1 Kings 19:1-13): sleep, hot food, refreshing water, time off and the Lord's gentle whisper.

These mini R & Rs worked for me. The point is, however, that each BAMer and family member will be faced with different emotional and psychological challenges. These must be faced and dealt with, but they will not be the same for everyone. This is normal, so we must listen to our bodies and keep a close eye on our families. After all, surviving comes before thriving. Developing healthy personal survival strategies is a critical element of BAM, because unless this occurs, BAM will not happen. The BAM enterprise will only be as successful and as healthy as the BAMers who manage it. Further, the mental state of each BAMer will also depend on the health and well-being of his or her family. In sum, taking care of the inner needs of the BAMer and loved ones is a definite BAM priority.

Fight or flight. In my case, while in Kazakhstan I returned to the United States to marry a woman I had gone to high school with but had not seen for thirty-three years. We met again on an R & R I took in California after my parents both died while I was overseas. Frecia is the light of my life, but I almost lost her the first week of our marriage! I took her from Newport Beach, California—the closest thing to Hawaii on the mainland—halfway around the world to Central Asia three days after we married. The entire trip took about twenty-seven long hours. When we landed in Moscow, she knew that things were not going to be as she had expected. We were met by a missionary friend and were taken three hours across town to the domestic airport, Domodedovo. There we forged our way through the hoards of people to board an Aeroflot plane to Almaty. The plane was a bare-bones steel shell with uncomfortable seats, obnoxious restrooms and a pile of greasy chicken pieces served on a cookie sheet for food.

After four miserable hours we landed in Almaty and were met by Ross and Martha King, who escorted us to our new home. It was a four-story walkup of poured concrete and austere Stalinesque architecture. Trash was piled in the courtyard. Graffiti covered the walls, and the hall lights were broken out with glass splinters covering the steps. The apartment itself had a bare lightbulb at the end of an electric cord dangling from the middle of the ceiling. The furniture was minimal, well-worn and gaudy. As I carried Frecia across the threshold, the cockroaches politely scattered out of sight.

Frecia took in the surroundings and, being exhausted from our trip, announced that she wanted a bath. I showed her to the bathroom with its antique, legged tub. She turned the water spigot, but it broke in her hand, flooding the bathroom. We cleaned that up, but the broken valve made hot water inaccessible. By the time she emerged from her cold bath, I was busy unpacking. She quickly found her hair dryer and, not being used to different electrical systems, looked for a place to plug it in. When the prongs didn't fit the wall sockets, she spied my two transformers and plugged into one of them. Each was the size and shape of a car battery and had been lovingly carried by me halfway around the world to solve my electrical compatibility problems. Frecia's hair dryer was too much of a load, and the transformer literally started smoking and melting down. Exasperated, but totally undaunted, she then plugged into the second one without thinking—with the same results. Needless to say, a life without a transformer in the former Soviet Union is challenging.

After trashing her smoldering hair dryer and toweling her hair, she wanted some tea. We quickly discovered, however, that the gas tank in the kitchen (affectionately known as a *bombbola*) was out of gas and a replacement was days away. The cooking gas was not an issue, I explained, as we had the local *stolovia* (school cafeteria). Her first meal there consisted of three medallions of horse meat and a mound of noodles. And that was breakfast. Lunch was much the same, but with a watery cabbage soup.

Frecia then decided she needed to call her children in the United States to let them know that we had arrived safely, but we discovered that in our absence the telephone had been disconnected. By this time she was feeling somewhat frustrated, until Ross arrived with the news that the GOK had announced a cholera outbreak in the city and that no one could leave the country. As it turned out, flight was impossible anyway, because Aeroflot was out of gasoline and their planes were grounded.

At this point my bride of three days showed her true character and, I could see, was already forming her own personal survival strategy. She bravely said, "Does it get any worse than this? If not, I think I can make it." But, for her, it did get worse. She was fine until she went shopping the next day and realized that no one spoke English (she didn't speak Russian) and she had no way to communicate. The market was a den of strange sounds, smells and sights. When she approached the meat market and saw chopped meat, with the heads of the animals lying above the meat (including horses—her father was a large-animal veterinarian), that was too much for one day.

Day after day Frecia adapted and, for a Southern California girl, showed amazing resilience, persistence and courage. She knew that she had a choice: go home and wait for me to return at the end of my contract in four months (flight), or stay, learn and not only make the best of a difficult situation but make it a fun challenge to test her mettle (fight). She bravely chose to stay and, as the apostle Paul did, "fight the good fight" (1 Tim 6:12; 2 Tim 4:7). In fact, she quickly became a major player in our mission and church, counseling the women, teaching Sunday school and ministering at a local orphanage. We ended up staying in Kazakhstan another two and a half years.

From a BAM perspective, Kazakhstan was a postcommunist nation that was just instituting the concept of private property. Up to its independence in 1991, all land and businesses were owned by the government. Frecia's twenty years of commercial real-estate-brokerage expertise were invaluable and led her to consult with both the GOK and local businesses and developers about private property ownership, development and taxation issues. She was also asked by the U.S. ambassador to organize the first international chamber of commerce. She did so and was elected its first president, which was no mean task in a male-dominated, Muslim-oriented society.

I do not write this as a tribute to my wife (although she richly deserves it), but to illustrate the realities of doing BAM on the field and to remind all BAM-ers of several points. First, it is not about us but our families. Second, each person, in the context of the family and the team, must develop a personal survival strategy, coping skills and support systems that will carry him or her through each day of acclimating to this new reality and its special challenges.

Third, God is in charge and may find totally unexpected ways to use our family members in support of his mission to the people we serve. Fourth, if at all possible, the BAM team spouses need a satisfying role in the BAM Company's holistic outreach to the community. They too have God-given talents, skills and gifts which can be used to bring people closer to our Lord.

LIFESTYLE ISSUES

I have already written about lifestyle and management-style evangelism, which are essential on the mission field if the BAMer is to effectively witness to the lost. There are four areas of possible conflict that deserve special comment: the watchers, compound living, the neglected spouse and BAM kids.

The watchers. The first point is the most obvious and is so critical that it deserves additional emphasis. Every aspect of our lifestyle will be watched, scrutinized, commented on and praised or criticized—not only by the government but also by the people. As foreigners (and as Christians and Americans) in the community or industry, our presence is an event. The locals see and hear everything: what we say, how we dress, where we live, what we spend our money on, what the source of our money appears to be, how quickly we pay our bills, how much we tip, how much we interact with the locals, how we treat them, how we treat each other and our family, how we react to the local context (including how much we complain, bemoan, gripe or criticize—as expats seem habitually inclined to do) and, perhaps most important, our daily countenance.

These things form the true message of our witness, not what we say on Sunday in church or on Wednesday in Bible study. It is our answers to the daily challenges of life that will indelibly define our status and character to the locals. They must see us as persons of integrity and honesty—filled with sunshine (Son-shine) and enthusiasm in our soul and on our face—before they will be curious about this Jesus we talk about.

Compound living. A singularly telling aspect of lifestyle communication is determining where the BAM team expats live and how they interact with the people. Traditionally, many missionaries have cloistered in compounds, even garrisoned ones. They flock together in a central place and use that as the platform for their ministry. Historically, that has not been a successful strategy and has tended to isolate and insulate the missionaries from the very people they came to serve.

Modern mission practice shies away from the compound mentality and urges missionaries to live among the people, dress as they dress and relate to them on their own turf, as Jesus did. When adopting a foreign culture, Ruth said to Naomi, "Where you stay I will stay. Your people will be my people" (Ruth 1:16). That must be the prevailing attitude of today's missionaries. It is especially appropriate for BAM, which by its very nature is both long-term and incarnational.

The neglected spouse. How a missionary divides his or her time and attention is a daily challenge. Each person and family has their own priorities, but through the years the following has worked for me:

- Priority 1. Love the Lord with all of my mind, heart, soul and strength.

- Priority 2. Love my wife.

- Priority 3. Love my children and grandchildren.

- Priority 4. Love others—family, friends, strangers, nations (neighbors)—through my life and relationships.

- Priority 5. Love others through my work (which is my ministry).

Notice that I put my spouse ahead of my children. This does not mean that a child should be neglected, but rather that the primary family unit is the husband and the wife and their oneness before the Lord. The children will grow up, leave the nest and have their own lives and families, but the primary relationship of husband and wife will (should) remain intact. We have seen far too many instances where the marriage falls apart after the children leave home, or where a person puts children before his or her spouse. When the children are young this may appear to be best, but the underlying reality must be that of parental unity.

Practically speaking, this does not always happen. The strains of marriage are considerable, even in one's own country. The strains on a marriage in the mission field can be even greater. With the dual mandate of BAM, the stress can multiply exponentially. Managing this risk is no small feat, but again, the answer may be found in 1 Timothy 5:8: "If anyone does not provide for his relatives, and especially for his immediate family, he has denied the faith and is worse than an unbeliever." I believe that God speaks through Scripture and is reminding us of the priorities in our lives as set forth by Jesus: first, love the Lord; second, love our neighbors. First among our neighbors, according to Paul, is our family, and first within our families is our spouse. It is not our church, not our business, not our employees and their families, not our community activities, not our recreation, although these are important.

In the final analysis, a neglected family is an unhappy family; and an unhappy family is a formula for disaster personally, professionally and missionally.

Accordingly, regardless of where they live, conscientious BAMers must establish their priorities with the BAM team and their families, then practice those priorities and hold each other accountable. Setting rigid work hours is one of the first requirements. Each BAMer should routinely leave work at a set time and observe weekend, holiday and sabbath times off. The time away from work should, first and foremost, be devoted to family. Only then should lesser priorities be allowed to intrude. This is far more difficult in practice than in planning. But if the BAMer families are weakened by neglect, the BAMer's joy in the Lord will visibly dissipate, his or her witness will be seriously flawed and the ultimate kingdom bottom lines put in jeopardy.

BAM kids. Both pastor's kids (PKs) and missionary kids (MKs) face particular stress points. They often have serious problems at home and in school.

They sometimes rebel against their parents' faith, are disobedient, drop out spiritually, emotionally and even physically, and keep friends and engage in activities that are at odds with the Christian lifestyle. Of course, this is not a universal rule. It is, however, sufficiently prevalent to have stirred considerable attention within the church and mission-sending agencies.

The reasons for these rebellious attitudes are legion, but some that I have observed in MKs are related to (1) resentment over having been dragged overseas away from their friends and the "good life," (2) neglect by parents because of the demands of the mission, and (3) exposure to the vicissitudes of life earlier than their maturity warrants, including a high degree of unsupervised freedom.

The point here is that BAM kids (BKs) are not immune from the same difficulties of the BAM mission. Their susceptibility may, in fact, be higher for two reasons. First, the BKs will probably be living at a higher socioeconomic level than the local MKs (i.e., the lifestyle of the business community rather than the marginalized), which allows for more freedoms and opens up more lifestyle opportunities. Second, the demands of the dual mandate on the time and energy of the BAMer is at least as severe as that on the traditional missionary. The likelihood of the BK being neglected or at least not closely supervised may therefore be greater than with the MK.

Of course what happens will depend on the age, maturity, and personality differences of the children, the attitudes and parental practices within their homes, the prevailing native cultural attitudes toward children, especially the girls, and the schooling and childcare arrangements the family makes. Would-be BAMers with young children should fully factor this into their risk management strategies and their risk tolerance assessments. Don't forget about your kids! It is their life too!

Discussion Questions

1. Given the dual mandate, family, church and personal responsibilities, how can a BAM Company CEO and team member find time to do all that needs to be done? What priorities must be set? What priorities should come first? What alternatives are there for managing time? What boundaries should be established? By whom?

2. What is a personal survival strategy? Do you have one and if so, what is it? How did it develop? How dependent on it are you? Describe and discuss some examples.

3. What can BAM team members do to keep their marriage healthy and their children well cared for while on the mission field?

4. BAM engagement: The author cites his personal priorities. What are yours? Examine your current work, family, church and personal time schedules. Do they align with your stated priorities? If not, what can (should) you do to achieve better alignment? Will you? Why or why not? What is the potential cost of continued misalignment?

Epilogue

THE NEXT GENERATION

*"We need to teach the next generation of children from Day One
that they are responsible for their lives. Mankind's greatest
gift, also its greatest curse, is that we have free choice.
We make our choices built from love or from fear."*
ELISABETH KÜBLER-ROSS

*"Hear now, O Israel, the decrees and laws I am about to
teach you. . . . Observe them carefully. . . . Teach them
to your children and to their children after them."*
DEUTERONOMY 4:1, 6, 9

IT IS APPROPRIATE TO END THIS PILGRIMAGE through the Marketplace Mission Movement by remembering where we started: BAM is defined
as a for-profit commercial business that is Christian-led, intentionally devoted
to being used as an instrument of God's mission *(missio Dei)* to the world, and
operated in a crosscultural environment, whether domestic or international.
BAM is a manifestation of God's plan for humanity and in his wisdom he has
graciously chosen to allow us as businessmen and women, business students
and entrepreneurs to be a part of that plan. He has called us to use our God-
given gifts for business and our God-ordained call to mission in a single, unified enterprise that is part of a larger divine purpose.

In short, he has called us to create and lead Christ-centered, Bible-based,
values-driven, socially responsible businesses that honor him by ministering holistically to hurting peoples around the world in the name and love of
Jesus.

God is moving across the face of the earth to see the fulfillment of his Great Commission, perhaps in our lifetimes. He is doing so in myriad ways, but the marketplace seems to be predominant on his agenda. The marketplace is, after all, perhaps the only human institution that directly or indirectly touches the lives of virtually every person on earth. Earlier I asked, In today's globalized world, is it any wonder that God would use business as a vehicle for mission? That he would deliberately choose the marketplace as a force majeure to call his people to himself and to seek a final reconciliation with humanity? Hopefully, this book has provided an answer.

On a more human plane, this book has been an effort to address those deep stirrings that I see in my students, colleagues, fellow believers and nonbelieving friends to have their lives count for something more, something higher, something profound and meaningful in the sweep of human history and in the midst of today's tragic human suffering. That feeling was eloquently expressed for me by James Emery White in *Serious Times: Making Your Life Matter in an Urgent Day*. While the quote is deeply personal to White, it speaks to all thinking humans today and, I suspect, to those of ages past. Hopefully it will speak both to you who are older and to the next generation, and convey one of the primary motives behind this book: to provide a path for you to make a difference with your life.

> Seeing that movie [*Star Wars*, for the first time] long, long ago in a city far, far away at the tender age of eighteen was a defining moment in my life. I walked out of the theater profoundly moved. I remember sitting in my car in the parking lot, overwhelmed with a single thought: *That's what I want for my life: to be caught up in the sweep of history. To be in the center of things. To be making a difference. To be at the heart of the struggle between right and wrong, good and evil.* My heart was almost breaking at the thought of a life of insignificance. I recall thinking, *But where can that happen in the real world? How can I be a part of something that is bigger than I am? Where in life can something so grand be found?*
>
> Then it came to me—as startlingly sudden as a rip of lightning and as poundingly affirmed as any thunder that could follow—*that's what God's invitation to the Christ-life is all about!* There *is* a galactic struggle going on, and I could be a warrior. I could give my life to something that

was bigger than I was, that would live on long after I was gone. What I did mattered and could impact all of history—even into eternity. The reality of the spiritual realm, the struggle for men's and women's souls, the cosmic consequences that were at stake—it became so *clear* to me—I could give my life to that! And there was *nothing* that would ever compete with its scale or significance. *Nothing....*

In the ancient world the influence of Christians acting as salt and light brought a stop to infanticide, ended slavery, liberated women and created hospitals, orphanages and schools. During the medieval era, Christianity kept classical culture alive through copying manuscripts, building libraries and inventing colleges and universities. In the modern era, Christians led the way in the development of science, political and economic freedom, and provided what is arguably the greatest sources of inspiration for art, literature and music. What will Christians do in our day? . . . The great danger is *nothing*.[1]

Through this book I hope to inform the next generation about the importance of their individual lives and careers and alert them to the dangers of doing nothing. Further, I want to stimulate and encourage them to discover God's mission, *missio Dei*, and to actively invest their lives in making this world a very different, far better place for the billions who inhabit it.

The next generation of BAMers includes both those Christians who are in business schools now and those entrepreneurs of every age—whether just out of school, deep in the throes of business or just entering midlife—who want to devote the coming years to making a difference for Christ and his kingdom through the marketplace. I want to help that generation systematically understand God's movement to, within and through the marketplace, determine their place in it (if any), and if business is their calling, to reenvision their life's work in the context of the movement and its four camps. Hopefully this book will have helped them understand its historical and biblical roots, its special burdens and rewards, and its importance to the future of this world and the Church. We have examined (1) what BAM is, (2) why and how to engage in BAM and (3) the possible costs of taking BAM seriously.

If this book is read and discussed but does not motivate Christian business-

---

[1]James Emery White, *Serious Times* (Downers Grove, Ill.: InterVarsity Press, 2004), pp. 11, 154.

people to action, it will have failed. As James reminded us, "Faith by itself, if it is not accompanied by action, is dead. . . . [F]aith without deeds is useless" (Jas 2:17, 20). So too BAM without action—without active businesses planted, growing and prospering in every nation and amid every tribe—is just another great idea that God had but we humans failed to act on. Without business there is no long-term relief from poverty, no potential for sustainable, improved standards of living and no hope for millions who are now being consumed by life's economic misfortunes.

On the other hand, if knowledge of BAM is translated into active, vibrant, growing, witnessing, Christ-honoring businesses by the hundreds of thousands worldwide, it could literally change the face and future of humanity, and lead to the abundant life Jesus promised. It can also change the face of the Church forever and lead to a new revival across the world.

Henry Blackaby urged us to see where God is working and to join him there.[2] God is working in and through the marketplace. He is commissioning BAM to be a major part of his mission strategy for the twenty-first century—the Marketplace Mission Movement. If you are a committed Christian with a call to business, don't miss being a part of it—to God's glory and your eternal joy.

■   ■   ■

I began this book by discussing what BAM is, why it is worth doing and how to do it. We examined the practical costs of engaging in BAM and how to engage in risk management so that the threats, risks and costs might be eliminated, avoided or hedged.

It would be disingenuous to end the book without unabashedly acknowledging that in spite of the risks and costs of doing BAM, I can think of no other mission strategy that has such a great prospect of reaching this lost world for Christ. Further, having experienced the mission field myself, I can say unequivocally that I loved it. There is a vibrancy and joy to life overseas in BAM that is unmatched in domestic, secular business. I would not trade those years for any others I have experienced and only wish that my wife and I could once again take on those challenges.

As for safety—an issue much on the minds of all of us today—I can hon-

---

[2]Henry T. Blackaby and Claude V. King, *Experiencing God* (Nashville: Lifeway, 1990).

estly say that I often felt safer on the mission field than at home. I definitely felt closer to the Lord and fully affirmed and embraced by the Holy Spirit. The risks were acceptable, the rewards eternal and exceptional, and the memories joy-filled.

To the would-be BAMer I say: Stay in Scripture, stay on your knees, pray without ceasing, lay each day's challenges and sufferings before Christ and claim his promises. Joy, fulfillment and enormous spiritual rewards will surely be yours, as will the satisfaction of knowing that your life and business have made a difference that matters temporally and eternally. Further, through focused prayer, keenly attuned sensitivity, selflessness and unconditional love, your marriages will not only survive but actually flower in the midst of the mission field. And, if you are blessed with children and practice compassionate parenting, the BAM experience can be a family adventure that will give your children a step up in maturity, global awareness and life that will keep them in good stead their whole lives.

In every sense, BAM is definitely *the gift that keeps on giving*.

DISCUSSION QUESTIONS

1. After reading this book, do you sense God's call on your life to be involved with BAM? Explain.

2. If you are feeling that call, what is the next step that the Lord is asking you to take? Spend time with God to discern what he is saying to you now and what the next steps might look like for you.

3. Is there someone in your life (spouse, colleague, child) with whom you could share your newfound understanding of BAM? Sharing this with them will assist you in thinking through the issues again and may very well help inform them about the link between business and the mission mandate given to God's people.

Appendix 1

LEADERS' VIEWS OF THE
MARKETPLACE MISSION MOVEMENT

THE FOLLOWING STATEMENTS ABOUT the movement of God to, within and through the marketplace are by various evangelical leaders within business, the church and the marketplace mission community. Together with the statements found in chapter three, these clearly illustrate the growing opinion that God is moving in a purposeful, powerful, new way in today's marketplace mission context.

- Bill Pollard, chairman of Service Master Corporation:
  In today's global community, the greatest channel of distribution for "salt and light" is the business community . . . the marketplace.[1]

- Edward Simon, president of Herman Miller:
  Business is the only institution that has a chance, as far as I can see, to fundamentally improve the injustice that exists in the world.[2]

- Glenn White, retired vice president, Chrysler Corporation:
  Learning to mobilize business for God's purposes is the future of foreign missions and is our responsibility in the emerging global economy.[3]

- Ken Eldred, CEO, Living Stone Foundation:
  I expect that Kingdom Business will be a primary tool that revolutionizes missions in the twenty-first century.[4]

- Steve Rundle, associate professor of economics, Biola University:
  This story [of Coca-Cola in the remotest parts of China] illustrates the remarkable capacity of business to reach people virtually any-

---

[1]Bill Pollard, quoted in Os Hillman, e-mail to the author, January 14, 2003.
[2]Edward Simon, quoted in Os Hillman, e-mail to the author, January 14, 2003.
[3]Glenn White, personal conversations with Scott McFarlane, November 15, 1999, as related in e-mail to the author, November 24, 2003.
[4]Ken Eldred, *God Is at Work* (Ventura, Calif.: Regal, 2005), p. 46.

where in the world, including places where the gospel still struggles to gain a foothold. It also helps explain why well-known evangelicals such as Billy Graham, Henry Blackaby and Wayne Grudem are focusing more of their attention on the heretofore neglected role of business—and those who run them—in mission. This increased attention is part of an even broader movement, in which laypeople from every profession are discovering, or rather, rediscovering, their role in *missio Dei*. That role goes beyond financial support, service on church committees and prayer, and extends into areas that were once thought to be the exclusive purview of professional missionaries.[5]

- Tom Sudyk, founder and president of EC Group:

  This is a huge movement. Around 1999, things started happening, people started coming to the ministry. . . . I think God is reclaiming the marketplace. I think that Satan has very, very effectively castrated business people from the kingdom market and has fed them a lie that all they can do is give money. . . . [T]here's like a glass ceiling on what Christians can do. And, I think that glass ceiling is a lie of Satan.[6]

- Mike Barrett, Colombia International University:

  Business as Mission is back with a bang! In fact, it never really left. The biblical and historical foundations of the BAM approach are embarrassingly evident. From Abraham to Paul to the Moravian Brethren, to William Carey, to today's tentmakers, God has used the marketplace as the *primary* conduit for his gospel and church. How could we have missed it?[7]

- Michael R. Baer, entrepreneur, business coach and executive director of an international mission organization specializing in microenterprise development and incubation:

  A great movement is beginning in North America and around the world—the kingdom business or "business as mission" movement. I say this is a great movement not because it is large but because I sense the hand of God in it and see a huge potential for impacting the world for Christ.[8]

---

[5]Neal Johnson and Steve Rundle, "Distinctives and Challenges of Business as Mission," in *Business as Mission: From Impoverished to Empowered*, ed. Tom Steffen and Mike Barrett (Pasadena, Calif.: William Carey Library, 2006), pp. 19-20.

[6]Tom Sudyk, personal interview with the author, September 16-18, 2002.

[7]Mike Barrett, conclusion to *Business as Mission: From Impoverished to Empowered*, ed. Tom Steffen and Mike Barrett (Pasadena, Calif.: William Carey Library, 2006), p. 323.

[8]Michael R. Baer, *Business as Mission: The Power of Business in the Kingdom of God* (Seattle:

- Henry Blackaby and Richard Blackaby, marketplace evangelists:

  God is *absolutely* concerned about the business choices you make. He expects his people to be a beacon of hope in a decaying, darkening world (Matt. 5:13-16). Those who conduct business are in a unique position to honor God. Don't call your work secular. It is (or can be) a vibrant, integral component of your Christian walk. Welcome God into your office. Seek his wisdom and trust his leading.[9]

- Ted Yamamori, president emeritus of Food for the Hungry International and past international director of the Lausanne Committee for World Evangelism:

  If the traditional Western missionary movement had some flaws this last century, surely one of the most obvious, in hindsight, was its failure to mobilize many Christian business professionals (beyond using their money) for the Great Commission. At the start of a new century and millennium, we can no longer afford this oversight.[10]

- Kent Humphreys, immediate past president of Christ@Work (AKA Fellowship of Companies for Christ International) and business owner and CEO:

  There is a great hunger among leaders in the business community, men and women both, small business and large business both. . . . I believe there is a movement in the marketplace because the Spirit of God is doing something among the individual hearts and lives of business leaders. And they're not being fulfilled in what the normal church or even the para-church is offering them. . . . God is doing this. There is momentum. People are hungry to be involved, they're hungry for significance. You can't control it, you can't organize it, you can't limit it, funds are not necessarily needed, leaders are definitely needed. But, it's a burning spirit within the hearts of people that God has placed there. God has done that for them to be a part of taking the gospel to the people in their sphere of influence and to other leaders in the marketplace.[11]

- Os Hillman, founder and president of the International Coalition of Workplace Ministries:

  I believe there is a remnant of men and women God is calling forth to

---

YWAM, 2006), p. 9.

[9]Henry Blackaby and Richard Blackaby, *God in the Marketplace* (Nashville: B & H, 2008), p. 57.

[10]Tetsunao Yamamori, preface to *On Kingdom Business*, ed. Tetsunao Yamamori and Kenneth A. Eldred (Wheaton, Ill.: Crossway, 2003), p. 7.

[11]Kent Humphreys, personal interview with the author, October 23, 2002.

understand their calling and purpose in the workplace. It is a global movement.[12]

There is a revival coming, revival that is returning us to our roots to understand what the early church understood—that work is a holy calling in which God moves to transform lives, cities and nations. . . .

Indeed, we live in historic times. Using the collective hands in companies, ministries, colleges, the media, and the local church, God has suddenly and providentially created a 9 to 5 window. Let us not miss this opportunity to fill it with stained glass.[13]

- Rich Marshall, a pastor and founder of two marketplace ministries, ROI and Nehemiah Partners:

  The Lord began to give me revelation about God's ongoing activity in the marketplace and in the lives of business and professional people. . . . The Lord has been speaking this message to many in the marketplace. . . . However, a new day is dawning in which the Lord is releasing into the marketplace an army of soldiers who will be used as frontline ministers for the work of the Lord. . . .

  I don't know how history will record it, and I am not sure what to call it today. But I know this: God is actively working in the marketplace. In city after city, nation after nation, I find men and women to whom the Lord has been speaking. Without benefit of a sermon, a book, or a teaching tape, He has been imparting His revelation into the hearts of marketplace leaders. He is calling; He is stirring; He is anointing. Everywhere you look you see God at work.[14]

- Ed Silvoso, founder of Harvest Evangelism:

  Millions of men and women who have been called to ministry in the marketplace feel like second-class citizens when compared to those who serve in a church or missionary context, and they often fail to rise to their God-appointed position. It is time to give marketplace people their rightful validation as full-fledged ministers, because the last revival—the one prophesied by Joel and quoted by Peter in Acts 2:17-21—will take place all over the city and not just inside a church building.[15]

- Bill Hamon, a bishop and head of the CI Business Network:

---

[12]Os Hillman, *Faith and Work* (Alpharetta, Ga.: Aslan, 2000), p. 90.

[13]Os Hillman, "The Faith at Work Movement: Opening '9 to 5 Window,'" ChristianityToday .com <www.christianitytoday.com/workplace/articles/issue9-faithatwork.html>.

[14]Rich Marshall, *God@Work: Discovering the Anointing for Business* (Shippensburg, Penn.: Destiny Image, 2000), p. 142.

[15]Ed Silvoso, *Anointed for Business* (Ventura, Calif.: Regal, 2002), p. 9.

Now, in this first decade of the twenty-first century church, it is God's predestined time for the Saints to fully come into their membership ministries. . . . In keeping with other restoration terminology, I have called this Holy Spirit-inspired time of activating God's people the "Saints Movement." It is destined to be a major restoration movement, not just a time of revival and refreshing. It will have the seven major attributes that have been a part of every major restoration movement. Church history reveals that there have been five major restoration movements thus far. The Saints Movement will be the sixth.[16]

- Tommy Tenney, popular revivalist and author:
  The anointing and power of God's presence are going to come upon us so strongly that His presence will literally go before us into our offices, plants, prisons, and shopping malls. Because this great revival is based on His glory and presence and not on the works of man, it cannot be contained within the four walls of the churches. God's glory must flow out to the world.[17]

- Tom Phillips, vice president of the Billy Graham Evangelistic Association:
  Someone recently said that the "First" Reformation took the Word of God to the common man and woman; the "Second" Reformation is taking the work of God to the common man and woman. . . . That time is now. The greatest potential ministry in the world today is the marketplace. Christ's greatest labor force is those men and women already in that environment.[18]

- Robert M. Anderson, founder of CEO, Inc. and a trustee at Fuller Theological Seminary:
  The marketplace is *the* great mission field of the century.[19]

- Allen Heneveld, founder of HIS Business and a California attorney:
  My personal observation is that the world is getting darker and darker, that the distinction between Christians and non-Christians is becoming more and more evident, that eventually it will cost us something to be a Christian, but in the trauma, the Lord desires to significantly impact our culture through Christ-led businesses which demonstrate his kingdom of love, peace and joy.[20]

---

[16]Bill Hamon, *The Day of the Saints* (Shippensburg, Penn.: Destiny Image, 2002), pp. 41-42.

[17]Tom Tenney, *The God Chasers* (Shippensburg, Penn.: Destiny Image, 1998), p. 97.

[18]Tom Phillips, "His Presence in the Workplace," conference platform speech at The Cove, Asheville, N.C., April 3, 2003.

[19]Robert M. Anderson, personal interview with the author, October 29, 2002.

[20]Allen Heneveld, personal interview with the author, November 12, 2002.

Appendix 2

STRATEGIC AREA/COUNTRY ANALYSIS (SAA)

THE ATTACHED STRATEGIC area/country analysis (SAA) stems from an effort to answer *how* a person comes to understand a culture other than his or her own.   For the would-be BAMer who is planning to start or develop a business in a foreign country or an alien cultural context within his or her own country, such an inquiry is absolutely essential. The following analysis is a work in progress. It is divided into eight basic dimensions: (1) geographic, ecological and environmental; (2) demographic; (3) historic; (4) societal; (5) cultural; (6) religious; (7) political and legal; and (8) economic and commercial.[1]

Before examining each of these dimensions in detail, five points are in order:

1. QUANTITATIVE DATA

Each of the dimensions primarily addresses the area or country in *quantitative* terms. This is not to denigrate or ignore the *qualitative* observations and analysis that are so critical to truly understanding a people group. Far from it. Such quantitative data is only a starting point in a much longer journey. The purpose is to gain as complete an understanding of a people and their context as is possible for an outsider, which will be imperfect and can only be enhanced through personal interaction with the people of a given culture. Even then, prolonged interaction still leaves the outsider's understanding deficient and, paradoxically, raises dangers of its own—the loss of objectivity in observations.

2. DECEPTIVE DISTRIBUTION

Quantitative data is quite useful, but it can also be quite misleading. It often fails to show the distribution of the data within the population. For example,

---

[1] This classification stems from my own experience and research, but I found support in Dean S. Gilliland, "Doing Theology in Context," MT510 class reader, Fuller Theological Seminary, School of World Mission, 2000, pp. 15-16.

the data may show an average income of $36,000 per family, which is probably quite good, but if there is a significant gap that is not disclosed between the wealthy few and the poor multitudes, the researcher may come to erroneous conclusions both as to the country's true condition and its capacity to support the business investment contemplated. Business requires a market, and that means, as the economists put it, *people with purchasing power*. Distribution variances can significantly reduce the number of people in the market who have the power to purchase the business's product, which leads to adverse business decisions.

3. SELECTIVE, SUGGESTIVE FACTS

By no means do I advocate that the BAM team's SAA include all of the factors listed here. They are given as suggested items to help the team discern those that are best suited to its particular purpose. The object is not to write a book on the country or area, but to focus on those factors that will affect the business, the mission and the people, especially the expats, local hires and targeted customers.

4. QUALITATIVE DATA

Qualitative data is only gathered by going to the country and actively interacting with the people and place. It is subjective, essential and complex. It brings a *reality check* to the quantitative study, but that study also keeps the BAMer from being blinded by the subjective experience. All too often foreign businesspeople are "wined and dined," shown what the host (possible would-be partner) wants them to see, told what the host wants them to hear and come away with a distorted, myopic view of the country and the BAM opportunity. It is only through the blend of both the quantitative facts and the qualitative observations and interactions that the BAMer can come closer to the reality-defining truth he or she seeks.

5. CONTINUAL QUESTIONING

At every stage along the path, the BAM team must continually interrogate each other, each observation, each relationship and each piece of data by asking questions such as, How does knowledge of this person, situation, fact or condition help me better understand how to (1) do business successfully in this place, (2) do holistic mission among these people, (3) bring them closer to Jesus (from an evangelistic perspective), (4) understand and perhaps ease their pain (from a holistic ministry perspective), (5) strengthen my relationships with them to develop trust and love, the key ingredients to properly honoring them while I seek to add value to their lives and community, and (6) live among them with my family in healthy, growth-filled, joyful ways? In many respects these questions underlie my entire approach in this analytical model.

✦   ✦   ✦

The following is one approach to gaining an overview of a people group or nation. It is intended to be used before entering into the BAM field and to give the would-be BAMer a cognitive, objective macro-overview before being injected into the physical setting (the visceral, subjective micro-environment). As such, this model of a strategic area/country analysis is only the first step in a much longer, richer enculturation process. A second, somewhat different approach is found in appendix three.

Geographic, Ecological and Environmental

- Location—hemisphere, continent, surrounding countries
- Features—access to oceans, rivers, terrain, weather, travel and trade routes
- Life resources—water, rainfall, soil, climate (climactic zones), temperatures (seasonal ranges), growing seasons
- Production of natural resources—forests, ores, minerals, petroleum (also economic)
- Environmental—history, problems and issues
- Primary regions and cities (specific data)

Demographic

- People
  1. numbers and locations (geographic distribution)
  2. density
  3. age distribution
  4. gender distribution
  5. total fertility rate (TFR)—a.k.a replacement rate
  6. mortality rates (e.g., infant mortality rate)
- Ethnicities
  1. type(s)
  2. numbers and percentages of populations
  3. densities and locations
  4. trends
  5. relate to governmental policies, where appropriate

- General living conditions[2]
    1. human condition indicators
    2. quality of life indicators
    3. freedom indicators
- Movements and distribution of people
    1. urban vs. rural
    2. trends
    3. relate each to economic conditions

Historic

- People group's story

- Relationships to other people groups

- Traditional conflicts and wars

- National historic milestones

- Political and military history

- Economic history

- Ethnic history

Societal

- Social groupings and composition—tribal, family, extended family, fraternal/maternal

- Generational issues

- General gender issues

- Power structures
    1. formal vs. informal
    2. patriarchal vs. matriarchal
    3. male vs. female
    4. attitudes toward women, children and the elderly
    5. decision-makers and spokespersons
    6. relate these to governmental, legal, economic and religious issues and structures

- Class structures or caste systems

- Relationships with children and elders

---

[2]Useful documents and report series are available from the United Nations and other multinational organizations. One highly informative report is the United Nations Development Programme's annual *Human Development Report*.

- Crime rates, types, issues and locations
- Education
    1. prevailing educational system(s)
    2. types and levels of education
    3. sources—public vs. private
    4. who is and who is not educated
    5. how many are and are not educated, and to what levels
    6. gender issues
    7. availability/access
    8. quality issues
    9. orientation (i.e., Western, non-Western, nationalistic, religious)
    10. resources—public funds, textbooks, buildings, etc.
    11. number of students per teacher
    12. level of teacher education
- Caregiving and death issues
- Communication[3]
    1. oral—major languages and dialects, greetings, tone of voice, direct or indirect style of speech, use of interpreters
    2. written—literacy assessment
    3. nonverbal—eye contact, personal space, use and meaning of silence, gestures, openness in expressing emotion, privacy, touch, orientation to time (both past and present)
    4. predominant nonprimary language(s)—what, where and prevalence
- Food practices[4]
    1. usual meal patterns
    2. special utensils
    3. food beliefs and rituals
    4. usual diet
    5. fluids
    6. food, drink and other taboos (e.g., tobacco)
    7. hospitality forms
- Health and wellness issues

---

[3]See, for example, Daisy M. Rodriguez, Carolina P. de Guzman and Arthur Cantos, "Filipinos," in *Culture & Clinical Care*, eds. Juliene G. Lipson and Suzanne L. Dibble (San Francisco: UCSF Nursing Press, 2005), pp. 178-80. Note that this article also contains substantive information regarding healthcare issues in other cultures. This book addresses these same issues in a variety of other countries.

[4]See ibid., pp. 180-81.

Cultural

- Language(s) (see "Communication")
- Shared/dominant values, understandings and assumptions
- Shared goals
- Shared or dominant allegiances
- Shared beliefs (e.g., mortality, causality and meaning of time)[5]
- Shared standards, codes of conduct and expectations[6]
- Basic attitudes toward such things as work, time, materialism, individualism and change[7]
- Primary subcultures—types, numbers and locations
- Cohesiveness of society/culture
- Dominant conflict resolution method(s)

Religious

- Religion(s)
  1. dominant religion(s) and organizational standards
  2. minor religion(s)
  3. influential religious leaders
  4. attitudes toward and tolerance of other religions
  5. global or local
  6. classic or folk
- Beliefs and practices
  1. basic beliefs
  2. basic values
  3. basic text(s) or holy book(s)
  4. forms and symbols of worship and religious practices
  5. piety requirements
  6. use of spiritual healing/healers
- Religious holidays
- Numbers/percentages of adherents
- Geographic location of adherents

---

[5]Helen Deresky, *International Management: Managing Across Borders and Cultures* (Upper Saddle River, N.J.: Prentice Hall, 2000), pp. 105-7.
[6]Ibid.
[7]Ibid.

- Social activism—influence on population and social and public policy
- Christian activities and history
    1. history of Christianity with this people group/country
    2. Protestant and Roman Catholic
    3. Protestant denominations
    4. mission—who, when, what, where, etc.
    5. dominant personalities and power structures

POLITICAL AND LEGAL

- Structure
    1. governmental structure and traditions (e.g., democratic, communist, totalitarian/dictatorial, monarchy, military junta, etc.)
    2. dominant and influential political figures
    3. police (public and secret) structures, traditions, strengths and influence
    4. military structure, traditions, strength and influence
    5. political parties structure, traditions, strength and influence
    6. legal structures—actual power, effectiveness, corruption, bias toward foreigners and toward business
    7. law—business relation (contracts, torts, taxes, private property, import-export, licenses, etc.)
    8. law—personal and organizational/freedoms (religion, speech, assembly, press, due process, etc.)
    9. bureaucratic controls and inadequacies
    10. bureaucracy
- Current social and political issues/events
    1. governmental stability
    2. trends
    3. attitudes and laws affecting religion and religious business or mission activities
    4. graft and corruption
- Threats to physical security and safety
    1. attitudes toward Westerners, foreigners, Christians and business
    2. to mission personnel—locals, expats and dependents
    3. to mission and personal property
    4. from criminals and bandits
    5. from organized crime
    6. from terrorists
    7. from police and military

  8. from governmental intrusion and espionage
  9. from war, revolution, insurrections, riots, civil unrest
  10. from mafia or secret police

- Governmental social policies—safety net laws and systems
  1. social security system
  2. welfare
  3. public housing
  4. food for the poor
  5. universal health care
  6. unemployment policies
  7. education
  8. gender development (gender bias and access to education)

ECONOMIC AND COMMERCIAL

- Multinational and global factors
  1. membership in global economic groups (e.g., World Trade Organization)
  2. membership in regional economic groups (e.g., free trade agreements, bilateral trade agreements)
  3. regional development agencies
  4. local history and influence of International Monetary Fund—economic stabilization process
  5. local history and influence of World Bank—economic restructuring process

- Macro factors
  1. type of economy (command/socialist, market/capitalist, mix, other)
  2. currency
     a. exchange rates and history—pegged, floating, etc.
     b. exchange rates to the U.S. dollar
     c. stability
  3. economic business freedoms
  4. legal factors of land ownership rights, mineral ownership rights (public or private?)
  5. GDP (Gross Domestic Product)
  6. GDP growth rates
  7. GDP per capita (PPP = purchasing power parity, based on hypothetical exchange rates)
  8. distribution of wealth and its patterns—standards of living; poverty
  9. inflation rates, history and trends

10. fiscal policy
    a. taxation types and levels
    b. fiscal soundness
11. government policies toward business, direct foreign investment, labor, etc.
12. government roles in the markets
13. unemployment rates
14. foreign investment
    a. external portfolio investment
    b. direct foreign investment (DFI)—main companies, products, locations and investments
    c. DFI as percentage of GDP
    d. legal and/or regulatory resources
15. imports and exports
    a. foreign trade—laws, regulators, government agencies, primary trading partners
    b. exports—products, markets, barriers
    c. exports as percentage of GDP
    d. imports—products, sources, local markets, barriers
    e. imports as percentage of GDP
    f. transfer payments—amount and as percentage of GDP
    g. current account balances
16. banking system
    a. nature, characteristics, health (safety and soundness)
    b. private banks
    c. accessibility
    d. services offered
    e. local interest rates on commercial and consumer borrowings
    f. central bank
17. major market sectors—types and statistics

- Micro factors
  1. local markets
  2. primary industries—types, products, buyers (markets), work force, revenues generated (both absolute and as percentage of local economy)
  3. illegal informal economy (e.g., drugs in Colombia and mafia in Russia)
  4. legal informal economy and cottage industries
  5. market traditions (e.g., local market every Tuesday)
  6. local unemployment

7. skill/education levels
8. labor pools—absolute and trends
9. transportation systems
10. foreign businesses in the local economy
11. BAM businesses in the local markets
12. governmental social policies (see "Economics")
13. economic development activities, players and indicators

- Local infrastructure (necessary to Christian business/mission)
    1. transportation systems—types and reliability (roads, rail, water, air)
    2. communications systems
    3. information systems
    4. utilities
    5. real estate (business and mission commercial property; expat housing)
    6. supply sources
    7. work/labor pool
    8. court system—common law, code system, ecclesiastical
    9. civil—contracts, torts
    10. criminal
    11. procedures—jury trials, rights, protections
    12. police

Appendix 3

Differential Diagnosis of Poverty

The following is from Jeffrey Sachs's *The End of Poverty: Economic Possibilities for Our Times.*[1]

> Many governments in these regions [Africa, the Andes and Central Asia] have shown boldness, integrity, and intelligence [in dealing with systemic poverty in their nations]. Yet development continues to fail. A clinical economics approach will point the way to a better strategy.
>
> The key to clinical economics is a thorough differential diagnosis, followed by an appropriate treatment regimen. In the course of a physical exam, the doctor runs through pages of questions: "Are you taking medications?" "Do you have allergies?" "Have you been operated on recently?" " Do you have a family history of the following diseases?" The clinical economist must do the same. In table 1, I describe a seven part diagnostic checklist that should be part of the "physical exam" of any impoverished country. . . . [For example], the first set of questions involves the extent of extreme poverty. . . [and so on].

Table 1: Checklist for Making a Differential Diagnosis

I. ***Poverty trap***

Poverty mapping
Proportion of households lacking basic needs
Spatial distribution of household poverty
Spatial distribution of basic infrastructure (power, roads, telecoms, water and sanitation)
Ethnic, gender, generational distribution of poverty
Key risk factors
    Demographic trends
    Environmental trends

---

[1]Jeffrey D. Sachs, *The End of Poverty: Economic Possibilities for Our Time* (New York: Penguin, 2005), pp. 83-84. Used by permission.

Climate shocks
Disease
Commodity price fluctuations
Others

II. *Economic Policy Framework*
Business environment
Trade policy
Investment policy
Infrastructure
Human capital

III. *Fiscal Framework and Fiscal Trap*
Public sector revenues and expenditures by category
Percent of GNP
Absolute levels in comparison with international norms
Tax administration and expenditure management
Public investment needs to meet poverty reduction targets
Macroeconomic instability
Overhand of public sector debt
Quasi-fiscal debt and hidden debt
Medium-term public sector expenditure framework

IV. *Physical Geography*
Transport conditions
Proximity of population to ports, international trade routes,
navigable waterways
Access of population to paved roads
Access of population to motorized transport
Population density
Costs of connectivity to power, telecoms, roads
Arable land per capita
Environmental impacts of population-land ratios
Agronomic conditions
Temperature, precipitation, solar insulation
Length and reliability of growing season
Soils, topography, suitability for irrigation
Interannual climate variability (e.g., El Nino)
Long-term trends in climate patterns
Disease ecology
Human diseases

Plant diseases and pests
Animal diseases

V. *Governance Patterns and Failures*
Civil and political rights
Public management systems
Decentralization and fiscal federalism
Corruption patterns and intensity
Political succession and longevity
Internal violence and security
Cross-border violence and security
Ethnic, religious, and other cultural divisions

VI. *Cultural Barriers*
Gender relations
Ethnic and religious divisions
Diaspora

VII. *Geopolitics*
International security relations
Cross-border security threats
War
Terrorism
Refugees
International sanctions
Trade barriers
Participation in regional and international groups

Appendix 4

Strategic Business Plan (SBP)

THERE ARE MANY FORMATS for workable business plans, but most follow the same general pattern as is recommended here. Nonetheless, each company tailors its own plan to the needs of its stakeholders and markets. As will be seen in the strategic mission analysis (appendix 5), a BAM Company plan must also maintain a Christian focus. For example, its purpose statement might include "to honor Christ and glorify his name" or "to fulfill the Great Commission through business." Similarly, its vision statement might include "to exemplify Christ so that all of our stakeholders see him through our products and services, practices, service and relationships."

When drafting the SBP, the BAM team should review the strategic area/country analysis (SAA) and determine whether/how it should be integrated into the plan.

Business Plan—CNJ BAM Company

Cover Sheet

- personalized cover letter (if applicable)

Executive Summary (prepared last)

- company's origins, activities, management and performance
- product or service distinguishing features
- market attractiveness

Table of Contents

Vision Statement

Mission Statement

Declaration of Core Values

Goals and Objectives

- multiple bottom lines
  1. financial
  2. social
  3. environmental
  4. kingdom
  5. other
- annual
- three to five year projected

Keys to Success

Risk Factors

- security—corporate, BAM team and families, and indigenous personnel
- country risks—infrastructure, stability, corruption
- macroeconomic issues
- political issues
- spiritual issues
- missional issues
- business issues
- expat and personal issues

Your Industry

- the industry in general
- major players
- industry stakeholders
- needs assessment
- statistics and trends
- issues

Your Business

- describe/define your business
- history—how the idea was born, company's origins, founders, etc.

- current circumstances—strengths, weaknesses, opportunity and threats (SWOT)
- products and services
    1. describe (as specifically as possible)
    2. product lifecycle, if applicable
    3. brand loyalties
    4. pricing (see later)
    5. patents, copyrights, proprietary features
    6. future of current product line(s)
    7. future product lines, if applicable
    8. research and development—needs and activities
- manufacturing and operations—what, where, why, how
- location(s)
    1. what, where and why
    2. advantages and disadvantages
    3. purchase or lease
    4. facilities and improvements
- human capital
    1. management personnel, backgrounds, experience (business, mission, international, etc.) and faith-work (Is this the right team with the right credentials?)
    2. operational and technical personnel (Is this the right team with the right credentials?)
    3. board of directors (representing the four "w's": wealth, wisdom, workers and web/network)
    4. board of advisors (corporate and spiritual)
    5. peer group(s)/mentor(s)
    6. consultants/professionals
- monetary capital (general—from financials, below)

Your Competition (know them well!)

- specifics—names, addresses, products, statistics
- their market shares
- their perceived differentiation in the market
- their strengths and weaknesses

Competitive Strategies

- your comparative, competitive advantage

- your market niche
- buying patterns
- points of differentiation, uniqueness
- what you do best and why that is true

Sales and Marketing Strategies[1]

- overview—manufacturing, wholesaling, retailing
- sales objectives
    1. challenging and attainable
    2. time specific
    3. measurable
        more than dollars and units
        transactions
        persons served
- target markets and customers
    1. wants and needs that are defined by the product
    2. segmentation—trade territory and market size
    3. target market segment strategy
    4. market research
    5. demographics
    6. product usage—buying habits and patterns
    7. frequency of purchase and purchase rates
    8. heavy users
    9. trends
    10. big box opportunities
    11. potential primary and secondary markets
- branding and positioning
- packaging
- service/fulfillment
- warranties
- sales and marketing structure
    1. in-house—wholesale/retail
    2. e-trading
    3. outsourced—marketing agencies, sales reps

---

[1]This section is adapted from Roman G. Hiebing Jr. and Scott W. Cooper, *The Successful Marketing Plan* (New York: McGraw-Hill, 2003).

- sales literature
- sales methods
    1. personal selling/operations
    2. promotions
    3. direct mail
    4. advertising message and media
    5. merchandising
    6. publicity
- marketing budgets and payback analysis
- marketing calendar
- evaluation and adjustment
- milestones
- strategic alliances

Pricing Strategies

- from pro formas—expenses and overhead
- profit goals and margins markup
- industry standards
- competition
    1. definitive comparison
    2. constant monitoring
- evaluation and adjustments

Operational Strategies

- timing—expected schedule of events
- tactical overview—setting up and running the business
- special equipment, capital investments
- suppliers
- market buyer
- servicing
- inventory controls
- shipping and distribution systems and controls

Structural Strategies

- organizational chart

- functional chart
- positional descriptions—vertical, horizontal and virtual
- partnerships
- alliances
- associations
- BAM strategies
  1. developing a strategic area/country analysis (SAA) (see appendixes 2 and 3)
  2. develop strategic mission analysis (SMA) (see appendix 5)
  3. dual organizational strategies
  4. planning process, goals and schedule
  5. coordination with chief ministry/mission officer (CMO) on SMA
  6. strategic master BAM plan—SAA, SMA

Relationship Strategies

- customers
- workforce (HR department strategies and functions)
  1. key officers and managers
  2. employees
  3. compensation and benefits
  4. working conditions
  5. training and development
- investors
- alliances and partners
- community
- board of directors
- peer groups

Legal Strategies

- corporate formation and maintenance—licenses, permits
- intellectual property—trademarks, patents, copyrights
- taxes
- contracts
- torts—premises, products, vehicles
- claims

- employment issues
- risk management and mitigation
- insurance
- conflict management
- compliance
- collections

Cash Management Strategies

- currency and investment strategies
- capital investments—land, equipment, vehicles
- funding strategies—credit, commercial paper, etc.
- banking relations
  1. depositories
  2. inventory financing
  3. working capital financing
  4. accounts receivable financing
  5. factoring contracts
  6. term notes—short (1 yr.) and long term (3-5 yrs.)
  7. demand notes (90-180 days)
  8. lines of credit
  9. letters of credit
  10. government assistance/guarantees
- operations-related financing
  1. supplier credit
  2. customer credit
  3. facility management

Financials and Capital Strategies

- company financial history (if applicable)
- capital sources, amounts and needs (debt vs. equity)
- fiscal year (if other than a calendar basis, provide dates)
- pro forma projections
  1. capital plan
  2. break-even analysis
  3. balance sheets—semiannual in first year; year-end thereafter

4. income and expense statements—profit and loss (P&L) (3-5 yrs.)
5. cash flow projections
6. statement of assumptions

- audits—internal and external

Appendix 5

STRATEGIC MISSION ANALYSIS (SMA)

THE FOLLOWING SMA OUTLINE is a suggested cafeteria list of possible avenues of fruitful inquiry for the company seeking to have a kingdom impact. It is far from complete and should be tailored by each company to fit its context, capacity, calling and priorities.

The SMA can be developed as a *stand-alone plan* that will later be merged into the strategic business plan (SBP) or as a *checklist* of areas (1) already included within the SBP and (2) not covered by the SBP but needing to be added to it to improve its kingdom impact. In each area, the drilling down method is recommended; that is, continue looking deeper than the surface function, product or situation to see more obscure areas where kingdom impact can be achieved. *The process is one of never-ending questioning and interrogation of the SBP, asking what can be done in each area internally and externally to identify and address heretofore missed kingdom impact opportunities.*

But remember: The SMA can (and should) initially be undertaken piecemeal over time. It does not have to be accomplished overnight and, indeed, should not be. It is an evolving, learning process that is approached incrementally as the company grows and gains maturity in its faith integration efforts. For more on this, see the discussion on the incremental planning approach in chapter thirteen.

The following SMA is (as with all elements of BAM) a work in progress. Readers and BAM practitioners are invited to offer constructive suggestions for improvement at the Bakke Graduate University School of Business website (BAM Research section, www.bgu.edu) where I serve as business school dean.

The SMA should be conducted in methodical steps and sequences, which are reflected below. You will notice that there are essentially only three key aspects to this process initially: (1) Identify the kingdom impact opportunities (KIOs), (2) list them into the SMA under the appropriate headings, and (3) provide certain listed details for each. To simplify your understanding of KIOs, just think of "ways to do good" or, more accurately, "ways in which we can do good for a stakeholder by the change we recommend or the action we proposed." By doing good, we "love our neighbor" and thereby promote the kingdom of God.

Strategic Area/Country Analysis (SAA)

Since everything in the SBP and SMP must be contextually appropriate to the context in which BAM is being done, you must first:

- Review appendixes two and three to understand what should be in the SAA.

- Review the company's SAA and determine whether/how it is integrated into the company's preliminary/initial SBP.

- At each point in the following analysis ask whether/how the SAA should be integrated into the SMP actions being proposed.

Strategic Mission Analysis (SMA)

- Review the initial strategic business plan (SBP) in detail: *At each point in the SBP, identify and list kingdom impact opportunities* (KIOs) into the preliminary SMP.

- *Functional Analysis Approach* (see chaps. 15 and 16). You should use this approach to drill down in each department and function to identify and list KIOs. The deeper you drill down, the greater grasp you will have of the latent potential the company has for kingdom impact; where possible, do this with the employees who perform these functions:

  1. department by department—start with the top echelons of the company to give the program greater credibility among the employees

  2. function by function

  3. product by product—do the same; drill down; identify KIOs.

  4. a list of important areas of inquiry is given below under "Internal Areas to Consider" and "External Areas to Consider."

- *Calling, Capacity and Priorities*

  1. Throughout the process, the BAM team needs to be in constant prayer and discussion to discern which of the KIOs are within the company's calling, capacity (resources—people, money, time, facilities, etc.) and priorities.

  2. The company is not a church or a social-service agency, and it cannot be all things to all people. Discernment, prayer and discussion are needed to determine which KIOs are right for the company and when—and which should be left for others to address.

3. They must remember the adage "Death by opportunity." Trying to do too many things too quickly can undermine the stability and sustainability of the company and cripple its ability to fulfill its primary mission.

The Workforce

The workforce includes all employees, full time and part time, and the community labor pool from which these and future employees are drawn

- *Employees:*
  1. Identify, analyze and prioritize the employees' expectations, urgent needs, noncritical but important needs (moderate needs), and other actions that would improve their safety, well-being, joy and satisfaction. Identify and list these KIOs
  2. On the job
     a. expectations
     b. urgent needs
     c. moderate needs
     d. improvements
  3. off the job
     a. expectations
     b. urgent needs
     c. moderate needs
     d. improvements
  4. their families
     a. expectations
     b. urgent needs
     c. moderate needs
     d. improvements

- *Community labor pool:*
  1. Identify, analyze and prioritize the community labor pool needs. List appropriate KIOs for each.
     a. expectations
     b. urgent needs
     c. moderate needs
     d. improvements
  2. Identify actions that would make these people more employable.

The Community

If the company has a presence in or impacts more than one community, each community should be considered separately, unless there is value in doing otherwise.

- If possible, retain or consult with a *Christian Community Development Specialist* to provide leadership and guidance in how to do community development in a way that wins the confidence of the community and is a win-win for them and the company.
- Analyze the community-at-large.
  1. Consult local employees.
  2. Consult formal and informal community leaders.
  3. Consult local churches, NGOs and other BAM companies in the area.
  4. Observe the life of the community.
- Determine and prioritize the community's needs. List KIOs for each.
  1. urgent needs
  2. moderate needs
  3. improvements
  4. develop a Community Impact Statement (CIS) on each community recommendation

The Cost of Doing Good—BAM Impact Statements

- Return to each KIO listed above and provide:
  1. an educated estimate of the direct, indirect and opportunity costs to the company for providing this service (see "Financial Bottom Line" below).
  2. recommendations for the department and person within the company who would be the point person for the proposed action.
  3. recommended priority (A, B, C or D) of the project in relationship to other proposals. Add the year(s) in which it should be undertaken (e.g., A-1 = top priority to be done within the coming year; B-1 = lesser priority, but also to be done this year; A-2 = top priority in planning for year 2; B-2 = lesser priority for year 2, and so on)
  4. a short-hand label after each recommended action supply for which bottom-line(s) it serves: Financial; Social; Green; Kingdom; Other—specify.
- BAM Impact Statement: With each recommendation, sharply focus on the SAA and determine if there is any variation in the recommendation that should be made to contextualize it to the BAM locale. If so, include that discussion in your SMA.

Coordination with SBP

- Recommendations—take the SMA recommendations to the COO or other planning officer who has prepared the preliminary/initial SBP and merge the recommendations into that plan under the appropriate SBP headings.

- negotiations—where there are disagreements as to the advisability and affordability of the SMA recommendations, the priorities, year, cost, point person, etc., or as to trade-offs with non-SMA actions found in the SBP, these disputes will have to be negotiated within the BAM leadership team. The negotiations should involve those whose input would help clarify the matters under discussion. Where possible, agreement should be by joyful consensus, or the proposed kingdom action may meet resistance in implementation.

- Reconciliation—once agreement is reached on each recommendation, it is melded into the SBP and becomes part of the initial SMBP.

■ ■ ■

The foregoing discussion gives the process for preparing the SMA. Other approaches can be taken that will certainly yield fruit, but this seems to be a user-friendly way of approaching the issue of faith-integration for kingdom impact. The following are specific details that may be useful to the BAM team as they go through the process:

Internal Areas to Consider
Internal areas to consider for identifying and listing KIOs in the SMA:

- *SBP vision and mission statements*—identify and list KIOs in the SMA
  1. draft or revise to reflect BAM commitment
  2. discern, describe and define core values from a kingdom perspective
- *Stakeholders*—identify and list KIOs in the SMA
  1. identify—as a class of people and, where appropriate, by individual names
     a. customers, clients and their families
     b. employees, contract labor and their families
     c. investors
     d. creditors
     e. suppliers
     f. partners
     g. alliances
     h. local BAM companies (including replicated companies)
     i. trade association
     j. labor unions
     k. community
     l. government

       m.competitors

       n. other

  2. for each stakeholder, consider their

    a. expectations

    b. urgent needs

    c. moderate needs

    d. improvements (especially vis-à-vis relationship)

- *People and products*—identify and list KIOs in the SMA

  1. board of directors

  2. management team

  3. professional services—company attorneys, CPAs

  4. employees

    a. human relations (see partial list of HR functions in chap. 16)

    b. employees' families

  5. products or services

  6. organizational structure

    a. operational departments

    b. operational functions

    c. quality control systems (see discussion in chap. 16)

    d. internal control systems

  7. resource management

  8. work environment

  9. special holistic projects (for the workforce and/or their families; e.g., training in personal finances, character development, personal hygiene, nutrition, literacy, first aid, prenatal care, child care, parenting, summer education, elder care, employee housing, etc.)

  10. other

- *Strategies*—identify and list KIOs in the SMA for the following strategies:

  1. competition

  2. sales and marketing (see partial list of M&S functions in chap. 16)

  3. pricing

  4. operations

  5. structural (organizational)

  6. relationships

  7. legal

  8. cash management

9. financial and capital (see partial list of financial functions in chap. 16)
10. partnership/alliance
11. entry and exit modes
12. other

- *Environmental (green) bottom line*—identify and list KIOs in the SMA
    1. BAM environmental impact statements
    2. conduct an internal audit from an environmental perspective of such areas as
        a. products and services
        b. packaging
        c. manufacturing
        d. waste disposal/usage
        e. pollution
        f. prevention vs. improvement vs. accommodation vs. minimization
        g. workplaces—space, lighting, air quality, noise, smells, colors, furniture and fixtures, safety, heating and cooling, cleanliness, restrooms, cafeterias, etc.
        h. vehicles and equipment
        i. policies on smoking
        j. other

- *Financial bottom line*
    1. Calculate the direct (net) monetary costs for each KIO recommended (including the compensation for anyone who is employed full time in organizing the KIO projects).
    2. Calculate the indirect monetary costs (e.g., time required by employees) for each KIO recommended.
    3. Calculate the opportunity cost (ask: What alternative uses exist for that money and effort?) for the major KIOs recommended.
    4. Calculate the impact on the company profit-and-loss statement of major KIOs individually and all KIOs collectively.
    5. List and weigh the benefits of undertaking such KIOs.
    6. Evaluate and resolve the tensions created between competing use of limited resources.

External Areas to Consider

External areas to consider for identifying and listing KIOs:

- *Social bottom line*—identify and list KIOs in the SMA
    1. BAM community impact statements

2. community *development* projects, addressing, for example:
   a. education
   b. health
   c. beautification and environmental improvements
   d. building/construction
   e. water quality and availability
   f. agriculture
   g. physical infrastructure
      i. transportation (roads, rail, air, etc.)
      ii. utilities (electrical power, gas, water, waste disposal, etc.)
      iii. communications (radio, television, telephone, internet, etc.)
      iv. airport and water-port facilities
      v. other
3. community *transformation* projects, addressing, for example:
   a. racial reconciliation
   b. gender equality
   c. homelessness
   d. elder care
   e. street children, disabled, marginalized
   f. adoption and foster homes
   g. crime
   h. drugs
   i. rehabilitation clinics
   j. social services
   k. human trafficking
   l. prostitution
   m. poverty alleviation
   n. job training
   o. social safety nets
   p. entrepreneurship
   q. other
4. peace and justice issues (political bottom line?)
5. other

- *Other (nonfinancial) bottom lines* (e.g., evangelistic or political)—identify and list KIOs in the SMA
  1. identify other bottom lines that are important to the company
  2. BAM impact statements
  3. local church partnerships
  4. mission agency partnerships

    5. measurements of progress

    6. other

- *Peer groups*—identify and list KIOs in the SMA

    1. forming and structuring

    2. alliances with national and international groups (e.g., Christ@Work, Full Gospel, CBMC, International Christian Chamber of Commerce)

    3. other

- *Replication*—identify and list KIOs in the SMA

    1. identifying opportunities and candidates

    2. methods of ongoing assistance

    3. incubation

    4. peer groups

    5. other

General Areas to Consider

- *Kingdom bottom line*—continually evaluate

    1. how to infuse kingdom impact into all aspects of the company, internal and external, and its various bottom lines

    2. how to institutionalize kingdom values and kingdom impact into the lifeblood and DNA of the company

    3. how to organizationally structure for sustainability of the company's kingdom focus

    4. when and how to move the company's faith integration efforts further toward the right side of the planning continuum (toward full strategic master BAM planning; see chap. 13)

    5. other

- *Prayer support*

    1. institutionalized (within the company)

    2. direct

    3. intercessory

    4. inner healing

    5. training

    6. prayer teams

    7. other

- *Planning process*

    1. senior management and board approval/buy-in

2. CEO led
3. planning coordinator and team
   a. appointment (selection)
   b. authority
   c. resources (capacity)
   d. goals
4. determining
   a. who is involved on each component
   b. preparatory stages (e.g., employee meetings, written questionnaires, department-by-department meetings and input, planning retreat, facilitator, facilities, etc.)
   c. how to obtain employee buy-in/ownership
   d. how to monitor results
   e. how much the KIO programs cost (see financial bottom line bullet point above)
   f. other
5. program evaluation and feedback systems
   a. 360-degree evaluation
   b. evaluation from all affected stakeholders
   c. other
6. program improvement and expansion

Name Index

Subject Index

Scripture Index